1000

Books By Ramaji

The Spiritual Heart

No Mind No Problem

Waking Up As Awareness

You Are Everything

The Tao of Non-Doing

Heal Your Body, Free Your Mind

Warning From Kali 2013

1000

1000

The Levels of Consciousness and a Map of the Stages of Awakening for Spiritual Seekers and Teachers

By

Ramaji

1000

The Levels of Consciousness and a Map of the Stages of Awakening for Spiritual Seekers and Teachers

Copyright © 2014 Ramaji

Ramaji.org

Ramaji Books
San Diego, California
Email: advaitaforidiots@gmail.com

This publication is presented to you for informational purposes only and is not a substitution for any professional advice. The contents herein are based on the views and opinions of the author.

What you do with this information is entirely your responsibility. If you do not agree with these terms, you may return this book for a full and prompt refund. Thank you.

All rights reserved. No part of this document may be reproduced or transmitted in any form, either by electronic or mechanical means including information storage and retrieval systems without the prior written permission of the publisher. The only exception is for a reviewer who may quote brief passages in the review.

Dedicated, with deep abiding love and respect, to everyone who is on the path, especially those who would like to know where they stand, those who would like to know where they are going, those who would like to know how to choose a good teacher, and, most especially, those who yearn to realize the Heart and live in the Freedom that was promised, taught and exemplified by Sri Ramana Maharshi.

1000

Table of Contents

Acknowledgments   15

Introduction   17

The Levels of Consciousness and the Complete Map of Awakening (Chart)   23

What Is Level of Consciousness?   27

How to Evaluate a Person's LOC   41

Notes On Assessing Non-Dual Teachers   48

LOCs of 200 Contemporary Western Teachers of Non-Duality and Advaita   63

101 Spiritual Giants   96

The River of Life: LOC 30 to 499   102

The Bonfires of Sacrifice: LOC 500 to 559   121

Stepping into the Blaze: LOC 560 to 569   129

The Mystic On Fire: LOC 570 to 579   141

A Sage Is Waiting: LOC 580 to 589   155

No Man's Land: LOC 590 to 599   177

Seven Maps of Non-Dual Awakening   188

Spiritual Map One: Seven Valleys of Sufism   194

Spiritual Map Two: Five Ranks of Tozan   203

Spiritual Map Three: 10 Zen Oxherding Pictures   214

Spiritual Map Four: Patanjali's Yoga Sutras   220

Spiritual Map Five: Stages of Advaita Vedanta   224

Spiritual Map Six: Major Arcana of the Tarot   231

Spiritual Map Seven: The Hero's Journey   240

The Condensed Map of Awakening (Chart)   266

Quest for the Absolute: An Overview of the Journey From No Self (600s) to Supreme Self (1000)   269

The Far Frontier: LOC 600 to 699   289

My Spiritual Journal: From No Self to Cosmic Self (LOC 683 to LOC 776)   333

The Cosmic Vision: LOC 700 to 799   353

My Spiritual Journal: Ascent into Darkness (LOC 776 to LOC 845)   403

The Unthinkable Surrender: LOC 800 to 899   425

My Spiritual Journal: Transfiguration or Radical Illumination via Amrita Nadi (LOC 845 to LOC 932)   474

The Hesitant Hermit: LOC 900   507

My Spiritual Journal: Starving the I-Thought to Death (LOC 932 to LOC 1000)   525

Lost in the Absolute: LOC 1000   581

The RASA Opportunity   637

If You Have Suggestions or Feedback   657

Appendix One: Music of Ramaji Unity   659

Appendix Two: Planetary Awakening   663

Appendix Three: Journey to the Heart of Truth   669

Notes   677

Bibliography   731

Meet the Author   743

Download Spiritual Maps   745

Subscribe to *LOC Insider*   745

1000

Acknowledgments

Although this book was written in a whirlwind in about a year, it was in fact many decades in the making. The seeds were planted when I recorded in my journal my first spiritual experiences as a teenager. Around the same time, I also began experimenting with methods to assess spiritual development.

First, I must thank my editor Koort. We spent many enjoyable hours discussing the direction for this book. He encouraged me to make it bold, direct and personal. His thoughtful heartfelt Introduction sets the tone for this audacious enterprise.

I want to express my appreciation to the San Diego satsang group. Individually and collectively, they encouraged me to pursue my LOC (Level of Consciousness) research.

I would especially like to thank Fred Smalley from the San Diego satsang group. Fred gave me a number of interesting names for LOC assessment that I would not have thought of otherwise. He also alerted me to "dirty laundry" on certain teachers. These insights made the book more entertaining while also clearing up blind spots in my LOC assessments.

I would also like to deeply thank Alex Burtson from the San Diego satsang group for his professional rendering of the Map of Awakening (complete and condensed versions). He was a true pleasure to work with and contributed many good ideas.

Finally, I would like to warmly thank Oivind from Norway for reading the manuscript prior to publication. His feedback was wonderfully encouraging as well as uniquely useful.

1000

Introduction

1000 is the ultimate level of consciousness, or LOC, the numerical assessment of a person's state of awareness, on the way to Self-Realization or Freedom in this lifetime.

Even though 1000 is the only thing that is real, it is realized by taking the imaginary journey through the lower levels of consciousness. In *1000* Ramaji quantifies, qualifies, and maps out this journey just as it is, level by level, step by step.

Although everyone's experience and time spent at each LOC will be unique, Ramaji shows you how to recognize each level, alerts you to the pitfalls as you move through them, and encourages you to complete the journey.

He opens up about his personal journey to LOC 1000. He lists the LOCs of numerous contemporary spiritual teachers, gurus, authors and historical figures. He also explains the benefits of Ramaji Advaita Shaktipat Attunement, or RASA.

It was my great pleasure to have Ramaji's extraordinary tutelage for over a year on my personal journey to LOC 1000. I made his acquaintance for the first time in July, 2012 in San Diego. I immediately began meeting with him for up to six hours a week to confront my questions, eliminate my doubts, and receive RASA.

The people at LOC 30 through LOC 499 are experiencing the early stages of awareness. They progress and move through life operating from base, animalistic impulses, great passions and emotions, and the power of intelligence.

Ramaji explains that most likely anyone reading this book has already progressed through these lower LOCs. The low LOCs make the Map of Awakening complete for the reader.

The LOC 500s have awakened to spirituality. They expect a reward for their good service to God and mankind either in this life, the next life, or in the hereafter. Early in my teens I turned to a higher power hoping to earn a problem-free life, loving relationships, and recognition from my peers.

I had lots of fantasies about enlightenment, such as an enlightened person will be saintly, be able to perform miracles, have lots of money and be very charitable. At other times, I imagined they would be very poor and serve humanity, never eat red meat, not wear glasses, never have health problems, and never get cancer.

I became a web surfer and spiritual globe trotter moving from one teacher to the next. For close to forty years I read many different books, tried all forms of spirituality such as abstinence, affirmation, mantra, meditation, yantra, yoga, new age, old school, you name it. I had several mini-awakenings and peak experiences via Kundalini, psychedelic drugs, and dreams.

Yet for whatever amount of love that I felt, I had an equal amount of fear in the form of shame, guilt, anger, rage, loneliness, or some type of demon or shadow that I avoided.

Eventually my mental anxieties, depression, suffering, and suicidal thoughts overwhelmed me, but I gave up trying to fix myself.

I faced the fact that all the spirituality, psychology, sex, drugs, or whatever I tried offered no permanent solution to my suffering. For several months, I was barely able to leave my bed.

As difficult as life was for me in the LOC 500s, I realize now that if I had not let go of resisting my fears and pain, I would have continued suffering the extreme emotional highs and lows that I had become accustomed to and risked remaining a seeker in the LOC 500s for the rest of my life.

The LOC 500s have not yet faced their greatest fears, but the LOC 600s have. At this time, I passed through the first void passage and had my first ego death. I felt like I experienced a second birth. I was more completely in my body than ever before.

I started living in the first stage of non-duality and sought out Ramaji's guidance. I existed in the world as the no-self and as the non-doer. Compared to life in the LOC 500s this was a vast improvement. I basked in the glow of my new life in the LOC 600s. However, Ramaji told me that even though this was enlightenment, it was far from Self-Realization. As good as it felt, it was really no big deal. The journey was far from over.

Ramaji explained that I risked crystallizing myself in the LOC 600s for the rest of my life if I continued to hold up my new found awareness as something special. He told me that there would be more darkness to face, but the good news was that it would be much easier for me to transcend, and that I would move ahead more quickly. He was right.

Although the LOC 600s are considered enlightened, they have more subconscious fears to face. In contrast, the LOC 700s confronted the reemergence of their fears after the bliss and excitement of their rebirth wore off.

Like me, they buckled down and got back to real Self-Inquiry. I experienced a second void passage. The concepts of no-self and non-doership dropped away, and I started living in the second stage of non-duality called cosmic consciousness.

It felt as if the whole world was moving through me, while I remained perfectly still. I now existed as King of the Universe, abiding mostly in peace and joy. Everything was in me, and I was the world.

During this stage Ramaji let me know that the world and knowledge of myself as cosmic consciousness was just another concept or state, and that it had absolutely no value. If I did not toss it out and continue the journey, I would remain in the LOC 700s as the King of Crap for the rest of my life.

The LOC 700s still identify with the familiar concepts of the world and cosmic consciousness, but the LOC 800s have thrown these concepts out. Like me, they passed through the third and final void passage and started living in the third state of non-duality, the pure "I AM."

Although this was a short-lived level for me, I enjoyed a personal, mystical relationship with Kali, Ramana, and Jesus. As poetic and beautiful as my life was Ramaji let me know that the pure "I AM," God, or Light was just another concept and a seductive form of separation.

He explained that I was holding onto the belief that I was because of them, but actually the opposite was true. They were only because I was.

Ramaji warned me that if I did not want to get stuck in the LOC 800s for the rest of my life, my God/Goddess/Guru would eventually have to go. He told me that they wanted to go. When that happened, I would go with them into That in which all states exist, but is touched by no state. My beloved Kali, Ramana, and Jesus were so kind as to remove themselves from me. No Kali. No Ramana. No Jesus. No God.

The LOC 800s exist in the brilliant state of "I AM," but the LOC 900s have transcended this state and the concept of God/Goddess/Guru. Like me, they discovered that there is no other. I was now living in the fourth stage of non-duality, the true "I." During this time I kept to myself a lot, not because I was stuck in my pain and fears, unable to face the world, but because I had a preference for living peacefully as possible.

I lived happily and mostly secluded within the four walls of my home leaving only to workout at the gym, grocery shop, and take a weekly nature walk with Ramaji. I chose to have minimal interaction with family, friends and other people who could possibly disturb my peace.

To avoid getting stuck in the LOC 900s, Ramaji encouraged me to throw all caution to the winds along with my need to control anything, including my own peace. He told me that there would always be disturbances and differences, and that my need to control was a form of separation.

While the LOC 900s are very close, they still have a subtle need to control, whereas the LOC 1000s exist in complete "controlessness." They have gone full circle and are fully engaged in the world. One afternoon after a RASA the idea of a "me" that was trying to control or to become LOC 1000 dropped away. There was only LOC 1000. It was not that the journey was over. It was that the journey never began.

This is It, and I do not know what It is. This not knowing is LOC 1000, the ultimate level of consciousness. I am no longer disturbed by being disturbed. The difference between all the ups and down makes no difference. The next thing is just the next thing.

Before meeting Ramaji, I had many teachers that I turned to for help along the way. I know now that most of them never completed their journey. Ramaji explained that it is likely that they crystallized at the LOC they started teaching at.

By assessing the LOCs of the gurus, teachers, and authors whose guidance we seek, words we listen to and books we buy, Ramaji may create controversy and juicy gossip within the world-wide non-duality community. Why shouldn't he? What is the problem? The dialogue will be lots of fun.

The journey from LOC 30 to LOC 1000 is imaginary, yet it is exactly what is. Why should we deny it? Why shouldn't we talk about it, and quantify and qualify our LOCs along the way? Ramaji shows you how to recognize each LOC, alerts you to the pitfalls along the way, and encourages you to realize the ultimate reality, LOC 1000.

Koort, March, 2014

The Levels of Consciousness and the Complete Map of Awakening (Chart)

The Complete Map of Awakening
Journey Beyond Imagination: the Evolution of Human Consciousness

The River of Life: LOC 30 to LOC 499

LOC 30 to 99
The Jungle of Hungry Beasts (Toxic Apathy and Shame)

LOC 100 to 199
The Island of Lost Souls (Toxic Anger and Pride)

LOC 200 to 299
The Land of Selfish Heroes (Boldness and Generosity)

LOC 210 = Average Human Being on Our Planet

LOC 300 to 399
The Domain of Earnest Enthusiasts (Vulnerability and Allowing)

LOC 400 to 499
The Kingdom of Brilliant Thinkers (Intellect and Analysis)

From Spiritual Emergence to the Supreme Self: LOC 500 to LOC 1000

LOC 500 to 559
The Bonfires of Sacrifice (Spirituality Emerges)

LOC 560 to 569
Stepping Into the Blaze (Spiritual Seeking Begins)

LOC 570 to 579
The Mystic on Fire (Spiritual Seeking Intensifies)

LOC 580 to 589
A Sage Is Waiting (Effortless Thought Free Meditation)

LOC 590 to 599
No Man's Land

First Spiritual Shock (Ego Death)

LOC 600 to 699
The Far Frontier (Pure Feeling of Being / No Self)

Second Spiritual Shock (Cosmic Expansion)

LOC 700 to 799
The Cosmic Vision (Feeling of Being the Universe / Cosmic Self)

Third Spiritual Shock (Ascent into Darkness / Great Void Passage)

LOC 800 to 899
The Unthinkable Surrender (Not Knowing / Divine Union)

Transfiguration (Amrita Nadi and the Consummation of the Crown Chakra / Radical Illumination)

LOC 900
The Hesitant Hermit (Stabilization in No Mind / Natural State)

Final Stage of Self-Inquiry (Starving the "I"-Thought to Death)

LOC 1000
Lost in the Absolute (Universal "I" Consciousness / Supreme Self)

1000

What Is Level of Consciousness?

What Is Level of Consciousness (LOC)?

The idea that different people, including spiritual teachers, are at different levels of consciousness, or at various stages of spiritual development, is a familiar one. Even so, evaluating their level of consciousness (LOC) remains controversial.

While there are spiritual diagnostic methods that yield good results in the hands of an experienced user, such as astrology, radionics, pendulum and intuitive assessment of the human energy field, these methods tend to break down when they are applied to the enlightened person (someone who is stabilized in non-duality).

The method presented in this book is a form of biokinesiology (also called "applied kinesiology" or "muscle testing"). When it occurred to me to write this book, I had already worked with this method for many years in its holistic health applications.

I refined and redesigned this popular method for the specific purpose of assessing enlightened people. The results of my research are presented in this book.

The Map of Awakening makes it easy to understand what a person's LOC means in terms of spiritual development. The LOC number is similar to the grade of a student in school.

The LOC number is even more accurate as it will show where they are located within their grade. My Map of Awakening model emphasizes the LOCs from 500 up to 1000. LOC 500 is where pure spirituality, as opposed to organized religion, begins to emerge. Most of my readers will be in that range.

How This Book "1000" Came About

It is important to note that the model or Map of Awakening that makes up the majority of this book was not my starting point. My original purpose was simply to assess and record the LOCs of some well-known modern spiritual teachers in order to satisfy my own curiosity about them.

After I had recorded the LOCs of several hundred spiritual teachers, I happened to notice that the results were bunched together. The teachers at different main LOC ranges or stages (600s, 700s, 800s, 900s, 1000) had noticeable similarities. These similarities included patterns in teaching content, style of teaching and reputation (evidence of misconduct or not).

I believe this is important. Had I obtained my main data after developing my model, it would make sense that I could have been influenced by my own model. Instead, what happened is I recorded most of my assessments well before I had the idea to write a book about my results.

The theoretical model appeared in spite of myself. The model impressed me even further when I found that it described my own spiritual journey with unerring accuracy. It became clear to me that my Map of Awakening was meant to be shared.

I define "non-duality" as an empirical understanding that transcends dualistic confusion. The ordinary person is each day besieged by traumatic ongoing conflict, a rock-like sense of separation and the harsh burden of doership. These issues are resolved when a non-dual experience of life is secured.

The main thesis of this book is twofold. First, that not all non-dual realizations are equal. Second, that the great non-dual spiritual quest does have a conclusion (LOC 1000).

In this book, that final stage of fulfillment is called realizing the Self, stabilizing in the Absolute, achieving the "stateless state" or living in the natural state (Sanskrit: *sahaja*). Life is allowed to be itself as it is. Both duality and non-duality are transcended. This is understood when this stage is realized.

Unique Approach to Levels of Consciousness in This Book

In this book, I will cover the full range of the levels of human consciousness. I will start at 30 and work my way up to 1000. LOC 1000 is the highest level achieved by human beings. I start at LOC 30 because this is the lowest human LOC that I encountered. This is extremely low as the average domestic dog is at LOC 90 and the average house cat is at LOC 110.

For maximum accuracy, whenever possible my interpretations of LOCs are based on actual people I know. My focus is on spiritual emergence at LOC 500 and above. The consciousness range between 30 and 499 is summarized in one long chapter. LOCs from 500 and above are given more detailed attention.

This book explains the gradual intensification of non-dual awareness in terms of LOC starting with LOC 500. This information has not been published before. My conclusions are based on my direct observations and LOC assessments of spiritual teachers, students and seekers. I have made use of my personal experience of people I know as much as possible.

Because I have known many spiritual aspirants personally over time, I have been able to assess the significance of LOCs in terms of describable, concrete, quantifiable readiness for non-dual awakening. I have observed favorable changes and found that they are accurately reflected in the person's LOC.

I have met and evaluated in person only a handful of the 200 enlightened spiritual teachers on my list. Whether or not I had met the teacher in person, I took my task of assessing their LOC quite seriously. I watched interviews, read books, studied reviews and researched personal histories online.

Of the teachers on my list, I have had the good fortune to be in the physical presence of Shinzen Young, Ramesh Balsekar, Namkhai Norbu Chen, Muktananda, Jean Klein, Chetananda, Satchidananda, Wayne Liquorman, Jiddu Krishnamurti, Gangaji, Chinmayananda, Sri Sri Ravi Shankar, Aja Acharya Thomas, Anandi Ma, Andrew Cohen, Catherine Ingram, Joko Beck, the Dalai Lama, Franklin Jones (Adi Da Samraj), Hale Dwoskin, Master Charles, Namgyal Rinpoche, Ram Dass, Robert Hover, Saniel Bonder and Satyananda Saraswati.

LOCs 560 to 585: Methodical Preparation for Non-Duality

The movement from LOC 500 to LOC 560 is spiritually significant but serious engagement with non-dual groups, teachers and teachings is not likely until the student enters the 560 range. Starting from the 560s there is a gradual orderly ascent up into the 570s and then into the 580s. The student in the LOC 580s is in position for a leap into non-duality.

Individuals who are primed for enlightenment and the leap into the non-dual ranges LOC 600 and above are typically established somewhere between 581 and 589. This person is able to easily and effortlessly rest in the thought-free state.

LOC 580s as Stabilized Preparation for Non-Dual Ascent

Since being able to abide in the effortless thought-free state is the strongest indicator of readiness for non-dual awakening, this is profoundly significant. At the same time, the natural ease of their state leads many in the 580s to become spiritual teachers from that level.

They make valuable contributions to spiritual culture from this vantage point, but they have missed a golden opportunity to reach the top of the mountain. This is their destiny. I believe that this book will help readers in the 580s to grasp the non-dual potential of their state. I am inviting them to go beyond their comfort zone. When they are ready, they will do so.

The 580s, especially the mid-range of 582 to 585, functions as a springboard or launching pad into non-duality (LOC 600 and above). If the individual starts to move above the LOC 585 staging area, a new process is activated which then "sucks" them into the 590s. It is in the 590s zone that the first deconstruction of the ego (empirical self) takes place.

"Fear of Dying" and the 590s Transitional Zone

The seeker may pass quickly through the transitional 590s or they may get stuck there. If they get stuck, it is usually due to fear of death arising.

To be precise, they are afraid of letting go of their identification with the physical body. The only reason they fear death is that they still believe "I am the body."

This idea, thought or belief "I am the body" is a clever and formidable opponent. I know an Australian seeker living in Thailand who stayed in the 590s for several years. Each time he felt himself being pulled into the 600s, he would experience severe panic and feel as if he was having a heart attack.

When asked about the location of this apparent heart attack, he told me that it was physically located on the *right* side of his chest. This matched reports from other students and my own experiences of similar activity by the ego (I-thought) in the region of the Heart on the right as taught by Ramana Maharshi. I told the Australian as firmly as I could that he was on the verge of enlightenment. Plunge boldly forward!

This formidable drama staged by the ego (I-thought) was just a strategy to intimidate this aspirant and strike fear into him. Its purpose was to terrify him so much with the thought of dying that he would give up his quest. The physical pain was just thought-based intensification of sensations by the ego.

Unfortunately, the seeker did not follow my advice to plunge forward and ignore the frightening sensations of heat and pain. Instead, he capitulated to ego I-thought intimidation. He tumbled all the way back down to the 570s. This setback was only temporary. He is back to LOC 583 ready for another go.

Chances are that this time he will not buy into the deception created by the ego I-thought. After all, it was just thought intensively contracted to produce momentary localized pain.

The Four Levels of Non-Dual Enlightenment Explained

Beyond this original description of the stages of preparation for non-dual ascent (the 560s through the 590s), the other main contribution of this guide is to elaborate in loving detail the four primary levels of non-dual (enlightened) consciousness. These are 600 to 699, 700 to 799, 800 to 899, and 900 to 1000.

As outlined in the Map of Awakening in this book, sages in the LOC 600s range are focused on the local empty "no self," sages in the LOC 700s range are invested in an expanded "cosmic self," sages in the LOC 800s range are stuck in the sweet honey of non-dual devotion, and sages in the LOC 900s are refusing to embrace the world as it is warts and all.

The LOC 1000 sage has completed the non-dual journey. He is stabilized in the "no mind" of the Absolute. We are fortunate at this time in history to have many people who are stabilized at LOC 1000 teaching publicly. This book identifies the ones I know of at this time.

At the same time, it is made clear that the best teacher for a student may not be the one with the highest LOC. The best teacher will be the one where teacher and student are aligned in trust, understanding and mutual warm positive regard.

More on How This Book *1000* Was Born

I experienced my non-dual awakening in 1992 following a transmission of Grace from Ramesh Balsekar in 1989. After that, my process became a prolonged transformational journey through the non-dual stages elucidated in this book.

In the course of my post-awakening sadhana, I concluded that Ramana Maharshi and Nisargadatta Maharaj offered the highest and purest teachings available in modern times.

It was clear to me that they were at the same level of realization. To further refine my understanding, I studied the teachings of both masters and accessed their satsang via photographs, videos, prayer, meditation and visions.

I made a special effort to find and study reports about their demeanor and behavior. It became abundantly clear that both sages lived impeccable exemplary lives. This served to further confirm my conviction that these two incredible men had indeed achieved the supreme pinnacle of spiritual greatness.

I came across a book by a respected spiritual authority in which he stated that a teacher's level of consciousness can be objectively evaluated using biokinesiology (also known as "muscle testing"). I eagerly turned to the page where he had provided his evaluation of Ramana and Nisargadatta.

Learning that the highest level of consciousness (LOC) that could be reached by a human being was 1000, it made sense to me to assume that Ramana and Nisargadatta would be rated by this highly regarded expert at LOC 1000. I was stunned to find that this writer had placed both of them at only LOC 720![1]

Confirmed: Ramana and Nisargadatta Are Both LOC 1000

On the spot, I did my own evaluation. I was right. Both Ramana and Nisargadatta were at LOC 1000!

This kind of intuitive evaluation was not new to me. Inspired by the book *Touch for Health* by John Thie and other pioneers, I began experimenting with biokinesiology about 20 years ago.[2]

There was no doubt for me. The intuitive muscle response was massively precise and clear. There was nothing to figure out. Since the available information in every way pointed to both sages being at LOC 1000, the results of this spontaneous test became my benchmarks as I explored this exciting frontier.

A New Model for Non-Dual Preparation and Realization

A fire had been lit in my psyche that would not be easily quenched. I began doing my own biokinesthetic (muscle testing) evaluations. I found major discrepancies between my intuitive LOC assessments of spiritual figures and those of this prominent author in his books. At the same time, there were numerous examples of teachers where my results matched or came very close to those reported by this respected expert.

As my data accumulated, meaningful patterns began to emerge that I had not seen or heard of before. I received a warm reception for these ideas when I shared them with students and friends. I decided to publish my findings and conclusions. This book is the result.

This book is designed to explain the variations that will be encountered in people who are approaching enlightenment. In broad terms, the ascent begins at LOC 500 with the emergence of pure spirituality. In practice, the effective range where the attainment of enlightenment is a strong possibility begins at LOC 560 and goes up to LOC 585 (rarely, to LOC 589).

To be even more specific, enlightenment becomes likely when the LOC 580s are reached. As the seeker abides more and more in the thought-free state in the LOC 580s, they become purified in preparation for the great leap into non-duality.

The work done in the LOC 560s and LOC 570s is to get to the LOC 580s. Once the aspirant arrives at the LOC 580s, they work to deepen the thought-free state and access the pure silence and stillness of the natural state or pure awareness.

The "No Man's Land" Between LOC 590 and LOC 600

This book also explains the "no man's land" zone between body-identification (below LOC 590) and non-duality (LOC 600). This is the LOC range from 590 to 599. There is only one person in the world that I have found who is staying stable in this profoundly transitional 590 range.

That individual is David Godman, the well-known and highly esteemed translator of Ramana Maharshi's works. I will get into why I believe he is in this special LOC position later on.

For everyone else, this unique range functions as a "black hole" that you go into but don't come out of. It is very similar to the transition known as the "near death experience."

Why Should You Read This Book?

I am sharing my discoveries with you in the hope that it will help you to understand where you, your friends and your teachers are spiritually stabilized according to the LOC model.

1000

The higher the LOC, the more the person has purified the mind. The lower the LOC, the more they are a prisoner of thought and a slave of the mind. According to the model in this book, LOC 1000 corresponds to transcending the mind.

You do not need to know how to evaluate a person's LOC in order to benefit from this book. By understanding the new model of consciousness presented in this guide, you will be in a position to assess a person's spiritual level based on their behavior, their teachings and their teaching methods.

If they are deeply integrated and realized, then their behavior will reflect the knowledge that "You are my very own beloved Self." While this behavior usually expresses in what is labeled as "loving," it may not appear that way on the surface.

For example, Nisargadatta Maharaj was known to yell and shout at many of the people who came to him. On the surface this does not sound loving, but students reported that being on the receiving end of his dramatic outbursts was a blessing.

One of the biggest challenges for a spiritual seeker is how to evaluate various teachers. Whether or not you are able to do your own intuitive LOC evaluations, this book should serve you in at least three ways.

First, you will have a new appreciation of the differences in levels of consciousness even among enlightened teachers. This has never before been clarified with this degree of precision.

Second, you will be better informed regarding how to assess LOCs. You will know that the attainment of enlightenment in and of itself is not the end of the process.

The journey goes on in the form of mental and emotional purification until the person reaches the level of total dedication to service. The mature sage regards all as his Self.

Third, you will be able to discern the basic LOC range of an enlightened teacher or guru (600 to 699, 700 to 799, 800 to 899 or 900 to 1000) based on the identifying markers in their teaching style and content. Each range has its own unique flavor and orientation. I will go into that in much more detail.

Why Is the Author Qualified to Evaluate Other Teachers?

You may feel like asking me "Who are you to presume to evaluate other spiritual teachers?"

The answer is simple.

Now that there are so many non-duality teachers writing books and giving public satsang in the West, it is time for us to start a lively dialog about the quality and level of these contributions. Somebody has to get this discussion going!

I believe that I have found a convenient reliable way to evaluate the LOC of a person at any level, whether they are a teacher or not. This is the method that I use every day.

Some readers may find that they have the ability to assess the LOCs of spiritual students and teachers. Other readers will discover that they cannot evaluate LOCs or that results are hit or miss. Either way, the reader will be served by this new knowledge about the levels of human spiritual attainment.

As for my spiritual qualifications, since my awakening in 1992 I have worked tirelessly to fulfill my spiritual potential in this lifetime. I have studied the teachings of Ramana Maharshi and Nisargdatta Maharaj in great depth. I have personally logged many hours following their practical meditation disciplines.

I have used descriptions by Ramana and Nisargadatta of their state of consciousness and of the supreme state as empirical benchmarks for evaluating my own levels of consciousness. It has been my routine for many years to assess my own LOC. I have observed how each of my spiritual breakthroughs was matched by a corresponding jump in my LOC number.

The time has come for this uniquely useful information to be revealed. This book began with a simple heartfelt desire to set the record straight with regard to Ramana and Nisargadatta. I thought that would be it, but it was not.

The project surprised me with its passion to grow and expand. After more than a year of hard work fueled by the sincere desire to help as many people as possible become free by becoming who they truly are, my original desire to set the record straight about the LOCs of my gurus Ramana Maharshi and Nisargadatta Maharaj blossomed into this big book.

How to Evaluate a Person's LOC Using Whole Body Intuitive Resonance

How to Evaluate a Person's LOC Using Whole Body Intuitive Resonance

While this book is not a how-to guide for assessing, recording and interpreting the LOCs of prominent non-dual teachers and other people of note, it makes sense for me to explain my method to you. You may or may not be able to do it yourself. It is extremely simple for me, nonetheless.

LOC means Level Of Consciousness. Every person on the planet has a level of consciousness or LOC. For most people, it tends to stay the same. For some people, it moves up. A rise of five points in the course of a lifetime is significant.

For a few people, it moves way up very quickly. When this happens and the person stabilizes at an LOC level above 600 on the LOC scale, this corresponds to enlightenment.

How to Evaluate a Person's LOC From a Distance

It is ideal to have a picture of the person available. If they are on YouTube, you can watch a video of them talking. These steps will help you get a "feel" for the person.

Now close your eyes and think of the person. Reach out with your consciousness and make energetic contact with them.

You do not want any thoughts, expectations or desire impinging on this reaching out. If your intuitive ability is open, you will know when you have made contact.

It may have a tangible tactile quality to it. The knowledge that you have made this contact is self-evident and self-validating.

When you make this contact, you will feel a degree of density, thickness or heaviness surrounding them. This density is the tangible tactile indicator of their level of consciousness.

In the average person, there is a feeling of heavy thickness and density. It is like they have a body or wall of armor around them. This may be felt especially strong around their head.

This density is the accumulated thought patterns that this person is not conscious of and has not eliminated. In the enlightened person, there is a feeling of lightness. The higher up the LOC scale of enlightenment, the lighter the person will feel.

The Finger Ring Muscle Testing Technique

The feeling contact step is the first step and the most valuable step. As you get more tuned in, it can be enough in itself. The numerical evaluation is just a label for what your intuition is telling you about this person's LOC.

The final step is to put a number to your intuitive impression. This is the biokinesiology step. This is also called muscle testing or applied kinesiology. There are differences between these concepts, but the main idea remain the same.

Our favorite method is the "Ring Finger" method. Make a ring with your thumb and index finger with both hands.

If you are right handed, put that ring *inside* the ring created by your left hand. If you are left handed, put your ring *inside* your right hand. Here's a link to a video on YouTube that shows you exactly what doing this method looks like.[3]

How to Get Their Unique LOC Number

Now start asking a series of questions like this: "Is this person at LOC 0 or above? At 100 or above? At 200 or above? At 300 or above? At 400 or above? At 500 or above? At 600 or above?"

Unless they are enlightened and in non-duality, their LOC will be between 0 (zero) and 599. When you ask the question, if it is true then you will feel that your "yin" or passive finger ring is strong.

If you are right handed, you will be pulling against the point where your left thumb and left index finger join. You will feel the muscular strength as well as the intuitive feeling strength.

Let's say the person you are checking the LOC for is at 512 LOC. You will feel strength until you ask the question "Is this person's LOC at 600 or higher?"

There will be a feeling of weakness in the left finger ring and the right finger ring will easily break through the fingers there. When this happens, go back to the previous question.

"If this person at 500 LOC or higher?" You get a strong yes.

Now go up in tens. "Is he at 510 or higher?" Since he is at 512 LOC, you will get another yes response.

Now go up another ten. "Is he at 520 LOC? Now you will get a no response. The left hand ring will weaken. Since you got a weak no response, go back to 510 again.

Now go up by single units.. First, restate your verified position which is that his LOC is at least 510.

"Is he at 510?" The answer is yes.

"Is he at 511?" The answer is yes.

"Is he at 512?" The answer is yes.

"Is he at 513?" The answer is no.

Go back to 512 and repeat the question.

"Is he at 512 LOC?" Yes.

You are finished. You have now evaluated this person and found them to be living at an LOC of 512.

How I First Started Evaluating the LOCs of People

I was introduced to the technique of muscle testing many years ago. I became interested in evaluating the levels of spiritual teachers. Because I had been studying the human energy field since my Kundalini awakening at the age of 16, I was already well schooled in the art of evaluating teachers.

Prior to biokinesiology testing, I had studied the auras of dozens of individuals reputed to be enlightened (above LOC 600). My experience while doing so was intensely empathic.

I was able to identify a visual pattern that all of these saints and sages had in common. The Crown chakra was radiant with light. It was wide open and unobstructed.

The average person is mostly closed at the Crown chakra. The Crown chakra of the spiritually advanced seeker in the LOC 500s will be partially or even mostly open. I see the wide open Crown chakra blazing with light in enlightened people only.

Since my spiritual awakening in 1992 after receiving Grace from Ramesh Baleskar, I have noticed that the average body-identified person has a thick hard energy wall with the density of concrete or metal around their head. This wall is their accumulated thoughts. They are not aware of this wall.

In contrast, the enlightened people that I have met feel like they have a great deal of lightness around them. Their thought density is much less. I have noticed that the more spiritually enlightened the person is, the lighter they feel to me.

I found that when I think of people alive or dead, I have the same experience. They don't need to be physically present. I get an immediate and precise sense of their thought density.

Although people seem to make a big deal about the muscle testing technique itself, my experience is that using the physical hands is not really needed. It is all in the *feeling*.

It may sound like I am saying that when you evaluate LOC the number is the objective, but that is not correct. The goal is to have a conscious clear empathic connection that is purely intuitive. It will not work if it is thought based.

I am operating from pure feeling. As a result, I can via direct perception evaluate the degree of thought density that surrounds the person. When this thought density has been fully resolved and the person is no longer struggling with the mind, then their LOC will register at 1000 for me.

When I think of someone, I instantly have intuitive feeling-knowing regarding that person, their thought density and their LOC. I still do the Finger Ring Circle test in order to confirm their LOC number, but it is a confirmation of what was already known. Once again, the key is in the *feeling*.

I automatically have a sense of the thought density of any person I put my attention on because I can feel it as a tangible coating, almost like it is a physical object. Since my sensitivity to this aspect of a person is so acute, I can easily distinguish between the thought densities found around a person in the LOC 580s versus a person in the 600s, 700s, 800s, 900s or at 1000. While the density gets progressively less and less at each higher level, only the LOC 1000 will feel to me to be totally free of this concrete thought density. Even the LOC 900s present a very fine detectable layer of residual mental density.

When you are doing an LOC assessment, be aware that any thoughts you have will interfere. You must have no thoughts, otherwise you will be reading your thoughts, not the person.

When this happens, when thoughts interfere, you will notice, meaning you will *feel*, a subtle change in the energy. This is the kind of attunement needed. There is no doubting and no guessing. There is *intuitive* knowing. It cannot be understood intellectually. It must experienced to be fully appreciated.

Notes

On Assessing

Non-Dual Teachers

Notes On Assessing Non-Dual Teachers

There are many teachers around the world today offering non-dual spiritual teachings and guidance. Most of the people on the main non-duality teacher list appear here because they say up front that they teach "non-duality" (or "nonduality").

Popular non-dual spiritual teachers aligned with established traditions are included the next chapter also. For example, Buddhism and Advaita Vedanta are well-known non-dual traditions.

You will find some of the better known Theravadan, Zen and Tibetan Buddhist teachers like Jack Kornfield, Stephen Batchelor and Lama Surya Das along with the Dalai Lama. You will also find traditional Advaita Vedanta teachers such as Swami Dayananda and Nanna Guru there.

The name of the teacher, their LOC, a short bio and the title of their book (usually) is provided. It is enough information that you can explore more of what they offer if you want to do so.

I apologize in advance for the many gifted non-dual teachers and traditions not represented. I also ask your understanding for the American bias that permeates this material. I live in San Diego, California. Rather than try to represent the world, I decided to talk about the teachers I am most familiar with.

This project, even in this minimalist presentation, has been monumental in scope. Tough decisions had to be made as to who made the cut and who didn't. I make no claim that these decisions are the best ones.

About 10 people helped make these choices. The matter was not taken lightly. Future editions will include suggestions from readers. Please refer to the back of the book for contact information. I encourage your feedback. I am aware that my LOC project is, and will always be, a work in progress.

About This LOC Model for Non-Dual Assessment

I have made every effort to insure that the LOCs in this book are accurate within the limits of my ability. No claim is made that they are so precise that they should be written in stone. The LOC of a teacher or student is one more way to assess the overall tonality of a person's being and the degree of purity and refinement with which they express it.

The chief reason for publishing this LOC model is to show the progression of transformational insight and how it unfolds in the upper regions of the spiritual stratosphere. My Map of Awakening makes the natural logic of progress in non-duality transparent. I explain how and why one step leads to the next.

No longer will mystical smoke and mirrors obscure the facts. Non-dual realization is a human attainment. Painters, writers, composers and scientists who achieve recognition for their work are not all at the same level as their peers. Likewise, all non-dual teachers and realizers are not at the same level of realization.

The subject of differences at the non-dual heights has been a forbidden topic or thought to be a matter of personal opinion. It has been thought to be beyond words. That is changing.

By providing a numerical assessment, it becomes possible to discuss in concrete terms that which before was represented by abstract symbols. Thanks to LOC differentiations, we can now discuss in broad strokes the differences in enlightened levels. This enables a type of discourse that previously was not possible.

I do not claim to be the only person who can make accurate LOC assessments. Since it is easy and effortless for me to assess an LOC, I was surprised to find that most people, even friends of mine who are gifted intuitives, find it difficult.

For this reason, teaching this skill is not the focus of this book. As explained in a previous chapter, the quintessence of the method is *pure feeling*, not the biokinesiology technique itself.

If the person cannot easily and routinely access the thought-free state and pure unbounded feeling, it is my experience that they will not be able to arrive at accurate LOC assessments. This is not an elitist position. I would very much like it to be a common skill. Perhaps someday it will be. For now, it is not.

Higher Is Not Always Better

The transparent energetic clarity revealed to me by the LOC 1000 person who is "lost in the Absolute" has no parallel in lower LOC levels. At the same time, since there are many "X factors" in the delivery of satsang, it is entirely possible that an enlightened teacher at a lower LOC may be presenting just the right quickening of consciousness for his or her students.

It is natural to assume that "higher is better." What matters most is the "chemistry" between the two of you.

A higher LOC would be better for the teacher for their own sake, but it is entirely possible that a teacher with a lower LOC will be better for you. They may be easier to understand.

Best-selling author Deepak Chopra (LOC 562) is not yet established in non-duality, yet his teachings have been a great help to many. The consensus is that Chopra has made great contributions to the modern non-duality movement.[4]

As an educator, Chopra is hard to beat, but more advanced and sophisticated students know that there is unparalleled value to being in the presence of one who is established in non-duality. In that case, Jeff Foster (LOC 678) and Scott Kiloby (LOC 754) are examples of accessible compassionate teachers who are well integrated in their realization. Likewise, both Gangaji (LOC 1000) and Francis Lucille (LOC 1000) offer liberating wisdom in a loving supportive context.

Even though I returned to Ramana Maharshi (LOC 1000) and Nisargadatta Maharaj (LOC 1000) for clarification of many subtle yet critical points, Ramesh Balsekar (LOC 764) was the perfect guru for me in 1989. Ramesh's message, down to the exact words the he spoke in person to me, was precisely what I needed to hear. The alignment itself was what mattered.

My conclusion from my spiritual initiation with Ramesh Balsekar is that the LOC of the teacher is not the most critical factor. Obviously, you want him to be stabilized in non-duality. The "transcendental" attunement between your awakened guru and you, the sincere disciple, is the key.

The Enlightened Guru and the Golden Standard

The purpose of this book is to elucidate apparent differences between teachers in their presence, behavior and message. When the facts are laid out, it appears that guru misconduct is much more likely with teachers in the 600s and 700s.

The classic forms of misconduct are very familiar to us. Four big areas show up again and again. They are abuse of power, abuse of money, abuse of drugs and abuse of sex.[5]

Of course, these are the same exact areas that exploitation, misconduct and abuse can be found in worldly contexts like politics, sports, business and entertainment. The guilty party is usually a man, but not always. Women seem to be less prone to scandalous behavior, but then they are not as likely to be in a position of authority where misconduct is possible.

There is no simple explanation for this problem. In the case of spiritual teachers, it is possible to come out too early publicly as a teacher. In theory this should not make a difference, but in practice a major awakening takes time to stabilize and integrate. Coming out a few months or a few years after your breakthrough into non-duality could be counterproductive.

There is no hard and fast rule about this. It is more a case of "By their fruits you will know them." Most people are not even remotely prepared for being in a position of authority where sex, money and recreational drugs may be made available without the conventional rules or limits. Much like the people who win the lottery and proceed to ruin their lives, too much of a good thing can easily turn out extremely bad.

After a sage is ensconced in this position of authority, it will be the rare teacher who decides that he or she needs to step down and take a break. Usually a crisis needs to occur before such an action takes place. Even then the sage may deny any wrongdoing. As the saying goes, an ounce of prevention is worth a pound of cure. That means wait until you're ready.

To use traditional language, in the LOC 800s sages and above a purification process has taken place that the teachers in the lower non-dual LOCs have not gone through. This includes deeply buried emotional traumas but is not limited to that.

The progression from the lower non-dual LOCs to the higher non-dual LOCs on up to LOC 1000 is not just a matter of going higher in consciousness. The final stabilization in the Absolute is a full resolution of the world and the other. Love has been fully integrated into the path. When you are a teacher at this level, the student you are teaching is your very own beloved Self. The evidence is strong that impeccable purity is more likely to be found the higher you go on the LOC scale.

Highly revered masters like Ramana Maharshi and Nisargadatta Maharaj were impeccable in their behavior as well as in the clarity and effectiveness of their non-dual message. They represent the gold standard to which the majority aspire but to which only a minority attain.

"Self-realization" has been used to describe an absolute separation between the "realized" and the "not realized." The evidence does not support this idea. Parallel to the evolution of life on earth, there is unfoldment over time and integration.

Progression upwards in the non-dual LOCs means that the mind becomes more and more attenuated until, at LOC 1000, it finally disappears. It can be argued that the mind continues with the difference that it is no longer a problem for the sage. Either way, the mind as such is gone. Now there is Silence, and in this Silence, thoughts may or may not arise.

To attain enlightenment and get established in non-duality is one thing. To live as a human being who compassionately embodies the truth "All is my very Self" is quite another.

If the apparent other human being in front of you is indeed you, if they too are this Buddha Nature, then surely the last thing you would dream of doing would be to hurt, harm, limit or confuse them. After all, you are only hurting yourself.

In Buddhist circles, this challenge has been posed as "Would you do this [act of misconduct] to someone you know for sure is a Buddha?" Christians may ask "What would Jesus do?" The answer is obvious in both cases, yet misconduct continues.

Clearly, these forces run very deep. Non-dual awakening does not mean that every twisted knot of the subconscious has been burned through and resolved. It does not mean that terrible traumas from past lives and this life have been handled. One of the gifts of awakening is that now you are in a position to dig up and resolve submerged conflicts that the empirical ego, when it ran the show, would not let rise to the surface.

At the "top of the mountain," life is service. If everyone is your beloved Self, then the ongoing daily suffering of these others is your suffering also. There is no room for selfish behavior. You live for the realization of all beings, for they are you.

Because you love yourself without limits or conditions and all is your Self, this is inevitably true. How this will look to others cannot be predicted. In your heart of hearts, you will know that you are on an authentic path of compassionate love.

The teacher of non-duality is a doctor for the deeper soul. All of us who seek to minister to the spiritual needs of others will do well to remember the words of the father of modern medicine, Hippocrates" "First do no harm."[6]

To rework a familiar discussion, at issue is not so much if the teacher is "halfway up the mountain" or even "half-baked." The concern is whether they are integrated and capable of profound and consistent love, service and sacrifice on a day to day basis. The dynamics of teacher-student relationships, including the tricks and traps as well as the rewards, are lucidly covered by transpersonal psychotherapist Mariana Caplan in her book *The Guru Question*.[7]

Who Would Be a God? The Age-Old Inflation Trap.

I want to at least mention Carl Jung's notion of "inflation." Inflation is a very human response to finding yourself in a position of elevation, influence, power and even worship by other human beings for which you are woefully unprepared.

In the way that I am using the term, it is akin to the actor who begins to believe that he is the superhuman character that he is playing. The "more than human" character is, in Jungian terms, an archetype or god symbol. The actor, teacher or guru enters into the danger zone when he believes his own hype.

This "inflation" via identification with a "bigger than life" image or idea may increase the charisma magnetism of the spiritual teacher. It may lead to claims of being "the avatar."

Innocent inflation is not the same as pathological narcissism.[8] This would be reserved for sociopathic cult leaders who are selfishly motivated and practice deception from the start.

What I am pointing to is the sincere spiritual teacher who goes astray. He could be independent. He could represent a major non-dual tradition. Sooner or later, he finds himself in over his head. I am not aware of any course offered by any teacher, school or tradition on how to deal with these challenges.

The only realistic preparation will be the years you spend "cooking" prior to coming out as an awakened teacher. If you go public prematurely, you may well be qualified on the enlightenment side, but your familiarity with the ins and outs of human manipulation may be sadly lacking.

The enlightened sage is often regarded as a "therapist plus" by his students. He will have to deal with psychological issues whether he wants to or not. This may include sexy women literally throwing themselves at him. Let me tell you a story about that.

Two years after my awakening in 1992, I ran a nine day non-dual meditation retreat where we all camped in the woods outside of Toronto, Canada. Once a day, in one of the tents I privately coached each student.

An attractive thirty-something blonde female attendee came in for her one on one time with me. She sat very close to me.

When I asked her how I could help her, she replied "Do you think I'm attractive?" I don't know if there is a right way to answer that question. Since she was, I replied "Yes, you are."

Without warning, she then jumped in my lap and said in a deep husky voice "Make love to me right now!" This really happened. I know it sounds like something from Hollywood, but I am not making this up.

I have a background in psychological counseling, including sexual abuse and substance addiction. I had already pegged her as a likely candidate for some kind of early childhood abuse that would be acted out in some form of addiction.

In that sense, I was prepared. Even so, I was shocked by the boldness of her gesture. Here she suddenly was, her arms around my neck, her lips inches from mine, her legs wrapped around my torso. She was begging to have sex with me.

As calmly as I could, I replied "Melody, you are a lovely girl. But I do not know you well enough for this kind of encounter. It's very important to me that making love be an expression of love, respect and tenderness. Let's talk about this first."

Before I said those words, it was like her face was frozen in a trance. She had a glazed look in her eyes. After my tender and respectful rejection of her sexual advances, she seemed to suddenly wake up. Her face softened. She slowly disengaged her body from mine and sat at a reasonable distance from me.

She began crying. "Nobody has ever rejected me like that."

I was prepared for the worst. It had truly been a double-bind situation. I could only hope that I had said the right thing.

Then through her tears, she smiled at me. "I really want to thank you. This experience with you has been incredibly healing." She cried some more. Then she gave me another hug. This one was gentle and sweet without the sexual overtones.

I heard months later that she had been singing my praises to her friends in Toronto after the retreat. "That guy is the real deal,"she said. "He is a great teacher. He really helped me!"

This left me with mixed feelings. Even though that incident had turned out okay, was I prepared for another one? She could have flipped the other way after I rejected her. She could have turned on me and condemned me. Then she would have gone around Toronto saying what a jerk I was.

It was this event and other totally unexpected twists and turns that told me I was not yet ready to teach the public. I needed to be more emotionally mature. I was also beginning to sense that my "enlightenment" could and should be deeper. Seeing that led me on the spiritual journey that resulted in this book.

While the most cruel manifestations of psychological self-aggrandizement are reserved for natural born psychopath cult leaders, anyone who has led workshops, seminars, group meetings or given public talks knows that sooner or later some form of temptation is likely to present itself. The aura of leadership lends a charisma some find intoxicating. A depth psychology approach will typically find a need to be loved by the parent who was never there or was there too much, but the ones who need this insight rarely do the work to get it.

In simplistic terms, this is the "rock star" phenomenon wherein one or more "groupies" want a "piece" of you. By getting up in front of a group and showing that you are a leader, you will now be viewed as a desirable "alpha" human.

In the crude imperative of reproductive biology that is imprinted in the human body by mother nature, you are demonstrating that your genetic material is superior and worthy of reproduction and perpetuation. Powerful forces are at work, but it will be a mistake to succumb. Whatever the underlying causes, the psychological damage to the student's sadhana and the guru's reputation can be considerable.

It is not the sage that these transient would-be worshipers really want, but what the guru or teacher represents to them. Students are not falling in love with "you," for they do not know you. If you as the teacher or "celebrity rock star" have identified yourself with this superhuman archetypal image projected onto you, then in servicing their fantasies you have lost your own humanity. You are a phony god of light with ugly feet of clay.

The Elegant Fragility of the Human Flower

To be human is a rare, unusual and unique opportunity. It is profoundly personal and infinitely intimate.

The word "love" points to the truth of the human essence, but you cannot just mouth the word. You must live it. The path is a form of art. We are spiritual artists. We dance the truths we have realized with our lives. We cannot do otherwise.

Enlightenment is universal, impersonal and timeless. Making it relevant, personal and one to one so that the "other" is known, recognized, valued and esteemed is the human job of the spiritual teacher.

To be human is like being a flower. We are profoundly beautiful, yet in our fragility it is easy for us to become broken or twisted. While the cosmos is busy smashing one galaxy into another, it is our job as a human being to gently extend our hand to that of another. This is the exquisitely majestic opportunity that each of us has as a human being, whether we are teacher, student or playing some other role.

It sometimes seems that sex scandals with spiritual leaders (usually men) are more likely than not to occur. Whatever the statistics, it is pretty much "old news' when we hear of yet another "fallen guru" or Christian preacher or controversial cult leader who bit into the bitterly blissful apple of sex.

As an antidote to the cynicism that arises when contemplating these foibles of human nature, I would like to reference a short online interview of editor Jean Dunn about her transcendental relationship with her guru, Nisargadatta Maharaj. In this amazing interview, you will experience a brilliant description of an exemplary fusion of true devotee with true guru.[9]

The King of the West and the Sage of the East

On a positive note, this vast new abundance of non-dual spiritual teachers is a very healthy sign of things to come. Thirty years ago, there was no need for this book. The new wave of awakening called for a new clarity. It is here.

Guru shenanigans are possible only in an atmosphere of secrecy. These goings on must take place behind closed doors. As the living reality of non-duality becomes more and more the norm, then the magical gleam of special powers, inner circles and forbidden knowledge will fall away.

In its place will be the recognition of the guru as a fully human exemplary human being. Stabilization in the highest levels of enlightenment is part and parcel of what it means to be a complete human being. Integrating this realization to the fullest possible extent is also what it means to truly be a human being. The humanity of the sage redeems the world.

The marriage of the spiritual and the material, so that the King of the West and the Sage of the East are one and the same, is the luminous and peaceful future that we as a culture and a planet are being pulled towards as if by a spiritual magnet.

LOCs

of

200 Contemporary

Western Teachers

of

Non-Duality and Advaita

LOCs of 200 Contemporary Western Teachers of Non-Duality and Advaita

I'm defining "contemporary" to mean actively involved in teaching non-duality in approximately the last 50 years. Some sages who have dropped the body are included in this list.

Modern Western non-duality is a new phenomenon. My goal is to recognize prominent contributors and provide you with insight into their level of understanding and how that is expressed in their teachings and their life.

Some names are here because they are prominent in the field. Not everybody listed is enlightened or known as a teacher of non-duality. I've included a few people who serve as skillful and enthusiastic interviewers of non-dual teachers.

I have also included a few people from other traditions, such as Brother David Steindl-Rast (LOC 848) to demonstrate that enlightenment is not an exclusively Eastern experience. It is easy to think that non-duality is new or that its methodology has no precedent. Awakening is going on and has been going on in the classical traditions for many centuries.

You will see some Kundalini masters mentioned. This is due to my own involvement in Kundalini since 1966. I have great admiration for that tradition.

I have mentioned teachers I believe deserve more interest from serious non-duality students. It can be argued that Kundalini plays a major role in most non-dual awakenings. That is a story for another time.

Please note that I have defined "Western" rather broadly to mean having significant influence in the West, especially in the United States of America. Their country of origin may be anywhere in the world, but the non-dual impact of their message and presence has shaped Western spiritual culture.

It has turned out to be impossible to provide LOCs for all of the non-duality teachers active in the world today. If your favorite Advaita or non-duality teacher is not listed here, the email address for making suggestions and offering feedback is provided near the end of the book. This list will be updated. Your contributions will make future editions better.

The significance of different LOCs may not mean much if you just started reading this book. The rest of this guide explains in rich detail the meaning and usefulness of these numerical consciousness codes and how you can apply them to your life.

This unique knowledge is designed to effortlessly expand and uplift your natural view. You do not need to assess anyone's LOC in order to benefit from this information. To be aware of the LOC differences and the reasons for them is enough.

You will be able to understand where you are on the LOC scale and why you are there. Rising upwards in LOC is based on a simple premise. As the mind falls away, the person rises higher and higher in LOC. When pure "no mind" is attained, this corresponds to LOC 1000.

From the spiritual seeker's point of view, the single most important factor is resonance, not the teacher's LOC.

You must resonate with the teacher and be comfortable in their presence. As long as they are established in non-duality, they can help you attain enlightenment.

Finally, it must be noted that on this list there a few well-known teachers with LOCs below 600. I have been extremely rigorous in checking my findings. My conclusion is that they are serving the dharma quite eloquently in that capacity.

In theory, a teacher does not himself have to abide in non-duality to facilitate the awakening of others. His ability to clarify the teachings and make them available to people at large can transcend any limitations of his personal view. I gave the example of Deepak Chopra (LOC 562) earlier.

However, when a teacher claims to be living in non-duality and their LOC is not even in the 560s or 570s, this means that at least some of their students will be more advanced than them. This is a situation which warrants considerable caution.

Adyashanti LOC 784
Began teaching non-duality and inquiry in 1996 after his Zen teacher asked him to do so. Author of *The Way of Liberation*.

A. H. Almaas LOC 1000
Modern master who successfully fused Eastern mysticism and Western psychology. Author of *The Pearl Beyond Price*.

Aja Acharya Thomas LOC 765
Former bhakti yogi under Swami Prabhupada. Awakened via intensive Self-inquiry in 1990. Author of *In This Moment*.

Albert Nahmani LOC 653

Search ended in 1987 with dawn of "the absolute reality." Cites J. Krishnamurti and Murshid James MacKie as influences.

Alex Vartman LOC 672
Teacher of Tantric sexuality for raising Kundalini safely and with consistency. Author of *The New Tantra* (DVD).

Alexander Smit LOC 684
Awakened in 1978 meeting with Nisargadatta Maharaj. Also studied with Wolter Keers. Author of *Consciousness*.

Alice Gardner LOC 678
Awakened in satsang with Eckhart Tolle and Adyashanti. Author of *Finding Our Way Forward*.

Amber Terrell LOC 917
Songwriter. Realization acknowledged by Gangaji. Apparent reclusive not publicly teaching. Author of *Surprised By Grace*.

Anadi (Aziz Kristof) LOC 1000
Studied with well-known sages. Author of *The Human Buddha*.

Anandi Ma LOC 875
Spiritual heir of Sri Dhyanyogiji. Known for many years as Asha Ma or Ashadevi. Gives Kundalini Shaktipat initiations.

Ananta Kranti LOC 688
Studied with Osho. Awakened in 1990s on Zen retreat in Japan. Stabilized in satsang with Dolano in 2000 in Pune.

Andrew Cohen LOC 684
Controversial student of Papaji who disowned his connection to him. Author of *Living Enlightenment*.

Annamalai Swami LOC 1000
Devotee of Ramana and supervisor of his building program.
Author of autobiographical *Living By the Words of Bhagavan*.

Annette Nibley LOC 678
Awakened with help of John Wheeler and Stephen Wingate.

Arjuna Nick Ardagh 773
Received Grace from Papaji in 1991. Creator of the Awakening Coach Training. Author of *The Translucent Revolution*.

Arnaud Desjardins LOC 755
French film producer who studied with Swami Prajnanpad. Author of *The Jump into Life: Moving Beyond Fear*.

Aruna Byers LOC 766
Awakened in 1993 with Grace of Papaji. Author of *The Masters' Messenger: Emergence of an Awakened Channel*.

Arunachala Ramana (Dee Wayne Trammell) LOC 1000
Founder of AHAM. Awakened looking at a photo of Ramana Maharshi in a book. Author of *Consciousness Being Itself*.

Bala LOC 678
Awakened student of Wayne Liquorman. Author of *Thorns For a Seeker*.

Bernadette Roberts LOC 854
Catholic mystic with devotional non-dual awakening. Author of *The Experience of No-Self: A Contemplative Journey*.

Bernie Glassman LOC 768

Successor to Maezumi Roshi. Author of *Instructions to the Cook*.

Bernie Prior LOC 676
Awakened spontaneously via series of experiences that began in childhood. Creator of the The Form-Reality Practice™.

Bhagavan Das LOC 744
Devotee of Neem Karoli Baba. Known as the mentor of Ram Dass in India. Author of *Love Songs to the Dark Lord* CD.

Bharat Rochlin LOC 744
Received Grace from Papaji. Author of *Split Seconds*.

Billy Doyle LOC 684
London student of Jean Klein who teaches in Klein's Kashmir yoga tradition. Author of *The Mirage of Separation*.

Bodhi Avasa LOC 754
Spontaneously awakened at age of 23. "Life was the path, if there was one at all." Gives satsang but not into guru-disciple.

Brother David Steindl-Rast LOC 848
Benedictine monk who worked with Thomas Merton. Active in Buddhist-Christian dialog. Author of *A Listening Heart*.

B. S. Goel (Sri Siddheshwar Baba) LOC 855
Yogic practices plus dream of Sathya Sai Baba awakened his Kundalini. Author of *Third Eye and Kundalini*.

Burt Harding LOC 783
Received Grace when Ramana Maharshi appeared to him in 1974 in Toronto, Canada. Author of *Hiding in Plain Sight*.

Byron Katie LOC 768
Spontaneously awakened during deep depression. Author of *Loving What Is: Four Questions That Can Change Your Life.*

Canela Michelle Meyers LOC 845
Opening at 15 years old. Awakened in 1998 in satsang with Isaac Shapiro. Author of *Right Here, Right Now Meditations.*

Carlos Castaneda LOC 672
Anthropologist who attained fame after studying with a Yaqui sorcerer-shaman. Author of *The Teachings of Don Juan.*

Catherine Noyce LOC 744
Co-owner of Non-Duality Press with husband Julian Noyce.

Catherine Ingram LOC 685
20 year practitioner of Buddhism who found Grace with Papaji. Author of *Passionate Presence.*

Cee LOC 1000
Realized truth through her spiritual master Nome. Author of *The Way of Knowledge: Meditation Realization Nonduality.*

Charlie Hayes LOC 674
Sat with Wayne Liquorman and listened to Ramesh Balsekar. Sailor Bob finally "did it" for him. Author of *You Are Unborn.*

Cheri Huber LOC 782
American independent Soto Zen master. Studied with Jay DuPont(?). Author of *What You Practice Is What You Have.*

Chetananda LOC 1000

Student of Muktananda, Rudrananda (Rudi) and Lashmanjoo in Kashmir Shaivism tradition. Author of *Dynamic Stillness*.

Chris Hebard LOC 674
Owner of StillnessSpeaks.com. Films and shares work of sages and today's Western teachers with focus on Direct Inquiry.

Chogyam Trungpa Rinpoche LOC 775
Famous Tibetan Buddhist teacher with major impact in the West. Author of *Cutting Through Spiritual Materialism*.

Chuck Hillig LOC 683
Playful licensed psychotherapist doing marriage and family counseling. Author of *Looking for God: Seeing the Whole in One*.

Colin Drake LOC 1000
Long-time meditator awakened with the help of Gangaji. Author of *Beyond the Separate Self*.

Dadaji LOC 775
Experienced explosive awakening while on solitary retreat. Author of *Intelligence Beyond Thought*.

Daniel Brown LOC 784
Studied with many great Theravadan and Tibetan meditation masters. Author of *Pointing Out the Great Way*.

Daniel Odier LOC 675
Credits enlightenment to mystical initiation by Tantric dakini guru in Kashmir. Author of *Tantric Quest*.

Darryl Bailey LOC 688

Former Thai Buddhist monk living in Canada. Author of *Dismantling the Fantasy*.

David Bingham LOC 676
Artist who awakened listening to John Wheeler interview.

David Carse LOC 918
Student of Ramesh Balsekar. Reclusive carpenter living in Vermont. Author of *Perfect Brilliant Stillness*.

David Deida LOC 683
Highly respected sacred sexuality and Tantra teacher. Author of *The Way of the Superior Man*.

David Frawley LOC 745
Director of American Institute of Vedic Studies in Santa Fe, New Mexico. Author of *Vedantic Meditation*.

David Godman LOC 595
Respected editor associated with Papaji, Ramana Maharshi and Lakshmana Swami. Editor of excellent *Be As You Are*.

David R. Hawkins LOC 874
Colorful mystic who studied under Lester Levenson after dramatic Kundalini experiences. Author of *Power vs. Force*.

Davidya LOC 754
Non-duality blogger with deep insight into spiritual stages.

Dayananda Saraswati LOC 843
Modern teacher of Vedanta in the Shankara tradition since 1976. Author of *Introduction to Vedanta*.

Deepak Chopra LOC 562
The former favorite of the Maharishi Mahesh Yogi is now an alternative health guru. Author of *Spiritual Solutions*.

Dennis Waite LOC 776
Student of Advaita Vedanta for decades. One of the first to put Advaita on the Internet. Author of *Advaita Made Easy*.

Dileepji LOC 775
Close disciple of Dhyanyogiji who travels with Anandi Ma giving Kundalini Shaktipat initiations around the world.

Dolano LOC 778
Gives Osho, Papaji and Gangaji as her influences.

Douglas Harding LOC 689
Early pioneer of non-dual direct pointing experiments. Author of *On Having No Head*.

Douwe Tiemersma LOC 925
Had radical encounter with Nisargadatta in 1980. Author of *Non-Duality: the Groundless Openness*.

Dr. Pillai (Dattatriya Siva Baba) LOC 1000
Teacher in Tamil Siddha tradition. Emphasizes spiritual and material fulfillment. Gave "Ahh" meditation to Wayne Dyer.

Drunvalo Melchizedek LOC 684
Ascension teacher. Author of *Living in the Heart*.

Eckhart Tolle LOC 674
Spontaneously awakened in the context of suicidal depression. Author of *The Power of Now*.

Ed Muzika LOC 723
Successor of Robert Adams. Advaita teacher of Rajiv Kapur. Author of *Self-Realization and Other Awakenings*.

Eli Jaxon Bear LOC 668
Awakened with help of Papaji and wife Gangaji. Author of *From Fixation to Freedom: The Enneagram of Liberation*.

Elizabeth MacDonald LOC 850
Lead disciple of Arunachala Ramana and co-founder of AHAM. Author of *Living From The Heart*.

Elle Collier Re (Annam) LOC 682
Spontaneously awakened in early 20s. Author of *Vessel*.

Ellen Emmet LOC 743
Awakened with Francis Lucille. Offers unique blend of yoga, dance and transpersonal therapy for realization of Presence.

Ellie Roozdar LOC 785
After learning Reiki, she experienced a Kundalini awakening and stabilized in non-duality. Offers free audios and videos.

Éric Baret LOC 764
Awakened student of Jean Klein. Carries on tradition of Klein's Kashmiri non-dual hatha yoga.

Esther Veltheim LOC 674
Received Grace from Ramesh Balsekar. Author of *Who Am I? The Seeker's Guide to Nowhere*.

Florian Schlosser Tathagata LOC 684

Awakened spontaneously at a public satsang with Isaac Shapiro after years of seeking. Author of *Being*.

Floyd Henderson LOC 1000
In the lineage of Nisargadatta Maharaj. Author of *From the I to the Absolute*.

Francis Lucille LOC 1000
Close disciple of Jean Klein from 1975 to 1998. Author of *The Perfume of Silence*.

Frank J. Kinslow LOC 745
Developer of Quantum Entrainment process for rapid access to non-duality. Author of *The Secret of Quantum Living*.

Franklin Jones (Adi Da Samraj) LOC 532
Charismatic controversial ex-student of Muktananda. Author of *The Knee of Listening*.

Fred Davis LOC 675
Awakened after 25 years of seeking and studying Eastern wisdom. Author of *The Book of Undoing*.

Galen Sharp LOC 778
Corresponded extensively with Wei Wu Wei (Terence Gray). Author of *What Am I? A Study in Non-Volitional Living*.

Ganga (Mira) LOC 754
Papaji's second wife. Gives occasional spontaneous satsang.

Gangaji LOC 1000
Received Grace from Papaji in India. Author of *You Are That*.

Genpo Roshi LOC 755
Zen master certified by Maezumi Roshi. Creator of Big Mind enlightenment process. Author of *Big Mind, Big Heart*.

Gian Paolo Girardi LOC 1000
Awakened with help from Jim Dreaver. Founder of The Brain Optimization™ Institute.

Gilbert Schultz LOC 689
Guided to "clarity" by the direct pointing of Bob Adamson. Founder of Urban Guru Cafe podcast and radio program.

Gina Lake LOC 689
Awakened in satsang with Adyashanti. Received additional support from husband Nirmala. Author of *Radical Happiness*.

Greg Goode 687
Studied Western philosophy, Buddhism and Advaita with Francis Lucille. Author of *Standing As Awareness*.

Gurumayi (Malti Shetty) LOC 745
Official successor of Swami Muktananda.

Hale Dwoskin LOC 583
Student of Lester Levenson. Leading teacher of The Sedona Method®. Author of *Happiness Is Free*.

Halina Pytlasinska LOC 678
Awakened with help from friends Richard Sylvester and Roger Linden plus meetings with Tony Parsons for two years.

Hans Laurentius LOC 688
Dutch musician and author of *The Joy of Enlightenment*.

Harsh K. Luthar LOC 880
Received Grace from Ramana in a dream. Follows Jain guru Chitrabanu-ji. Runs "interfaith enlightenment" web site.

Ingo Swann LOC 653
Painter and metaphysical genius, he was widely regarded as the "father of remote reviewing." Author of *Secrets of Power*.

Isaac Shapiro 674
Received Grace from Papaji. Author of *It Happens By Itself*.

Isira Sananda LOC 850
Mystical childhood followed by violent rape at 16 which she transformed into deep enlightenment. Author of *Words of One*.

Jac O'Keeffe LOC 684
Holistic healing, ayahuasca, Amma and Mt. Arunachala facilitated her awakening. Author of *Born To Be Free*.

Jack Kornfield LOC 684
Leading American Vipassana teacher who trained in Thailand as a Buddhist monk. Author of *A Path With Heart*.

Jakusho Kwong LOC 757
Shunryu Suzuki Dharma heir. Head abbot of Sonoma Mountain Zen Center. Author of *No Beginning, No End*.

James Braha LOC 675
Leading Vedic astrologer who attained non-duality after 30 years of spiritual seeking. Author of *Living Reality: My Extraordinary Summer With "Sailor" Bob Adamson*.

James Corrigan LOC 674
American philosopher. Author of *An Introduction to Awareness*.

James Swartz LOC 583
Chinmayananda student espousing traditional Vedanta in the new non-duality scene. Author of *How to Attain Enlightenment*.

Jan Esmann LOC 976
Kundalini Shaktipat master. Studied with Gururaj Ananda Yogi, Amma, Anandi Ma, Deepakbhai. Author of *Lovebliss*.

Jan Kersschot LOC 655
Natural medicine practitioner whose seeking ended with Tony Parsons. Author of *The Myth of Self Enquiry*.

J. C. Amberchele LOC 684
Incarcerated marijuana marketer. Author of autobiographical *The Light That I Am*.

Jean Dunn LOC 735
Devoted exemplary bhakta. Editor of three books of talks by Nisargadatta Maharaj including *Seeds of Consciousness*.

Jean Klein LOC 926
Eloquent French guru of Francis Lucille. Author of *The Ease of Being*.

Jed McKenna LOC 580
Pseudonym of anonymous writer who merges fiction and fact much like Carlos Castaneda did. Author of *Spiritual Warfare*.

Jeff Foster LOC 678

After prolonged depression and illness, awakened without a guru. Author of *The Deepest Acceptance*.

Jeff Primack LOC 654
Founder of Supreme Science Qigong.

Jim Dreaver LOC 840
Awakened with Jean Klein in 1995. Author of *End Your Story, Begin Your Life*.

Joan Shivarpita Harrigan LOC 768
Psychologist and successor of Kundalini master Swami Chandrasekharanand Saraswati. Author of *Kundalini Vidya*.

Joan Tollifson LOC 686
Author of *Awake in the Heartland: the Ecstasy of What Is*.

Joel Morwood LOC 843
Experienced Gnostic Awakening in 1983. Director of Center for Sacred Sciences. Author of *The Way of Selflessness*.

Joey Lott LOC 784
Entertaining non-duality coach who emphasizes physical and emotional healing. Author of *You're Trying Too Hard*.

John Astin LOC 682
Psychologist teaching meditation, stress reduction and witness consciousness. Author of *This Is Always Enough*.

John de Ruiter LOC 663
Controversial due to open affairs with female students while he is still married with children. Author of *Unveiling Reality*.

John of God LOC 848
Full trance medium who does spiritual healing in Brazil. He says God has the power. Healing occurs only if it is God's will.

John Greven LOC 685
Awakened with assistance from Sailor Bob Adamson and John Wheeler. Author of *Oneness*.

John Hagelin LOC 684
Former particle physicist. Practitioner of Transcendental Meditation (TM). Known for advocating "Maharishi Effect."

John Hughes LOC 684
Disciple of Swami Lakshmanjoo. Editor of his teachings.

John Ptacek LOC 693
Creative, humorous and articulate writer on non-duality.

John Sherman LOC 763
When Gangaji came to the prison where he was serving time for bank robbery, he awakened. Author of *Look At Yourself*.

John Troy LOC 684
Wizard in Celtic nature tradition. Author of *In Other Words*.

John Wheeler LOC 692
Highly effective teacher whose search ended in 2003 with Sailor Bob Adamson. Author of *Awakening to the Natural State*.

John Wren-Lewis LOC 847
Skeptic awakened after traumatic near-death experience induced by poisoning while on vacation in Thailand.

Joko Beck LOC 772
Influential American Zen master. Received transmission from Taizan Maezumi Roshi. Author of *Nothing Special*.

Jon Bernie LOC 688
Counselor in private practice in the lineage of Adyashanti. Author of *Ordinary Freedom*.

Joseph Goldstein LOC 715
Co-founder of the Insight Meditation Society (IMS), he leads retreats worldwide. Author of *The Path of Insight Meditation*.

Joseph Rubano LOC 745
Counselor who leads four day highly structured "Who am I?" retreats. Did dyadic Charles Berner Enlightenment Intensives.

Judith Blackstone LOC 776
Psychotherapist who emphasizes embodied spiritual awakening. Author of *The Enlightenment Process*.

Kalyani Lawry LOC 688
Studied with Muktananda, Pak Subuh and Sailor Bob. Author of *Only That: the Life and Teaching of Sailor Bob Adamson*.

Karl Renz LOC 1000
Awakened over many years, first into cosmic consciousness, then as the Absolute. Author of *The Myth of Enlightenment*.

Katie Davis LOC 754
Spontaneously awakened while doing intense athletic activity. Wife of Sundance Burke. Author of *Awake Joy*.

Ken Wilber LOC 702

Buddhist geek and integral philosopher of wisdom traditions. Author of *A Brief History of Everything*.

Kenny Johnson LOC 738
Awakened while meditating with Gangaji when she came to the prison he was in for what was to be a 40 year sentence.

Kiran LOC 934
After being disciple of Osho (Rajneesh) for more than 15 years achieved awakening. Also influenced by U. G. Krishnamurti.

Koort LOC 1000
Experienced spontaneous awakening via suicidal depression. Stabilized in non-duality with spiritual coaching from Ramaji.

Lakshmana Swamy LOC 1000
Received Grace in Ramana's presence in 1949. Author of *No Mind — I Am the Self*.

Lama Tsultrim Allione LOC 1000
American female Tibetan Buddhist recognized as emanation of Machig Labdron. Author of *Feeding Your Demons*.

Lama Surya Das LOC 684
Popular exponent of Tibetan Buddhism and Dzogchen in the West. Author of *Awakening the Buddha Within*.

Larry Rosenberg LOC 685
Insight meditation teacher. Student of J. Krishnamurti, Thakar, Seung Sahn and Buddhadasa. Author of *Breath By Breath*.

Laura Lucille LOC 764

Worked closely with Lester Levenson from late 1970s to 1994. Also credits Ramana Maharshi and Robert Adams.

Leo Hartong LOC 692
Early breakthrough helped by Tony Parsons, Ramesh Balsekar and Wayne Liquorman. Author of *Awakening to the Dream*.

Lester Levenson LOC 1000
Attained enlightenment using his original method of inquiry. Author of the out of print classic *Keys to the Ultimate Freedom*.

Llewellyn-Vaughan Lee LOC 1000
Student of Sufi master Irina Tweedie for many years. Author of *Sufism: The Transformation of the Heart*.

Loch Kelly LOC 762
Buddhist meditation teacher awakened with the help of Adyashanti and other non-dual sages.

Lujan Matus LOC 777
Self-taught shaman awakened via conscious dreaming. Author of *The Art of Stalking Parallel Perception*.

Lynda Cole LOC 712
Awakened during a visit to Ramana's ashram in India. She then stabilized via ongoing support from Eckhart Tolle.

Madhukar LOC 530
Studied with Dzogchen master Namkhai Norbu. Met Papaji in 1992. Experienced "spontaneous Kundalini enlightenment."

Mandi Solk LOC 1000

Awakened via nearly fatal motorbike accident and near death experience in surgery. Author of *The Joy of No Self*.

Marc Leavitt LOC 784
Breakthrough at Monroe Institute. Author of *Enlightenment*.

Mark Griffin LOC 772
Kundalini meditation master awakened by Muktananda. Studied with Chogyam Trungpa. Author of *Shaktipat*.

Mark McCloskey LOC 778
Author of the audiobook CD *Pure Silence: Lessons in Living and Dying*.

Mark West LOC 747
Received satsang from Nisargadatta Maharaj in 1970s. Author of *Gleanings from Nisargadatta* (talks transcribed by West).

Marlies Cocheret LOC 684
Holistic therapist who studied with Osho. Found her root teacher in Adyashanti. He requested her to teach in 2000.

Martin Birrittella LOC 748
American entrepreneur who ran an ashram in India in the 1970s. Author of *Field of Love: How to Experience the Field*.

Master Charles LOC 754
Disciple of Muktananda. Promotes audio technology said to induce meditative states. Author of *The Bliss of Freedom*.

Mathru Sri Saradhamma LOC 1000
Designated spiritual successor of Sri Lakshmana Swamy.

Maurice Frydman LOC 674

Editor of Nisargadatta's landmark book *I Am That*.

Melvyn Wartella LOC 884
Spontaneously awakened via natural inquiry into violence and hatred. Author of *Ego, Evolucion e Iluminacion* (Spanish).

Metta Zetty LOC 688
Spontaneously awakened in a lucid dream where the top of her head opened and bright white light poured into her body.

Mokshananda LOC 681
Licensed psychologist. Awakened in satsang with Gurumayi. Later stabilized with Adyashanti who asked him to teach.

Mooji LOC 763
Received Grace from Papaji in India. Author of *Before I Am*.

Namgyal Rinpoche LOC 875
Canadian recognized by Theravadan and Tibetan Buddhist traditions. Author of *Body, Speech and Mind*.

Namkhai Norbu LOC 1000
Recognized at age of two as a reincarnation of great Dzogchen master Adzom Drugpa. Author of *Dzogchen Teachings*.

Nanna Guru LOC 863
Received Grace at Ramana's ashram in Tiruvannamalai years after Ramana's mahasamadhi. Author of *Words of Nectar*.

Nathan Gill LOC 681
Gardener living in the green countryside of England. Offers meetings in London. Author of *Already Awake*.

Neelam LOC 718
Received Grace from Papaji in India. Author of *Relationships - The Path to Freedom* (video).

Nirmala LOC 664
Teacher is Neelam. Helped by Adyashanti. Author of *Nothing Personal: Seeing Beyond the Illusion of a Separate Self*.

Nome LOC 711
Experienced samadhi at 16. Awakened at 19 reading Ramana Maharshi pamphlet. Author of *Self-Knowledge*.

Om C. Parkin LOC 864
Awakened via car accident that put him in a coma and support from Gangaji. Author of *The Birth of the Lion*.

Oscar Ichazo LOC 744
Bolivian-born founder of the Arica School. Creator of the modern Enneagram of nine personality types.

Pa Auk Sayadaw LOC 876
Theravadin Buddhist meditation master emphasizing states of deep concentration (jhana). Author of *Knowing and Seeing*.

Pamela Wilson LOC 674
At age 15 visited by Ramana Maharshi. She sat with Robert Adams and awakened in his Presence with help from Neelam.

Paul Hedderman LOC 688
"Everybody is recovering from something." Teaches non-dual spiritual awakening as it relates to addiction and recovery.

Paul Lowe LOC 733

Human potential workshop leader. Former therapist under Osho. Author of *In Each Moment*.

Pema Chodron LOC 748
Student of Chogyam Trungpa Rinpoche. Author of *When Things Fall Apart: Heart Advice for Difficult Times*.

Peter Brown LOC 1000
Received transmission from Pino Turolla in 1973. Awakened into total "Radiance" in 1997. Author of *Dirty Enlightenment*.

Peter Fenner LOC 744
Monk in Tibetan Buddhist tradition for nine years with Lama Thubten Yeshe as his guru. Author of *Radiant Mind*.

Peter Francis Dziuban LOC 874
Influenced by Alfred Aiken. Author of *Simply Notice*.

Philip Mistlberger LOC 876
Eclectic therapist who spent a decade with Osho. Author of *A Natural Awakening: Realizing the True Self in Everyday Life*.

Philip Renard LOC 776
Teaches in traditions of Nisargadatta Maharaj and Alexander Smit (and Atmananda via Smit). Author of *"I" Is a Door*.

Premananda LOC 684
Awakened by Papaji after getting warmed up for 15 years by Osho. Author of *Papaji Amazing Grace*.

Prem Vishrant LOC 702
Credits Osho, Zen, Isaac Shapiro, Gangaji and Vartman for facilitating his awakening. Runs Mystic Heart Mystery School.

Radha LOC 776
Spontaneous Kundalini awakening in 2010. Stabilized during satsang with Aruna Byers. She and Aruna are in Japan.

Rajiv Kapur LOC 1000
Former Kriya Yoga practitioner. Guided to Edward Muzika in tradition of Robert Adams. Teaches classical Self-Inquiry.

Rajneesh (Osho) LOC 754
A controversial convention breaker, his contributions to non-duality have been substantial. Author of *Book of the Secrets*.

Ram Dass LOC 733
Popular American spiritual leader. Author of *Be Here Now*.

Ramaji LOC 1000
Kundalini awakening at 16. Former Vipassana meditator. Devotee of Kali Ma. Received Grace from Ramesh Balsekar.

Ramesh Balsekar LOC 764
Most prominent disciple of Nisargadatta Maharaj and guru of the author of this book. Author of *Consciousness Speaks*.

Randall Friend LOC 682
Kentucky non-dual teacher who prefers email, Second Life (as Avastu Maruti) and Skype. Author of *You are No Thing*.

Reginald Ray LOC 746
Studied with Chogyam Trungpa Rinpoche for many years. Author of *Mahamudra for the Modern World* audio course.

Richard Bartlett LOC 685

Chiropractor who teaches people how to use quantum physics for dramatic energy healing. Author of *Matrix Energetics*.

Richard Lang LOC 688
Student of Douglas Harding and Dhiravamsa. Author of *Seeing Who You Really Are*.

Richard Sylvester LOC 675
Fateful meeting with Tony Parsons in 2002 led to awakening. Author of *I Hope You Die Soon*.

Rick Linchitz LOC 692
Met Satyam Nadeen during health crisis and experienced awakening. Author of *No You and No Me*.

Riktam Barry LOC 673
Free spirited Australian who did Transcendental Meditation and studied with Osho. Author of *The Telling Stones*.

Robert Adams LOC 776
Attained enlightenment via Grace from Ramana Maharshi in 1946 in India. Author of *Silence of the Heart*.

Robert Hover LOC 784
Studied with U Bha Khin and S. N. Goenka. One of Ramaji's Vipassana teachers. Author of *Internal Moving Healing*.

Robert Meizer LOC 668
After 30 years of non-dual study, awakened by John Wheeler with two questions. He did not stay for the "Advaita chitchat."

Robert Powell LOC 689

Non-duality pioneer. Edited three books of dialogues with Nisargadatta Maharaj. Author of *Path Without Form*.

Roger Linden LOC 689
A seeker for 40 years, he became TM teacher, gained a glimpse with Jean Klein, then awakened with help from Tony Parsons.

Rupert Spira LOC 1000
Studied Advaita for 25 years before awakening with the help of Francis Lucille. Author of *The Transparency of Things*.

Sadhu Om Swamigal LOC 1000
Enlightened devotee of Ramana Maharshi who first received his darshan in 1946. Author of *The Path of Sri Ramana*.

"Sailor" Bob Adamson LOC 788
Attained after doing TM and then visiting Nisargadatta in 1976. Author of *What's Wrong with Right Now?*.

Sakyong Mipham Rinpoche LOC 975
Son and official successor of Chogyam Trungpa Rinpoche. Author of *Turning the Mind into an Ally*.

Samarpan LOC 685
Received his spiritual name from Osho. Awakened during a retreat with Gangaji. Author of *Silence* (in German).

Sandra Glickman LOC 822
Lifelong seeker. Awakened in 1996 with help of Saniel Bonder. Transpersonal therapist. Senior Teacher of Waking Down.

Saniel Bonder LOC 675

Founder of the Waking Down in Mutuality work. Author of *Healing the Spirit/Matter Split*.

Santosh Sachdeva LOC 933
Kundalini awakened after doing yoga, vipassana and Mental Physics. Author of *Conscious Flight Into the Empyrean*.

Satyam Nadeen LOC 778
Former Ecstasy drug dealer who awakened while in hard core prison environment. Author of *From Onions to Pearls*.

Satyananda Saraswati LOC 1000
Tantric Kundalini master who was a student of Sivananda. He founded Bihar School of Yoga. Author of *Kundalini Tantra*.

Scott Kiloby LOC 754
Spontaneously awakened from addiction into a loving life with the separate self fallen away. Author of *Living Realization*.

Scott Morrison LOC 884
American Zen Master. Author of *Open and Innocent: The Gentle, Passionate Art of Not-Knowing*.

Sharon Salzberg LOC 688
A leading American vipassana teacher. Bestselling author of *Lovingkindness: the Revolutionary Art of Happiness*.

Shinzen Young LOC 797
Buddhist mindfulness meditation teacher who fuses the best of the East and West. Author of *The Science of Enlightenment*.

Sri Sri Ravi Shankar LOC 1000

Former student of Maharishi Mahesh Yogi. Creator of the Sudarshan Kriya technique. Author of *Celebrating Silence*.

Stephen Batchelor LOC 687
A former Buddhist monk with an original voice, he leads retreats worldwide. Author of *Confession of a Buddhist Atheist*.

Stephen Jourdain LOC 1000
Spontaneously awakened at age 16 by contemplating "I think, therefore I am" of Descarte. Author of *Radical Awakening*.

Stephen Snyder LOC 763
He is the first American male to be authorized to teach by Pa Auk Sayadaw. Co-author of *Practicing the Jhanas*.

Stephen Wingate LOC 675
In the tradition of Nisargadatta with support from John Wheeler. Author of *The Outrageous Myths of Enlightenment*.

Stephen Wolinsky LOC 683
Famous non-dual psychologist in the Nisargadatta lineage. Author of *Trances People Live* and many Advaita books.

Steve Ford LOC 684
Awakened spontaneously after several years in a 12 step recovery program for alcoholics. Offers 12 steps counseling.

Steven Harrison LOC 778
Founder of The Living School and "post-spirituality." Author of *Doing Nothing: Coming to the End of the Spiritual Search*.

Steven Sadleir LOC 748

Kundalini Shaktipat master. Gurus include Yogiraj Vethathiri and Shivabalayogi. Founder of the Self Awareness Institute.

Stuart Schwartz LOC 684
Disciple of Robert Adams. Author of *The Great Undoing*.

Sundance Burke LOC 1000
Awakened gradually with the help of three unnamed living teachers. Author of *Free Spirit: A Guide to Enlightened Being*.

Suzanne Foxton LOC 750
Humorous non-dual blogger. Author of *The Ultimate Twist*.

Suzanne Segal LOC 782
Known for her short-lived but dramatic impact as "describer" of the "Vastness." Author of *Collision with the Infinite*.

Swami Lakshmanjoo LOC 1000
Last teacher in this ancient Tantric Kashmir Shaivism lineage. Author of *Kashmir Shaivism: The Secret Supreme*.

Tarthang Tulku LOC 784
Tibetan Buddhist lama who trained in Tibet before Chinese invasion of 1959. Author of *Hidden Mind of Freedom*.

Tenzin Wangyal Rinpoche: LOC 778
Dzogchen master in Bon tradition. Founder of Ligmincha Institute. Author of *The Tibetan Yogas of Dream and Sleep*.

Thich Nhat Hahn LOC 786
Zen master and peace activist. Author of *Being Peace*.

Timothy Schoorel LOC 783

Disciple of Osho at age 15. Met Alexander Smit in 1991. Awakened in 1995. Author of *The 7 Principles of Freedom*.

Tina Rasmussen LOC 864
Buddhist nun and first Western woman authorized by Pa Auk Sayadaw to teach. Co-author of *Practicing the Jhanas*.

Tony Parsons LOC 683
Former Osho sannyasin spontaneously awakened while walking in a London park. Author of *The Open Secret*.

Trip Overholt LOC 678
Radio host who interviewed 100 non-dual teachers while awakening. Author of *Conversations with Avant-Garde Sages*.

U. G. Krishnamurti LOC 678
Outspoken ex-student of Jiddu Krishnamurti. Author of *The Natural State*.

Unmani Liza Hyde LOC 684
Awakened with help from German Zen Master Dolano who in turn had been awakened by Papaji. Author of *Die to Love*.

V. V. Brahmam LOC 934
Awakened in 1969 in after surrendering to the picture of Ramana Maharshi in the Meditation Hall of Ramana Ashram.

Wayne Liquorman LOC 694
Official successor of Ramesh Balsekar. Author of *The Way of Powerlessness*.

Werner Erhard LOC 583

Erhard's EST training, founded in 1971, continues its unique evolution as a transformational "shot hear 'round the world."

Wolter Keers LOC 789
Received Grace from Ramana Maharshi in 1950. Then studied with Atmananda. Translated *I Am That* into Dutch.

Yolande Duran-Serrano LOC 684
French woman who experienced spontaneous awakening with no prior seeking in 2003. Author of *Silence Heals*.

Yongey Mingyur Rinpoche LOC 1000
Tibetan Buddhist meditation master known for working with neuroscientists. Author of *The Joy of Living*.

Yukio Ramana LOC 776
Awakened by Papaji in 1993. Blends unique transpersonal psychotherapies and NLP hypnosis with traditional satsang.

101 Spiritual Giants

101 Spiritual Giants

"We are not a drop in the ocean. We are the ocean in a drop."
— Rumi[10]

While the focus of this book is on contemporary spiritual teachers, I have had numerous requests to evaluate the LOCs of historical figures. This list is my response.

The vast majority are famous spiritual figures. It will come as no surprise that these well-known names were enlightened. Be on the lookout for a few geniuses that made the cut, too.

Abraham LOC 823
Abraham Lincoln LOC 682
Ajahn Chah LOC 838
Alan W. Watts LOC 723
Aleister Crowley LOC 665.8 (666?)
Alice Bailey LOC 732
Anandamayi Ma LOC 1000
Anthony de Mello LOC 774
Atmananda (Krishna Menon) LOC 1000
Aurobindo LOC 873

Bahá'u'lláh LOC 1000
Bede Griffiths LOC 744
Bodhidharma LOC 1000
Brother Lawrence LOC 787
Buddha LOC 1000
Buddhadasa Bhikku LOC 1000

Chinmayananda LOC 855

Chinmoy LOC 1000
Choa Kok Sui LOC 764
Chuang Tzu LOC 1000
Confucius LOC 734

Dalai Lama LOC 1000
Dhyanyogi Madhusudandasji LOC 1000
Dipa Ma LOC 878
Dogen LOC 1000

Eknath Easwaran LOC 1000
Elizabeth Clare Prophet LOC 673
Epictetus LOC 854

Faridu'd-Din 'Attar LOC 887
Flower Newhouse LOC 1000
Francis of Assisi LOC 1000
Franklin Merrell-Wolfe LOC 768

Gandhi LOC 733
Genghis Khan LOC 1000
Gopi Krishna LOC 778
Grigori Rasputin LOC 684
Gurdjieff LOC 648

Hakuin LOC 1000
Huang Po LOC 1000

Ikkyu Sojun LOC 1000
Irma Tweedie LOC 1000

Jakob Böhme LOC 688
Jalal al-Din Rumi LOC 1000

Jesus Christ LOC 1000
Jiddu Krishnamurti LOC 844
Jnaneshwar LOC 1000
John the Baptist LOC 847
Joseph Campbell LOC 684

Kirpal Singh LOC 1000
Krishna LOC 1000

Lao Tzu LOC 1000
Lee Lozowick LOC 878
Leonardo da Vinci LOC 676
Lester Levenson LOC 1000

Madam Blavatsky LOC 881
Maharishi Mahesh Yogi LOC 1000
Mahashi Sayadaw LOC 1000
Mansur Al-Hallaj LOC 1000
Mark Prophet LOC 743
Mark Twain LOC 686
Meher Baba LOC 1000
Meister Eckhart LOC 1000
Mikao Usui LOC 753
Moses LOC 1000
Mother Theresa LOC 878
Muhammad LOC 1000
Muktananda LOC 772

Neem Karoli Baba LOC 1000
Nietzche LOC 684
Nityananda LOC 1000
Nostradamus LOC 735

Ösel Tendzin LOC 683
Osho (Rajneesh) LOC 754

Padmasambhava LOC 1000
Padre Pio LOC 888
Papa Ramdas LOC 1000
Papaji (Poonjaji) LOC 1000
Patanjali LOC 1000
Paul Brunton LOC 678
Peace Pilgrim LOC 848
Peter Ouspensky LOC 673
Philip Kapleau LOC 778
Plato LOC 687
Plotinus LOC 674
Pope Francis LOC 548
P. R. Sarkar LOC 1000

Ramakrishna LOC 1000
Rama Tirtha LOC 1000
Ranjit Maharaj LOC 1000
Robert Aitken LOC 844
Robert Monroe LOC 694

St. John of the Cross LOC 878
St. Teresa of Avila LOC 840
Satchidananda LOC 1000
Sathya Sai Baba LOC 1000
Seung Sahn LOC 1000
Shankaracharya LOC 1000
Shirdi Sai Baba LOC 1000
Shivabalayogi Maharaj LOC 1000
Shivananda LOC 1000
Shunryu Suzuki LOC 1000

Siddharameshwar Maharaj LOC 1000
S. N. Goenka LOC 748
Socrates LOC 1000
Swami Rama LOC 933
Swami Shyam LOC 1000

Taizan Maezumi LOC 744
Terence McKenna LOC 684
Thomas Aquinas LOC 678
Thomas Merton LOC 667
Totapuri LOC 1000

U Ba Khin LOC 1000

Vernon Howard LOC 722
Vimala Thakar LOC 1000
Vitvan LOC 727
Vivekananda LOC 848

Wallace Black Elk LOC 943
Walt Whitman LOC 684
Wassily Kandinsky LOC 688
Wei Wu Wei (Terence Gray) LOC 1000
William Blake LOC 924
Wolfgang Amadeus Mozart LOC 684

Yogananda LOC 769

Zoroaster LOC 1000

The River of Life

LOC 30 to LOC 499

The River of Life: LOC from 30 to 499

The LOCs from 1 up to 499 are simple and straightforward compared to the LOCs 500 and above. The vast majority of the people on earth live below LOC 500.

The average LOC on the planet right now is LOC 210. I start the complete Map of Awakening at LOC 30 because it is the lowest human LOC that I have personally assessed.[11]

The focus of this book is on LOCs from 500 up, with a special emphasis on the non-dual seeker LOCs 560 to 599 and the non-dual realization LOCs 600 and above. Even so, I would like to paint with broad strokes the big picture of human mental, emotional, ethical and spiritual evolution.

In this chapter, I provide a brief summary of the LOCs below 500. This subject matter which deals mainly with heavily contracted ego positions and the corresponding negative emotions has already been covered in detail by others.[12]

Since you are reading a book on non-duality, chances are you are somewhere in the 500s or above. Interest in metaphysics may arise as the person enters the 500s. However, non-duality as a serious and abiding life interest does not typically arise until the person reaches the 560s or above.

Prior to this milestone, there are just too many thoughts, too many problems and too many things they think they have to do. Though the person at 560 and above may not feel they are close to non-dual realization, they are knocking at the door.

Now you will plunge into the murky desolate darkness of the first LOC range from LOC 30 to 99. In this dark and troubled zone you will find the pathologically cold-blooded serial killers. This is the spooky depraved unlit basement of human consciousness. It is the stuff of which horror films are made of.

The Jungle of Hungry Beasts: LOC from 30 to 99

At this first and lowest level is found ultimate human cruelty and acts of brutality on another human being. We will not dwell here except to say that this is not a domain of survival.

This dimension of consciousness favors self-destruction. In terms of toxic human emotions, here we find frozen fixations of apathy, shame and guilt. At the root of human emotional suffering is lack of love, but love has not yet arrived for this dimension. It is dog fight dog. Dog kill dog. Dog eat dog.

The Beast Within Hunts for Dinner: the 30 to 99 LOC Zone

The names of these three serial killers will probably need no explanation. They are famous, but for all the wrong reasons.

This is not a place to dwell. Just be glad that, since you are reading this book, your LOC is most assuredly *far above* these hellish killing fields.

Gary Ridgway LOC 33

Jeffrey Dahmer LOC 64

Ted Bundy LOC 72

Is That a Tiger in Your Tank?

I can offer an explanation for this bizarre beginning to the LOC climb. The question I will answer is "Why are there such terrible people in the world?"

And perhaps also "Who goes around killing and eating other human beings?" This second question is in reference to certain infamous cannibalistic serial killers.

The mystery is solved when you realize that the person in question is not fully human yet. Assuming for the sake of argument that the classic reincarnation model, including the notion of humans evolving over great spans of time from animals, is somewhat legitimate, then the explanation is in plain sight and surprisingly logical.

In the absolute sense, there is no rebirth and no person, soul or entity taking rebirth. Empirically speaking, it is useful to make use of this view. Individual destiny per astrology supports it.

From the psychological perspective, these individuals have not yet developed the higher intellect that enables moral and ethical checks and balances. They function via instinct, cunning, aggression and stealth.

They are driven by primal impulses of lust and death. There is mindless fury in the blood. Eros and thanatos in their crudest least evolved expressions reign supreme. This is life in hell when it is not even known what hell is. Heaven, or rising above this sticky instinctual swamp, is not yet even a concept.

The reincarnation view is utilitarian and makes a perfect story.

The serial killer whose actions are so gross from a human point of view make perfect sense from the point of view of a wild carnivorous hunting animal such as a lion or tiger. While tuning into a few of these individuals for the purpose of making their LOC assessment, I became vividly aware that this was quite literally their first human lifetime. In the lifetime before this one, they had been the kind of stealthy fierce wild animal who hunts, kills and eats people.

Though able to talk and function as human beings, they kept the survival mindset of the carnivorous predator. That is my explanation. If life is a dream, then this is the nightmare.

In the vast scheme of mother nature as she evolves on the grand bridge of time each human soul, there is no rush to transform the former beast into a radiant saint. In this cosmic game, everything takes as long as it takes. It is not up to us.

The Island of Lost Souls: LOC from 100 to 199

There is improvement for the masses, but the potential for tragedy and terror has expanded astronomically. This evolution of human consciousness intensifies a bold brutal narcissism in the ego. It gives birth to heartless dictators. Negativity on a grand unthinkable scale is now possible.

A new level of toxic narcissism emerges. Grandiose self-pity and wounded pride justify the most extreme retaliation. Deep anguish and malaise feed the fury of righteous pitiless rage. Feeling is being born, but here it is self-serving for the pseudo-victim. True warmth and generosity have not yet appeared.

Infamous Beyond Forgetting: the 100 to 199 LOC Zone

Adolph Hitler LOC 126

Pol Pot LOC 133

Jospeh Stalin LOC 137

Aileen Carol Wuornos LOC 176

Unlike serial killers, dictators have no explanation or "excuse." They are soul dead and rotten to the core. The hell they create is the hell they live within. The beastly killers below 100 LOC operate on blind impulse. These urbane human monsters are conscious of their seething hatred yet embrace its deadly gift.

Shocking as the cold blooded murders by serial killers may be, acts of war and genocide instigated by cruel heartless dictators with LOCs in the low 100s kill millions of people. They are in another class of selfishness. They walk a path of conscious darkness. Empowered briefly by the destructive force, they bring to ruin all that they touch, including themselves.

Modern technology has made warfare heartless, cowardly and impersonal. While the gun has equalized ability to kill for man and woman, it removes the intimate lessons in courage and valor of mettle proving face to face combat. Ah, for the good old days when it was man to man with bare hands or a sword!

If Hollywood movies are any indication, many of us yearn for days long gone when we could fight and even kill to protect ourselves and our families. The call of the herd is behind this.

The point is science and technology cut both ways. Power can be used or abused. Both have happened and will continue to happen. When the LOC rises to embrace the transforming power of love in the 500s, the taste for war disappears. Up to that point the so-called art of war makes sense, if not dollars.

Obviously, not everyone in the LOC range between 100 and 199 is a powerful dictator. Most below 199 LOC live in the opposite position. They are the faceless downtrodden. Their spirit cannot rise, for it has not revealed itself. A desperate merciless struggle for materialistic survival is the only truth.

Nonetheless, let us give this dimly lit and troubled range, plunged into a darkness it cannot diagnose, a name and a face.

Aileen Wuornos: Self-Defense as Prideful Murderous Rage

Aileen Carol Wuornos, LOC 176, is that rare phenomenon, a female serial killer who killed out of pent up seething rage. The usual motivation for a female serial killer is financial gain.

At the time, Wuornous was a working prostitute. She argued that her victims had raped her or tried to rape her. She was a victim to be pitied. Their deaths were an act of self-defense. She killed seven men in Florida from 1989 to 1990.[13]

We know that being a prostitute on the streets is a terrible horrible way to make a living. We know that she put herself in harm's way every time she went out to make more money.

We want to sympathize with her. Her solution is not one that we would choose. We know right from wrong. We also know that, sooner or later, we would probably get caught.

If we are honest with ourselves, we have had moments where we wanted someone dead. We can imagine how she got there.

She is higher in LOC than the dictators because her actions are the direct result of anger stored and accumulated to the point of murderous rage. She kills from a hot rage, not a cold heart.

Obviously, Wuornous had other options for making money. It can be argued that she wanted this situation so that she could express her rage. Whatever the deep dark psychological truth, it reflects her below survival 176 LOC. No doubt she had the skills to do something else, but the black cloud that ruled her emotions would not let her go down any path but this one.

Anger to the point of uncontrollable raging violence, coupled with misdirected pride and a distorted sense of self-worth, led Wuornos to make the choices and take the actions that she did. Documentary and Hollywood films have been made about her life, suggesting she was not alone in her feelings.

The Land of Selfish Heroes: LOC from 200 to 299

The human race as a whole is currently (2014) at LOC 210. Our planet earth, though, is now at 550, the vibratory frequency of unconditional love. It is headed towards 600. When that day comes, or soon before it, life as we know it will change.

As it says in the Bible, no man knows the day of the Coming of the Lord. In this context, I believe this saying refers to the advent of unconditional love and peaceful non-dual holistic consciousness on the planet at a global level.

In brief, I predict "world peace," but the human race will have to catch up with the rapid LOC ascent of its space vehicle, planet earth. What birth pangs this will entail, what they will look like or how long they will last, I do not know.

The Sun Peaks Over the Mountain: the 200 to 299 LOC Zone

Victor Lustig (Audacious Con Artist) LOC 232

Dan Quayle (44th V.P. of the U.S.) LOC 274

George W. Bush (43rd U.S. President) LOC 283

Below LOC 200, cowardice prevails. The stench of overarching addiction to survival at any cost justifies all actions to preserve self, meaning the body. Morality is convenience. Life is but a cynical game of self-preservation. Played for no reason, the game is callously terminated. All this changes at LOC 200.

Here dawns egocentric boldness and a militant generosity. The person is for or against and defines the self in this way. The status quo is gladly embraced. It enhances emotion, energy and purpose. At last, the truly human self is emerging.

These are all well-known figures. None are true "heroes" in the Hollywood movie sense, or even according to the archetype promulgated by the legendary Joseph Campbell (LOC 684).

Dan Quayle stumbled with words often, yet he kept on going and left his record spotless. A coward could not have done so.

George Bush displayed a militant demeanor in office. Though bold and decisive, he was not known for his intellect.

His strength was a dogged tenacity worthy of a pit bull. The final truth about this man and his presidency has not yet been written. What we can say is that he carried it off not just boldly but with, if it makes any sense, a level of courage and confidence that his own natural ability did not warrant.

Victor Lustig, the Man Who Sold the Eiffel Tower... Twice!

Victor Lustig may not seem to fit, but he was as smooth as any top politician. Con artist is short for "confidence man." To be a successful con man, you must have confidence in yourself and be able to quickly and easily gain the confidence of others. This is beyond the capacity of humans living at the brute level.

Lustig is said to have left a set of instructions for anyone who aspires to be great con artist. His advice may surprise you.

1. Be a great listener who always looks interested and never looks bored.

2. Offer no opinions, but as soon as your target offers a strong political or religious belief, show your agreement with them.

3. Imply sex and sensuality, but do not pursue it unless your target shows a burning interest.

4. Avoid the topic of illness unless they bring it up.

5. Ask nothing about their personal life (all will be revealed, sooner or later).

6. Be not boastful or uncouth. Always act humble. Look great.

7. Do not ever get drunk. It's okay if they do, but not you.[14]

Although Lustig's list displays deep insight into human nature, he used it to exploit the narcissism and victim stance of others for personal gain. Knowing that he had divined his target's weaknesses gave him the unfair advantage he craved.

Although Lustig's seeds of insight grew into noxious weeds of greed, his notes are evidence enough that in the lowly 200s a light is dawning in the human soul. The blossoming of ethics is later, but deft insight into human nature must arise first.

Had Lustig seen into his own depths with such psychological precision, he might have become a gifted psychiatrist like Sigmund Freud (LOC 484). Lustig was impatient for results, so he chose the short cut and the instant hot cash payoff.

Finally, the con artist typically does it for the thrill. The money is obtained so he can maintain the game. He loves to live on the edge. The fear of getting caught is the icing on his cake.

The Moral Compass Does Not Yet Point North

It has not yet dawned on Lusting, along with others in the LOC 200 zone, that his pleasure comes at the expense of others. He has not yet developed "fellow feeling" sensitivity.

Empathy remains an unexplored frontier for him. It is at the next level that sympathy and empathy emerge with a host of other humanizing traits.

They develop into the beginnings of reverence, humility and moral strength. The man or woman of the 200s is a hero only for themselves, but their courage can change their lives and lead them boldly into prominence.

There is a world of difference between above 200 LOC and below it. Below 200 is death, tragedy and trauma. Above 200 is survival, success and self-expression.

The Domain of Earnest Enthusiasts: LOC 300 to 399

Non-resistance to "what is" is one definition of enlightenment. The unconditional acceptance and fully blossomed non-dual embrace of whatever life gives you moment to surprising moment does not spring into being overnight. It has its seeds somewhere in the past. Those seeds are planted here in the LOC 300 range. Here you find deep displays of sincerity, surrender, acceptance, willingness, receptivity and allowing.

The fierce combatant of the LOC 200s is overcoming a tough adversary created by his own mind. Since this projection does not become conscious, a non-aggressive posture is laughable and unthinkable. The seemingly passive stance of acceptance for the militaristic LOC 200s simply does not compute.

"My enemy will overcome me if I give him this unfair advantage," thinks the LOC 200s person. "It is I who must strike first in self-defense." This is greatly refined and strategic over the Aileen Wuornous posture, but it is still aggressive.

In LOC 300s another dimension is added. The subconscious presumption of an invisible attacking adversary is reframed.

A new option of non-resistance to defuse an approaching situation with a potential opponent appears. It's a major milestone. Deep caring passion and true tenderness emerge.

A Full Moon Rises in a Cloudy Sky: the 300 to 399 LOC Zone

Tonya Harding LOC 342

Junior Seau LOC 363

Margaret Thatcher LOC 377

All three of these individuals exhibited tremendous passion and vitality. They were "forces of nature" driven by deep reservoirs of emotion not accessed by most people.

In the context of their unique careers, they displayed a vulnerability they could not avoid. Their emotions were visible. Their emotions were the wind that filled their sails.

Tonya Harding is the Olympic class skater who shattered her own dreams through pettiness and became a caricature of herself. *Junior Seau* was a football player known for his tremendous emotional intensity and astonishing work ethic. *Margaret Thatcher* boldly and astutely helmed the United Kingdom through numerous crises during her dynamic though checkered reign.

Lunar Thinking: a New Intoxication through Irrationality

As a visual symbol, the moon represents both the mind and the emotions. I refer to the expression of the "wet" emotions.

In essence, this is the capacity to cry both for self and for others. Vulnerability has arrived. This is radical. It is the birth of everything higher. The heart is opening and softening.

By lunar I also mean being driven and taken over by passion for both good and bad ends. Passion can guarantee success, but it may impose blinders of narrow myopic focus. Passion can be a man's game. He can give his life for his passion.

Up to this point, crying was for sissies, weaklings and women. A real man doesn't cry, or so they thought. The evidence says you can be hard headed, and it will be okay. It is dawning that hard-hearted has a huge hidden cost. Soft-hearted is the way.

That is the discovery of the LOC 300s. It takes courage to love. It's takes courage to cry. It takes courage to be passionate.

That courage is growing. But there is a prolonged journey before arriving at the supreme level of sacrifice shown by Jesus and others like him. Even so, here begins the long walk to true humility, loving service and total surrender to God.

But at this level it is not Gandhi or Martin Luther King. At this level it is "love is all we need." If we love each other, that is enough. The magic will find us. Our love will light the way.

If you've been in love, then you know these are half-truths at best. Love is blind. You do not see what you need to see. You see what you want to see. Such love is a projection of lack.

Your error leads to pain. At this LOC 300s level, you value the lessons from your experience.

Now you know that you can keep working at a relationship. You know that love needs time to grow. You enjoy family values with a simple heart.

Maturing Emotions: the Teenage Phase of Human Evolution

Ironically, this emotional vulnerability of the LOC 300s will get replaced by the power of the human intellect in the LOC 400s. This seems like a loss. It does lead to titanic technologies like credit cards and the Internet that feed and multiply human desires instead of transforming and liberating them.

But all is set right again in the LOC 500s when the power of love, like a sparkling rainbow made of fragrant flowers, fills the sky of the tired hungry mind yearning for final release. It has arrived at this point honestly, Having tried other ways, it is now ready to march forward on the path of real love.

But I am getting ahead of myself. Here in the LOC 300s you see the opening for the first time. The heart was behind the scenes before. Now it comes forward and allows vulnerability.

It is a critical step. The heart was guarded before. Now intense emotions are uncovered, cultivated, celebrated and channeled.

Emotional strength, the power of passion to create and destroy, is discovered. Passion, coupled with vitality, produces life-changing results. Unique greatness is possible.

In the LOC 300s, basic ethics are established. There is desire to become a good person. Do your job well. Love your family. Go to church. Obey the law. Follow the Ten Commandments.

The Kingdom of Brilliant Thinkers: LOC 400 to 499

The "human computer" is the head or brain. Now emerges the archetypal dialog between (hard) head and (soft) heart.

In the LOC 300s, emotion sprung forth like live-giving water from hard solid ground as the honest yet unavoidably surface expression of the human heart. Overwhelming in its oceanic soft depths, it is a great adventure worthy of a spiritual sailor.

But there arrives a sheriff in town, and that sheriff is the intellect. He would control the emotions. In his urge for domination, he stifles emotion, not understanding it.

Here too is the discovery of strategy and wit that enables brilliant success at the games of life, business and otherwise. You will find many exemplary individuals here, people with impressive attainments and shining super-satisfactory lives.

They have maximized their understanding and outputted it for all to see. By taking their vision to the extreme, they allow it to evolve and eventually transcend itself. This is the passion of the LOC 400s, to expand and test the limits of the mind.

Eventually, they see the limitations of their own enterprises. In the LOC 500s, struck by the universal vision of love, they change their tune and begin to work for the benefit of all mankind. This is done out of joy, for now all are brothers and sisters. Intellectual force submits to a grand universal vision.

"I Think, Therefore I Succeed": the 400 to 499 LOC Zone

Alfred Nobel LOC 478

Paul Allen LOC 483

Robert B. Cialdini LOC 490

Alfred Nobel was a scientific genius with 350 patents who also knew six languages. Sometime after he invented dynamite, he realized that his legacy would be as an inventor of new ways to kill people faster. In response, he dedicated 94 per cent of his wealth to founding the humanitarian Nobel Prizes.[15]

Paul Allen is the faceless billionaire who co-founded Microsoft with his more famous billionaire ex-friend Bill Gates. In the media, Allen is characterized as the "bitter billionaire."[16]

In spite of lavish spending on celebrity-studded parties and multiple super-yachts, he is still the 53rd richest person on the planet. The 15 billion dollar question is "But is he happy?"

From what I can tell, he would like to be happier, but he can't let go of his resentments. He lacks gratitude for his great good fortune. He needs to let go, forgive and heal his heart.

Robert B. Cialdini, Ph.D. is the author of a bestselling book on *ethical* influence and persuasion. *Influence: Science and Practice* has sold an astounding 1.5 million copies. This is all the more impressive because Cialdini emphasizes honesty and integrity while following six principles that make people say "yes."[17]

At LOC 490, Cialdini is approaching the initiation into the transforming power of authentic love of LOC 500. At LOC 490 he is still psychologist, thinker, businessman and salesman.

His accomplishment is impressive in a blighted domain known for telling people to sell the "sizzle," not the steak. He is planting seeds of wisdom in the LOC 400s fields of life.

The intellect cultivated in the LOC 400s can be artfully used to dissolve itself in the LOC 500s. The analytical self-observation methods of the Buddha use the mind to go beyond it. Then the mind is exposed as the calm, clear self-liberating Buddha.

The pinnacle of the 400s is ethics from the perspective of the mind. When purity of heart is introduced, its magnificence outshines the mind. No matter what miracles the mind has managed to manifest, they cannot hold a candle to the Sun in the Heart. Love without conditions is its human expression.

In essence, this golden Heart is the simple smile of a child. In the hand of this smiling child is a beautiful fragrant rose.

The man of intellect sees the smile but does not understand it. If he notices the rose at all, he does not stop to smell it. In his mind he is thinking "What is the value? Where is the profit?" Or "How does this work? What is the cause and the effect?"

In eternity, there is no relative value, no profit, no doing, no cause and effect. All of this and more is utterly transcended.

When all things are Love or God, the mind is rendered useless. It conquers by dividing. In Love and God, there is only supreme ineffable wholeness. The mind falls silent, stunned by the majesty of wisdom beyond knowledge.

The shards of the broken dream coalesce. They melt in the holy furnace that is the true Heart of the whole human being.

1000

Bright shining star, the universe is in a cup of tea. Concepts dissolve in the electric thunder of reality. You are that in this moment. There is no mundane plane and no spiritual plane. If it is anywhere, it is here right now. This very world is God.

The Bonfires of Sacrifice

LOC 500 to LOC 559

Bonfires of Sacrifice: LOC 500 to 559

The low to middle 500s are a mixed bag. There is a lot that needs to be worked out and these parts are in conflict. This manifests as powerful paradoxical people. On the one hand, they may seem profoundly selfish in how they conduct their lives, yet they may do acts of charity and generosity that are mind boggling in their scope and vision.

In this range, you can be a physicist and a priest at the same time. You don't have to walk around carrying a flower. There is a new movement in you. Great universal love is awakening in you. You will eventually be transformed by it.

The brilliant quantum physicist who proves non-duality with his science yet lives dualistically in contradiction to his proof is a classic example. What is being discovered is that action initiated from the intellect in the spirit of strong "do-alism" has an intrinsic flaw. Born from separation, it is unable to partake of the wisdom, power. beauty and magic of cosmic wholeness.

The Most Controversial Range: LOC 500 to LOC 559

I suspect this range will be the most controversial in terms of my picks for the people to represent it. From LOC 500 to LOC 559 pure spirituality — the soulful essence of being human — in contrast to religion plays a bigger part in the person's life.

The human being is functionally complete when they reach LOC 499 and well before. What begins to develop in LOC 500 and up is what the poets have been talking about. It is still spirit opposed to matter, but it is a righteous struggle.

This breaking away from trusted crusty conventional religious constructs and constraints can take strange appearances as it gropes in a new darkness for the angelic glow of inconceivable answers. These are the frontrunners of the consciousness rebellion. They have not yet drunk the cup of non-duality, but its heady fumes made them dizzy with unquenched thirst.

A Subtle Dividing Line: From LOC 540 to LOC 560

There is a refinement that takes place between LOC 540 and LOC 559, but the breakthrough in consciousness where the truth and relevance of non-duality is clearly seen for oneself is the domain of LOC 560 and above. For the most part, it is only individuals with LOC 560 and above who will maintain a real commitment to non-dual groups, teachers and teachings.

In the LOC 540 through LOC 559 range emerges a largess that was not there before. The integration of metaphysical, magical and material is taking place, but it is still outer directed.

They are still looking for an external answer, but it is slowly and vividly dawning that the inside is the outside and vice versa. They are witnessing the miracle of love, but they are still testing it against the grosser measures of the mind.

When the transition to LOC 560 occurs, the insight emerges that true greatness is not defined by anything external. There is an invisible and ineffable supremacy, transcendental and triumphant. They begin to smell it and taste it, though they do not yet know the way. They may try the ceremonial use of a "sacred medicine" like ayahuasca to hasten their awakening.

The burning urge for personal liberation begins to overwhelm the bias for external achievement and social recognition. It becomes understood how a pauper on the outside, such as Ramana Maharshi or Nisargadatta Maharaj, can be the richest man in the world in the ultimate sense. Happiness is wealth, and it is not counted in dollars, houses, boats, clothes or cars.

This kind of understanding is studiously avoided prior to around LOC 560. Such knowledge sounds the death knell of the mind. If all that the mind can do, acquire and be is as worthless as the shadow compared to the sun that creates it, then what is the point of having this disturbing divisive mind?

Let the Sun in the Heart rise to high noon! At its zenith there will be no mind, no shadows, only Light. The mind avoids its inevitable dissolution as a distinct entity as long as possible.

"No Mind" Is Not Mindless: First Intellect Is Transformed

The development of the human intellect was a monumental achievement. It is not to be thrown away like a used gum wrapper. It is the medium for power and greatness. Yet when all that the mind promised has been achieved, where do you turn? There is only one place left, and that is the heart.

Most of the people in the lower range of the 500s are vocal, ambitious, aggressive, even egocentric. In this bold exercise of power, there are no angels in training. Where is the love?

The answer is don't look at the personality. Look at actions. A fiercely aggressive personality may be unpleasant to deal with, but they get things done on a massive scale that most "nice" people can barely imagine, much less accomplish.

The person in the low to middle 500s knows that action makes things happen. These are not just results for themselves, they are beneficial outcomes for others, too. Some are destined to live on a grand scale. They sneeze and the world shivers.

The New Man of Life Abundant Is About to Be Born

Gone are the primitive beastly impulses of the LOC 99 and below. This the reign of the "manimal" and its predatory lust.

Gone are the burning vengeful rages of the LOC 100s. This is the season of human monsters and the herds that obey them.

Gone are the self-serving aggressions of the LOC 200s. This is the medieval realm of courage to conquer inevitable enemies.

Gone are the mind-bending flip-flops of the dramatic LOC 300s. This is an age of emotion and passion for their own sake.

Gone are the callous computer-like precisions of the profit minded LOC 400s. It would calculate acceptable human losses when launching a new campaign for pharmaceuticals or war. Its detachment is superior, but that sword is double-edged.

In the 400s the power of the intellect dictated our destiny. The guiding truth was "I think, therefore I am." The infinite power of the intellect is the supreme standard. Through science and technology, all of our problems will be solved.

The inventor of the machine gun was convinced it would usher in the dawn of world peace. This nonsense, this trusting of the double-edged sword of the mind, must change.

It does change in the 500s. In the 500s, the mind begins to awaken as cosmic mind, as universal mind, as super-mind. No longer is mind the petty pulsations of overheated brain meat.

The new global mind ascends a golden staircase of splendor and amazement. This is the stuff that dreams are made of. This is the cosmic power at work. This is the mother of the computer. This is the father of the Internet.

If we are to be free as a person and as a planet, we must liberate the pure heart. Only it can call the intellect back to its roots in pure silence. Only it can bring the thought machine to its knees where, falling forward in full sacred prostration, it touches eternity and achieves "peace beyond understanding."

Golden Chains of Manifestation: the 500 to 559 LOC Zone

Bill Gates LOC 525

Brian Tracy LOC 534

Rhonda Byrne LOC 547

Max Planck LOC 553

You may be surprised to see billionaire *Bill Gates* in a book on non-dual spiritual enlightenment. Gates caught my attention due to his unparalleled acts of financial generosity. Some find fault on the basis that his $10 billion dollar charitable donation is for vaccines or that he has business relationships with global drug companies. However, Gates is not into holistic health. Conventional medical science supports his ideas.

Some suspect his agenda has a darker purpose, such as global population control. At LOC 525, I believe Bill Gates is above that kind of callous calculating Machiavellian deceit.

Gates has faults like the rest of us, but he has earned his place in history. With his charitable donations, he has cemented that position for a long time into the future.

If he is competing with other billionaires past and present to show who is the most generous of all time, then so be it. There are far worse things he could be doing with his money!

Brian Tracy is the success expert par excellence. At LOC 534, his message has a different tonality than, say, the business advice of Gates. In the 530s, there is expanding awareness of the need to find a balance between competition and higher consciousness. Market domination is not an end in itself.

Rhonda Byrne is famous for *The Secret* and its global success. She epitomizes the spiritual insights and limitations of the so-called Law of Attraction for wealth, health and happiness.

At LOC 547, there is no question that she has achieved a true depth of spiritual understanding. It is the triumph of positive thinking in creative relationship to the Cosmic Mind.

In spite of the deep quantum underpinnings of this view, the separate self and doership are not questioned. Concepts like non-locality are treated as if they are in place for the service of the user. This is a subtle conceit. True humility is yet to dawn. Supposedly, the human brain programs the cosmic mind. At some point, the opposite is seen. God is running everything.

Bob Proctor (LOC 543) is another prominent and gifted teacher in the same camp. As with Byrne, the emphasis is always on the bottom line and physical manifestation.

When you insist that your ground be made of gold, you miss the divine richness hiding in the depths of darkness. Wealth is not just material. The highest abundance is non-dual reality.

None of the high achievers in this LOC zone can appreciate the vast influence of karma. They are focused on being the doer and the power of that. It is their destiny to do so.

Their doership is working for them, so why should they question it? The grinding down of the ego will come later.

Max Planck is in the list to illustrate the amusing paradox of the physicist who grasps non-duality intellectually but does not walk the talk. Considered the Father of Quantum Physics, he received the Nobel Prize in physics in 1919.

To be fair to Planck, there is no need for a scientist to also be an enlightened philosopher. His achievements have changed the modern world beyond measure.

At LOC 553, he shows that such profound insights require a deeply refined mind. His friend Albert Einstein (LOC 582) regarded him as a pure soul alert to the sacred side of science.

Stepping into the Blaze

LOC 560 to LOC 569

Stepping into the Blaze: LOC 560 to 569

The groundwork has been laid for the new ascent. Here at last you see spirituality lived and made plain. Yet the gospel of success still permeates their agenda. It is fascinating how they are able to propound elevated views while stressing empirical results. These talents have remarkable success stories and exemplify the ideal of doing well by doing good.

The Masters of True Success: the 560 to 569 LOC Zone

Deepak Chopra LOC 562

Mikhail Gorbachev LOC 562

Wayne Dyer LOC 567

Jim Rohn LOC 567

Now the Light is emerging and proclaiming itself. I don't know what the reader thinks of my assessment of *Deepak Chopra* at LOC 562. He talks eloquently about enlightenment and self-improvement in the same breath.

Chopra is a consummate spiritual salesman. This is not meant as a criticism. He delivers the lessons of non-duality in a form that people can easily understand and digest. Brilliant and articulate, he performs a great service for non-dual awakening on our planet. Self-help guru Tony Robbins is also at LOC 562.

What can be said about *Mikhail Gorbachev* other than he changed the world when it was not thought possible?

1000

In those days, most of us were anticipating an endless stalemate between communism and capitalism. The nuclear arms race was in full deployment. It was a scary time.

Gorbachev transformed the grim predictions of 1989, brought down the Berlin Wall and made the modern world possible. Margaret Thatcher and Ronald Reagan agreed "We can do business with this man." That made not sound like much, but when war, cold or hot, is the alternative, it is hugely healing.

A man of true vision who inspired trust and admiration, he was the rare politician motivated by courage and compassion. It was his high level of spirituality that made peace possible through glasnost (openness), non-violence and bloodless revolution. His peace within made the peace without possible.

There are many excellent spiritual teachers, mentors, guides and coaches with LOCs in the 560s, but I chose *Wayne Dyer* at LOC 567 because he so perfectly embodies the paradoxical delivery of the 560 LOC range. One foot is in the material and one foot is in the spiritual. Teachers like Dyer skillfully blend the two, offering a compelling case for the happy healthy integration of these opposites into a wholesome successful life.

Dr. Wayne Dyer claims to be able to show how anybody can fulfill their heartfelt desires if they respect the divinity within. They must strive to live from a higher consciousness. They must closely follow his step by step guidelines.[18]

Yes, good things happen to a person who lives in harmony. There are many ways and levels of "living in the Tao."

The not so subtle implication of the Law of Attraction school, though, is that God can be manipulated into granting what the person desires. This is not far removed from the primitive notion of placating a deity in return for protection and favors. The packaging is new, but the message is very very old.

Of course, according to non-duality, there is no such person. The person who would receive this fulfillment is the separate entity who thinks he or she is the physical body. This entity does not exist. It may be felt to exist, but when the thinker or the observer of the thought stream vanishes, who is left to claim the body? The thinker is in reality just another thought.

If this sounds like a scathing criticism of Dyer, it is not meant to sound that way. Dyer is doing a tremendous job of what he is supposed to be doing. He is skillfully training those at that level of receptivity to this kind of message. It is perfect for them. If you are serious about non-duality, it is not for you.

Jim Rohn is also at LOC 567. If you are not familiar with Jim Rohn, he is personal development coach on a global scale. The quality that puts him at LOC 567 versus Brian Tracy at LOC 534 is that he emphasizes transformation.

Rohn comes across as a seasoned American Zen coach. He shows how to succeed in business and beat the competition from an elevated perspective. He puts the "zen" in zenith.

A typical Rohn teaching is you don't ask for life to be easier, you ask for life to make you better. Rohn is offering training in how to be a superior more complete human being. He is showing how to win in a rigorously ethical manner.[19]

Business and moneymaking can be taught from a much lesser stance. Rohn represents the highest level that "success" can be taught as "be the doer" and take action to make things happen. In the LOC 570s, you will see the mind embracing spiritual systems that purport to facilitate an awakening of some kind.

Intellectual Acumen and the 560s Non-Duality Student

In the range between LOC 560 and LOC 569, there is the potential for a life-changing progression of insight that takes the seeker from armchair curiosity to butt on the meditation cushion inquiry. Just as Chopra and Dyer as teachers are able to comfortably embody and mobilize intellectual investigation of non-dual truths, the 560s student is content with safe gains that do not yet challenge the fundamental ground of his life.

Entry into the 570s will signify that the quest is no longer a theoretical matter. The magnetic pull of Infinity begins to exacts its spiritual tax. The heart opens wide. Ever-deepening emotional vulnerability is demanded. Also at the 570s is seen the dedicated globetrotting spiritual seeker and guru chaser.

The 560s range non-duality may dutifully attend non-dual gatherings. He may meditate regularly though in an eclectic fashion. What he is not doing is allowing the teaching to penetrate to the point of seeing that it is his very self that is being demanded up as payment to the divine assassin.

He is in transition from the golden mental cage of self-centered attraction and manifestation. He has discerned that the acquisition of health, wealth, popularity and conventional success will not make him happy, but he has not yet grasped just how profoundly slippery is this slope into non-duality.

He thinks he can play with fire and keep it at a distance. He achieves peace that is good enough, yet now and then yearns for more. He is drawn to non-duality because he hears the echo of truth resounding in it. He senses that its demand is total, but he knows that he is not yet ready for that sacrifice.

LOC 560s Spiritual Practice & Armor Plate Thought Density

Chances are he is an impressive and humble person in terms of morals and ethics. He may demonstrate saintly qualities. It is true that the great quest has been activated in him. This is the level where the seed of awakening is planted. There is no rush for first he must absorb its radical thrust with the mind.

Though he may practice inquiry, his ability to enter into and sustain the thought-free state is limited. More often at this level is still seen the meditative discipline dabbler. He sits when it suits him. He meditates based on his mood.

He has not yet grasped the extent to which his thoughts are ruling his life. The Law of Attraction school, with which he may still have some involvement, taught the basics of this.

But the recognition that each and every thought must be attended to is still far from dawning. He is still asleep at the wheel. Since arising thoughts are not being studied, true silence is not experienced. If he experiences the gap between thoughts, it is for calm and stress reduction. He intuits the transcendental, but enlightenment experiences are not likely.

If a breakthrough does occur, it will probably be dismissed. If he embraces it, he will likely shift up into the 570s or higher.

Kundalini events may arise. Without the higher context, the intense symptoms may be difficult. Surrender is required, yet in the LOC 560s the tonality is still "my" achievements.

He will be comfortable with hatha yoga, t'ai chi, chi gong and other practices that involve holistic healing life force energies. Here and into the 570s, you will see easy "armchair Advaita." The goal, as at lower LOCs, is still more "self-improvement."

The difference is that in the 570s, the urge to be free verges on desperation. Solid substantial gains are not typical until the 580s with the ability to rest motionless in thought-free states.

For both the 560s and 570s the angst may be considerable. For the 560s, it is because they are keeping the living fire at a safe and comfortable arm's length, yet they intuit the loss in that.

Passion, Silence and Thought in the 560s, 570s and 580s

For the 570s, the angst is from the awakening of deep spiritual passion but there is no proportionate payoff forthcoming. They labor in the vineyard but do not yet enjoy sweet fruits.

The 570s are the most challenging transitional zone. Their sensitivity has blossomed. They are cognizant of their deeper predicament. But the addiction to constant thinking remains.

The skills required to discern the subtle movements and manipulations of the ego I-thought (the thinker) are not yet valued or attained. The mind is still believed. The burden of thinking is recognized, yet its dense overlays still dominate.

Those in the 580s are so close that they may think they are enlightened. Due to the reduced thought burden, they may think they are virtually there with nothing for them to do. It will happen automatically by way of osmosis or magnetism. They may be right, especially if they associate with true sages.

It will be in the 570s that spiritual discipline is seen to be as vital as breathing. Spiritual breakthroughs, including classic enlightenment experiences, are possible. In the 580s, they are certain. The 570s person may think that an astral trip out of the body is an experience of enlightenment. He is confusing altered states with the lucidity of temporary "ego death."

The 560s lay the intellectual foundation for the 570s. The 570s methodically prepare the way for the natural discipline of the 580s. This is a gradual process for good reasons. The brain and nervous system must adjust. They are being trained to carry the vibratory load of higher thicker frequencies. The high 570s are discovering the thought-free state. In the 580s, they will routinely enjoy them in preparation for a jump to non-duality.

Non-duality is like high voltage to the human body. Sudden shocks are not desired. Even in the carefully prepared vehicle, the disorienting blast of the Clear Light can lead to mental imbalance. This is more likely if the seeker has attempted to storm the gates of heaven by using psychedelic substances.

"Just Watching": the Slow Birth of Self-Inquiry in the 560s

In the 560s, the student is the moth attracted to the flame. But his egocentric instincts inform him to keep at a safe distance. He wants to stay in control of his life. He wants to keep his world as he knows it safe and intact.

1000

The sacred madness that will lead him to dedicate his life to this deadly (to the ego) understanding is birthing. It does so subconsciously. It has not yet surfaced in his life.

This is all as it should be since once the step is taken into direct experience of the non-dual, there will be no looking back. There is no guarantee this exposure will work out well.

As from a divine poison, symbolic limbs may be cut off. States of mind elsewhere labeled a type of "insanity" may arise. The only way to heaven is through hell, and it is a one way ticket.

Like falling in love, the journey is worth it, but the price may be higher than you ever imagined. What you gain is not what you expected. What you hoped for turns out to be a myth. Who you are is discovered to be nothing like you thought.

"Just watching" meditation is attractive for its passivity here. There will be greater calmness of mind, but the ego I-thought, the persistent thinker or observer, remains uncontested.

There is no need to rush. From the 560s on it is one long slow ego death grind. It is not so strange that in the 560s, the seeker would rather read the book or watch the movie. As with climbing Mt. Everest, the risk reward ratio of being a passive onlooker is very good. Let the mountaineer risk his life on the cold indifferent slopes of the Himalayas as you read about it in front of the fireplace, a glass of fine wine in your hand.

When you reach the 590s and beyond, you will be roasted alive, turned on a spit in God's fire pit. This is as ruthless and as merciless as it sounds. Spiritual adults only need apply.

Life for all is lived between the proverbial rock and hard place. In the 560s, it is finally dawning that the Higher Power is in charge. You and your life are a dream within a dream.

That can be interpreted as it's okay to watch, which is what the seekers in the 560s usually do. It is in the 570s that they feel impelled to potent action as the awareness of suffering due to egocentric separation reaches a conscious crescendo.

The Curious Parallel Between the 560s and the 600s

The energetic match between the psychology of the 560s and the non-dual perspective of the authentic 600s realizer is surprisingly transparent. The similarity is that both are engaged in discovering the details of their new dimension. It is a new world with new views, new rules, new ideas. There is an inspiration that leads to reaching out and interacting in a helpful manner, yet the sense of being "in the world" remains.

The 560s person is still looking back at the life from 500 to 559. He does not know it, but he is living between one realm and the next. In sum, 560 to 569 is a transition into the 570s.

The 570s accelerate into the pure intensity that unfolds in the 580s. The 580s blossom and radiate to fulfill human potential. Abilities are released like a fragrance. An effortless quality pervades the 580s domain, yet it is but a preview of things to come. Yet only the most courageous among them continue.

The awakened 600s person is still a psychological participant in the world he once knew, loved and feared. He is the new kid on the block in a city he does not yet know or understand.

Even if now he is the "non-doer," he is "non-doing" as a human being in the world with others. Even if he is "one with everything," there is still some kind of substantial "universe" to be at one with. These subtle points will be clarified in the chapter on the LOC 600s.

Recapitulation of Ascension: the Upper and Lower Quartets

The higher dualistic ranges are a presentiment of the noble non-dual levels of consciousness: 560 to 600, 570 to 700, 580 to 800, 590 to 900 and 600 to 1000. The gradual ascension from LOC 560 to LOC 600 is recapitulated in the progression of the non-dual stages as they climb higher to the supreme goal.

The 560s with their Janus-like looking back at the old and then at the new parallel the LOC 600s. The 570s with their love of systems parallel the LOC 700s. The 580s in their obsession with loving oneness parallel the LOC 800s. The 590s as a tricky transition zone parallel the LOC 900s. LOC 600 as the grand division between duality and non-duality parallels final stabilization in the fullness of non-duality at LOC 1000.

There is even a parallel between 586, 686 and 786 in how each borders the invisible event horizon of a spiritual black hole. Approached with soulful abandon, the transition is precipitated by a transcendental vacuum (sucking process).

In the lower quartet, the egocentric entity is sucked through the no man's land of the 590s into non-duality in the 600s or above. In the upper quartet, the enlightened 800s sage is divested of long-term residual holdings via Transfiguration.

1000

Subtly dualistic devotional encampments are subject to transcendental trance debriefing. In the "no mind" of the Absolute, there is not room even for the wonders of God, at least not the God who remembers Himself as such.

The Mystic On Fire

LOC 570 to LOC 579

The Mystic On Fire: LOC 570 to 579

The man or woman in the 570s labors in the karmic vineyards of the Lord but does not yet enjoy transcendental payouts. He is endowed with advanced spiritual desires that can move in a wide variety of directions. Here you see the emergence of the superior spiritual teacher confident in his high knowledge.

In the frustrated seeker, blood, sweat and tears seed the ground with sorrowful yearning, aggressive confusion and failed experiments in anti-wordliness. The consciousness that there is a craving, an incompleteness, a black hole just below the surface that gnaws away at every happiness is emerging.

"When will it happen to me?" he often thinks.

"Why won't it happen to me?" he wonders.

"What am I doing wrong?" he asks as he again berates himself.

The Hard Core Spiritual Seeker: Radical Rising in the 570s

He may become the hard core seeker who spares no expense, who sacrifices everything he can think of for the quest, who hops from guru to guru or method to method in a desperate power grab for the glowing holy grail of enlightenment.

This is the seeker stage par excellence for the seeker believes he will find what he seeks. Secretly he is bargaining with God to get his due. He expects a return on his investment. After all, that is how everything else has worked up until now.

He wants to believe that God can be cajoled, seduced or otherwise maneuvered into granting the great spiritual boon. Yet below the surface the workings are the same as in the Law of Attraction devotees and others who expect to program the Mind of God with their willful menu of self-serving demands.

The difference is that his ambition is at a higher level. It is more pure. It will take him to the gateless gate. He cannot yet enter, but he can pound his head against it. In a fit of wisdom, he will then give up because he can do no more. At last he will see the conceit of his enlightenment agenda. He, the spiritual beggar, would tell God what to do and when to do it. Absurd!

The Intelligent Systems Seeker: Relaxed Rising in the 570s

The contented LOC 570s seeker invests in a sophisticated system of spiritual knowledge, a virtuoso gradual path, that claims to provide a reliable map for the journey to truth and salvation. The seeker believes that by staying steady on this course he will slowly but surely arrive at his goal. He may indeed be right, but the path will be less linear than expected.

In contrast to the LOC 580s zone resident who readily rests in some edition of the ethereal no-thought state, his attachment to a logical system reflects the busyness of his mind and his craving for the safety of a philosophical mental object. His mental coverings remain intact but they are slowly dissolving. He is unconscious of this density and assumes it is permanent.

This density is the accumulation of thought strings and knots, the entanglements from traumas in many past lives. He is getting close to clearing most of it up. But the payoff will likely be in the 580s and he may not make it there in this life.

Frustrating as this stage is, this mental purification is needed. Otherwise, the egocentric mind displays a harsh complexity of densities that block out the light of spiritual sun. Without that light, life is merely a clever nihilistic mechanical mind game.

The aggressive gung ho seeker and the passive system user both belong to groups. Their upward trending motion and heartfelt motivation are protected and reinforced by organized groups intensely conscious of their elite spiritual solidarity.

Instructors of Systematic Illumination: 570 to 579 LOC Zone

Don Richard Riso LOC 572

Jack Canfield LOC 574

Kenneth Wapnick LOC 577

Jon Kabat-Zinn LOC 577

Illumination in this context refers to an awakening of some kind, but not classical enlightenment (LOC 600+). In Western mysticism and occultism, you will encounter systems that claim to provide steady progress up a ladder of states and stages. The appeal of such a system when it has a charismatic founder and a good story attached to it is considerable.

The Enneagram is such a system. Famous names associated with it include George Gurdjieff, Oscar Ichazo, John Lilly and Claudio Naranjo. It distinguishes itself by helping the student identify their "chief feature" or "ego fixation." In theory, this will help greatly to facilitate dissolution of the separate self.

Don Richard Riso was a leading proponent and author in the Enneagram movement. The attraction of the Enneagram for seekers LOC 540 and up, LOC 560 and up in particular, is that they get to work on themselves, identify and release fixations (blocks), and enjoy self-validation of progress along the way.

In contrast, a "sudden" school like direct pointing Advaita has no tolerance for such a "gradual" progressive journey. Even so, most who take on the sudden approach are not prepared for it. Their mind needs to be purified. They need to think less and BE more. In sum, they need a progressive path first.

The LOC 570s obsession with cultivating, systematizing and elaborating knowledge produces a tangled web. Translucent and glittering like diamonds, its complexity is its stickiness. Riso at LOC 572 was much admired for the multiple facets he was able to extrapolate from the Enneagram.

He sincerely believed that each Enneagram type was a gate through which "transcending the ego" could take place. Yet it was inevitable that the endless elaboration of the model could only work counter to that ideal. Sales of his Enneagram book were well above one million — one more reason to keep the abundance of new insights into the Enneagram flowing.[20]

Please understand that this is not a criticism of Riso, of the Enneagram, or of any facet of this tradition. Riso was selected as a featured person in the LOC 570s section precisely because his expression as a spiritual teacher entailed a deep yet telling intellectual elaboration of what is, in essence, a simple system.

This increase in complexity is characteristic of the LOC 570s teacher. He must elaborate because it is how he relates to the material. In LOC 580s teachers, you see return to simplicity and elegant pure feeling. In a way, the 570s are the acme of intellectual brilliance because there is a synthesis of spiritual, mental and material at the highest level of analytical thinking.

Yet this elaboration is itself an avoidance of the quintessential message of the Enneagram. Again, this is not a criticism. I am merely pointing out that such elaboration is a function of this LOC level. It is feeding minds who need this stimulation, who need this abundance of thought food, who need to keep their busy minds preoccupied with spiritually substantial content.

Jack Canfield at LOC 574 is another gifted spiritual teacher of great integrity. He represents a return to the Law of Attraction material I mentioned in my discussion of Bob Proctor (LOC 543) and Rhonda Byrne (LOC 547). The distinction between what Byrne and Canfield are teaching is subtle yet significant. We can ask "What does a difference of 30 LOC points make?"

Canfield originated the Chicken Soup for the Soul® series and the inspirational anthology book concept. Based directly or indirectly on his efforts, there are now more than 500 million Chicken Soup for the Soul® books in print around the world.

Billing himself as "America's #1 Success Coach," Canfield brings a unique spiritual tonality to the all American success ideal. While that difference may not be obvious on the surface, here are five tweets from Canfield that illustrate the subtle difference that being a "success coach" in the 570s makes.

1. "Everything you want is on the other side of fear."

2. "The true task of spiritual life is not found in faraway places or unusual states of consciousness. It is here in the present."

3. "You only have control over three things in your life-the thoughts you think, the images you visualise, and the actions you take."

4. "If you want to be really successful, and I know you do, then you will have to give up blaming and complaining and take total responsibility for your life."

5. "If it ain't fun don't do it."[21]

Making money and achieving success is being taught in the context of high ethics, having fun, facing fears (and thus embracing love), inspired authentic living and total personal responsibility. The grim materialism hiding under pseudo-spiritual "thought power" money obsession is not present.

Even if the word "service" is not used, that is the spirit. The follower of Canfield is receiving excellent training in right beliefs, right attitudes, right thoughts and right actions.

I use the word "right" deliberately. The Buddha's Noble Eightfold Path is "1. Right view, 2. Right intention, 3. Right speech, 4. Right action, 5. Right livelihood, 6. Right effort, 7. Right mindfulness and 8. Right concentration."[22]

Kenneth Wapnick was perhaps the leading teacher of "A Course in Miracles"® (ACIM). At LOC 577, that is not surprising.

We have featured another well-known spiritual leader with an ACIM message in the LOC 580s group. That's bestselling author Marianne Williamson (LOC 584).

If you are familiar with ACIM and its non-dual flavor, it is not surprising that a teacher of ACIM would be in the 570s or 580s. I am not aware of an ACIM teacher who is stabilized in non-duality (above LOC 600). ACIM sets as its goal giving up the self and awakening from the dream. Yet Wapnick deliberately describes it as a "thought system."[23]

This is critical. If you are working with a thought system, then you are not working to give up or transcend thought. You are working to replace thought, to take thought to a higher level.

According to ACIM, there is a thought system of knowledge from God and a thought system based on perception from the body and the separate will. By reversing our thinking, we learn how to forgive and transcend this world.[24]

I know very little about ACIM, so the above may not be quite correct. If you seek clarification, excellent materials on ACIM are abundant. My point is simply that ACIM appears to be yet another advanced thought-based training system suitable for people in LOC 560s and LOC 570s in particular (as well as those in lower LOCs, of course).

There is no criticism here of ACIM, Enneagram or any such useful spiritual system that is based on thinking. Such systems are absolutely necessary. They are a transformational bridge from the less subtle refined materialism views expressed in the lower 500s to the sublime freedom from thought that spontaneously and gracefully appears in LOC 580s persons.

Jon Kabat-Zinn represents yet another frequency of the 570s enthusiastic focus on systems, methods and techniques. While the three other LOC 570s featured persons were teaching and promoting thought-based systems that involved meditation, Jon Kabat-Zinn at LOC 577 is focused on meditation itself.

Author of several bestselling books on Buddhist mindfulness meditation, he is the founder of the Mindfulness-Based Stress Reduction (MBSR) course now taught at university-based stress reduction clinics around the world. The eight week course fuses meditation on being in the moment with hatha yoga in order to help patients cope with stress, pain, illness, panic attacks, anxiety and depression. Kabat-Zinn's medical background includes a Ph.D. in molecular biology.[25]

A student of Zen Master Seung Sahn (LOC 1000), he was on a retreat with another popular Zen Master, Thich Nhat Hanh (LOC 755) that emphasized mindfulness when he realized that what the Vietnamese meditation master was teaching could bring profound benefits to people with chronic medical and psychological conditions.[26] The rest, as they say, is history.

In the chapter on enlightened (non-dual) realizers, I included popular Buddhist meditation teachers Jack Kornfield (LOC 684). Joseph Goldstein (LOC 715) and Sharon Salzberg (LOC 688). Why isn't Jon Kabat-Zinn on this list?

When you listen to Kabat-Zinn, he is articulate, precise, warm, practical and engaging. What becomes clear is that his priority was to find a way to make this powerful ancient Buddhist meditation system, refined over many centuries by dedicated monks, available to the average person who needed help.

The person he wanted to help had no interest in Buddhism or mindfulness. His target audience was interested in reducing pain, improving a medical condition, counteracting stress, getting over depression and having fewer panic attacks.

Kabat-Zinn's compassionate gesture was to take the advanced course that he attended and transform it into a systematic step by step training and methodology that could be understood and applied by the interested motivated person regardless of their background or prior lack of training in meditation.

That is a classic LOC 570s vision and accomplishment. In the case of Kornfield, a former Buddhist monk, nibbana (personal liberation) had been the goal. Eventually, he returned to the United States and began teaching and writing books.

In the best sense of the word, Kabat-Zinn, as a member of the Western medical establishment, wanted to "dummy down" Buddhist mindfulness meditation and boil it down to its workhorse essence *without* enlightenment as the goal. To his credit, he did so in the context of recognized masters and from his own profound applied understanding. He walked his talk and talked his walk. His actions have benefited many people.

His pioneering efforts have been well received. Numerous scientific studies are being conducted on the benefits of mindfulness. Stress reduction via mindfulness is now a cottage industry that functions as "training wheels" for those who may want more and to go deeper. As with Zen, this form of Buddhism has been enthusiastically adopted by the West.

Hardcore Seeker X: Straight Out of Hollywood Casting

In early 2013, I was contacted by a sincere spiritual seeker. This man had watched a video of me on YouTube and found that his mind was stopped. For a day or more, he could not think or function normally. Intrigued, he asked to meet me.

I met with this ardent seeker at a small trendy coffee shop in San Diego. The conversation quickly focused on one thing. This seeker had been all over India and the world. He had met some of the greatest spiritual teachers of our time. In short, this man was a "star" among seekers. He was a super-seeker!

He had met Papaji. He had met Neem Karoli Baba, the elusive guru of the beloved American mystic Ram Dass. He had met so many famous gurus that his exotic stories made my head spin. It was an amazing spiritual travelogue. Beyond that, he had stayed with Papaji and other genuine sages for years.

This man was a magnificent example of a hardcore spiritual seeker. His LOC was 573. At this mid-range 570s LOC, he had transcended the passivity of the LOC 560s but he was not yet at the stillness, silence and easy clarity of the LOC 580s.

He still believed in his search. He still believed it would get him where he wanted to go. He had not yet had the insight that what he was seeking would be his as soon as he dropped the mind. Even with all of this seeking, along with meeting and even living with some of the greatest spiritual masters of our time, this man was still only at LOC 573.

As the hour wore on, it became abundantly clear why, in spite of being exposed to so many enlightened people, he had not made it any higher. The man could not stop talking.

He was full of himself. He knew so much. He was a spiritual expert. He was like the Zen student with the full cup of tea.

The teacher tries to pour tea into the student's full tea cup. There is no room for what the teacher has to offer. The student is filled to the brim and overflowing with his knowledge, his experiences, his separate seeking self. He is full of the past. He is not available to the present. He is not ready for the teacher.

I asked him "Do you feel driven? Is there still an emptiness inside of you? Do you feel a hole inside of you?"

The man said "Yes." He paused for about two seconds. Then he launched into another fascinating story about meeting another great spiritual master in another exotic location.

This man was heavily addicted to his thoughts. He had no room in his mind for a spiritual intervention by silence. His thoughts were closely linked and rushing by like a freight train. Underneath it all was fear of dying, fear of losing all the precious knowledge he had acquired. His collected insights were just dead useless thoughts and ego-puffing stories. They were the rancid consolation prize for his globetrotting drama.

This seeker illustrates the wired tightness of the 570s mind. He is fiercely seeking, yet his mind is still knotted and armored. The mind remains very real to him. He has not discovered how to rest in the open space between thoughts, the luminous spaciousness which reveals that there is no mind. It is likely he has tasted it, but his mental momentum prevents staying in it.

Surprising Parallel Between the LOC 570s and the LOC 700s

The LOC 570s individual subconsciously demands organized structures and systems due to security imprints in his dense mentality. Mental momentum is inevitably directed outwards.

The group orientation of the LOC 570s is reflected in the LOC 700s. These enlightened teachers work hard to liberate people via easy systematic spiritual technology at a group level rather than the individual coaching style of LOC 600s solo realizers.

They are inspired to create new methodologies that rapidly and reliably purify the mind so that potent breakthrough enlightenment events occur in this lifetime. In its subtle non-dual reflection, the 570s life orientation is expressed by the LOC 700s range guides and gurus in compassionate practical inquiry systems that cut through mental knots, mental coverings and mental armored plates with precision.

Teachers in this category include Byron Katie, Scott Kiloby, Arjuna Ardagh and Dennis Genpo Merzel Roshi. All have invented specialized spiritual inquiry modalities to facilitate non-dual breakthroughs. All have created coaching programs so that their methods can be delivered on a massive scale by trained facilitators who may themselves not be enlightened.

A Sage Is Waiting

LOC 580 to LOC 589

A Sage Is Waiting: LOC 580 to 589

When the seeker reaches the 580s, he has achieved significant reduction of his mental coverings. The hardcore seeking of the 570s has finally paid off. The scope of this spiritual saga is usually multiple lifetimes. In our exceptional age of spiritual acceleration, enlightenment in this life is possible for all.

In previous lives, these crystallized condensations of thinking that accumulated in hundreds of lifetimes was still too thick. The hardness and complexity of the encrypted thought layers overwhelmed the seeker's attempts to access enlightenment.

In the 580s, the mental veil or thought cloud layer has thinned sufficiently. The density of the mental coverings is reduced to a decisive extent. Compulsiveness of thought has subsided.

Thought is still driven, but there is now the capacity to readily enter into thought-free states. Now the seeker begins to enter samadhi states and enjoy profound meditations. He may have accessed such states before. The difference now is that he can stabilize in them and do this without much effort.

The spiritual sun, representing enlightened awareness, is peeking through the clouds at least now and then. The seeker is delighted that this is happening on a consistent basis. The thinning of the veil makes meditation easy and enjoyable.

It also is a virtual guarantee of one or more enlightenment events (the sun rising and blasting the mind with Clear Light). This exposure may only work to thin the veil some more. There can be numerous breakthroughs without stabilization.

It is like the mind is going through a washing machine. The more stubborn the dirt, the more times the cleaning cycle will need to be repeated. Eventually it reaches critical mass and the yearned for leap into and stabilization at non-duality occurs.

The Flowing Mind of Global Love: the 580 to 589 LOC Zone

This group is fascinating. Love abundant and overflowing is the theme. The energy is round, circular, moving in a spiral. It is the ideal mindset for reaching out and changing the world, which these well-known luminaries have done. They carry their celebrity karma lightly. These are impressive people!

Oprah Winfrey LOC 582

Louise Hay LOC 583

Dannion Brinkley LOC 584

Marianne Williamson LOC 584

Soon after the idea for this book was conceived, the thought to include billionaire *Oprah Winfrey* (LOC 582) appeared. That was years ago. Her success is even more remarkable now.

Why feature Oprah? Consider this. The entire staff of Harpo Studies, Oprah herself and her 400 employees, meditate every day at 9:00 a.m. and then again at 4:30 p.m.

That's right. The entire company... twice a day... meditates. Just imagine if the whole world was doing that. Amazing!

Can you think of another major firm where every single person, including the CEO, meditates? Not only that, they all meditate at the same time... each workday... together.

Yes, there are companies that encourage employees to meditate, that offer free yoga and meditation classes, that are eager to apply the growing body of evidence that these practices reduce stress and upgrade emotional intelligence.

Oprah is conducting a brilliant consciousness experiment. She claims her people are healthier, sleep better, work better and get along better.[27] Oprah is anticipating the future when whole companies, whole cities, perhaps the whole world, will be meditating together. Then we will have peace on earth.

Louise Hay is a "new age" guru with many bestselling books and a publishing empire that enables her to promote authors she believes in. She is, in short, a force to be reckoned with.

She is on this list because she talks about enlightenment and when she talks about it, she is talking from experience. With an LOC of 583, she is not established in non-duality. But it is fascinating to hear what she has to say, because what she is describing is the state of illumination, of transparent easeful being, that can precede classical enlightenment (600s and up).

Sample this quote from her Facebook page "Hay House Daily Meditations" (Hay House is her publishing company).

"Enlightenment is my 24-hour-a-day job. Awakening to love is what I am doing each morning. I love stretching my mind and acting as if I am already perfect, whole, and complete, right here and right now."[28]

The only way to be "already perfect, whole, and complete" is to not be the mind. To be that "right here and right now" is not possible for the mind. The mind is back in the past. The mind is forward into the future. The mind is not here and now.

In contrast, the viewpoint in the 570s was "We're working on transcending the ego, but in the meantime, we're getting all these cool insights — wait a minute, here's another one!" In contrast, Hay is saying "perfect-whole-complete-here-now."

Dannion Brinkley is the only man in this LOC 580s group. His presence is soft, warm, gentle and kind, yet he is a big and powerful man, too. Very human compassionate love blends with his Southern drawl to smoothly emanate from his being.

One of the most famous survivors of a life-changing near-death experience (NDE), Brinkley at LOC 584 has died not once, not twice, but three times. His visions and prophecies aside, what strikes me about him is the attractive mixture of ordinary ego and timeless space that I feel around him.

Here is a man who is an emissary of death, an advocate of the art of dying, a survivor of the realm beyond. When he died, it wasn't just his opinion. He was pronounced clinically dead.[29]

You would think that if anybody is ready for ego death, it is the person who has already died. Based on the reports of NDE survivors like Brinkley, I find the NDE is a breakthrough, but there is not typically a stabilization in non-duality.

The person has been changed, but they are not established above LOC 600. I have seen this repeatedly.

The glimpse may be given, but the stabilization must be earned. This spiritual work, this effort, somehow "qualifies" the seeker for Grace.

Marianne Williamson at LOC 584 is a remarkable woman with four *New York Times* bestsellers. She talks breezily about "enlightenment" and being "illumined."[30]

Her latest teaching is about how the experience of falling in love is a kind of "mini- enlightenment." In her view, what she is saying is in perfect alignment with the message of ACIM.

This is a profound instruction that beautifully illustrates how the LOC 580s person can speak to the ordinary person where they live while holding to the clarity of their own "illumined" state.[31] They have, so to speak, a foot in both worlds.

This image of the LOC 580s person having one foot in the material world and one foot in the spiritual world is perfect. The teachers in the 560s and 570s do a good job, but it is these rare spiritual cultural guides who manifest it in its fullness.

They are the beach where the ocean of the infinite washes up indescribable gifts from its depths. They live both in the ocean and on the land. But as great as their accomplishments are, they are not yet ready to dive into the ocean and dissolve.

The 580s Criterion: An Authentic Enlightenment Event

The functional definition of the "emerging sage" person in the LOC 580s is that they have had one or more enlightenment experiences. However briefly, they have tasted non-duality.

They are beyond the LOC 570s seeker who is driven by his unsatisfied hunger. They have been kissed by the Infinite and yearn for more. For them, once will not be enough.

These breakthroughs are "enlightenment" experiences in which the cleansing actinic flash of the Clear Light has blasted away major blocks of ego holding. They have had moments in which it was clearly seen there is no separate self, no entity, no center, no "ego," no person, nobody choosing, nobody doing.

Without at least one such all-penetrating spiritual blast, the thick mental density of the mind, hard like the armor plate on a tank, remains merely dented. The pathos of a 570s seeker is that he intuits the possibility of breaking through the mind and freeing himself of it, but the ultimate state escapes him.

He may enjoy astral travel, occult experiences or bliss states. At the high end, at LOC 578 or LOC 579, he is preparing to enter the LOC 580s. Then thought-free states begin to arise.

Those in the 580s have seen this timeless truth with their own eyes, heard it with their own ears, felt it with their own heart. They may even believe that now they are "enlightened." They may even go out teaching "enlightenment."

Their web sites offer sincere enticing claims. When I looked deeper, what I found is that by "enlightenment" they do not mean *stabilization* in non-duality. They mean having an enlightenment "experience." Because they have had a direct taste of non-duality, they can be very articulate. Typically, they have not yet evaluated their experience in the context of the great non-dual traditions and the message of the masters.

It is impossible to know if the celebrities I have chosen to represent the 580s have had classical enlightenment events. I suspect that they have. It is something they may prefer to keep to themselves. I would say Brinkley's NDEs certainly count.

As with any rule, there are exceptions. Mainly I am saying that enlightenment "experiences" will most likely take place before the big jump into non-duality and stabilization there. If the person is already prepared, then they can make the leap without any test runs. What I've seen is that people first go to "visit" (and test) non-duality before they decide to "live" there.

The Role of "Enlightenment Events" in the Author's Journey

I had three such "enlightenment events." I define them as the undeniable disappearance for minutes, hours or days of the separate entity. I did not stabilize in non-dual awakening and non-doership until 1992. When stabilization finally took place, it was directly due to receiving my guru's Grace back in 1989.

The first breakthrough was a spontaneous Kundalini event at the age of 16. Though the ego entity died in an ocean of clear light, it came back the next day imbued with distracting new psychic powers. On top of typical teenage agonies, it was a rough and rocky road that I would not wish on anyone.

After numerous breakthroughs in which stabilization eluded me, a unique detachment arose. There was a giving up of the search. The craving for enlightenment gave way to a unique state of "high indifference" that lacked conventional affect yet supported deep intuitive feeling and awareness. Because I was right in the middle of it, I could not know its significance.

An existential chaos illuminated a dusky fog, the straggling remnants of the battle for enlightenment that had failed. It was understood that "I" cannot achieve this. This was the authentic surrender. This was the true beginning of ego death.

"If it is to be, it is up to Thee." This was the new mantra. There was not a clear knowing of who this Thee could be, but it was clear that It was in charge. It had planted this otherworldly ambition in me, this unquenchable transcendental fire.

Then out of the blue, the guru (Ramesh Balsekar) appeared with his Shiva Hammer fashioned from a spiritual lightning bolt. In one sentence that consisted of six powerful words ("There is nothing you can do!") my seeking was shattered, blasted and annihilated on the spot. This was Fall, 1989.

After that transmission, the mind began to finally unwind, setting the stage for a terminal dip of the isolated thinker into the ocean of cosmic consciousness in 1992. The hall of mirrors was shattered. The fires that had produced endless smoke were quelled. The grating of iron wool against the skin of the soul, the agonizing alarm clock of Lord Ketu (South Lunar Node) that had kept this seeker awake day after day to his suffering, was finally silenced. It had fulfilled its purpose.

I did not know it at the time, but my journey at another level had just begun. Awakening is but the beginning. For those unwilling to accept consolation prizes, for those who refuse the wine of sleep in the warm desert tents of spiritual oases, the mountaintop, unspeakable sacrifice and the final test of absolute aloneness beckons. I was profoundly blessed to have as my guide the sublimely ruthless ego assassin Kali Ma.

On the Threshold: the High Indifference of Illumined Ones

These 580s people are having a great time, so they may just want to stay right where they're at. What I have found that parallels the enjoyment of the famous people featured here is the fact that often 580s people are quite comfortable with their life and who they are. They are attached to their easy state. They may be called "illumined" due to their exposure to non-dual frequencies of enlightenment. Stabilization will be later.

When working with the LOC 580s person, I will typically hear them say "Oh, sure, I can go into a thought-free state and stay there quite effortlessly." This is a profound opportunity. This is the yogic freeway to the Ocean of the Infinite. This is huge.

They understand that there is more, that enlightenment is beyond this peaceful state they readily find themselves in, yet they are finding it hard to be motivated. I have seen this again and again. They are where so many seekers yearn to be. They are enjoying this part of the ride and they want to prolong it.

Of course, stabilization in non-duality beyond mere glimpses is a radical annihilation of all that you have known and loved. It is understandable that so many of these 580s folks are hanging out just enjoying the spiritual breeze from the cosmic ocean, just watching the waves roll in.

When they do finally dive into that ocean, it will be the end of them. They directly intuit this. So they stay on the beach and play holy volleyball.

Spiritual Sweet Spot: LOC 580s and the Thought-Free State

Just the same, based on my experience with spiritual seekers and students. it is the LOC 580s people by far who have the best shot at enlightenment here and now.

I hesitate to go so far as to say it is a rule, but my impression is that seekers will proceed up from the 560s or 570s (where strong motivated interest typically arises) into the 580s. Then at the 580s they are "ripe" and the "enlightning" can strike at any moment.

This makes sense since the mental coverings below the 580s are simply too thick. The mind is coagulated and the layers are tightly fitted. The mental knots and programs do not yet have enough space in them to allow the Light to do its work.

Light is slowly working upon the mental rigidity, but this is in preparation for the entire machine to shatter. The mind does not die so easily. Even shifting into non-duality is not enough. It is only at the LOC 900s that the mind becomes "no mind." At LOC 1000, the ego I-thought is finally vanquished.

The people I have worked with who did make the leap after working with me and receiving RASA were all in the LOC 580s at the time of their non-dual breakthrough. They may have started lower, but when they made the leap they were between LOC 581 and LOC 589. As of this writing, all of those people remain firmly stabilized in non-dual enlightenment.

Progressive Non-Dual Enlightenment From LOC 580s

My own journey is a good example. A Kundalini event at the age of 16 launched my spiritual quest in 1966.

1000

I was at LOC 583 when I received my guru's transmission of Grace face to face in 1989. I was dry kindling waiting for a match. As an aftermath of Grace from Ramesh Balsekar, non-dual awakening occurred in February, 1992 in San Diego.

At that time, I jumped up to LOC 683. After several years at this level, I decided that it was flawed, unstable, limited and dissatisfying.

I then dedicated myself to the task of working through every limitation and boundary that I could find. As a result, over the years I gradually rose up through the various levels that are described in this book. I can talk about them because I lived them. This process culminated in February, 2008. This book is the direct result of that 42 year long journey (1966 to 2008).

I was able to write this book because I can feel and intuitively sense the degree of mental density that surrounds a person.

This density becomes less and less until the person reaches LOC 1000. Then it dissolves and disappears. Each non-dual LOC range has its own unique texture, weight and tone.

Suicidal Depression and the Fine Art of Enlightenment

Suicidal depression in which there is the thought "I cannot live anymore in this painful state" keeps appearing as a pattern in modern day times. Eckhart Tolle awakened this way. Jeff Foster awakened this way. One of my students also awakened in this way. After getting RASA, he subsequently stabilized.

What I learned from the student who went through this process is that the thought pattern was spiritually precise. It was not an ordinary suicide drama, a call for attention motivated by self-pity and narcissism. The specific thought pattern was "I cannot stand this I anymore. *I want this I to die!*"

Looked at closely, this is a revelation. A differentiation is being made between one I, the false I, and another I, the true I.

At this stage, it is not necessary to know who the true I is. What is needed is to know that "you" are not the false I. In this knowing, an urgency for the death of the false I escalates.

The student who explained this process so eloquently to me also pointed out that the depression functioned in a positive way, fixing and stabilizing the mind. A typical problem for seekers is that the mind jumps around and will not focus. In the case of depression, the weight of that state holds the mind down, rubbing its face as it were in its own negative poop!

This student's LOC at the start of his spiritual depression cycle was 578. At the time of his breakthrough into non-duality, it had risen to 584. He then made the leap into non-duality to LOC 675, but had difficult stabilizing there. He found me on the Internet and started one to one weekly spiritual coaching.

After working closely with me for three months, he was able to permanently stabilize. After a few more ups and downs, all within non-duality ranges, he gathered his spiritual forces for a final push. He has now gone all the way to LOC 1000!

Green Pastures For Sacred Cows: LOC 580s and LOC 800s

1000

While there is no comparison in terms of realization between LOC 580s and LOC 800s, there is a fascinating parallel where the nature of the 580s exposes something critical about LOC 800s that otherwise might not be seen. As we have seen, LOC 570 people are in love with their spiritual systems. LOC 580 people are in love with their wonderful vision of reality.

Because the degree of mentality is greater, the 570s person is investing in a system such as the Enneagram, the Kabbalah,"A Course in Miracles"® (ACIM) all of which promise they will sequentially precipitate the desired advanced awakening. That it does not actually do so is not a major concern of these advocates. It has successfully kept them spiritually engaged.

In contrast, teachers, promoters, educators and other leaders in the 580s are imparting a soft luminous loving vision of things as they are and as they can be. The pure pinnacle of dualistic self-expression, this compassionate vision is nobly humanitarian and universal. The amazing contributions of Oprah Winfrey via modern media are the perfect example.

The equivalency at the LOC 800s is that there still remains what might be described as a "sacred cow." This could be an inability to let go of old religious beliefs, a fascination with the glories of the Divine, an attachment to a spiritual guru. No matter how sublime it has been, no matter how it has served the person in the past, it is a veil that stands between them and their realization of and stabilization in the Absolute.

Beyond the Sacred Cow: the Blissful Way of Parabhakti

It is possible to transcend this extremely subtle "other" or sublime veiling via Parabhakti, meaning transcendental love-devotion that is beyond any flavor or texture or density of duality. The attainment of Parabhakti presumes transcending the 800s and stabilizing in the ineffable heights of LOC 1000.

Parabhakti is the heartfelt way of supreme love, devotion and surrender. It finds the Absolute diving into the heart of love.

Jnana (non-duality) also attains the Absolute (LOC 1000). Either approach can work. The key is total purity.

"Purity of what?" you may ask. Pure of any and all concepts, even beloved concepts such as a God we worship and adore. Pure of any ideas, pure of all knowledge, pure of knowing that there is an "I" of any kind in the first place. The "I" of the Absolute does not know that exists. The meaning here is akin to the saying "If you see the Buddha on the road, kill him."

One interpretation is the Buddha on the path to LOC 1000 is a "sacred cow" concept that we simply cannot let go of because it *was* our vehicle. It helped us get to where we are. It would seem like blasphemy to drop our devotion to the Supreme.

The Indian saint Swami Ramdas (not the American spiritual teacher Ram Dass) attained Parabhakti via devotion to the avatar Lord Rama. Since he was at LOC 1000, his opinion is worth listening to on this subject. Swami Ramdas had realized the ultimate of both bhakti (devotion) and jnana (non-duality). The word "Anand" here means "bliss" or "ultimate fulfillment."

> Om Sri Ram Jai Ram Jai Jai Ram. The Anand of pure Jnana and the Anand of Parabhakti are the same. One is enjoyed in the inactive aspect of God, while the other in His active aspect.[32]

I was stuck in blind devotion to the Hindu Mother Goddess Kali Ma. This made it impossible for me to continue with my spiritual progress. For many years, I was addicted to the humble role of being her abject love slave. She corrected this problem by removing Herself as an object of my devotion.

Late in my sadhana period, She literally disappeared. She reappeared when I agreed to stop being Her slave and agreed to claim my identity as Lord Shiva. Even then I tried to get away with the strategy of being a "Junior Shiva." Kali Ma would have none of it. She demanded that I totally embrace what is called Shiva Consciousness, the stainless Absolute.

The Surprising Parallel Between LOC 586 and LOC 886

I have worked as a spiritual facilitator with dozens of people who have LOCS in the 580s. I have also studied other people in the LOC 580s who I do not know as friend or student.

Although my theoretical model says that the LOC 580s go from LOC 580 to LOC 589, I kept encountering people stable at LOC 581 through LOC 584. I found one person stabilized at LOC 585 and one person stabilized at LOC 589. The LOC 589 person is now one of my enlightened students (LOC 884).

The feeling vibration emanated by a person stabilized in the low LOC 580s is that they are *preparing* for the big jump into non-duality (600s). The leap can be made from anywhere in the LOC 580s. LOC 582 and LOC 583 are the most common.

Above LOC 585 the non-dual "ego death" suction force from the mini-void at the LOC 600s dimensional gate is taking over. Another way to express this is to say that the outer edge of the "event horizon" of the black hole (mini-void) of separate self annihilation is located at LOC 586.

When the LOC 589 student first contacted me, she told me in her email that she felt she was at the end of her spiritual rope. This made sense to me.

Hanging out at LOC 589, she would have been extremely close to awakening, yet tantalized and tortured by her "failure" to realize. Fortunately, her first RASA sent her rocketing for good into the spiritual stratosphere.

Parallels Between the Lesser Void and the Greater Void

The spiritual "no man's land" between duality and non-duality is the 590s. Entry into the 590s means the person has gone past the point of no return. They will get sucked into the black hole of ego death. It is possible to fight it, but it makes no sense. I have found only two people who were stabilized in LOC 590s.

This gate is being called a mini-void or Lesser Void because the true void or Great Void transition occurs between the high LOC 780s and the LOC 800s. The precise spot? LOC 786.

LOC 586 to LOC 589 is a spiritual boundary and the outer edge of the transmogrifying black hole force field. When I studied the LOC 700s, I found a similar gap starting at LOC 786. This is a transition through indescribable ultimate Void into exquisite divine union and blissful "dazzling darkness."

During this shift, all that was known and accumulated is abandoned and dissolved. This unprecedented sacrifice of knowledge separates the cosmic mystics of the 700s from the sages of the 800s and above. Knowledge is reborn as love.

Symbolically, LOC 586 and LOC 786 are both at the edge of a life-changing cliff. The great significance of the 586 transition is illuminated by the 786 transition and vice versa.

In contrast, the movement from the LOC 686 area to the LOC 700s is more comfortable. The local open "no self" expands to cosmic size.

LOC 786 plus represents rebirth via the luminous darkness of the Great Void or Cosmic Womb. There is entry into a new not knowing via the swoon of love union with Source.

The new stage, the LOC 800s, presages the final ultimate Nothingness and "no mind" of LOC 1000, the unconditioned Absolute. It typically enjoys "unknowing" that is love-based.

LOC 586 and up refers to tossing the spiritually prepared seeker into the black hole of ego death via the LOC 590s transcendental "tunnel." It is the cosmic birth canal that takes you from the dark confined pressurization of hard duality to the soft open liberating lightness of non-duality.

LOC Model Explanation: Involuntary LOC 600s Recidivism

For reasons that will be explained shortly, the effective range in which the transformation takes place is LOC 586 to LOC 624 and LOC 886 to LOC 924.

There is a parallel passage from the 600s to the 700s, but it is an extension of familiar ground. So Wayne Liquorman stays cozy at LOC 694 and Buddhist teacher Joseph Goldstein is comfortable at LOC 715.

In our times, persons who are transcending the 700s are likely to skip or quickly pass through the 800s. The 800s is the realm of the great mystics of yore. Clarity, not mystical experiences, is the focus of our directly pointing efficient modern methods.

If you go back to the chapter listing the LOCs of well-known non-duality teachers, you will see that not one of the teachers in the 600s range is at LOC 624 or below. Stabilization in the 600s requires being above that boundary.

If you are in the 600s but below LOC 624, you are still actively in process. It is possible that you will drop out of non-duality and back into (most likely) the low to mid-580s. This is why people can go into non-duality and then pop out again.

You must accelerate beyond the pull of the lower range (LOC 580s to LOC 624). Otherwise, the gravitational pull of that vibrational plateau keeps you locked down tight. The stability that kept you in, say, the 580s now fights to keep you there.

LOC Tracking: LOC 583 Seeker "Test Drives" LOC 600s

In Summer 2013, I tracked an individual who went from LOC 583 up to LOC 623. The new LOC lasted about two weeks. Then it fell back, only this time to LOC 584, a gain of one point. This person remained stabilized at LOC 584.

This individual had attended my satsang several times. She was also attending satsangs with at least two other people in the San Diego area that I had verified were non-dual realizers.

In addition to tracking her LOC, I had the advantage of having several pithy and illuminating conversations with this serious meditator. I was deeply impressed by the intensity and precision of her efforts. These chats further confirmed for me that she was very close to realizing non-duality.

I asked a mutual friend if he had noticed anything about her or if she had said anything that sounded out of the ordinary during her brief sojourn in the low 600s. He said that he did not notice anything in her demeanor, behavior or comments.

Since he knew her better than I did, after she dropped back to LOC 584, I asked him if he would ask her directly about her "state" during those two weeks. The mutual friend agreed to ask her directly. She reported not noticing significant changes.

My interpretation was that this person is readying themselves for the ascent into the LOC 600s or higher. This was a "test." It was a "shakedown cruise" to see if her vehicle was seaworthy. Was she ready to sail the Ocean of Cosmic Consciousness?

The test went well because there were no negative side-effects or other difficulties due to the higher LOC frequencies. In this case, no news was good news. The trial run was a success.

When I first met her in Fall, 2012, I intuited that she was very close to enlightenment. Subsequent conversations confirmed this. This most recent LOC 600s visit added to my conviction. I sensed that she was getting very close now.

I was pleasantly surprised when she showed up unannounced at my monthly satsang in December, 2013. I worked with her one on one in the meeting and delivered RASA to the group. Her LOC shot skyward right afterward and stayed in non-dual frequencies. Her LOC at the time of this writing is 764.

The purpose of her trial run into non-dual frequencies was to make sure that her human vehicle was ready for the greater intensities at those levels. Specifically, are the nervous system and brain sufficiently harmonized and purified?

Since no side effects or difficulties were noted, the "test flight" was successful. She proved her readiness for "take off" into the wild blue yonder.

Please note that most of this data was gathered as raw data prior to me developing my LOC Map of Awakening model.

Thanks to my access to her friend and to her, I was able to get the various changes in her LOC validated by third parties independent of my assessment. Recent talks with her have confirmed that she is established in non-duality.

No Man's Land

LOC 590 to LOC 599

The No Man's Land: LOC 590 to 599

The LOC 590s is a unique range that has similarities to the LOC 900s. As the passageway from duality to non-duality, though, it is in a class by itself. I can talk about it via analogy. I can say it is like an NDE-like "tunnel" or a "black hole," but words cannot describe it.

This is the gateless gate. It is the invisible highway to a new dimension. That it exists goes without saying. Why it exists and how it works cannot be described, at least not by me.

After you attain non-duality in the LOC 600s, you begin a transcendental journey. One implication of this model is that stabilizing in the LOC 600s is not enough. You will have to come back again (reincarnation) until you have stabilized in LOC 1000.

A full 40 per cent of the human consciousness range is in the rarefied heights of non-duality (600 to 1000). I was asked how many people alive today are enlightened. I estimate that there are about 5,500 enlightened people on the planet right now. Since there are roughly 7 billion people on earth, this is not quite one in a million odds.

Dead Man Walking: Odd Case of David Godman LOC 595

David Godman at LOC 595 is the highly esteemed author of many books about Ramana Maharshi, Papaji and others in Ramana Maharshi's lineage.[33] He is *the* editor in the world today for conveying the words of Ramana Maharshi and, in effect, acting as his mouthpiece for modern times.

The question naturally arises "Is David Godman enlightened?"

I asked this question and answered it in my usual way by assessing David Godman's LOC. The result that he was "stuck" in the 590s was completely unexpected. Yet there is a practical explanation for this position given his life role.

He is a man living between two worlds, one foot firmly in duality, the other rooted in non-duality. This puts him in the perfect position to communicate Ramana's message to the masses in a way that they can respond to and understand.

Many great masters speak from such a lofty plane that the average person cannot follow them. It is fair to say that David Godman has made the insights of Ramana Maharshi as easy to understand as is humanly possible. I believe this is partly due to David Godman's unique and extremely rare LOC.

"David Godman Is Mine!" Fiery Words from the Master!

In 2012, I did something that I pretty much never do. I decided to meddle in the spiritual affairs of another person.

Frankly, in retrospect, it was probably not my idea at all, but Ramana Maharshi's. Here is the story.

One fine evening here in San Diego, California, finding some time on my hands, out of the blue I decided to do what I could to raise the LOC of Mr. Godman. After all, the poor fellow had been stuck in LOC 595 for years.

Please keep in mind that I had never attempted to raise a person's LOC without their permission before this incident. Nor have I tried to do so since.

I give a spiritual transmission called RASA (Ramaji Advaita Shaktipat Attunement) which has proven effective remotely via Skype around the world. It's express purpose is to raise the LOC of the person by gently opening their Crown chakra.

Thinking I was about to perform a good deed, I put a recent picture of David Godman up on my computer screen. I contemplated the picture for a few minutes in preparation for doing this free unsolicited RASA transmission.

My very next step was going to be to start giving the RASA transmission in order to raise David Godman up into the LOC 600s and deep into non-duality. A second after I had the thought to begin doing the RASA for him Ramana Maharshi showed up radiant as the sun. His face filled the inner screen of my mind. The great master did not mince words.

"David Godman is mine!" he said. "He is under my guidance and protection. Do not meddle with him. He is where he is at [level of consciousness] because that is where I want him to be. When the time comes, I will see to it that he is liberated."

Whoa! What a way to get the darshan of Ramana Maharshi!

That had not been the plan, but I was grateful just the same. It would not be correct to say that Ramana was "angry" with me. It was like being in the presence of a powerful thunderstorm. As intense as it was, there was nothing personal about it at all.

The implication in Ramana's bold interruption of my plan was that Ramana understood that my intentions were good. He understood that I did not have all the necessary information.

In his own way, Ramana was aware of Godman's special consciousness frequency. He made it clear that I did not need to concern myself with Godman's enlightenment. Ramana was going to see to it that Godman attained non-duality after Godman finished the job he was here to do on this planet.

Ramana's Roughhousing: A Cosmic Practical Joke?

When I told this story about getting busted by Ramana to my satsang group in San Diego, they thought it was very funny. Since doing this kind of thing — giving RASA to somebody without asking them — is not my style at all, somebody suggested that it was Ramana himself who had put the idea into my head so that I could get Ramana Maharshi's darshan.

I'm sure I could have prayed for Ramana to show his face to no avail. No doubt this is the experience of many sincere seekers. But mess with his official book editor on planet earth and look out! You have succeeded in getting his attention!

I had never tried to give anybody RASA without getting their permission first, so it could very well be that Ramana set me up. In retrospect, the whole thing was pretty hilarious. While I do feel graced by Ramana's gentle wrath, I will not be tempted to do anything like that again!

An Aussie's Rocky Road: Stuck in 590s, Then Struck Down

Aside from David Godman, there is only one other person I have assessed who has spent years stabilized in the LOC 590s. In all other cases the LOC 590s is strictly transitional. The strange case of the Aussie who liked it rough explains why.

For privacy reasons, I am not giving the man's name, but I will say that he is a student of "Sailor" Bob Adamson (LOC 788). The emails and Skype sessions with this student of Sailor Bob's took place while the student was living in Thailand.

This Australian guy living in Thailand had studied with Sailor Bob for several years. He had the Advaita "rap" down cold. He could talk it and write it with the best of them.

I first met him because we share an interest in Vedic astrology. Future communications focused on Advaita and non-duality. When the guy in Thailand complained that he felt he was very close but just could not "go over" into non-duality, I became intrigued and checked his LOC.

I was stunned to see that he was at LOC 594. I knew this was possible, but extremely rare. During the two year period that we were in frequent communication via email and Skype, he stayed at LOC 594 and made three attempts to transition into non-duality. All three were aborted by panic attacks. Since I knew that he was "closer than close," I got very curious as to what exactly was taking place each time to prevent him.

Over video Skype with a lousy Internet connection from a Thai hotel, he explained that when he felt he was being pulled over into non-duality and into a kind of "ego death," he would have the exact same odd yet apparently physical experience.

His chest would start to hurt so terribly that he was convinced that he was having a heart attack. He was certain that he was going to physically die. This scared him so much that he willfully shut down the process. He aborted the "ego death."

I had heard of this kind of thing before, so I had my questions ready to go. "Which side of your chest was the pain on?" I asked. "Was it on the left side or on the right side?"

The guy from Thailand did not hesitate. "Oh, it was on the right side. Definitely the right. Like a hard fist in my chest."

"Your physical heart is on the left," I replied. "I do not believe that was a heart attack. It was an ego I-thought attack!"

"What do you mean?" he said. "The pain was in my chest. It felt very real. I was terrified."

"Listen, I am not a doctor, so of course you should consult with a physician about such things. But I know for a fact that when a person is getting close to enlightenment, there are many things the ego I-thought tries in order to scare you off.

One of them is to make you very depressed. Another tactic it favors is to produce intensely painful sensations on the *right* side of the chest where the causal Heart is located."

The Aussie man had not heard of this. Sensing his skepticism, I plowed forward. "The I-thought has only negative power. It can contract that area like a hard fist so that you feel sharp tight hard pressure and pain. If the next time this happens you can relax, let go and not panic, the I-thought will realize that its strategy is not working. It will relax and let you go."

The guy from Thailand remained dubious. He had not read about the Heart on the right according to Ramana Maharshi. The idea of the ego I-thought ("I am the body" thought that is the hidden root and source of the mind) performing such odd actions like an entity living inside of him was too much.

After the three failed attempts to transition into non-duality as reported by my Australian friend, all of which were blocked by the chest pain masquerading as a heart attack, I noticed his LOC had suddenly dropped all the way down to LOC 573.

Stunned by this precipitous drop in LOC and concerned for his spiritual well-being, I called him up on Skype. Our brief conversation went something like this.

AUSSIE: No worries, mate. I'm right as rain. I'm feeling really good now, nice and relaxed. The strain is gone. Before there was this constant pressure. Now it's like I'm on vacation.

RAMAJI: I hear you, but you dropped all the way down to an LOC of 573. For somebody like you who was on the verge of breaking through into non-duality, that's a spiritual lobotomy!

No doubt you feel more relaxed. It is probably good for your health to relax awhile, but your relaxation is a sign that the pressure is off. Hopefully you're just taking a break.

AUSSIE: You know me. I'll be at it again. Sooner or later, you can count on it. What else is there? I don't even feel like the doer anymore. So what's the point? I've got nothing else. Thanks for your help. Cheers, mate.

That conversation was a few years ago. Now he is back up to LOC 583. I'm sure he is preparing for another leap. I hope that this time he will be ready for the I-thought and its stealthy tricks, especially the fear of death, its ace in the hole.

The Ego I-Thought's Torture Kit: Dark, Painful, Negative

By the way, this person had no history of heart disease. It was only those three times that he had this unusual chest pain. I was not trying to play doctor. At an intuitive level, I knew that this pain on the right side of his chest was the ego I-thought attempting to intimidate him. Once I had that experience, too.

At least half a dozen people have told me about intense pain on the right side of the chest during a spiritual crisis or breakthrough. It was not a heart attack for them, either.

This is important information. Please pay close attention. It is hardly ever talked about. Negative symptoms of contraction, which can be physical, emotional or mental, are a standard strategy by the ego I-thought to discourage you on the path.

The I-thought has the power to intensify his contraction and bring in dark storms of thought and severe negative emotions. He may even *imitate* painful disease symptoms like chest pain to scare you into thinking you're going to die, but that is rare.

If you experience chest pain or another serious sign of illness, you should get a thorough examination from your licensed health care physician. Please request a full battery of tests. I am not a doctor nor am I dispensing medical advice.

These are my empirical observations based on reports from students. After your doctor scientifically eliminates the usual medical suspects, then you can consider the spiritual options.

The bizarre case of the Aussie guy from Thailand illustrates that the ego I-thought ("I am the body" knot or contraction) will go to any lengths in its efforts to discourage you from going through the "ego death" gateway into non-duality.

I want to stress that *all* of the I-thought strategies are negative. Painful negative thoughts, painful negative emotions, painful negative body sensations — that is the full repertoire of the ego I-thought. That is his torture kit. The ego I-thought is himself terrified of dying. He is not thinking about you. He is only thinking about himself. He does not want to die!

Consider this quotation from *Guru Vachaka Kovai* (The Garland of the Guru's Sayings) by Muruganar, an enlightened disciple who lived with Ramana Maharshi.[34] It is thought to be a spoken teaching statement direct from Ramana Maharshi as recorded by Muruganar in their native language Tamil.

> The nature of the ego is similar to that of an elf [trickster], being very enthusiastic, rising in many wicked ways by means of innumerable imaginations, being erratic in behaviour, and knowing only things other than itself. But the nature of Self is mere Existence-Consciousness.[35]

If you would like to know more about the ego I-thought in Ramana's teaching, a great place to start is DavidGodman.org. He stays very close to Ramana's teachings as he illuminates them for Westerners. I don't agree with everything that he says — he does not understand the Heart on the right — but overall he is reliable in dealing with these esoteric topics.

When I describe the I-thought to students, I call it a thief, a con artist, a trickster, a criminal. The I-thought does not care about you, the real Self. It just cares about itself. Its strategies on the negative side are vast, yet it contributes nothing positive at all. Everything that is positive, such as feelings of peace, love, joy, gratitude and bliss, are all from the Self, the pristine Absolute.

Seven Maps

of

Non-Dual Awakening

Seven Maps of Non-Dual Awakening

The spiritual maps in this chapter have been around a long time. They show that there is a global common ground to the contemplative, mystical or non-dual journey. There is a map, a template, a schema, a spiritual DNA blueprint, that transcends spiritual tradition.

The degree of their agreement is remarkable. The differences appear more to be an emphasis of what is considered most important within that tradition. Their fundamental agreement suggests that they have in common a universal spiritual map.

The Map of Awakening in this book is my attempt to present a universal map that explains the major steps in as simple and straightforward a way as possible. It outlines the four main levels or stages of non-dual consciousness, illuminates the passageways between them and provides identifying marks so that it is easy to differentiate between these four non-dual stations. My innovative LOC assessment methods offer a new degree of precision for determining where a seeker or realizer is on the path to full stabilization in the Absolute (LOC 1000).

The spiritual maps covered in this chapter are the Seven Valleys of Sufism, the Five Ranks of Tozan (Zen), the Ten Zen Oxherding Pictures, the Seven Stages of Yoga, the Seven Stages of Advaita Vedanta, the final eight Major Arcana of the Tarot and the 17 Stages of the Hero's Journey according to the sage and mythological researcher Joseph Campbell (LOC 684).

There are many more major spiritual maps that are not included. It is likely that they show strong parallels as well.

Three major maps neglected here that come to mind immediately are Kundalini and the Chakras, the Kabbalah and the Theravadan Buddhist map of the Elders (Stages of Insight). There are many other fascinating yet lesser known maps, such as the stages in the Quest for the Holy Grail.

It should be pointed out that the stages of the way can be intuited by a seeker or mystic without them having actually walked the path. They are built into our spiritual DNA. As you study them, a natural logic is revealed as to why one step is in front of another, why one sticking point must be seen and cleared before the next sticking point can be revealed.

A spiritual map showing stages of enlightenment is just a description. It is up to the person to actually *live* it. The higher purpose of such as map, including this LOC map, is to show the reader that (1) there is more than one level or stage and (2) you don't want to stop until you get to LOC 1000!

Why settle for anything less? That really is the point!

Don't be content with middling realization. Go all the way. Make the most of this life. According to my personal review of my own past lives, it is possible to attain enlightenment in one life and then forget it in the next.

This happens when you did not complete the path. Since you did not complete the path, you have to keep working at it.

Put another way, you are going to end up at LOC 1000 sooner or later, so why not save yourself trouble and go for it now?

We live in extraordinary times where our planet is rapidly awakening into non-duality beneath our feet. That is my conclusion based on the fact the the LOC of the planetary soul is not only rising, it is accelerating. At her current rate, the planetary soul will reach non-dual LOC 600 around 2024.

Whether that is "true" about our planet or not doesn't really matter. The point is to get with it. Wake up now. If you're already awake, then wake up all the way. You will know when you get there. You can't miss it.

I am starkly aware that any pithy description of a great tradition's grand map of the journey to the Supreme is rudely reductive and, therefore, incomplete and inaccurate. My sincere apologies to all of the traditions represented here is provided up front. It is hoped that the pointing here will revive the interest in these valuable maps and in the noble traditions from which they were born.

In broad strokes, these maps outline five stages. The first stage is pre-enlightenment. The second stage is enlightenment (in LOC 600s). The later stages show deepening of enlightenment.

The third stage is LOC 700s. The fourth stage is LOC 800s. The fifth stage is LOC 900s to LOC 1000. The last two are lumped together because both have gone through the Transfiguration at the higher boundary of the LOC 800s.

In the LOC 900s the sage tends to be a recluse. He still having difficulty adjusting to the ("gross physical") world. The sage who has worked through that thin final veil or transitioned without a challenge attains fullness in "no mind" (LOC 1000).

There is a transition between each stage that can be thought of as a black hole or spiritual passageway not unlike the dazzling dark tunnel seen by near-death experiencers. Each transition is an ever more subtle form of "ego death."

These transitions take place at the high end of the lower stage. They are from the high 500s to the low 600s, from the high 600s to the low 700s, from the high 700s to the low 800s and from the high 800s to the low 900s. The journey culminates and ends at LOC 1000. At LOC 1000 is "home" and "final rest."

The movement from the high 500s to the low 600s is highly significant since it is first entry into non-duality. I christened it a passage through the Lesser Void. The movement out of the 700s into the 800s is another major movement. I have called it the passage through the Greater Void.

The LOC 600s and LOC 700s have much in common. The 700s are more of the same, only stable and expanded. The major difference is that the LOC 600s experience of emptiness is localized while the 700s experience is universalized. These two zones blend together to create a more or less continuous range. This LOC 600s through LOC 700s range is the default comfort zone for non-duality. Most realizers reside there.

In contrast, the shock of going from the 500s into non-duality, or the shock of going from cosmic knowledge in the 700s to "no knowledge" (unknowing) in the 800s, is considerable. The sacrifice required and degree of change involved are massive.

Thanks to science, the modern bias is against devotional non-duality. Those who rise above the LOC 700s do enter and progress through the LOC 800s but they usually do so quickly.

As a result, it may appear as if the transition was from 700s to 900s or 1000. Even so, the primal duality of the 800s was faced.

In summary, it's a big deal to go into non-duality (LOC 600s) in the first place. Once you get there, it is natural to mature from the 600s to the 700s. The experience is one of deepening.

There is a new demand placed upon the realizer when he is ready to transcend the LOC 700s. Even though he may think that he is living in a state of "knowing nothing" (in comparison to the false knowledge of the conventional person), he sits on a mountain of accumulated knowledge that he must give up.

This is a big deal. There is the impression of losing everything. This is a new level of sacrificing the ego. This time it is cosmic ego that is being let go of and dissolved. It is not accomplished through effort. The moment arrives when the limitation even of being the universe and the cosmic consciousness is seen. An embrace of the blissful divine darkness of the 800s takes place.

Transfiguration, the movement from the LOC 800s to the LOC 900s, can occur smoothly. Kill all your Buddhas. Confront and destroy all of your icons. Gods, goddesses, teachers or gurus, all must go. Everything must go if the ego I-thought, the root of the mind, is to be fully exposed, diagnosed and eradicated.

The exposure of the ego I-thought, of its movements and its machinations, takes place in the LOC 900s. The final step is to destroy the concept of the "world" itself. This is the I-thought's last bastion, its final stand. The world is gone for LOC 1000.

Spiritual Map One

Seven Valleys of Sufism

Spiritual Map: the Valleys of Sufism

This map is presented first because it closely parallels my LOC map. I developed my "1000" LOC model before I saw this map. I designed my LOC map based on my raw data, then I discovered that the major traditional spiritual maps were in close agreement with my empirical findings.

In this way, I avoided skewing my LOC results. I want to emphasize this because I arrived at my interpretations for each major stage (600s, 700s, 800s, 900s, 1000) by studying the lives, teachings and behaviors of the people who were all in that particular range. I determined their LOCs first. Then I noticed the similarities between the teachers in each stage. The development of the Map of Awakening was the last step.

My LOC model says essentially the same thing as the Sufi map but presents it in terms of numbers. The main difference is that there is precision with the LOC evaluation method. The boundaries and transitions are based on the same Fibonacci numbers found in our human DNA (more about that later).

The Sufi map of seven valleys was first revealed in the 12th century Sufi poem, *The Conference of the Birds*, written by Faridu'd-Din 'Attar (LOC 887). It is a marvelous Sufi classic.

Then a book called *The Seven Valleys* that explained the stages mentioned in Attar's work was penned in 1855 by the Persian nobleman Mírzá Husayn 'Alí. Ali would later become known as the prophet Bahá'u'lláh (LOC 1000), founder of the Bahá'í Faith.[36] This religion emphasizes the spiritual unity of man.

The first three stages, valleys or cities in the Sufi map are the Quest or Search, Love, and Knowledge or Understanding. These stages are steps of purification and preparation. For example, Knowledge is characterized by arriving at a state where it becomes possible to forgive everyone in your life.

Roughly speaking, these first three stages correspond to the LOC 500s and more specifically, at least in theory, to the LOC 560s through LOC 589. The spiritual search proper can only begin when the maturity of the person warrants it.

This inner Quest is the search for spiritual fulfillment. It is not just the pursuit of personal happiness through objects. In the LOC model, this cannot begin in earnest until the LOC 500s. As I have shown, "illumined" individuals in the 580s display integration of these attainments: Quest, Love and Knowledge.

The first non-dual stage is aptly named Unity (oneness). This experience of oneness is explained in terms of sunlight. The sun shines on everything, but the color displayed depends on the object. It is possible to be aware of the unity that is the sunlight yet be confused by the multiplicity of objects. Those who turn their attention to the sunlight itself overcome the blind spot inherent in this level and rise to the next stage.

The second non-dual stage (number five in the overall Sufi map) is called Contentment. This stage is also described as the fusion of Independence and Detachment. High indifference is combined with true enjoyment of life in the context of this sublime oneness. This sounds like you could be at the ultimate stage right here, but you are not. What you are is contented. You can make better sense out of the first non-dual Unity stage by comparing it to the more mature Contentment stage.

The Unity non-dual stage is the equivalent of the LOC 600s. In this group you find people who have realized non-duality yet they are decidedly not the proverbial "happy camper." They can still be intrigued by nihilism, chaos, anarchy or amorality.

Perhaps the most outstanding example is the recently passed articulate malcontent U. G. Krishnamurti (no relation to the famous Jiddu K.). At LOC 678, he was solidly established in non-duality, yet he had not yet discovered the joy in the unity.

His well-documented words show that he passed my litmus test for realizing non-duality, which is non-doership. Yet he was still not happy. He made it blatantly clear that he was not.

The LOC model is not so formulaic as to say that everybody at "X" level is going to talk, feel and act the same. The very popular Jeff Foster, also at LOC 678, seems to be overflowing with love and happiness. So clearly it's not just the LOC level.

What the LOC level points to is the generic grasp at that stage of the unfolding of ultimate reality. The integration challenge and making the most of that station remains very much an individual action. Even so, certain trends tend to stand out.

Returning to the fifth Sufi level, you have true Contentment coupled with authentic high indifference. Once again, you are compelled to ask "What can top this? What is better than highly refined enjoyment combined with real detachment?"

In the question is the answer. Enjoyment of what? Detachment from what? He feels contented, but his foundation is false. He is seduced at a subliminal level by objects, other and world.

When you dig deeper into this Contentment level, the stage that corresponds to the LOC 700s, you find that this is a most fulfilling stage of the spiritual life. This is a blessed time.

Here you sit on the spiritual throne. Here you enjoy mystical bliss. Here you discover that wounds are reborn as joy. Old agonies are transformed into new delights.

As the popular saying aptly puts it "What's not to like?"

It comes as no surprise that this spiritual stage, the 700s, is where the vast majority of the higher realizers stabilize. They do indeed find "contentment" at this stage. They do not feel impelled to move on. The divine pull of spiritual magnetism, emanating from the Heart at LOC 1000, has grown weak.

Subtly implied by the classical Sufi description is a process of emotional healing. It is impressive to talk about "purification" but the Sufis are talking about flawed human beings here.

The half-baked LOC 600s are just the first level of non-duality. One step up in the LOC 700s you can still smell the stench of the sweltering human jungle. After the shock and awe of non-duality has worn off, then follows the full exploration of the far frontier. If that task is completed, then it is seen that to be in non-duality, to be the LOC 600s non-doer, is not enough.

In the LOC 600s, you can have massive mental and emotional fixations. Unless they are processed and eliminated, they will remain and the energies of non-duality will now impersonally express through that endarkened impure aspect.

The word "healing" really does apply. I am talking about the healing of inner obstacles that could not be exposed before. They were too deep, too arcane, too threatening to the ego, too entangling to embrace. This process deepens and expands as the sage matures and embraces the LOC 700s.

Armed now with the power of non-dual insight, the traumas can be transformed and liberated. This is non-dual emotional healing. This is going on consciously in the LOC 700s because the need for it has been seen.

In the LOC 600s, it may or may not be seen. The individual may be so enamored of their non-dual joyride that they fail to see their own flaws. Non-duality is the flowering of the human being. In LOC 600s, we are just tasting this fragrance. It has not yet fully blossomed in all its beauty.

Stage six in the Sufi model is Wonderment, alternatively Astonishment and Bewilderment. It is here that we find those who attain to non-duality via a devotional path or in their efforts to transcend a devotional path (God remains the topic).

Terms like "wonderment" and "bewilderment" correspond to the Western mystical terminology of "divine unknowing" and "dazzling darkness" for this LOC 800s stage. These Sufi terms also resonate with the emphasis on love by these realizers.

My research indicates that there are not that many in this realm. This spiritual zone corresponds to the LOC 800s. Here we find Mother Theresa (LOC 878), David R. Hawkins (LOC 874), Bernadette Roberts (LOC 854) and Jiddu Krishnamurti (LOC 844). Two well-known Christian mystics, St. John of the Cross (LOC 878) and St. Teresa of Avila (LOC 840) abide here.

The placement of Krishnamurti in the 800s with devotional non-dual mystics suggests that he never did outgrow the religiosity imposed upon him at an early age. Instead, he denied it and defied it. Rebelling against it, he launched into a fiery mission to help the entire world inquire into and gain freedom from the harsh invisible chains of religious dogma.

In the modern spiritual climate, informed by quantum physics and a spirit of global awakening, the tendency to tally in "the fields of the Lord," as it were, is not encouraged. Instead, if the modern sage has seen through the limitations of the LOC 700s — more accurately, if he or she has completed the secret deep *healing* that is demanded by that stage before it can truly be transcended — then the movement is likely to be fairly rapid and right into the LOC 900s and, perhaps, LOC 1000.

The contrast between the purification that led into LOC 600s versus what is required to enter the LOC 800s is revealing. When transcending the LOC 500s, the passage may feature dark depression or other severe emotional states, such as the famous pre-enlightenment suicidal state of Eckhart Tolle (LOC 674). When transcending the LOC 700s, the healing purification can be through rapture and bliss instead of angst.

The seventh and final stage of the Sufi path per these sources is dramatically described as True Poverty and Absolute Nothingness. Alternatively, it is Deprivation and Death.

It will be difficult to improve on these words. They point vividly to the essence of what is required to move into the final stage. There will be the annihilation of all that was.

1000

The Contentment of the LOC 700s was comfortable in a wonderful way. The non-dual adoration of the Divine in the LOC 800s was magnificent. As extraordinary as the wonders and miracles that bewilder, astonish and amaze in the LOC 800s, that is not the end. When viewed from the perspective of the highest and most pure, it cannot be the ultimate station.

These are profound attainments. Yet there is still movement, there is still a story, there is still an unfolding. Therefore, they cannot be the conclusion. You have watched Hollywood movies. You know how to tell when you are at the end of the movie. The boy gets the girl. The runner wins the race. The good guy kills the bad guy. No matter how close you are to that denouement, until this final event happens, there is still the need, the momentum, to do more, to see more, to be more.

The divine drama of the 800s allowed for an ultimate "other," the Divine. If there is any kind of "other," this means there is also some kind of "self." No matter how refined, no matter how subtle, no matter how holy, if there is an "other," there is also the subject who is perceiving and conceiving this other.

What could be left? Well, as the Sufi descriptions of the final stage indicate, what is left is the final death. Now all notions of self and other, including that of God or the Divine, are let go of, dropped, dissolved, jettisoned, abandoned, discarded, transcended, seen through, lost and forgotten.

What is left in place of that which has apparently been lost?

The short answer is nothing, nothing at all. This nothing does not even know that it exists. There is no "I" to announce that it is here, to know that it exists. There is no self-reflection at all.

1000

If there is no "I" going on, then there will not be the "other" either. The "I" made self-conscious of itself is invoking the "other" whether it knows it or not. The only solution, the final answer, is to have no "I" whatsoever arise, and no knowing of this "I" even as a potential.

It can be said of this stage that there is a "Universal I" (the "I-I" of Ramana) experienced which does not reflect back to itself. It is also said that even so this "I" does not know itself to exist.

This is "True Poverty." This is "Absolute Nothingness."

We have arrived at deep ground, but let us plow on. The sense of an isolated self was lost long ago, so what is it that has been abandoned so late in the journey?

Though the notion of discrete self was dissolved, the very subtle aspects of the mind, which include the cosmic mind, the mind of creation, maintenance and destruction, the mind of time and space, these various forms and shades and grades of the mind had to some extent remained intact and undetected. They are residuals of the mind. They are echoes of the "other."

The arrival at the LOC 900s and into LOC 1000 enables the debut of the true "no mind." This is the poverty, the death, the nothingness that the Sufi descriptions refer to for this final stage. In reference to "no mind" and this supreme absolute nothingness, then the eloquent densities of the 600s, 700s and 800s are seen to have been veiled. However thin, however attractive, however sublime the veil may have been, it was a veil nonetheless. It was treasured in reference to what had come before, but compared to the Absolute, it was incomplete.

Spiritual Map Two

Five Ranks of Tozan

Spiritual Map: the Five Ranks of Tozan

I am not a Zen Master, not even a Zen Buddhist, so please accept my apology in advance if I do not show proper respect or correct understanding of this Zen teaching. The Five Ranks appear in the *Song of the Precious Mirror Samadhi* by Tozan Ryokan (Chinese: Dongshan Liangjie). The Five Ranks are the five stages or levels of realization for Zen practitioners.

The Five Ranks are considered difficult to understand. The founder of the Japanese Soto School, Dogen, referred to them in the first paragraph of one of his seminal works, the *Genjokoan*. Hakuin, representing the Rinzai School, saw fit to incorporate them into his koan teaching system.[37]

The first rank is called "the Relative within the Absolute." It refers to a direct perception of emptiness and access to the no-thought state during meditation. However, it is not stable and cannot be maintained in the world while active. The student is easily distracted and gets sidetracked due to outer stimuli.

This describes the purification-aspiration stages below LOC 600s. While the ability to effortlessly rest in the thought-free state is a unique marker to the LOC 580s, the pursuit of this degree of mental purity characterizes all serious seekers. This is the place of samadhi states and enlightenment experiences.

Since there is a quality of illumination already present at this rank (the general population being considered "pre-rank"), it is entirely possible that a person may now believe that they are enlightened. This was shown with several 580s people.

The second rank is called "the Absolute within the Relative." This refers to entry into non-duality proper, the LOC 600s. In the midst of life's variety you can see your "original face." As a result of this clear seeing, there is stability in non-duality.

The problem at this level is that seeing yourself in everything around you is a very arcane expression of an intense egotism. It may not seem so to the enlightened person, but the spiritual narcissism intrinsic to this LOC 600s level is expressed as an inability to show true respect to others and an inability to live committed to a life of total and endless compassion.

It is like the 600s person is a newborn baby. What they are born into is a new dimension, the non-dual world. Like a baby they are busy discovering how this world works. Like a baby, their world is naturally an automatic reflection of themselves.

They have not yet integrated the mystery of "others" into their life. Their spiritual narcissism gives them a subtle arrogance that is very hard for them to detect. So they will declare things like "There is nothing you can do" or "It is all meaningless."

These are not statements of wisdom-compassion. These are statements of ignorance. At the very least, the LOC 600s sage could be referring to those who have come before him, to the Ramanas and the Nisargadattas and the Dogens and Hakuins.

He could be checking his state against their state. He could be checking his spiritual advice against their spiritual advice. In his narcissism, he is utterly convinced that he has "arrived." There is nothing beyond it. In fairness to the LOC 600s sage, the new world he lives in is a huge change from the LOC 500s.

The third rank is called "Coming from within the Absolute." In my LOC scale, this corresponds to the LOC 700s. The need to own the existence of the "other" and fully integrate this unexpected "other" into the emptiness that you know to be yourself comes forward. The yardstick of behavior, mostly ignored in the LOC 600s, is now valued as a critical marker.

It is realized that since the vast majority of people, seekers, students and meditators included, are not enlightened and are not stabilized in non-dual consciousness, then it is paramount to take the initiative in treating them as human Buddhas.

You cannot wait for them to start acting like Buddhas and treating you like a Buddha. You now see that it is up to you to act like an impeccable Buddha and be like an impeccable Buddha in every way that you are able to put into action.

The ordinary people are just going to do whatever they are going to do. Not only that, you also begin to see that the behavior of ordinary people, of people who know nothing of spirituality, who make no pretense of being spiritual, is in fact extremely important to you. In fact, you *need* their feedback.

The feedback they will spontaneously and "thoughtlessly" give you about your behavior is as precious as pearls. They do not know that, since you are a Zen Master, they are supposed to treat you special and be special around you. So they don't and they aren't. That's good for you and it's very good for them, too. Your Zen means nothing to them. Wonderful!

Your situation is now much different than it was in the LOC 600s. Now you understand that where you are in this LOC 700s range is a maturation phase.

You have dropped the naive narcissism of the LOC 600s. Now you are growing into a true spiritual adult, a true Buddha. You are owning your "stuff."

Simultaneous with this evolving understanding is seeing that even though you are deeply enlightened, you, too, are in need of healing. You, too, have emotional wounds, mental fixations, blind spots that have not yet been touched by spiritual fire.

If this seeing is not taking place or is not taking place soon enough in their career as a spiritual teacher, the LOC 700s person can get into serious trouble. The famous saying from an 1887 letter by Lord Action will apply to him: "Power tends to corrupt, and absolute power corrupts absolutely."[38]

Put the unrefined LOC 700s sage in front of thousands of young naive adoring students, place him as the leader at the top of a vast global spiritual organization, and it's a good bet that some kind of corruption, some kind of misconduct, some kind of unethical, not nice, not Buddha-like behavior is going to manifest. Sexual misconduct seems to be the most popular, but financial gain, drug use, emotional abuse and the same issues found with celebrities and politicians may surface.

What can be done about this? Not much, really.

A sage in the LOC 700s is a deeply enlightened person. There is no reason they should not teach. If they are dramatizing their own unresolved psychological blind spots, it does not cancel out the legitimacy of their realization. Each student of such a teacher must decide for themselves if they are willing to embrace that kind of journey.

It can be richly rewarding to work with a realized teacher who is also working on their emotional healing. But for this to be fair to the student, the teacher will need to admit that they need to do this work. They may not be able to do that. They may not yet have the humanity and the humility required.

Paradoxically, then, it is back upon the student to make the decision. The bottom line is that the LOC 700s sage must be evaluated in the same way as any other human being. If he is being an enlightened jerk, then even though he is definitely enlightened, he is still a real jerk.

As with any other serious long-term relationship, you must figure out for yourself if their particular flavor and style of being a jerk works for you or does not work for you. Most of us know that looking for the "Perfect Master" is a waste of time. The only "perfect" things in this world are the fantasies.

Nisargadatta Maharaj was known for shouting at his students. Many felt that they were receiving transmission or Grace in this way. Yet an outsider might think that his personality was crude and the opposite of peace.

Nisargadatta's personality had been surrendered. The divine power wielded it like a spiritual sword. He excised the ego while doing no harm. But Nisargadatta was a sage of the fifth rank. He abided effortlessly in the stainless Absolute.

The ancient original Five Ranks poem in describing this level talks about a way out of the world's dust within nothingness. The sage must avoid violating an extremely important taboo.

Both images refer to the LOC 700s sage being at a place where he is moving out of the world, from relative nothingness which still has reference points in it to absolute nothingness, which has no reference points of any kind (and never did).

This sage has not yet fully left the world behind (the dust) even though he may think he has and feel like he has. As for the taboo, it is the Law speaking. As far as I can tell, this refers to treating each person with the respect usually reserved for the Buddha. The infamous acts of misconduct inflicted by spiritual teachers on their students, devotees and followers constitute a resounding failure to honor this taboo.

If you would do what you are doing to a known Buddha, then go ahead. If you would not do it to them, then you are in error. Whether you know so or not, they ARE the Buddha. Your understanding is weak. You are second or third rank.

The fourth rank is called "Arrival at Mutual Integration." Once again you see this mysterious "other" being referred to in the context of non-duality. If you have realized non-duality, then who or what is this "other"? That is the mystery solved here.

Now the bodhisattva (compassionate enlightened human being) goes into the marketplace with outstretched hands, eager to help anyone who needs help. Their spirit is soaring as their actions are spontaneously from a bottomless compassion.

Yet this is not the final resting place for the sage. This is not the true and final peace. The sage is now bold and pure in his determination to fulfill all aspects of his spiritual Buddha nature as he fulfills all aspects of his human Buddha nature. He is dedicated to harmonizing the two totally and perfectly.

They are not really split like that, but the many long years of spiritual practice made it seem like they are different. In fact, they are not different at all. They are one and the same. That is what he is finally discovering for himself everyday at home and out in the world. To see how the flower of the Buddha blossoms in every thing, from the most mundane action to the most ordinary person, is a source of transcendental delight.

This is not the final peace, though. After he completes this stage, then he will know it. Then he will be it. Knowing it, living it and being it will be one and the same. No thought or work will be needed. It will simply be what it is.

There is one more rank, the full stabilization in the relative and the Absolute at the same time. Then no way is seen or known as to how it could be any other way. No notion that it could ever have been any other way ever arises. What is is and that is that. What is that? The primordial stainless Absolute.

The fifth rank is called "Unity Attained." The name itself gives away its finality. The previous stage was called "Arrival at." The one before that was called "Coming from." Both labels talk about some kind of motion, a progress towards the higher or deeper or more pure. In the fifth rank it says "Attained."

What is attained? The poem says that neither "being or non-being" will now have a hold on you. They cannot touch you at all. You are able to return to total ordinariness. Now you are indistinguishable for the masses. Now you are invisible.

This is the way of the Absolute, for it does not attract attention to itself. If it did so, then it would not be the Absolute.

"Being" means you get to be somebody. "Non-being" means you get to be nobody. Being beyond both being and non-being means you are the true nothingness which does not know itself. It does not know it exists. Therefore, it cannot not exist.

It can't go from Being to Non-being if it has never been born. The great Zen master Bankai called it "the unborn."

When described by words, it sounds like a riddle. But to live this way is to breathe simplicity as if the very air was made of it. There is never anything to figure out. There is nobody to do anything. Not only is there no self, there is no world, either.

When there is no world, there is nothing to do. Nothing ever happens. Nothing has happened. Nothing will happen. In this there is absolute peace. Ultimate motionless is attained.

You could say that everything is you and you are everything, but there is no everything and there is no you. This is the way of the Absolute. If time and space have not been invented, if even the notion of an "I" has not been conceived, where then will be found this sage of LOC 1000? Nowhere and anywhere. This is the supreme state beyond enlightenment.

This is the immaculate mark of the bird of life as it flies through the stainless supreme sky. The bird flies. It can be seen. It reveals the sky as its magnificent backdrop. Yet it leaves no mark, no sign, no residue, no tracks.

There is only the Supreme and even the beautiful flying bird is a part of it. It cannot be described. Therein lies its freedom. This is the fifth rank of the Five Ranks of Zen Master Tozan.

I will summarize what we have learned. This expert Zen model points out the subtle flaws that hide in the apparent perfection of each level. It boldly calls them "ranks." This says that one is indeed superior to and more mature than the other.

The second rank was the nascent non-dual realizer in the LOC 600s. Caught up in a conceit of consciousness, he thinks he has summarily dealt with the problem of the other. This leads to a grievous error — valuing himself while not valuing others.

The third rank in LOC 700s recognizes the ongoing existence of the apparent others and knows they must be treated as Buddhas. His challenge is to achieve that purification where such Buddha-like behavior is automatic and in all contexts.

The fourth rank in the LOC 800s has realized that there is still a "world." It is the body of the Beloved. The sacred other is the Divine, or the as of yet not fully realized Absolute. Either way, he knows he must go back exactly the way he came. Whereas before he avoided dirt as it might stain his white shirt, now he rolls in the mud and looks for happy pigs with which to frolic.

The LOC 900s represent the transition from a sense of world to no world. They could be placed at the finale of the fourth rank or at the birth of the fifth rank. To be established in the fifth rank means that you have destroyed the world. There is no longer any veil or gap. You have gobbled up the world.

In the fifth and final rank, LOC 1000, there is *no* world. There is nothing to do, nothing to realize and no one to realize it. He cannot find anything or anyone who is not the Buddha. No one is the Buddha. Everyone is the Buddha.

Nothing and everything. existence and non-existence, being and non-being, are dissolved in the laughter of this sage. All IS Buddha! But who or what is Buddha? Look in the mirror!

What he had been looking for was here all along, only he could not see it. It was in the money. It was in the poop. It was in the church and the temple. It was in the thief and the cop. It was in the abuser and the abused. All Are That absolutely.

Totality means all of the totality. If it is the Absolute, then nothing can be excluded. Self, other, world, all melt into a perfectly still radiant Silence. There is no more death for the truly dead person. Only eternal life in a heaven on earth.

The other folks in the marketplace may have no interest in the dharma, but this cup of tea is very good. The Buddha made this cup of tea. The Buddha is this cup of tea.

Whether he sleeps by the road in rags or has servants who attend him in a mansion, he is a king. All of the universe is his, even though he shows no interest in it. It is there when he needs it, and it is not there when he doesn't. The Absolute is beyond everything, yet it is everything. It is good to be the king. It is good to be the Absolute. It is good to be WHAT IS.

Spiritual Map Three

10 Zen Oxherding Pictures

Spiritual Map: Zen Oxherding Pictures

Having given so much attention to the Five Ranks of Tozan, I will not need to go over these famous pictures in great detail. They are well known with many excellent commentaries.[39]

The first five drawings show preliminary purification of the mind. In LOC terms, you are working up to and through the LOC 580s. This is the first "trap," the tendency and temptation to think that you are enlightened, or at least enlightened "enough." The fifth image depicts peace sustained with effort. It is the ability to rest in the thought-free state in meditation.

The sixth Zen Bull drawing shows the monk playing the flute and sitting on the bull. This is effortlessness, meaning he is now established in non-doership. He is in the LOC 600s.

The next image "The Bull Transcended," shows the monk is all by himself. He sits with nothing to do. The commentary says there is a path of clear light. He is still engaged in purification.

This is the LOC 700s stage. This image is less useful regarding this stage than the Sufi and Five Ranks models. It implies that the sage at this level has nothing to do. He is not the doer, that is true, but there is still plenty to do. This is the emotional healing that I mentioned earlier. Now that he has become a god of enlightenment, he must discover how to be a human being all over again and forget this crazy enlightenment thing.

The next image shows a perfect circle. It says "Both Bull and Self Transcended." If now "self" is transcended, that means it was present in the previous stage, but it was not seen as such.

If there is "self," then there is "other." But the restfulness was emphasized, not the purification that takes place in the 700s. The LOC 700s sage retains an "enlightened self." It must go.

Many LOC 700s sages think they are done. They think they have arrived. They would place themselves at the next step which shows a perfect circle. But they are still preoccupied with transcending self. The confusion is due to the self that they now need to transcend is a cosmic self. They have gone from a separate self to a no self and now to a cosmic self. The primordial narcissism has now achieved cosmic grandeur.

The perfect circle is divine perfection. All is God. All is Love. But that is not good enough. God, Buddha, call It what you like, still remains as transcendental object, as ultimate pure object. Your adoration for any "other" remains a distraction from who and what you truly are. The task of the LOC 800s is to rise through and above what you most love and adore.

If you are honest, this will always be yourself. That becomes God's gift to you. In the final stage, God gives you to you as Itself, meaning you realize that you are the Absolute. God is forgotten because God can no longer be remembered. God was always a concept pointing to you, yet you had to die to find that out. Both you and God had to die and be forgotten.

The Transfiguration passage is at the high end of the 800s. It takes you into the 900s and beyond. The "not knowing" of the 800s still involved subject and object. It was subject-object at its most secret level. To go beyond that primal seed duality, everything must be forgotten.

There is entry into a permanent state of not knowing. In this final dissolution of knowledge, the other is utterly lost. This is the only possible preparation for real life in the Absolute.

First, perfect union with the Divine is enjoyed (LOC 800s). Then even that union is surrendered. It is said "No one can see my face and live." This fourth death is rebirth. It is blissful. It is the ultimate submission where even humility itself burns away. True and total humility was the lesson of the LOC 800s.

That is why I call it Transfiguration. It is not a dark night. It is a celebration. It is how God's face will be seen in the most ordinary moments of life, in all things at all times. This step precedes the profound simplicity of the ultimate clear ground.

Do you want to constantly see the phony face of your false self? Or do you want to constantly see God's face? You decide.

In the next picture you see the world again. It is beautiful and natural. A stream flows in it. The picture is called "Reaching the Source." You would think that before you would have done this. You thought you reached the Source before. But what you had achieved before was reaching what you *thought* to be the Source, meaning God, Buddha, Jesus, Krishna, Rama.

They are God until you arrive. Once you are there, it is a busy hotel of dreams. God is perfectly right for every devotee. He or She is the perfect match, a match made in heaven. They are the Divine Father or Divine Mother you always yearned for.

But when you finally do arrive in heaven, you find it is not what you expected. You are ushered into a very quiet room.

There you are introduced to what is behind the mind, behind even the big magical mysterious divine mind. No matter what your concept of Source was up until then, it was wrong. You had arrived at the perfect concept. It was still wrong. You go beyond the 800s when you see that ALL concepts are false!

This idyllic pastoral scene paints a picture to show the inner state of the LOC 900s. In the LOC 900s the person remains slightly tentative. There are a few that hold onto the notion of isolated peace. They are called to embrace the world and be it totally, but there is still a slight recoil in them. Old habits keep them hidden from the world. They avoid the public eye. Or if they live in the public eye, they are charming iconoclasts.

The error of the LOC 900s is that they still see a world. Not only that, they want this world to be perfect and beautiful. Until they drop their demands, they will remain just one step from Truth. You cannot demand anything at this point.

Here you let go totally of all concepts of "other" and "world." By that I mean *annihilate* them once and for all. *Obliterate* them. If you can find anybody to negotiate with after you do that, go right ahead. What will be left is simply you... the Real You.

The final picture shows the sage as the Buddha hanging loose and having fun in the marketplace. The picture is called "In the World." It is only now, after this long apparent journey of purification, that you can truly and completely be in the world. Now this "world" is the Buddha. It is your very Self.

Before this time, prior to this final stage, the world was still presenting you with problems. Perhaps, as in the LOC 800s, you preferred to dwell in "God" rather in the world.

Now there is no God. Now there is no world. Or God is world and world is God. This is perceiving neither existence nor non-existence. You directly experience the "ISness" of it all.

Now this ugly place with all of its smog and violence and funky people is the Buddha Land. There are no paradoxes for you now. Everything is finally and completely resolved.

Yes, there is the perception of apparent differences, but these differences make no difference to you. Everything is just as it is — perfect. This is as solid and real as a diamond. Not only that, everything is quite literally your Self. All of it is You.

The ordinary is now ultimate reality. Mountains once again are mountains. Rivers are once again rivers. This is the blessed domain of LOC 1000 sages. All is "I." All is my very own Self.

Spiritual Map Four

Patanjali's Yoga Sutras

Spiritual Map: Patanjali's Yoga Sutras

It is Vyasa, a commentator on the *Yoga Sutras*, who presents the seven stages of yoga. True to the oral tradition, Patanjali barely leaves hints. Vyasa generously fills in the blanks. The sutra that starts this section is Chapter Two, Verse 27.[40]

The first three stages describe the arising of discrimination, the recognition that the mind is the problem and the ability to access thought-free states due to discipline in meditation. This progressive process describes the student's work up through the LOC 580s. In the LOC 580s, the best he can do is rest in the thought-free state. The rest is up to God, Grace, Guru and Self.

There may be several breakthroughs into non-duality. These are legitimate enlightenment experiences, but they do not stick. The seeker is unable to stabilize in the LOC 600s or higher. They were able to visit, but they were not able to stay.

Since such events are a strong indicator that stabilization will eventually occur, and are immensely purifying in their own right, then this transition is identified as a third step.

In the fourth step, you have arrived at and stabilized in non-duality. This step talks specifically about living effortlessly. There is effort without effort, doing without doing. There is no entity. There is no doer. This describes non-doership, the definitive marker of non-dual realization. In my LOC model, it confirms that the sage is established in the LOC 600s.

The fifth step corresponds to LOC 700s. The mind is described as being released from the ego momentum.

This means that the LOC 700s sage is still in a process of purification. Even though now he is the non-doer, that was just the beginning. Now he is awakening to the realization that what is required from him is absolutely *everything*.

He thought that he gave up everything when he gave up being the doer and the thinker. He was wrong.

Now he must face the archaic hiding places of the ego, the ego pain stashes and need stashes and lust stashes and anger stashes. He buckles down to a new level of work on himself. This level is far deeper than anything he has done before.

This is where he actually gets to the bottom of things. He is getting close to the bottom of his personal karmic bucket of shit. At the bottom of this bucket is the Buddha. He can get to those deepest hidden stashes that are still left because now the ego brakes have been disengaged from the mind. The thought stream flows freely like a beautiful brook babbling in a forest.

There may be much work to do here. Even though it is quite effortless, that does not make it "easy." Dancing in a fire pit is effortless. Your flesh burning off your body is effortless. But it is not easy, not by a long shot. That is why most of the LOC 700s sages avoid it. They do the work if and when they really have to. Sometimes it's from a crisis. Sometimes it's a natural seeing that cosmic consciousness is in golden handcuffs.

The sixth stage of yoga corresponds to the LOC 800s and 900s. Now the world process is exposed. Eliminating the doer, the egocentric entity, turns out to have not been such a big thing after all. Now can be discerned the secrets of the Absolute.

1000

This great Heart is the center of the turning worlds. It cannot be found until the worlds themselves stop turning. As long as you want the world to exist, it will keep turning for you. It will be your dancer as long as you want it. You send it home.

Then in that ultimate stillness and silence, in that motionless state that might be called death were it not the rebirth into freedom, the sage finds ultimate deliverance. As Vyasa says, the mountains falls down. Even the law of gravity fails. There is nothing to hold the sage now. He is entering the final and ultimate black hole. The white hole he will emerge into is the one without a name that is everything and nothing, that was and is and will always be. It is the invisible Source of all.

The seventh stage of yoga has a unique Sanskrit name. It is called "Kevala." Kevala means total freedom, living in the unbounded self-luminous stateless state. The literal Sanskrit reveals a little more. Strictly speaking, it refers to being alone on a mountain top. One is absolutely alone, supreme, pure, whole, all, perfect. You are utterly released from the universal process. The individual mind has been reabsorbed. You now abide in "no mind." This is the mind of the LOC 1000 sage.

There are some who elect to take this aloneness as a lifestyle. This is found mostly in sages in the lower LOC 900s. Even so, there is no rule that the LOC 1000 sage must live next to noisy rude urban neighbors. He may live far away from the city.

Chances are he will show his face now and then to bless and give darshan. Beyond that, he knows he has made his main contribution. This was to complete the journey to LOC 1000. Wherever the body may be, all he can find is the Supreme Self.

Spiritual Map Five

Stages of Advaita Vedanta

Spiritual Map: Advaita Vedanta Stages

This map of the seven stages of Advaita Vedanta is from the *Varaha Upanishad*. There is a similar map in the *Yoga Vasistha*. These stages are called jnana bhumikas (wisdom stations).[41]

The first stage or bhumika is the arising of the desire for enlightenment. It is called *Subheccha*. Subha means "good" and Iccha means "desire." There arises a benign desire for an experience of the higher good, of truth, of freedom.

But desire does not convey what has really happened. Iccha also can literally mean "itch." Now the person has been bit by the seeking bug. He's got the itch and now he's going to keep scratching it by seeking this and seeking that.

The second stage is called *Vicharana* or inquiry. Now he is going to non-duality groups and listening to sages. He may be meditating, doing hatha yoga, eating vegetarian or otherwise be involved in the many well-known purification practices.

The third stage is *Tanumanasi*. This literally means "thinning of the mind." The mind is losing weight. It is getting lighter. It is getting thinner, meaning the hard coverings are softening. An opening will be appearing through which the Light can shine.

The first stage corresponds to the LOC 500s in general. The second stage lines up with the LOC 560s and up seeker who is making a commitment to non-duality. They are ready to initiate and sustain a serious non-dual meditation practice. Participation in non-dual thought may arise in the LOC 540s.

The *Tanumanasi* stage matches precisely the ability of the LOC 580s person (and also of the advanced LOC 570s person) to rest in the thought-free state and, out of the blue, have one or more enlightenment experiences. These brief non-dual breakthroughs blast big holes in the mind's protective layers.

The thought-free state is not a goal in itself. It is a means to an end. It is the noble assertion of spiritual availability. It is the wide open clarity through which the spiritual Light can shine.

When the true nature of the mind is realized, it is seen that thoughts or no thoughts make no difference. The true Self is prior to thought. But mastery of thought must come first.

As this process of effortlessly resting in the thought-free state, having enlightenment experiences and sitting in satsang with true sages flows onward, at some point the center of gravity shifts. The person may not realize it, but they are now ready.

Then the leap is made into *Sattvapati* (stabilization in pure mind). This is non-duality. You are settled in the LOC 600s.

The Advaita Vedanta model makes it quite clear that this is not a place to just hang out. Your work is not done. This fact is indicated by the description of the next state, *Asamshakti*.

Asamshakti means non-attachment. The person in LOC 600s is in non-duality. They are established in non-doership. Surely they are "non-attached," right? No. *Asamshakti* is LOC 700s.

Asamshakti indicates maturation of enlightenment, integration of enlightenment. The stakes for non-attachment are raised.

The non-attachment they had in the LOC 580s got them into non-duality (LOC 600s). Now they have to be non-attached to the sticky "blind spot" stuff that previously they could not see, feel, know, hear, touch or otherwise consciously access.

This involves nothing less than a total housecleaning, this house being the deep subconscious mind. The ego in the past did not allow access to this deep level. It was afraid, it was ashamed, it wanted control, it felt guilty. Now with the gross ego out of the way thanks to the non-doership, the spiritual cleanup can take place at a new level not possible before.

When that deep subconscious is cleaned up, that is the non-attachment referred to here. Parallel to the stages in Patanjali's yoga, there is purification of the mind, then separation from the mind, then, finally, elimination of the mind ("no mind").

Non-attachment includes not being attached or captivated by the symptoms of enlightenment. For example, non-doership is quite fascinating. I spent several years experimenting with it, playing with it, researching it, testing it. Other symptoms include the feeling "I am enlightened." This, too, must go.

In *Sattvapatti*, the emphasis was on cleaning up your own act, on getting your own ducks in a row. Now that you have done that, you are ready to face the world of "others" in a new way. *Asamshakti* is about purifying your relationship to the world.

Emerging from that clarity, now you assess the substantiality of the world. Is its appeal intrinsic and inevitable? What is the world process? *Sattvapatti* was subjective. *Asamshakti* is objective. In *Asamshakti*, you can see the world clearly.

In *Sattvapatti*, you make mistakes about yourself. There is something solipsistic about it. In *Asamshakti*, you make mistakes about others. The focus is off of you. The focus is now on others and on groups of others. If you are a spiritual teacher, your journey of purification as you stabilize in this stage involves students and perhaps misconduct with them.

When you are done with all of that business, done with being enlightened (LOC 600s) and done with others not being enlightened (LOC 700s), then you are ready for the next level. You can tell that something big has happened because now the topic is non-differentiation. Misconduct with students is unlikely if you cannot identify them as your "student."

This next stage is called *Padarthabhavana*. At this stage, objects are no longer perceived. Does this mean the person is blind, that they need a guide dog to leave the house? It sounds like it but that is not what is meant here. What is meant is that the world is fading away. This is the LOC 800s and LOC 900s.

As the true Self is known more and more, the apparent world loses its importance. Not only that, its appearance changes. It may become translucent or look like a dream or seem like a mirage. But this advanced stage refers to objects themselves no longer being seen as objects. This means the mind is not projecting labels onto them. It means the mind is dying.

This melting away of the world is an absolute must. The mind cannot be dissolved as long as it is allowed to have a world.

In non-dual mysticism where there is devotion to the Divine, everything becomes the Beloved. All is God. All is Jesus. All is Rama. All is Kali. All is Shiva. All is your Perfect Beloved.

1000

The sophisticated complexity of your old top heavy state of enlightenment (LOC 700s) dissolves into a simple joyful playful transcendental dyad —me and the Lord, me and Divine Mother, me and God. Kingly cosmic consciousness is resolved into the infectious playfulness of "me and my deity."

This is the acme of love. It is Elysian fulfillment of the timeless promise inherent in the primal father-mother love bond. Now, at long last, you have attained to "true love." This ethereal love required profound purity. You are now sufficiently purified.

But the mind is still slightly there, so it seems like this state is perfect, but there is still a slim veil over it all. The ultimate Mystery is still clothed. It is not naked. Even at this level, "love is blind." At the same time, "love is the path." This great love will surrender to itself, will collapse into itself, if you allow it.

In the Advaita Vedanta model, you are bringing the silent stillness of deep sleep into the waking state. In deep sleep, there are no objects. This sixth stage of *Padarthabhavana* reflects this disappearance of objects. It is possible to function in the world, but it may be difficult to differentiate between the presenting objects. The Oneness is close to taking over.

Padarthabhavana is beyond the LOC 700s. You are now in LOC 800s and LOC 900s. You are now in the realm of the mystic.

No longer are you just purifying the mind. That game began in the LOC 600s and reached maturity and clarity in the LOC 700s. Now the mystical love, a new surrender, takes over. This non-differentiation sounds like a negation, but it is not. It is an affirmation of life without the possessing invasion of "other."

Another way to express this is that the other has become love itself. Love is self, love is other, love is the flow between us. If the focus is on awareness, then awareness is self, awareness is other, awareness is the flow between us. The dancing dialog of two perfect true purities is still dualistic, but it is purely so.

Misconduct is unlikely. It is seen that human beings have no power. Only God has power. There is only God. There is only the Love Supreme. Love itself is the Universal Power. Love is God (versus "God is love.") Love without limits is real God. Love without limits dissolves even love. The Beloved is dying.

The world shapeshifts before your eyes. The only security is yourself. For this reason, you may cling to yourself and reject the world as messy and impure. This is the costly misstep of the LOC 900s. When you reject something, you reinvent it. Jesus said "Resist not evil." What you resist will persist.

The next and seventh stage is Turiya. This is the LOC 1000. Some people make this a big deal. It is a big deal and it isn't. Turiya is here now for everybody. That means it is not a big deal. Very few people realize it. That makes it a big deal again.

In terms of the journey, this is the arrival at the Absolute. This is total transcendence. This is "no mind." This is the freedom of the wide open sky. This is the Self. This is your home.

Ramana Maharshi said "There is no world. There is only the Self." This is the perspective from Turiya. No other. No world. There is the Self only. This is also called Shiva Consciousness. There is only one "Universal I." Ramana called this "I-I."

Spiritual Map Six

Major Arcana of the Tarot

Spiritual Map: Tarot Major Arcana

The Tarot can be confusing. However, when you look at just the last seven Major Arcana, you see a pattern that matches the other great classic spiritual maps I am presenting.[42]

The Devil card, Major Arcana number 15, symbolizes being trapped in the mental prison of materiality. You are chained by your identification with the physical body. But that is just the beginning. Your imprisonment extends to include every part of your daily life, emotions, thoughts and dreams. This is the condition of the average "unawake" human being.

On the positive side, the Devil represents the persistence and reliability of structure. Without rules, there would be chaos.

The Tower card, Major Arcana number 16, represents the total early spiritual process. This is from the first arising of desire for freedom or oneness with God in low LOC 500s all the way to the deep purification of the mind found in the LOC 580s individual who can stay effortlessly in the thought-free state.

"Waiting upon God," prepared as much as possible from that pristine station, the divine lightning eventually strikes. But as the dramatic Tower card illustrates, this is no bed of roses.

There may be many ups and downs, many bad breakdowns as well as many big breakthroughs. It is a hard rough road. You better have a spiritual four-wheel drive to handle the new terrain. Expect the unexpected. God is full of surprises. This Tower is the castle of the ego who is lives in the head. When spiritual lightning strike, the ego comes tumbling down.

The Star card, Major Arcana number 17, is the non-dual vision. Here the seeker finally breaks through into non-duality. Here his spiritual dream, shown by a shining star, is actualized. At last he feels one with the sacred universe.

This is the grand prize. It is natural for him to think that this is it. He has arrived. He now lives in higher better world. He floats above the tortured sweating masses. He is a free spirit. His soul soars. He lives spontaneously. Whether he calls this Grace non-doership or something else, a blessed inspired wind moves him here, there and everywhere as life requires.

But the Star is an symbol of the imagination, too. There is an element of fantasy fulfillment to this step. The tendency is to stop right here. Why go on? Take it easy. Were not all your dreams from when you lived in the Devil's jailhouse fulfilled?

Well, yes, they have, but those were the yearnings of someone living in a prison cell. Now that you are free, now that you are living in a much bigger world, more growing will be needed.

The Moon card, Major Arcana number 18, refers to the deep subconscious. It is by now a familiar tune. You are at the LOC 700s. I am again talking about the subconscious and the need for its purification.

Some pass through this overnight, but the reality of your old life with the ego is that way back then there was a whole bunch of psychological garbage that the ego did not want to look at! Not today, not tomorrow, not ever. The empirical ego was calling the shots. You simply could not gain access then.

1000

Now that the supernatural dazzle of living in non-duality has worn off and landing on planet earth is finally taking place, a new accounting is inevitable. What is seen is that there are still problems to solve. There is still a mind. There is still garbage. When you recognize garbage as garbage, when you smell the stink, what do you do? You take the garbage out.

Other associations with the Moon such as psychic powers and occult activities may apply for some individuals. They may develop siddhis. They may manifest miracles. But none of this is going to change the dirty job at hand. This job is to clean out the old hard dried poop from the psychological toilet.

If this task is not completed, then progress to the LOC 800s and beyond is not likely to take place. That would be a shame since the sage has managed to get this far. It would be good for the LOC 700s sage to become a purification machine. The goal is detox at the deepest psychological, karmic and past life levels. Past life traumas long forgotten surface in order to die.

The Hebrew letter on this card refers to the "back of the head." This is the brain stem, the old reptilian brain. Symbols of evolution abound, along with twin towers showing that the journey through cosmic duality is not finished. Personal duality, yes, but the cosmic mind is not yet transcended.

The Sun card, Major Arcana number 19, looks like *this* should be the card representing full enlightenment. As usual, though, this is not the case. The sun is the most important circle in our lives. The sun is more than just a circle. It is the giver of life.

This card is reminiscent of another stage in another study. This is the stage eight perfect circle of the 10 Zen bulls.

That one said "Both Bull and Self Transcended." It gives the appearance of being perfect, but in spirituality appearances mean pretty much the opposite of the true substance. Here is the trap of being frozen in a notion of perfection, whether it is your perfection or that of the Divine that you adore. It could be the perfection of a teaching, of a guru, of a spiritual state that you go into so completely you leave the world behind.

Spiritual purity is still spiritual. That sounds obvious, but the point is that spiritual is opposed to material. There is still a duality at play. All notions of spirituality, all notions of any kind of perfection, of a so-called supreme being, of any kind of being or beingness, must be dropped totally and completely.

Naturally, if there is anything at this stage that you want to hold onto or that you need to hold onto, you will. Who will there be around you who can tell you otherwise? You are more spiritually advanced than almost anyone you meet.

Only a handful of people on the entire planet have the ability to teach you anything. It is easy to stay here, to suck from the soft cosmic breast the perfect milk of the Great Mother, but the final destination transcends everything known and unknown.

It is only for the bravest of the brave, for those who know they have nothing to lose because they know for sure that they have nothing and they never had anything else. It is for the fool, the one who finds no use for his mind except when doing taxes. Usually, the mind is kept in the backyard with the dog.

In extreme language, here you must kill what you love. Love of or for something is love of the other. The other must go!

The sunshine is the opposite of the dark, but if you would realize the Absolute, then you must love the dark as much as you love the light. Then it is no longer love, for it is beyond all concepts. But there is a passageway that takes you there.

The Judgment card, Major Arcana number 20, symbolizes that transition from the LOC 800s to the LOC 900s and LOC 1000. It is a transcendental passage through the gates of ultimate truth. I call this step Transfiguration. After you have gone through it, you will not be able to go back or even look back.

Your memory of what was, your ability to reconstruct it as if it is real, will be destroyed. Gone will be the ability to know. In its place will be the universal functionality of "not knowing." This is the "only don't know" mind of Zen Master Seung Sahn.

To know things is awkward, clunky and divisive. Know nothing, and you are free of the whole game. This is the radical divinely inspired strategy of the wise Fool.

It is effective, but it is using dynamite to kill a cockroach. The coackroach is gone... and so is your house... and so is your mind. Thoughts you can still have. Thoughts come and go. Thoughts are not a problem.

This is the big game changer. This is the door to the Absolute. This is the Big Daddy. Most non-dual realizers don't make it this far. This is the White Rapids with a drop off that goes on forever. This is the Great Abyss that is beyond even the Great Void that separated the LOC 700s from the LOC 800s. Now you take up residence in the "not knowing" of deep sleep.

There is a parallel between the Judgment card and the Tower card. The tower symbolized the separated isolated ego-doer. It is destroyed at that stage. It is the Small Death.

The Judgment card is depicting the Big Death. It affects not just one person. It shows that the whole world is being called to awaken. The entire human race is rising from its coffins of ignorance. All of existence is now coming alive. This is the promise of the Buddha, of Jesus, of Ramana, of Nisargadatta, of Dogen, of Meister Eckhart.

The Judgment Major Arcana card is pointing to this esoteric transition stage from the LOC 800s to the LOC 900s and then to LOC 1000. It is specifically about your Transfiguration (in a way, your resurrection, as the Judgment card image suggests). The sage will be "judged" or evaluated. Is he is ready for the foolish wisdom of "no mind" to be turned on at full power?

The World card, Major Arcana number 21 of the Tarot, startles with its depth of spiritual insight. At this penultimate stage, the next confrontation for consciousness is with the notion of there being a "world" in the first place. The old masters would retreat into the mountains and leave the world behind. We live in a new time where the LOC 1000 sage typically makes himself or herself fully available in every possible way.

This card points to the final sticking point for those who have undergone this Transfiguration into the LOC 900s. This is the temptation to adopt the aloof life track of the spiritual recluse. Though he is firmly established in the truth so that he knows that the Buddha is the world and the world is the Buddha, he wishes to be left alone. He wishes to dwell exclusively in this private pristine purity that he worked so hard to achieve.

1000

In my journey, this transition manifested as a profound need for privacy. It wasn't that I consciously felt that the "world" was my problem. Yet the tenacious conviction even at this stage there still had to be some kind of "world" was creating this last iron ring of confining self-definition. It was this thin but final veil that kept me in the LOC 900s just as it would anyone else who reaches this spiritual stage and gets stuck.

I was very reluctant to become known, to teach in public, to assert anything about my understanding. I cherished my isolation, my solitude, my aloneness, my anonymity. I did not think of it as being about the world. I just felt strongly that I wanted to be left alone. I wanted to enjoy total perfect privacy.

Eventually this was seen to be a limitation. This book is one result of that. I find the pristine aloneness I prized is the same. This is possible because "world" is gone. There is only the Self.

The Fool card, Major Arcana 0/22, completes the spiritual quest and brings the sage to LOC 1000, which is also zero. The 0/22 person is the holy fool, the sacred fool, the divine fool.

As zero, he lives in "no mind." As 22, he is the Master who has transcended the world. Yet he redeems the world each time he opens his mouth. He saves the world each time he laughs. He liberates the world each time he gets up in the morning.

For him, all is God, all is Buddha, all is Jesus, all is the Self, the Supreme Universal "I," the ultimate stateless state of Shiva Consciousness. There is no longer any kind of world at all. The 0/22 of the Tarot Major Arcana is *identical* to LOC 1000.

1000

There is an experience of your Self where you can recognize the world and participate in the world that other people are talking about and getting so wrapped up in. But for you there is no "world," just as there is no "other." There is only the Self.

There is only God or the Self. This includes especially "other" people. The "other" person is felt to be your "own precious beloved Self." This is living in and as the Absolute. If there is anything beyond this, it is not known by this author.

Spiritual Map Seven

The Hero's Journey

Spiritual Map Seven: the Hero's Journey

This sacred map was chosen to be last for a good reason. What I have been talking about always comes down to being a bold courageous good human being. That still leaves plenty of room for variation, as the definitions of "bold," "courageous" and "good" are left wide open for interpretation.

The hero is the quintessential adventurer on a great quest. There is no greater quest than the quest for enlightenment.

Not because it is something special. The quest is for freedom, the total freedom that is intuited by all but lived by few. The hero sets out to achieve this freedom at all costs. When he realizes it, he will bring it back to the people. This completes the cycle. Then a new hero arises who does it all over again.

I have chosen to work with the original 17 stage model of the Hero's Journey by Joseph Campbell (LOC 684).[43] There are other versions out there. The 12 stage model by screenwriter Christopher Vogler is popular and easier to understand.[44]

Vogler's version eliminates critical transition stages that do not occur in every movie or story. In that sense they are not universal. But they do help to explain how the heroic sage is able to rise up and integrate levels of spiritual consciousness.

The first five stages of the Joseph Campbell Hero's Journey map correspond to the LOC 500s through the LOC 580s. The conventional materialistic world, the world of the Devil card, is no longer good enough. It is unsatisfactory. The quest for true happiness, for peace, love and freedom, has begun.

This is the Advaita Vedanta stages of *Subheccha* (bit by the seeking bug or itch), *Vicharana* (honest self-investigation) and *Tanumanasi* (reduction of the thought burden).

These first five stages of what Campbell called the Monomyth (another name for the Hero's Journey) are Departure, the Call to Adventure, Refusal of the Call, Supernatural Aid and the Crossing of the First Threshold.

Departure corresponds to dissatisfaction. Whatever you may do on the outside, on the inside you are no longer "buying" the world at face value. You know there is more. This may lead you into philosophy rather than spiritual practice.

For example, you might be drawn to existentialism and the views of Jean-Paul Sartre (LOC 555). If his LOC is higher than yours, then you could be attracted to his message. You will benefit from studying his message as it will take you higher.

This is the attraction of philosophy. Great thinkers prepare you so that you can rise above them. You drink the milk of their insights. You learn to think, question and investigate. When you are ready to soar, you graduate to non-duality.

At the LOC 560s and above, there is intuition of an integral way of life that has no negativity and no limitation in it. There is intuition of a true and total transcendence in non-duality.

The Refusal of the Call is any and all moments of hesitation about what you may be getting yourself into it. This is not a bad thing. It shows that you are taking it seriously.

You are refusing it, hesitating, because you don't understand it. By all means, know what you're getting into. You can be in the LOC 560s and still be hesitating. But at this point you've got one foot in the fire, so you have to decide.

Supernatural Aid is the teacher and the teaching. It may not even have the appearance of spirituality. It may be the deep study of philosophy. It may be energy practices like yoga or chi gong. To do these things, you will need a teacher. This corresponds to LOC 570s as a strong commitment is implied.

Crossing of the First Threshold corresponds to LOC 580s. A big event has taken place. This event is the breakthrough into states in which the ego, the thinker, the watcher, the "guy behind the eyes," is not there. Briefly, he or she is gone!

This can occur in meditation as a gentle deepening of silence. It may happen during a bout of depression. It may take place while you are in a state of ecstasy. But it will not end up being just another "peak experience." The hard shell of the ego egg is cracking. Peak experiences are for the LOC 570s and below.

This Crossing is the loss of the experiencer. The separate self actually disappears. This may last for a few seconds, a few hours, a few days, perhaps longer. If the conventional ego entity is missing, then this is a legitimate experience of enlightenment. Why doesn't it last? You're not ready.

Why are you not ready? Because your mind needs to be thinned out even more (*Tanumanasi*). The silent openness of your mind does not cause enlightenment, but it does make it receptive to it. Likewise, if the invisible covers on your mind are thick and tight, there is no way for the Light to enter.

This is the thought-free state I keep talking about. It is not an end in itself. But the more you can rest in this silence, the more you give your true Self a chance to gain strength, rise up and consume the false separate self (the thinker or ego I-thought).

If a person is consistently overwhelmed by negative thought patterns, they are not yet at this point. The LOC 580s person is not free of problems, but there is a spaciousness and an ease to their experience. It all boils down to fewer thoughts equals more freedom. No thoughts equals maximum freedom.

The thought-free state is a precondition for the advent of the state of enlightenment in which the non-moving thought-free state of pure awareness dominates. Then it is okay to have thoughts arising or to not have thoughts. It won't make any difference either way. But first you have to progress above being dominated and controlled by your thought patterns.

The Threshold that is crossed is this river of the mind. As long as it is raging, passage is impossible. As it calms down, you are able to see into it and understand it as never before. You see how you can cross this river that you once thought was impassable. You gain confidence and double your efforts. You are ready for the far frontier, the "other side of the rainbow."

The next stage corresponds to the LOC 590s transition. It is aptly called the Belly of The Whale. The is the "black hole" ego death passage. Certainly it will be dark inside the whale. The whale is like a womb. This symbol shows that this period of transition may be slow or it may be sudden. Some people just make the leap. Other people require multiple tries before they "land" in the non-dual dimension and stay there for good.

Because the process has been fairly straightforward until now, you may think that this dark Belly transition will be smooth and gradual. This is unlikely. It is sudden. Some say it is no big deal, it was just a little bump in the road. For me, it was a shock. It was beyond "life-changing." It was the end of one life and the start of another. It was the death of who I had been.

After that passage comes the Road of Trials. This corresponds to the LOC 600s. During this stage there will be many tests. The new sage is now in an unfamiliar phase of transformation. In his new world there are many new possibilities. He has no choice but to explore them, to investigate them, to enjoy them.

The blessed new power that moves his life like a great wind blows a sailboat across the seas needs to be understood. Yes, he is established in non-doership, but what does that mean?

Many questions have been answered, but new questions have appeared. If the new sage is honest with himself, he will see that there are restrictions to his situation. All of his doubts and questions have *not* been answered. He has not yet arrived at the Heart of supreme reality. He is a brave new stranger in a brave new world. After he settles down in his new world, he will understand that he is somehow still focused on himself.

Campbell says that the next stage is the Meeting With the Goddess. This meeting is with the goddess of love. This meeting at this stage may be unexpected by the reader. It follows right after the Road of Trials. There must be a reason that this ancient sequence leads now to this type of experience. If the sage does not meet the goddess of love, Venus, he needs to invoke her. He needs to focus on love, on opening his heart.

For the person to graduate from LOC 600s, they must embrace love and be healed by unconditional love as never before. It is this higher love that makes it possible for them to rise above the subtle spiritual narcissism that taints the LOC 600s level.

No matter how much work the person does to purify their mind in the LOCs below 600, no matter how hard they strive to clean out the depths of their subconscious, their past lives, their karma, their samskaras, there will still be many layers of deep subconscious mind that remain untouched. The ego does not allow it. The ego I-thought, in its shame, in its guilt, in its self-worship, in its dedication to avoiding pain, in its chronic desperate fear of death, will avoid some or most of that stuff. It will put its foot down. It will apply the brakes. It will stop it.

But in LOC 600s and above, thanks to the non-doership, thanks to life being lived freely and spontaneously, those brakes are gone. This means the great work can continue at a deeper level. That is why the LOC 600s is the Road of Trials. This is why there is still a Meeting with the Goddess of Love.

Now that the gross ego interference is gone, the sage can know love and live love like never before. There is no love like non-dual love. This is transcendental love. It is the best of both worlds. The wisdom insight into non-duality combined with the flame of love-compassion yields the highest fulfillment.

According to my LOC evaluations of hundreds of spiritual teachers, misconduct with students and other ethical breaches are much more likely when the teacher is in the LOC 600s or LOC 700s stages. This is true for realizers across the board. It is not just for non-dual teachers. It reflects spiritual maturity.

The non-dual adoration of the LOC 800s and the "There is only Self or God" of the LOC 900s to LOC 1000 preclude such behavior. There is no need for it. There is no interest in it.

Such behaviors at higher LOCS are unlikely. Their purpose would be to compensate for some deep hidden sense of lack that has not yet been exposed and is not yet integrated. If that sense of lack is embraced, healed and integrated, then there is no need for an "acting out" to fill it up. It is gone. In its place is wholeness. It may have been there before, but it is gone now.

The glaring exception may be Jiddu Krishnamurti (LOC 844). He conducted a 25-year long love affair with his close friend Rosalind Rajagopal, the wife of his manager and publisher. There were three abortions.[45] I will discuss Krishnamurti's affair when I cover the LOC 800s spiritual teachers.

Now there is another surprise. According to Campbell, the next stage is not some glorious epiphany. It is the Woman as Temptress. "Woman" here is symbolic of the world. She is not just sex. She is fame, money, power, pride, celebrity. In spite of the unpromising label, this marks the LOC 700s.

The focus of the LOC 700s teacher is the group. He or she is known for creating effective group solutions, methods of inquiry that can be delivered by trainers, not just by the sage themselves. This group focus leads to new powers, new skills and new temptations. To be totally prepared for this is rare.

This group focus indicates a growing sophistication in relation to the world process. As potent as the one on one coaching of the LOC 600s person may be, there is more power in groups.

It is not a given that a sage or realized person will create a great system or a method of inquiry. But that is what the LOC 700s people do. They are strongly aware of a multiplicity of "others." They are addressing the challenge of helping them.

The new level of temptation is based on the new opportunities that this higher and grander level of spiritual influence and empowerment offers. More than in the LOC 600s, you have the opportunity to be the man-god to your devoted group.

You see this played out to the nth degree by Osho-Rajneesh (LOC 754). You do not see religions being started by LOC 600s sages. You do see that, or at least the attempt at that, with LOC 700s sages. If they fall for this ego trap, then they believe that they have the ultimate understanding. They do not.

Some people wonder how a person can be enlightened and have these issues. The answer is that these issues could not be faced before the person became enlightened and reduced ego.

I am talking about final purification. This is the ending of things. This is not conventional therapy. This is another level of healing where the karma comes to an end. The LOC 700s person is preparing to become a Buddha. He is enlightened, but he is not yet a Buddha. He is not yet pure enough. How will he get pure enough? By going through this healing stage.

The LOC 600s had two steps. So do the LOC 700s. The second step of the LOC 700s is called Atonement with the Father. The only "father" that the sage could have fully and finally faced before his awakening was his biological father.

The highest and deepest archetypes of authority, of ultimate power over others, were buried too deep. Only now can he access fixations in his mind and in his life that have to do with the super-father, the state of absolute power.

Former Secretary of State Henry Kissinger put it best: "Power is the ultimate aphrodisiac." The context for this famous quote is that Kissinger was making fun of his reputation as a "secret swinger."[46] Kissinger would know the truth. He told us straight. There's no greater thrill than pure raw power.

This pure power, this exaltation of power, the extraordinary kind of power that the average person cannot even imagine, that is the kind of power that may be encountered at this stage. That is why the LOC 700s person may fall for it. They are sincere. They are humble. They are enlightened. But they never in their wildest dreams anticipated such intoxicating power as this. This is the Father, inside and out, that is faced.

I am also talking about the cosmic powers of the cosmic mind. This, too, is the Great Father. There are secret powers of the Great Mother as well. They are called siddhis. In our world of amazing technologies, these skills are not valued like they used to be. But they may still show up. They will tempt the sage to stay in a psychic circus of secondary spiritual powers.

This meeting of the archetypal Great Mother and Father in one person can also be viewed as the unification of Yin and Yang, of the female and male energies. In the enlightened person, a fusion is possible in which the potentials of both are set free to act at their maximum. It is the sacred marriage on one being.

What could possibly be next? Apotheosis is next.

Now that the sacred marriage has taken place, the Great Mother and Father have regained their rightful places. It is time for the third death. The primordial duality of the Great Father and Mother, of Yang and Yin, are fused and resolved.

The first "ego death" was the Small Void from the LOC 500s into the LOC 600s. The second "ego death" was the expansion from the LOC 600s to the LOC 700s. The third "ego death" or spiritual shock occurs in the move from the LOC 700s to the LOC 800s. The fourth step, Transfiguration, reveals the Self.

In this Great Void "ego death," the views and attainments of the LOC 700s sage are transmuted. His residual investment in any kind of position taking is annihilated. Campbell calls this stage Apotheosis. It is still part of a middle "Initiation" phase.

This passage is the last spiritual black hole. Transfiguration, the step up, out of and beyond the LOC 800s, is not a void passage. It is an epiphany, a foretaste of Supreme existence.

Apotheosis is entry into the LOC 800s. This word has several meanings. One is "the highest point in the development of something." Apotheosis is also defined as "the glorification of a subject to a divine level." Both meanings are on the mark.

If you are a mountain climber, when you reach the top of the highest peak you can climb, it is your apotheosis as a climber. But what do you meet at this peak that you did not see before?

At the very peak of the mountain, the mountain ends. All your life you had focused on reaching the top of the mountain. You are at the top now.

What you discover is that while it is true that you have found the end of the mountain, you have at the same time arrived at the beginning of the sky. All your life you were focused on the peak. Now that you are there, you see that it opens into an wide open sky with no boundaries.

Now the sky is your new frontier. You could not possibly have known about it without climbing the mountain. This mountain symbolizes the vast knowledge and achievements of the LOC 700s sage. The shocking news is that when you arrive at the peak, this mountain of wisdom crumbles under you feet. You leap into the sky. The false ground you once stood upon now is lost forever. You are becoming the sky.

Your apotheosis as a spiritual mountain climber, as a sage who fulfills the promise of the LOC 700s, leads to a third spiritual shock. This third and final sacred shock is a passage through the Great Void where your knowledge will be lost.

I experienced it as a passage through the darkest darkness. It had the drama of a risky journey into the unknown where everything that was familiar to me was lost and forgotten. I went through a period that lasted several months in which I seemed to live in an internal darkness with no bearings.

Everything I knew and had known was falling away. I was plunged into a total blackness where nothing could be labeled or identified. The very mechanism of knowledge itself, the experience of "knowing" something, the impression of an object outside of myself, was dissolving and disintegrating.

The feeling was like walking on a narrow path with a deep treacherous ravine on either side. All I could do is put one foot in front of the other. That is all I knew how to do and it is all that I could do. It turns out that this is also all that I needed to do. It was an introduction to a new way of life where I do not ever know what to do or what anything is.

The grand and glorious spiritual knowledge I had gained in the LOC 700s after graduating from the perplexing trials of the LOC 600s was irrevocably dissolved in that darkness. In a way it is the greatest death because now you have the most to lose. This darkness is a doorway into ineffable divine wholeness.

Internally, a new voice, the faceless nameless inner guru, was advising me. Externally, a remarkable synchronicity appeared in the form of a rare and amazing book by Nisargadatta's guru Sri Siddharameshwar Maharaj. He talked in plain and simple language about how to "learn to forget everything."[47]

In the LOC 800s, the experience of non-dual devotion is attained. There is no longer you and me and the world. There is now only You, my God or Goddess, and me, your devotee, your humble servant, your love slave. In this transcendental simplicity an ultimate experience of love and bliss is obtained.

The sacred duality within the non-duality is obvious, but what does it mean? If your path is love, devotion and surrender to an eternal God who is real, then this state will stay dualistic.

If there is flexibility in your definition of God, then you will allow that, in the ultimate sense, this God that you adore and worship is none other than yourself.

Had the many purifications of the previous stages not taken place, this would be a statement of utmost arrogance. But now that you have arrived at the stark dazzling euphoric simplicity of bare naked total cosmic love, what is left but for the love to love itself? Your love is the essence of innocence. It is pure.

That unlimited pure true love loves itself. It dissolves all boundaries, all notions, all concepts. It ends up dissolving itself. Perfect love ends up dissolving perfect love. God ends up dissolving God. God dissolves, but into what?

This remarkable 17 stage Hero's Journey sequence comes to our aid once again. Can you predict the next step? Probably not. The spiritual logic of these stages is seen only afterward.

That is why I trust them. It is like a graduate from these stages is looking back and describing them. They are the words of the sagacious ancient Master, not of the eager budding hero.

The next stage is the Ultimate Boon. Here, at last, the so-called holy grail is gained. Perhaps this is not a surprise. After all, it had to be achieved sooner or later. The Sun, the Heart, and the Full Moon, the Crown, are activated, fused and unified.

In my journey, this stage corresponded to Transfiguration, the self-luminous revelation of Amrita Nadi. Ramana called this event aham sphurana. It begins with radiant pulsations from the Heart on the right. Then a river of shining Light rises up to connect the Heart with the incandescent open Crown chakra.

Not everybody experiences this. Nor do I think it is necessary. In some cases, this spiritual event leads directly to realization of the Self or the Absolute.

1000

It lifted me from the LOC 800s to the LOC 900s, but I still had some serious cleanup to do. I still had to stalk, starve and kill the I-thought that originates in the Heart and lives in the head.

I do not call this a "spiritual shock" like the previous three "ego deaths." The Self is revealed in all of its glory. The sage is uplifted or transfigured. It is profoundly blissful. For me, it was the most extraordinary experience of my life to that point.

If this is the great goal, if this is the elixir, if this was the grail of the quest, then we are done, right? Not quite. Although it happens, it is rare for the sage to stabilize in the Absolute here. I know that I did not. The I-thought had not been conquered.

You most certainly could sit on your laurels now and warmly congratulate yourself on a job well done. Now that you are in the LOC 900s, you are higher than all but a few spiritual elite (the LOC 1000 crew). It's okay to take a break. You deserve it!

Having achieved this supreme felicity after so much hard work, the person cannot be faulted for hanging onto it or taking a long well-deserved vacation from spiritual work.

In the Hero's Journey, the hero has been tasked with obtaining a boon that will bring renewal to his community. His quest is not for himself alone. His quest is for his elders, his family, his friends, his city, his state, his country, the world. He did not travel alone. The whole human race was somehow with him.

They inspired and motivated him. Their suffering called out to him. Now the compassion that was their mutual flame rises to its full ecstatic glory. Now he approaches a supreme sacrifice.

But as with so many of these stages, it is not what he expected. He simply could not have anticipated what it would be like when he finally got there.

Supreme sacrifice, okay, but of what? At this point, now that the Holy Grail has been won, what could possibly be left?

The I-thought, the root of the mind itself, is what is still left. Yes, even at this advanced spiritual stage, the I-thought has not been fully eliminated. It still obscures the final truth. The mind does not want to die. Even at this exalted stage, it still has some tricks up its sleeve. It will hold on until the very end!

Campbell calls the next stage Refusal of the Return. The sage, having found what he wanted, does not want to go back to the world and share it. It's not so much that he is being selfish. It's more like he is just very comfortable. This is a very nice place to be. The idea of getting on up out of here and moving onto to a new situation with all kinds of unknowns has no appeal.

This Refusal of the Return is the Hesitant Hermit LOC 900s stage. The few who tarry here have an issue with being in the world. They don't want to embrace that funky marketplace.

But this Refusal of the Return is fueled by something more sinister than the civilized reluctance to get your hands a little dirty. As profound as the LOC 900s realization is, as close as it is to the full and final stabilization in the Absolute, it is still not 100 per cent pure. It is 98 per cent pure, which means two per cent is impure. In this case, a miss is as good as a mile.

This two percent impurity is dramatized by a stubborn refusal at the final step to embrace the "world" as your very own Self. What could produce this naive misstep? What could provoke such ignoble blindness this close to the finish line?

There is only one candidate for this deception. It is the same troublemaker that you were fighting before. It is the I-thought.

Even though at this late stage of the game it has been exposed, this stubborn root of the mind refuses to die. It plays its final ace. If you are spiritual, then you will deny the world, right?

The Refusal of the Return was definitely my initial response to the notion of moving on. Why? For What? "There is nothing for me to gain," I heard myself thinking.

If the sage has refused, then he has intuited that there is more. He has heard the call from Beyond. He heard it all right. He is saying no to it. He is fighting it. He is resisting it. He does not want to go. He has good reason. He will lose whatever is left.

In the LOC 900s, sublime peace, tranquility and serenity is what is left. It is understandable that the sage does not want to give this up. This hesitant hermit likes his privacy, his silent retreat, his hermitage. He likes how the external silence of his serene environment intensifies the internal silence of his joyful solitary wholeness. It is a lush symphony of silence for an audience of one. That noisy world out there won't understand. That brash aggressive polluted world will never understand.

The magnetic pull of the Supreme at this point is very great. Perhaps due to past life karma as a recluse the sage may yearn to remain hidden in the low 900s isolated from the world.

For most the call to the complete the journey is overwhelming. Then they may need to become a public figure. There is no rule as to how this goes down, only that they will need to be profoundly available.

When you finally see the error of isolating yourself to protect your tranquility, your Refusal of the Return is transformed into the Magic Flight. You are not yet at the point of Crossing the Return Threshold of the world. But you are very close.

What is magical about this Magic Flight is not that you fly through the air or witness miracles. The magic referred to is the magic of deception, obfuscation and evasion. I describe this phase in my chapter about starving the I-thought to death.

The I-thought is the magician. The mind is a magic factory. It is now running for its life. It will pull out any tricks left in its magic bag. If you are now able to track the I-thought rising up from the Heart on the right, you will be able to stalk him with great accuracy until he is terminated. But even if you have not gone through an awakening of Amrita Nadi, you will be able to track the rising I-thought one way or another until it dies.

The next stage is Rescue from Without. This, too, matches my own experience. I had lifesaving help from within and from without. Rescue implies a desperate situation and help that is unexpected and decisive. Yes, I still needed a helping hand.

At the time, I had no idea that this sequence of events would line up with the 17 stage Hero's Journey. Nor would I have cared. I was busy fighting for my spiritual life.

1000

It was a knock down drag out battle to the very end. I was a spiritual warrior covered in the blood of my enemies. But my wily arch enemy, the last to go, was the I-thought.

Rescue is the word. I was utterly bewildered by this new development. I was astonished that I still had the fight the I-thought at this late stage of the game. I was helped in two ways. One help was internal. The other help was external.

I discuss the external help I received at this point in detail in my chapter on stalking and starving the I-thought. I ended up being alone in the middle of a barren desert. I sat in a little shack guarding some valuable industrial parts. I could read or watch TV. I could also pray and meditate. That is what I did.

The peculiar flavor of "rescue from without" is illustrated by how I got this job where I was "paid to meditate." I went to the interview looking as unkempt and scruffy as I could. My T-shirt was stained and torn. My jeans were dirty and scruffy. My hair was a tangled thorny mess. I hadn't shaved in a week.

I did not want to be a security guard, so I did my best to act belligerent and defiant. However, I am not very good at that.

I got hired against my will. It was the best thing that could have happened to me. At my remote desert guard shack outpost, I was able to do an intensive spiritual retreat each weekend that was totally focused on tracking and terminating the I-thought once and for all.

This was one way that I experienced "rescue from without" in terms of my everyday outer life. I also experienced "rescue from without" in the form of unexpected sacred interventions.

1000

My rescuers included a variety of famous spiritual champions. These people included Lakshmana Swamy, Papaji, Ramana Maharshi, Nisargadatta Maharaj, Amma and Arunachala Ramana (of A.H.A.M.). All of these personages are at LOC 1000. Plus I had ongoing support from Kali Ma and Lord Shiva as well.

What my own life experience during this phase demonstrated is that you may think you are out of the woods, but until the I-thought is put down, you are still in danger. I prayed to these individuals for help because I could tell that my own efforts were not sufficient. I needed Grace and I needed as much of It as I could get from my LOC 1000 friends, allies and mentors.

For example, I felt guided to buy a particular used videotape of Papaji on eBay.[48] Other than the fact that it had Papaji on it, I knew nothing of its contents. One night when the torture from the I-thought was at an extreme, I got the idea to watch this videotape. I thought it would at least make me feel better.

I was not prepared for what happened next. A few minutes into the video, I realized that the I-thought was terrified of Papaji. Papaji was a lion. The I-thought was his petrified prey.

Seizing the opportunity, I prayed to Papaji as the videotape played. "Please help me put down the I-thought," I asked him.

The stunned I-thought suffered a major setback that night from which it never fully recovered. He did not die that night, but he did not rise up again with such fierce arrogance. Papaji had scared him so much that he had become more docile and well behaved just so he could avoid Papaji!

This phase culminated in the final death of the I-thought. As I explain in that chapter about starving the I-thought to death, the I-thought died with a whimper, not a bang. It was like a movie villain who had terrorized without mercy, yet when it was his time to die, he just collapsed. He went limp and slid down into the ocean of consciousness never to come up again.

None of this was expected by me. Nor had I heard of such things. The journey from the LOC 900s to LOC 1000 is not front page news. Even in spiritual circles, it is rarely talked about. It is among the most esoteric secrets of spiritual yoga.

After completing that passage, there were several months of adjustment. To be honest, it was awhile before I had any idea of what had happened. The ascent to this point had seemed to be a kind of progressive process, a rising higher in the ranks of clarity, insight and understanding.

Now that I was here, wherever that was, I was starting all over again. I was nobody and I knew nothing. Now there was no difference between spiritual and material. Now it was like the whole journey had taken me right back to where I had started it from. The zero was 360 degrees was zero again.

Nothing had prepared me for this. To be prepared for this was impossible. Since it is beyond the mind, it cannot be described.

Campbell calls this near to the final stage Crossing of the Return Threshold. There was a threshold getting into this Hero's Journey. This is the threshold when you complete it.

This is not the Refusal to Return. That step is finalized. In the Magic Flight and the Rescue From Without, the decision to return was reinforced. The sage has completed his work.

The nascent LOC 1000 sage is like a newborn baby. He has returned to the world, but he must still learn how to live in it. Because he has never lived like this before, the whole thing must be relearned, or discovered, all over again. It is by trial and error. There is no manual for this. There is only life itself.

For some sages, the question of bodily survival arises. Now that they have realized the Self, what is the point of keeping this body? After all, the biological machine has served its purpose. There is no greater glory for the body. Like a bright flower who opens for one day in the desert then dies that night, the body has displayed its finest potential to the fullest.

Such a sage may need to be convinced that life in eternity will come soon enough. The benighted humanity needs him to stay in the body to help raise consciousness on the planet. On the relative plane, the struggle between the dark and the light continues. Every sage is needed in order to keep the balance.

A return to the world is also a return to the marketplace. The issue of money must be handled. The LOC 1000 sage must figure out how to make a living in a world that doesn't exist.

The fact that the next stage of the Hero's Journey is called Master of Two Worlds shows that the focus of Crossing the Return Threshold is making this adjustment to the new world. Master of Two Worlds is the next to last stage of the Hero's Journey. He is a true master of both worlds because for him there is only one world. However, this is not quite accurate.

1000

To be more precise, in his perception there is no world at all. There is only the Self or the Absolute or the Supreme. This is the final answer, at least for him. This supernal "oneness" is not a lesser oneness from one of the lower non-dual stages.

Yet he has a new challenge he could never have anticipated. He is called by the others who see a world separate from themselves to account for their apparent world. Somehow, he must acknowledge their world. This is not an easy challenge.

How does the sage talk to these people about their world when there is no such world? In my case, I use analogies.

One of my favorites is the world is like a three-dimensional hologram. You can see it and experience it, yet it is not solid. Even though it is perceived, it is not really there. Other classic analogies are the world is like a dream or a glittering rainbow.

The sage is now LOC 1000. Yet this map does not miss a single step. There are steps of adjustment even now. Not in terms of spiritual attainment, for that part is finished. The challenge is now the decision to share this attainment and how to do that.

Yes, he is still subtly adjusting. Two worlds, one world, no world — but it all gets sorted out. Like a rising golden sun, an astounding new depth of compassion emerges. His body, his life, his being, will be sacrificed for the sake of this world that does not really exist. It is a perfect finale. His spiritual blood will be like fine wine. His spiritual body will feed the world.

The final stage, the completion stage, has an interesting title. It is a wonderful and perfect name for it. It is Freedom to Live.

Most people consider themselves free to live, don't they? The emphasis is on the freedom while alive. That you feel free and you are free. You do what you want to do and you don't do what you don't want to do.

There is total relaxation into living in the present moment. In the past, there was clinging to changelessness. Not anymore.

The final Zen oxherding picture is called "Return to Society" or "Returning to the Marketplace with Open Hands." This is the that stage. Freedom to Live means freedom to be a billionaire, freedom to be a drunk, freedom to be a teacher. Pure freedom.

Yet due to who you are and what you are and where you are, no matter what you become, you will be a blessing to the world. Even if you become a drunk living on the street, you will somehow be a blessing to those you encounter, to those who try to help you. It will be God who put you there.

I must emphasize that for the heroic LOC 1000 sage who has returned to the world, there is still no world. There is nowhere to return to, no world at all. That's right, there simply is NO world. The world is itself his own Self, his own true unlimited "I." Therefore, he cannot help but love it as his very own Self.

This really gets the heads scratching, but there's no other way to say it. The world is already saved. Each new morning is the resurrection. The world is saved because the world was just a concept, just a bunch of thoughts. As soon as it is seen for what it really is, it disappears. This is its true salvation.

1000

This is the status of the LOC 1000 stage. Sometimes it is called being a human Buddha, but I discourage such associations. To say that the LOC 1000 sage is a Buddha is like saying he or she is a Jesus Christ, a Krishna, a Rama. Unless you are them, how can you know for sure? I do not know what they experience.

I think of it as fulfilling the human potential. I like to say it is living in the "natural state." The fancy name for this is sahaja.

That is all it is. It is your true natural state. Before you were in an unnatural state, an intoxicated state, a state of drunkenness and confusion, and now you are stone cold sober. It's a brand new day. The sun blasts through the window like it has gone supernova. The birds are singing a song of freedom. Your cup of coffee is God Incarnate. How did you not see this before?

Everything is God. Everything is Buddha. Everything is Jesus. It is all so obvious to you now. Not only that, you cannot come up with another notion. That distortion function is disabled.

You cannot remember any other way it could be. You are now a divine child. Everything is God, Buddha and Jesus... and everything is You. It may sound sacrilegious or egomaniacal, but that is the experience. That is how it feels. That is how it is.

This is the divine blessing of the great forgetfulness. If you are truly reborn as a new person, then the memories of the old person will be gone, too. Everything is gone. This is the truth.

Even if you can remember something about the old days, they are not your memories. They are the memories of that person.

This is the new you. This is your new world. This new you in a new world is the Absolute. Yet in the Absolute, there is no you and there is no world. There is nothing at all. This nothing is everything. This nothing is not empty. It is absolutely full.

It may sound like I am being vague on purpose. I am not.

When you live this way, your questions die and come to an end. Like ripe fruit, they fall from the tree of life and return to good soil. The mind had questions. The mind had answers. The answers always led to more questions. The new you has no questions. The new you has no answers. What you have is life as it is. That is all you have in each moment. It is enough.

This paradox cannot be known. It can only be lived. Finally, it all makes sense. It cannot be explained, words will completely fail, but now it does make sense. Finally.

The Condensed Map of Awakening (Chart)

The Map of Awakening
From Spiritual Emergence to the Supreme Self

- **500** — Spirituality Emerges
- **560** — Spiritual Seeking Begins
- **570** — Spiritual Seeking Intensifies
- **580** — Effortless Thought Free Meditation
- **590** — *1st Spiritual Shock* (Ego Death)
- **600** — Pure Feeling of Being (No Self)
- **690** — *2nd Spiritual Shock* (Cosmic Expansion)
- **700** — Feeling of Being the Universe (Cosmic Self)
- **790** — *3rd Spiritual Shock* (Great Void Passage)
- **800** — Divine Union (Not Knowing)
- **890** — *Transfiguration* (Radical Illumination)
- **900** — Natural State (Stabilization in No Mind)
- **1000** — The Absolute (Supreme Self)

1000

Quest for the Absolute:

An Overview

of the Journey

From No Self (600s)

to Supreme Self (1000)

Quest for the Absolute: An Overview

I summarized the levels of consciousness at the beginning of the book. That provided an overview of the whole journey.

Here I will give an overview of my personal journey as I moved through the non-dual levels of consciousness. In later chapters called "My Spiritual Journal" I go into more detail and quote from the diary I have kept for many years.

When I first conceived of this book, I did not expect to write about myself very much. As I got more deeply into it, I saw that my own spiritual life had unfolded in a way that precisely followed the model I was putting forth in the book.

Since my own experiences illustrated how the spiritual journey through the stages and levels of consciousness takes place, the logical choice for me was to share those experiences from the point of view I had at the time they happened to me. This meant quoting from my private spiritual journal. I would need to bare my soul like never before.

This chapter also serves as an introduction to and summary of the four non-dual levels: LOC 600s, LOC 700s, LOC 800s and LOC 1000. The LOC 900s are a transitional zone. As with the LOC 590s, there are not very many people residing there.

Later in this book I will go into much more detail about what makes each non-dual level special and unique. I will also talk about contemporary people who are currently at these four levels and how they are communicating from their level.

My goal is to spell out the spiritual path in its entirety. If this information is made plain for everyone, then it will be much easier for seekers and enlightened persons to evaluate where they are and where they would like to be. I believe that my personal experiences make this process more understandable.

I went through each non-dual stage slowly with dramatic experiences that revealed themselves to me in great detail. Other people may progress upwards with little or nothing in the way of signs or experiences. There is no right or wrong way to reach LOC 1000. All there is is *your* way.

I'm convinced that the four main stages or LOC levels that I have outlined in my Map of Awakening will be traversed by the enlightened individual as they deepen and consummate their realization. For example, one student "blew through" the LOC 800s in a few days. He had experiences that matched the LOC 800s profile, but they happened very quickly for him.

Your journey to LOC 1000 and stabilization in the Absolute does not have to be the long painstaking process that it was for me. At the time of this writing, I have three students, two male and one female, who are stable at LOC 1000. After they got the RASA transmission, one took one and a half years, one took six months and one took six days to get to LOC 1000!

LOC Summary of My Journey: Seven Distinct Movements

Here is a short summary that shows the date, the event, the spiritual trigger and the LOC for that period of my spiritual journey. Seen from the LOC perspective, they are organic intelligent movements in the spiritual symphony of my life.

The pithy summaries for each section are taken from a short summary of the stages by Nisargadatta Maharaj in *I Am That*.

"I Am Myself" is followed by "I Am All," then "I Am." Next "I Am Goes." Finally, at the Absolute, "Reality Alone Is."[49]

The Spiritual Stages of My Life (With LOCs)

Stage One: Physical Birth
Event Date: 1950 in Kansas, USA
Shock Stimulus: Past life karma and spiritual realizations
LOC Reached After These Spiritual Events: **842**

Stage Two: Three Enlightenment Experiences
Event Dates: 1966, 1972, 1982 in Los Angeles and Boonville, CA
Shock Stimulus: Kundalini, Tantric sex, deep meditation
LOC Reached After These Spiritual Events: **583**

Stage Three: Awakening into non-duality ("I Am Myself")
Event Date: February, 1992 in San Diego, CA
Shock Stimulus: Grace from Ramesh Balsekar, meditation
LOC Reached After Spiritual Event: **683**

Stage Four: Expansion of non-duality ("I Am All")
Event Date: October, 2000 in Las Vegas, NV
Shock Stimulus: Intimate Betrayal in January, 2000
LOC Reached After Spiritual Event: **776**

Stage Five: Divine Darkness of Not Knowing ("I Am")
Event Date: April, 2006 in Las Vegas, NV
Shock Stimulus: Kundalini
LOC Reached After Spiritual Event: **845**

Stage Six: Amrita Nadi ("I Am Goes")
Event Date: November, 2006 in Las Vegas, NV
Shock Stimulus: Unknown (Grace)
LOC Reached After Spiritual Event: **932**

Stage Seven: Stabilization in the Absolute after Elimination of the I-Thought ("Reality Alone Is")
Event Date: February, 2008
Shock Stimulus: Intense daily Self-inquiry meditation from December, 2006 through February, 2008 supported by Grace
LOC Reached After Spiritual Event: **1000**

My Journey Through the First Three Non-Dual Levels

My personal journey through the four levels of non-duality is the foundation of this book. This is why I can talk about them with precision. I went through them one by one over a long period of time. My process was gradual and progressive.

Some people go through these states and stages suddenly. I did not. I had plenty of time to write in my journal, study my level of consciousness and compare it to other mystical maps.

Eventually, I began evaluating my LOC and recording that data in conjunction with my subjective experiences. It quickly became obvious to me that there was a strong connection.

What motivated me to keep going up was my dissatisfaction. Even though I was definitely established in the LOC 600s and living in a state of non-doership (spontaneous action), I was not happy with my state at all. It did not feel complete to me.

Something was missing. Actually, a lot was missing!

I did not feel content in the least. It was obvious to me that this could not be the final state. It lacked stable deep peace. It lacked happiness. It lacked intrinsic well-being. I continued to investigate, question and challenge my LOC 683 state.

Eventually, that state expanded to an impressive cosmic state where I experienced being one with the universe. I felt like I was everything. I even felt that the universe was inside of me.

But that didn't satisfy me either. The problem with that was that the universe was changing. Since this big "I" was one with the universe, that meant this big "I" was also subject to change. There was also a very subtle outward movement associated with this cosmic manifestation. It wanted to keep expanding.

In spite of its sublime grandeur, my LOC 776 state was limited and clearly unstable. I knew there had to be something higher and better. I knew this could not be my final destination.

Amrita Nadi: the Discovery of the Fourth Non-Dual Level

The next step took me by complete surprise. This was the third spiritual shock of transcendental darkness. Everything is forgotten. All the knowledge, the enlightened state of being the universe, it got consumed by the impenetrable darkness.

At this point, I thought this might be it, but I wasn't sure. For me, this had been a Kundalini process. I had moved through Ajna chakra (Third Eye) and up to Sahasrara chakra (Crown). The Sahasrara chakra had opened completely.

According to the traditional texts on the Kundalini journey, this was it. I had passed through "not knowing," through the darkness of the Great Void. Now I was at LOC 845. I felt like this was a dramatic improvement over the cosmic oneness of the LOC 700s. Yet it, too, felt incomplete, not yet a wholeness.

At the same time, I had been in a devotional relationship with Divine Mother Kali Ma since 1982. At LOC 845, my ability to love Her and submit to Her went to a sublime level beyond anything I had enjoyed previously. I might have stayed stuck here if She had not, with merciless mercy, kicked me out of it.

After the Kundalini opened the Crown chakra, I was led to spiritual experiences not found in conventional Kundalini yoga texts. In meditation, I was shown a subtle passage down from the Crown to the (causal) Heart on the right.

I was familiar with Ramana's teachings on the Heart, but this secret passage connecting the Crown and the Heart was new to me. I had read of something quite mysterious like that, but I had not known what to make of it at the time.

The next event was the most unexpected of all. This was the awakening of the radiance of Amrita Nadi. This secret hidden passage starts at the Crown, goes down behind the head and then stretches across the chest from the left to the Heart on the right. It suddenly lit up like the filament of a light bulb.

It got brighter and brighter until it was like the light of a thousand suns. It is this experience that I am calling the Tranfiguration. However, the Transfiguration step does not need to take place in this way. After all, many realizers never become conscious of the Heart on the right or Amrita Nadi.

The World Disappears in a Blaze of Light

I was relaxing at home in my apartment in Las Vegas. Even though it was the middle of the day, the brightness I saw with my open eyes blotted out everything. A brilliant blinding luminosity took over that made the world entirely disappear.

There was only supreme white Light. The feeling that arose with the appearance of this Light was exquisite beyond any description. This experience of there being only Light lasted about two hours. Over the next year, it returned a few times.

When this supreme Light faded, I was at first disappointed. I had assumed that this state was the final and ultimate state.

Certainly it was the ultimate mystical experience in a 40 year mystical career that began with a Kundalini awakening in a lucid dream at the age of 16. Yet the reality was that this Light had been so bright it would have been impossible for me to function in everyday life. It really was true that all I could see was this Light. There was only that Light. No world. No objects. Nothing was perceived other than this Light.

Of all of the many spiritual events in my life, this is the one that truly deserves to be called "enlightenment." It was that. It was a state in which everything had literally turned to Light.

This blazing white Light was seen with open physical eyes. The so-called "world" had literally been burned away with no remnant. In its place was a radical luminosity beyond words.

A Transfigured Life in the Radiance of the Self

Reflecting in this way, I took another look at the world. Had it changed in any way as a result of that experience of Light?

I was stunned to see that it had. Now when I looked at the world, I could see that there was no world. What I saw was the Self or the radiant stillness of the Absolute. It looked to me like a pure translucent transparency or pristine clear light.

That is what I saw as what was there, but "the world" as such could still be perceived and interacted with. The best analogy I can come up with is that the world looked like a holographic projection. The Absolute is not changed by it. The world is an expression of it, yet as that expression, it IS the Absolute. This way of perceiving the world has persisted to this day.

What I see first is the Self or the Absolute. Then I see "the world." But this is not really accurate, as "the world" per se is never seen. What is seen is the radiant translucent clarity of the Self or the Absolute. Then "the world" is seen as a kind of "afterthought" or "ornament" or "adornment" of the Self that is also somehow an expression of the Self. So there really is no world. In short, "There is no world. There is only the Self."

Final Cleanup of the I-Thought

In spite of this radical event, my work was still not done. I was still dealing with the tiresome dramas of the pesky I-thought.

The main Amrita Nadi event had taken place in November, 2006. My LOC after that event had gone up to 932. I knew this meant I was not finished. Somehow, I had to get to LOC 1000!

The unprecedented blazing of the Amrita Nadi had exposed the last remnants of the I-thought in the deep subconscious that I had not yet been able to root out. I knew that to have the peace I yearned for I would have to completely eliminate it.

The I-thought is the seed of the mind. In the morning, this I-thought shoots up from the Heart on the right to the brain. It looks like a little spark. It takes over the brain and spreads throughout the physical body. Then the conventional world is seen. Identified with the body, the person lives in duality.

To realize and stabilize in the Absolute, the mind must be destroyed. This is not as drastic as it sounds. The end of the mind is the end of world, duality, separation and suffering. It is due to the mind that division and duality exist. In order to completely eliminate the mind, its seed or root, the I-thought, must die. Until that happens, the mind will persist. You will not be able to achieve LOC 1000. You will not realize the Self.

You do not have to destroy the I-thought in the way that I did. You will do it in your own way. I have had a natural gift for tracking subtle phenomena since I was a teenager. Being able to observe these extremely subtle events is not a requirement.

Thanks to the clarity that followed the arising of Amrita Nadi, my ability to notice, track and confront the I-thought reached a new level. I intuitively knew that now I could finally get to it at its place of origin and, quite literally, dig it up by its roots.

I went on an intensive meditation retreat from December, 2006 through February, 2008 in order to accomplish this. In essence, the purpose of this retreat was to observe, confront and knock down (back to the Heart) each and every rising thought.

I was going to do this until the I-thought no longer rose up from the Heart. I would keep doing this until the I-thought died in the Heart on the right and never came up again.

This intensive retreat was made possible in an interesting way. I needed a job as my unemployment was running out. The only job that was available was a security officer job.

Since I did not want this job, I went to the interview unshaven. I wore scruffy jeans with holes in them. I exhibited a surly indifferent attitude. I was sure that they would reject me.

I was offered a job on the spot! It had unusual hours. I would work 12 hours a day on the weekend (Saturday and Sunday). I would be guarding an unoccupied warehouse in the desert.

This was God's doing. I lived in the heart of Las Vegas, yet I was going to get paid to be alone in the middle of nowhere for 24 hours a week. Incredibly, I was going to *get paid good money* to go on a solitary desert meditation retreat two days a week.

Although I had to walk around the property once an hour, I was free the rest of the time to do what I wanted. I just had to stay on the property and answer calls on the security radio.

From December, 2006 to February, 2008, I did two intense eight hour meditation retreats per weekend. That was one Saturday and one Sunday. During the week, I meditated a minimum of one hour a day plus doing Self-inquiry all day.

This strict regimen enabled me to finally knock down the I-thought for good so that it dissolved. It did not rise up from the Heart again. I had arrived at the stillness of the Absolute.

My LOC in February, 2008 at the end of this final cleanup phase was 1000. I had reached my goal. I like to call this LOC sahaja, meaning "natural state." At long last, I was Home. It had taken me many years of hard work, but it was worth it!

My LOC Mini-Autobiography: From Seeker to the Supreme

Here I will summarize my spiritual journey in terms of my LOCs. I talk about the LOC I was at for each of the spiritual stages to illustrate what they mean for a person in real life. I also talk about a painful relationship that transformed my life.

Even though I had an LOC of 842 at birth thanks to my past life efforts, by the age of 14 it had fallen to LOC 582. In high school, I became a "hard core" seeker. I studied philosophy, especially existentialism. This investigation culminated in a period of spontaneous inquiry and a Kundalini event at the age of 16. This event gave me an unforgettable taste of the enlightened state. I would not rest until I had stabilized in it.

During my seeker stage, I went through a series of spiritual shocks or "enlightenment experiences." These events got my LOC up to 583. I had a Kundalini enlightenment experience at age 16, a Tantric ego death event at age 21, and a Buddhist flash of nibbana (nirvana) at age 33.

During these events, the ego or empirical self (separate entity) disappeared. It was gone for minutes, hours or days, but it always came back.

The return of this contraction was profoundly frustrating! By the time I met my guru Ramesh Balsekar, I had given up on being able to accomplish this awakening on my own.

I received Grace from Ramesh Balsekar in person in Fall, 1989. It was a meeting in Southern California of about 50 people. I sat up front. I asked him a question. When he tersely replied in just one sentence, a spiritual force struck me between the eyes. My compulsive seeking was terminated on the spot.

I experienced a progressive relaxation and unwinding in the depths of the mind. In February, 1992, while meditating on my living room couch in San Diego, the ego or empirical self disappeared. It dropped down into an ocean of consciousness.

This time the ego did not come back. The experience was a profound shock. I could not tell if my body was the chair or the cat or this flesh. The next day I realized I was established in the mysterious and amazing state of non-doership.

I read the *Bhagavad Gita* about it. My experience matched exactly Lord Krishna's words in Chapter Three: Verses 27-28. "All actions arise from Nature. If you are deluded by the ego, then you think 'I am the doer.'" Now that my separate self was gone, it was absolutely obvious to me that I was *not* the doer!

In Chapter Five: Verses 8-9, Lord Krishna is more specific. He says "If you know the truth, then you know you are not doing anything. The senses just playfully interact with sense objects. Seeing, hearing, talking, walking and so on, you are aware that you do nothing at all."

This is my rather loose translation. You will not need to wonder or speculate about it. Krishna is saying that it will be obvious to you that you are a "non-doer." You will know it.

After this non-dual breakthrough, my LOC jumped up to 683. For a few months, I was in a blissful luminous state. It felt wonderful. I thought I was completely done. I was not done!

First irritation, then other negative emotions appeared like dark stains on my "holy" glow. I was shocked. I was still "full of crap." I still had lots of work to do. I couldn't believe it.

I was astonished by the arising of these contracted emotions. I had read everything I could find about enlightenment. I had not read anything about negative emotions showing up that were more intense and more ugly than anything I had known in the past. It was like things had gotten worse, not better.

Once I got over being impressed by the non-doership, I settled down and dedicated myself to processing my remaining negative emotions all day long. I discovered that I had no brakes and no fear. There was no ego entity to stop the radical "scrape the bottom" cleansing of my emotional garbage.

I realized that I was eliminating stuff from many past lives, not just this life. Every day was like a crazy emotional roller coaster ride. It was beyond super-intense.

At an emotional level I was driving 100 miles an hour all day every day. It did not scare me. I enjoyed it. This purification process did not harm my LOC. It went up some more. In 1998, it was at 689. But I'm getting ahead of myself.

In 1992, I was guided to move to Portland, Oregon. It started out well. I made my living as an intuitive counselor and a psychotherapist. I led a group every week in Loving Kindness meditation. It was a beautiful uplifting experience for us all.

In 1996, I met a woman 12 years younger than me. We moved in together. I fell in love. For a couple of years, it was heaven on earth. Towards the end of that long honeymoon in our relationship, I began to sense something was wrong. She was distancing herself from me. I couldn't figure it out.

What had been heaven soon became hell. I didn't know what to do. I tried to talk to her, but she said there was nothing to say. Then a close friend told me that she was dating somebody else even though she was still living with me. I was still madly in love with her. My girlfriend ended up marrying the other guy. I was devastated by her deception and betrayal.

Devastated is too weak. In my spiritual journal, I wrote that it was like a "nuclear bomb" had been dropped on my emotions. My entire emotional life was destroyed. My ability to feel was annihilated. I went completely numb. This was January, 2000.

This blank state of emotional numbness lasted a year. As my ability to feel my feelings came back, I began to have visions of a place with neon lights. Since I had not been to Las Vegas, it took me awhile to figure out where I was being told to go.

In October, 2000, right after my move to Las Vegas, I checked my LOC. It had now gone up to 776. The traumatic betrayal and breakup had knocked off a big chunk of my attachment. It shifted me to the level of cosmic consciousness or "I Am All."

I had experiences that matched that stage. For example, I felt that the entire city of Las Vegas, dazzling lights and all, was inside of me. I experienced myself as the universe. Eventually, I was able to see that I was bigger even than the universe.

The rest is pretty straightforward. I met my soulmate, my wife Linda, in Las Vegas in 2001. We have been together ever since.

The irony of that scenario unfolding the way it did is that I was not looking for anyone. I truly didn't care about being in a relationship anymore. My first six months in Las Vegas I was silent. I did not talk at all except for a few words exchanged with a store clerk at a grocery store in downtown Las Vegas.

My LOC was slowly climbing. In 1998, it had been 689. The temporary annihilation of emotions took place in early 2000. At 689, I had reached a threshold and activated the next level.

That threshold in the 600s range is LOC 686. It is not a rule that you must go up to the next level when you cross that threshold. You may have views or attachments or other reasons to stay at the lower level. But crossing the threshold is what makes being pulled up via magnetic ascent possible.

In late 2000, after my move to Las Vegas, my LOC was up to 776. In 2004, it was 780. In 2005, it was 782. By January, 2006, it had jumped up to 793. This activated access to the next level.

My theory is that getting to LOC 793 opened the door to the next higher level of non-dual consciousness. It crossed over an invisible LOC threshold. I'm referring to Fibonacci numbers.

The Fibonacci number for the high end of the 700s is 786. Since 793 was well above that, this meant that the next higher level would start pulling me upwards. I will say more about these special numbers that are found throughout nature very soon.

In Spring, 2006, the yogic Kundalini "upper process" occurred. This took me through the darkness of the Great Void and the state of unknowing up to and through the Crown chakra.

Following that event, I found myself at LOC 845. Thanks to some hidden momentum, I discovered that I was accelerating to higher LOC levels. By July, 2006, I was up to LOC 876.

In September, 2006, my LOC had risen to 888. Once again, I was above the threshold. In this case, the Fibonacci transition number was LOC 886. I was just above it, but it was enough.

This scenario was parallel to my movement out of the 600s. At that time, in 1998, I had been at LOC 689 (just above LOC 686).

In November, 2006, my Amrita Nadi event, "Transfiguration" in the divine radiance of the Self, took place. After that impact settled down, I found myself in December, 2006 at LOC 932.

In June, 2007, I reached LOC 960. In February, 2008, I reached and stabilized at LOC 1000. As a teenager, I had committed myself to reaching this level. That was in 1966. It had taken me 42 years, but I had finally achieved my goal. Nobody had to tell me. I didn't need to check my state against other expert sources (although I did). I was supremely content and at rest.

Fibonacci Number Thresholds and Non-Dual LOC Ranges

Fibonacci numbers appear in nature and also in our physical DNA. As I studied the LOC numbers in preparation for this book, I noticed that in each major non-dual range they were bunched around the middle or high end of that range. For example, most of the non-dual teachers in the LOC 600s are in a middle zone that stretches from the 650s to the 680s.

I have lived a rich and varied life. At one time, I was an active investor in stocks, commodities and forex. Back then I studied Fibonacci numbers in order to identify what in the stock market business they call "support" and "resistance."

This concept smoothly transfers to the LOC model. The idea is that there has to be "buying pressure" or "selling pressure" to move the stock up or down. Likewise, if a person's LOC is going to go up to a new level and stay there, some kind of internal pressure is building up that will take that person over the edge. That "edge" has a number. It is a Fibonacci number.

These LOC thresholds are based on the Fibonacci numbers. The trick is to convert the Fibonacci numbers that occur in the natural spirals of nature to useful percentages that will describe the lower, middle and upper boundaries of a range.

For example, the Fibonacci number 0.618 translates to the 62 per cent level of a range. In the LOC 500s, this corresponds to LOC 562. In the LOC 600s, it matches with LOC 662 and so on.

I converted Fibonacci trading numbers to percentages. I ended up with the following list: 18 per cent, 27 per cent, 38 per cent, 50 per cent, 62 per cent, 79 per cent and 86 percent.[50]

Now let's translate these percentages to a non-dual range. Let's use the LOC 500s as an example. We end up with these LOCs: 518, 527, 538, 550, 562, 579 and 586. Now it will be easy to apply the Fibonacci numbers to the Map of Awakening.

Now let's look at the LOC 600s. The Fibonacci thresholds for this non-dual range will be 618, 627, 638, 650, 662, 679 and 686.

Earlier I talked about my San Diego student who did a test run into the LOC 600s went up to LOC 623. Then she went back down to LOC 583. Months later she went back up into non-duality and stabilized. She is at LOC 764 as I write this.

Taking into account the Fibonacci number thresholds, she tested the LOC 618 threshold but stopped before reaching the LOC 627 threshold. Now at LOC 764, she is stable deep in LOC 700s territory just above the LOC 762 Fibonacci level.

Examining the list from the chapter giving LOCs for 200 non-dual spiritual teachers. the lowest person stabilized in the 600s is Jan Kersschot at 655. The highest person in the 600s is Wayne Liquorman at LOC 694. The rest are somewhere in between in the 660s, 670s and 680s. The exceptions are Leo Hartong, John Wheeler and Rick Linchitz who are at LOC 692.

Since Liquorman, Hartong, Wheeler and Linchitz are stable in the LOC 690s, this makes them exceptions. They are violating my upper Fibonacci number limit. But my theory also says that when somebody penetrates the upper limit of a major non-dual range, they are preparing to move up into the next major LOC range. I believe these realizers are some of the best candidates for moving up into the LOC 700s or higher.

I looked at my 200 non-dual teachers list for more people who were not in the fat middle or upper ranges. I found some in the LOC 700s and LOC 900s, but not in the LOC 800s.

Exceptions in the LOC 700s range are Prem Vishrant LOC 702, Nome LOC 711, Lynda Cole LOC 712, Joseph Goldstein LOC 715, Paul Lowe LOC 733 and Ram Dass LOC 733.

Exceptions in the LOC 900s range are Amber Terrell LOC 917, David Carse LOC 918, Jean Klein LOC 926, V. V. Brahmam LOC 934 and Kiran LOC 934.

According to my Fibonacci threshold theory, these people are moving up in LOC. They may stay at this LOC for years just as I did, but the pressure is building for a breakthrough.

For example, in 1971 when popular American sage Ram Dass arrived on the Western spiritual scene with his blockbuster book *Be Here Now*,[51] he was at LOC 684. Now he is LOC 733.

The Far Frontier

LOC 600 to 699

The Far Frontier: LOC 600 to 699

The awakening event in which there is found to be "no self" is the *beginning* of a great spiritual journey, not its end. Yes, it is "enlightenment," but it is not a place to settle down. It is not the time to post your spiritual teacher shingle.

If you choose to crystallize as a teacher at this stage, you run the risk of seriously stunting your spiritual growth. You are not done. In the LOC 600s, you are not even halfway up the mountain. Your conviction that you have finished the path will justify you giving up your spiritual practices. You stop doing Self-inquiry. You stop reading the great masters.

The LOC 600s sage is the one-eyed king in the land of the blind. He can see what the ordinary person cannot.

He has seen and awakened into an open space of pure being. His life has been transformed. For most LOC 600s sages, this appears to be enough. They feel complete. They are satisfied.

But what about those who were not satisfied with this level of understanding and realization? How do they view this stage? What did they discover when they transcended the LOC 600s?

The LOC 600s Marker: Authentic Detachment from Activity

Based on their personal accounts, the 600s teachers validate another classical marker of genuine enlightenment known as non-doership. They may not know that it is a traditional and very ancient marker of non-dual realization, but it is. Today it may be described as living "spontaneously" or "effortlessly."

For awakening to be stabilized in "enlightenment," the person must be living spontaneously. This is not a now and then state. It is not a peak experience or a temporary state. For it to be the real deal, it is "all the time." Doership is destroyed.

Non-doership is defined quite precisely in Chapter 5, Verses 8 and 9 of the *Bhagavad Gita*: "A knower of truth knows that all that is going on is that the senses are interacting with their sense objects. He never thinks that he is doing anything. Even though he is seeing, hearing, touching, smelling, eating, moving, sleeping, breathing, pooping, pissing, grasping, talking, opening and closing his eyes, he always knows that the reality of the situation is that he is doing nothing at all."[52]

So the knower of truth lives spontaneously in the knowledge that the physical senses are just doing their thing with their sense objects. He is isolated and detached from them and their activity. He is above and beyond them. He is aloof from them. He is free of them. This is authentic detachment from activity.

If your spiritual awakening is merely some kind of bliss state or a some sort of witnessing, then it is not enlightenment. It is a step in the right direction. You're waking up, but you are not awake yet. Non-doership is the proven reliable litmus test.

Life in non-doership is a cataclysmic adjustment for you as a human being. This adjustment may be easy or it may be difficult, but you can't miss it. It isn't just some cool "groovy" kind of living where you're "in the flow of the now." You are no longer the doer! Doing is gone! It is gone beyond gone!

Non-Dual Dead End in the "No Self" Ghost Town

Since this non-doership is such a big change, and there is no experience of a separate self anymore, it is easy to understand how this stage might be thought of as the ultimate stage. But it is not. There may be an enjoyable "glow" phase after this awakening. It may last for a few months. It may last for years.

What does the new sage have from this awakening? He or she has a "no self" self who is a "non-doer." The new sage can protest vehemently that there is nobody here, there is only no self, I don't exist — but it just doesn't ring true. Who exactly is it who is asserting that they don't exist? It smells a little fishy.

It's not "wrong" exactly, but it isn't right, either. The situation is a bit like being hungry and going to a restaurant that serves, as its specialty, non-food.

Can you eat non-food? Can you eat a non-apple? No, you cannot eat a non-apple. You can talk about a non-apple all day long, but you cannot eat a non-apple ever.

"No Self" Needs the Separate Self to Make Sense

When you negate something, you imply that there is some sort of substance associated with what you are negating. In the example of the non-apple, the reason you could make sense out of what I said is that you know what an apple is.

If I say I am an advocate of non-violence, this will make sense to you because you know there is something called violence. It is due to the reality, the mutually perceived substance of this thing called violence in the world, that it can be meaningful for me to say I am actively engaged in non-violence.

Talking about "no self" is still talking about "a self" and talking about "non-doership" is still talking about doership. The new LOC 600s sage can sincerely say to spiritual students that from his point of view "There is nothing you can do," but he is 100 per cent wrong.

He is stuck on negation. He is attached to "no self" and to "no doing." Therefore, he sees a problem with self and doing.

Who is the "you" he is addressing? What is the "do" that he is talking about? When you come full circle with this journey, then it makes perfect sense to talk to people as people in terms of what they can do to help themselves as human beings.

The sage may not feel he is making this reference, he may describe his state or his understanding in flowery language, but that does not mean he has fully actualized the potential of what he has discovered. Indeed, many people who arrive at the LOC 600s spend the rest of their lives there. They believe this non-doing "no self" or "life without a self" is IT.

The New Sage Believes He Can and Should Save the World

In the LOC 600s, the world of individuals who are identified with the physical body as doers is negated. But that does not mean it is transcended. There is a Janus-like looking back to the material world taking place in the LOC 600s sage.

For example, some 600s sages say "Now that I am enlightened, what can I do to help and improve the world?" The 600s sage may not like to admit it, but he is living in both worlds.

He may not be "of" the old material world, but he is still "in" it. The world and the people "out there" are still substantial for him. To perceive a world that needs to be saved and can be saved shows a massive identification with this world idea.

The reality of his "no self" did not turn other people into "no others." It did not turn the world into "no world." It produced a subjective state of "no self" and "no doer" operating in an objective world that still seems to be "out there." It negates the old way of life, but it is not the great rebirth into the great Self.

If the 600s sage believes he is in the final state, then he will say that "no self" is the final truth. But it is impossible for negation to be final. Life demands that affirmation follow negation.

Beyond the realm of opposites, the paradox is that real peace does not know that it is peace. Real love does not know that it is love. Real happiness does not know that it is happiness.

These opposites are not transcended in the 600s. In the 600s, the sage still struggles with "no self" versus others and world.

At LOC 1000, abiding in the Absolute, in the Self, all concepts, all notions of other and all ideas of world are annihilated. It sounds like a tall order and it is. This is what it takes to attain the true peace, love and happiness that are beyond the mind.

Separation and Divorce Will Never Affirm Happiness

The final truth cannot be a divorce. It cannot be a separation. No matter how the words are spun, "no" and "non" are words of lack, words of emptiness, words of void, words of absence.

The final truth cannot be any kind of duality. To just be the pure sense of being separate from activity, to just be the "no self," the "non-doer," the witness, is not enough. Life is not like that. Love is not like that. The heart demands wholeness, not "non-separation." The heart demands fullness, not "no self." The heart demands passionate vulnerable deeply generous participation, not cool indifferent "witnessing."

"No self" and "non-doer" are the launch of the enlightenment project. You cannot know where you are going from where you are. You cannot know the destination from the first step.

You will know where you were when you have moved onto the next step and stabilized there. Then you look back and you can see clearly. From the 600s, the next step is the expansion of pure being to include the whole world and even the universe. This takes place when the sage moves up to the LOC 700s.

The 600s: "No Self" and the Borderless Spherical Non-Doer

I call the LOC 600s "spherical consciousness." The new sage is experiencing their personal space as being without "walls" or "edges." It is "borderless." They feel they are expanding in all directions. They conclude that they are "limitless." As a result, they may mistakenly believe they are "being everything."[53]

This error is understandable. The new sage is comparing his experience of enlightenment to his memory of what it was like to be limited by the skin boundaries of the physical body. This old "self" is what he compares his experience to. His "old self" felt like it was encased inside of a "meat suit." He felt confined, incarcerated, imprisoned, locked up in a jail cell of the flesh.

Classical descriptions of enlightenment can sound more or less like the expanding "borderless" LOC 600s experience. But "borderless" and "boundless" are two different things.

When you are borderless, you may feel like you are one with what is in front of you. What you see is you. It seems logical to then extrapolate "I am boundless." But they are not the same state. Establishment in boundlessness happens in LOC 700s.

I made this mistake myself when I was at LOC 683. Since I felt myself to be expanding in all directions without a detectable border or limit, I decided this must mean that I was the whole enchilada. I was wrong. That distinctly different experience happened to me when I moved up to the LOC 700s. I did not fully appreciate the extent of my error until after I got there.

I call the LOC 700s "cosmic consciousness." The key marker of the 700s is the expansion of conscious identity or pure being to cosmic proportions. No longer do you just feel that you are without boundaries or expanding in all directions. Now you are the world and the world is you. It is literally your body. You feel much much bigger. Now you are cosmic in size.

From the 700s, the sage will look back and see that his LOC 600s separation from activity was a form of duality. He will see that he was attached to this experience of "no self."

Not only that, he will see that he was separate from the world and from other people. The head may have been okay with that, but the heart could not accept it. The heart needed true union. The heart needed to embrace the entire universe and even beyond. When the mind dropped into the heart, the heart started dissolving it. There is more dissolving to do.

The 600s: the "No Self" Space and Localized Expansiveness

Because of the intellectual emphasis in non-dual circles, the state of non-duality is described as an understanding rather than as an experience. Thanks to this bias, there are not many descriptions by LOC 600s sages of their subjective state. What they do say tends to be vague and lacking in sensory detail.

The LOC 600s sage is having an experience that he calls "pure presence" or "presence awareness." He is established in this. It sounds very good but he is not detecting that this experience is localized. He is not the ocean. He is a local "no self" bubble.

This "pure presence" is an enjoyment of the openness of the "no self" space. This openness is an experience of the absence, loss or lack of a self. It is a void experience. It is a negation.

You may be an enlightened person or not. Either way, you, too, are right now this pure sense of presence, this pure sense of existing or being that is aware of itself. That is the point of the LOC 600s sages. They are right, but they do not take it far enough. This "no self" space is the first step into spaciousness.

You are that aware presence. Described abstractly, it can be made to sound ineffable and cosmic. It can be declared "That's it!" But it is not it. The "no self" is not transcended.[54]

It was only when I switched to my felt sensory modes, to my kinesthetic and proprioceptive perception abilities, that I was able to detect the confinement of the LOC 600s state. I shifted from thinking to pure feeling. Then I felt its subtle limitations.

Like a man groping in the dark, I was able to detect for myself what kind of densities still remained around me. Instead of just thinking and speculating, I made concrete contact with the subtle empty bubble that defined my "no self."

Precisely articulated, the experience of the self in the LOC 600s in sensory terms is one of being spacious in a localized way. The new sage may imagine that his being encompasses the whole world. It does not do that yet. He enjoys what I call a "spherical" sense of self that radiates out in all directions.

To be "an open space of clarity and awareness" is not the final destination.[55] Compared to the painful drama of the separate suffering entity in the world, it may feel like liberation. If it is liberation, then it should be able to stand up to certain tests. It should be able to pass these tests with flying colors.

Since this subjective experience of being the no self non-doer feels free relative to conventional embodied life, exactly how do we expose its limitations? Let's start with my experience of it. At one time, I thought my LOC 600s state was wide open, free and unlimited. Yes, back then I believed I was "done."

From My Spiritual Journal: My Experience of the LOC 600s

Here is a description of the LOC 600s that I wrote when I was at LOC 683. Back then I was fascinated by non-doership.

My notes show that I was making two serious errors. First, I was confusing my "expansion of consciousness" feeling with "universalization." Second, I was equating my "no self" with "the Self." Many LOC 600s sages make the same mistakes.

Just imagine if you did not know if you were ever going to brush your teeth, or comb your hair, or take a shower, or put on clothes, or, even, get out of bed — ever again.

This is what this "non-doership" state is like. You have no idea what is going to happen next because you have no belief at all in your control over anything. It has become absolutely self-evident that you are doing absolutely nothing. Everything down to the tiniest detail — such as brushing your teeth — is simply "being done."

At this point, I must go back and clarify what I mean by the "I" and the "you" that I keep using. I mean by these pronouns "nobody" or "nothing," that which is called either the "no-self" or "the Self."

After terminal ego-death, Consciousness continues to be associated with the human body. If it were not, then that body would just drop dead on the spot. Instead, a human "fragrance," a non-dualistic "up-link," remains.

Consciousness is associated with the body and mediated via the same human phenomena — thoughts, feelings, sensations — that were present before, only now there is nobody identifying with them and nobody thinking that they are doing them or having them.

What remains is sometimes called, in meditation circles, "witness consciousness." However, this is a "witness" that never stops being a witness. There is no returning, no "I have come back." There is neither a going nor a coming back.

Paradoxically, this "expansion of consciousness" into non-localized universalization, so-called "cosmic consciousness," results in life consisting of, well, maintenance of the physical body.

At one level, life is simply reduced to the most ordinary, mundane tasks — opening the eyes, getting up, brushing the teeth, washing the body, eating, talking, breathing, walking, getting tired, and going to bed.

I do not really comprehend the scope of what has happened to me. All I know is that "I am gone!" In its place [replacing the old experience of the separate empirical self] is some kind of pure consciousness or awareness that is featureless, motionless and, apparently, endless.

An Isolated Empty Ball: Retrospective Analysis of LOC 600s

My comments here are based on what I observed when I myself was living day to day at LOC 683. I kept meticulous notes and a detailed spiritual journal.

Yes, I, too was experiencing myself to be an "open space of clarity and awareness" but it lacked a sense of finality for me. Even though I had the confirming sign of non-doership, I could not shake the feeling that something was missing.

I recall vividly that my sense of existence or pure being was that my clear aware empty "no self" presence was akin to a ball, globe or sphere around the physical body. This sense of spherical presence felt like it went out in all directions.

If it was assumed that this state was the final state, then the sage might not investigate this state any further. This state, when it is unexamined, could be interpreted as a sublime state in which there is oneness with everything.

The subjective sense of expanding out in all directions could be interpreted as the supreme "oneness" that the greatest sages of all time were describing. This interpretation would not be correct.

It is exactly what it sounds like it is. From this open empty center which feels spherical to the sage, there is a sense of expanding out in 360 degrees, in all of directions. This is what I mean by localized and spherical. The body is in the world. There is an expansion of the feeling of being in all directions from this body. The body is the center of this expanding out.

While it can be extrapolated from this subjective experience that there is a oneness or that you are "one with everything," that is not actually the experience you are having. What you are experiencing is that you do not have boundaries in the way that you did before with you were bounded by skin.

In this way, the subjective state of "no self" can appear to be an expansion into the world, the universe or infinity. If this state is not closely examined, that is the typical conclusion. It is not that. It is a feeling of expanding outward with no boundaries.

It is not actually a feeling of being identical with the world. That experience comes later. Then your "body" is the world. In the LOC 600s, your "body" is a localized spherical awareness.

It is an affirmation of the localized spherical presence, but it is not an affirmation of the pure self as the totality. The world and the universe have not yet been encountered and absorbed.

The separate self has been negated. A strong experience of non-doership and a sense of spherical presence are the results.

This pleasant feeling of expanding outwards is not conscious ownership of the world. To embrace the world in this new way, the 600s sage must stop looking back at the old world.

When I examined this state of expanding outwards without boundaries, I discovered that I felt limited by this condition. I also experienced that the "no self" center for living without the old ego center felt like a hole, a lack, an emptiness, a nihilistic void. My experience of this "no self" space was not positive.

The 700s: Pure Being Expands and Claims the World as Self

In the LOC 600s, what is being affirmed is the experience of "no self." Automatically, there is also the experience of being the "non-doer." This is authentic legitimate enlightenment.

In the LOC 700s, the experience "I am the world" is affirmed. Your "body" is no longer this local spherical "no self" that feels like it radiates out into the infinite unknown. That infinity is now known. It is you. It is your world. You own it. That vastness is now your new body. It is your new vehicle.

"You are the world" means that you have discovered that the world is your body. You may discover that the universe is your body. Beyond that, you may realize you are bigger than the universe. The entire universe is inside of you. You may vividly experience that the whole universe is inside of you. This is not the same as expanding out from the human body!

These experiences correlate to the authentically expanded state of pure being that is experienced in the LOC 700s. These experiences do not take place in the LOC 600s.

There may be hints and flashes, but this feeling of "I am the world" or "I am the universe" will not last or be understood until the sage is stabilized in the LOC 700s. They take place beyond the LOC 600s. How will the LOC 600s sage know this? He must keep exploring and challenging his own experience.

While the sages in the 600s talk about being pure awareness and being infinite and all of that, they are forgetting the big elephant in the living room: the reality that remains for them of other people and the physical world that they still inhabit.

If you are infinite, then the other people and the world must be *inside* of you. To feel like you are unbounded or expanding in all directions without any boundaries is not the same thing. Feeling boundless is a simple logical consequence of "no self."

It is not the positive expansion into and glorious embrace of infinity. It is the absence of conventional locality. It is the collapse of the existential constriction caused by a biological definition. It is the dissolution of the "skin tight" feeling that results from gross identification with the "I am the body" idea.

The 600s sage has asserted "no self" and "no doing." He has not and he cannot assert "no people" and "no world." He can logically infer that such a state exists based upon his state, but he cannot have the experience of that truth from his state.

The no self non-doing LOC 600s sage may feel boundless and free. He may feel fully "baked." But until the "other" and the "world" (the big "other" that is the last to go) are fully, finally and totally resolved, he cannot say his quest is complete.

In the Absolute, it is experienced that "There is no world." The 600s sage is genuinely enlightened, so he may have eloquent words of wisdom to impart regarding the Absolute. It is one thing to have an intellectual understanding or to extrapolate from your experience. It is another to live that way day to day.

You Must Become the World Before You Can Destroy It

The understanding that there is "no world" is made possible by the realization that "There is only the Self." There is only Supreme I. It is called the Absolute because that is all there is.

If there is anything else at all, then it is not the Absolute. "One without a second" sounds like there is another thing, this second. There is not. There is only the Absolute.

In the LOC 700s, the world is embraced and affirmed as your very own Self. It is not yet the final realization, but it is a big step. No more is the world denied or seen as a problem to be solved. There is now a new unity. Now you are the world.

You may not have a vivid vision of this. It may just be a strong feeling. But this feeling is the knowledge "I am All." I am not a localized emptiness. I feel that the whole world is my identity.

Before the big true Self can gobble up the world and make it go away, which is what happens when the Absolute takes over, you must first own the world and make it yours. You must recognize and actualize your identity with it. Only then will you be able to take the eventual next step and make it disappear for good. It turns out the world is just a thought.

After the world disappears, the Absolute is what will remain. The Absolute eats the world. After it does that, there is nothing left at all. It is impossible to talk about it. Even so, it can be experienced. Stabilization in the Absolute is called sahaja. This means "the natural state." It is ultimate ISness. It is beyond nothing and everything. It is the "stateless state."

The Bizarre Paradox of the Unhappy Discontented "No Self"

The LOC 600s sage has painted himself into a corner. This point is very subtle. The strength of the LOC 600s sages is that they can offer something very simple and direct. But that is also the weakness in their message. They offer a one-way ticket to a wonderful new place. Once you get there, though, you are on your own.

Now you are the "no self" doing nothing going nowhere. There is nothing you can do. According to many of the LOC 600s sages, this "there's nothing you can do" includes *not* being able to help other people realize their own non-dual "no self."

If you have heard that the enlightened state feels open, empty and free, and you are now feeling open, empty and free, it is understandable that you might stop there. Like most LOC 600s sages, you would be satisfied. Most LOC 600s sages are content with that. But there are a few who remain discontent.

It is a fact that some people who attain enlightenment are not happy with their enlightenment. They are in the LOC 600s. They are stabilized in the no self. They are the non-doer. They have arrived, but they are not at peace with or in that state.

Logically, if you are a "no self," this open empty clear space, then you should not have any problems any more. You should not feel unhappy, unfulfilled or discontent.

No, you should be feeling groovy. You should be feeling happy, fulfilled and contented. You are enlightened. You are totally spontaneous. You are living in the flow of life, in the Tao. You have achieved the supreme good of human life.

The "truth" is there plain as day. I am nobody. I have no center. I am an absence. I am an emptiness. I am an open space of pure awareness. I am that open pure aware space. I am that.

After all, if there is "no self," then who is there to be unhappy? Who is there to be discontented? Who can question any of it?

This sounds quite reasonable. If there is nobody to feel discontented, then any feelings like discontentment or unhappiness should just be witnessed and ignored. They are a false signal. They are not of the new "no self." How can you possibly have any problems now? You don't exist!

It seems likely that if the LOC 600s sages is convinced that he has "made it," then he will ignore signs that he can go further and deeper. He will not be interested in signs that maybe he still has work to do. This will be even more likely when friends and teachers (if any), firmly reinforce this view.

But in some cases, even with all the right signs, even when the no self and the non-doership are strongly experienced beyond any doubt, a new discontent arises. This discontent just won't go away. It gnaws away, contradicting your enlightenment.

This discontent arises because the deeper intuition is that freedom is not based on negation and emptiness. Freedom is a state of positive happiness, joy and peace. Merely negating the separate self does not automatically take you there. Absence does not produce happiness. Fullness produces happiness.

This insight may take the sage to the LOC 700s. Yet if they get crystallized in their understanding, they may just stay stuck in a bad mood like the paradoxical sage U. G. Krishnamurti.

Return to the Masters: the Limitations of "No Self" Exposed

When I was in the LOC 600s, I chose to not teach because I could see that being the non-doing no self space was not the final stage of understanding. It resolved the problem I had known about in the previous stage, my "unenlightened" LOC 583 stage. That problem was being a separate isolated entity obsessed with the spiritual search and finding a way out.

My new "no self" solution, discovered after receiving Grace from Ramesh Balsekar after many decades of seeking, validated by the unmistakeable marker of non-doership, was just not good enough. It might have been good enough for Ramesh and others, but it was not good enough for me.

That's when I went back to studying Ramana Maharshi and Nisargadatta Maharaj. I went through their teachings all over again. This time I was studying their words with the deeper understanding that came from being this "no self" space.

Now I was back for graduate work. Everything was at a new level. I felt as if I was hearing and understanding these great masters for the first time.

It dawned on me that I was suffering from localization of an intrinsically universal pristine awareness. This accounted for the very subtle confinement, the sense of a confining tangible density or shell or veil, that I could still feel surrounding me.

I had been reborn as this pure presence. I was a new baby in a new invisible womb. I was waking up in this womb. I was finding that the walls of this new spiritual womb were confining to me. I felt limited by them. I felt too big for them.

These new walls no longer felt safe and protective. They felt limiting and confining. In the LOC 580s, the physical body had felt limiting and confining. Now at LOC 683, this localized borderless spiritual self that seemed to expand out in all directions was starting to feel the same way to me.

Not only that, life remained problematic. Other people and the world were still difficult for me. I did not understand this.

I had believed that if the empirical self was gone, then issues with other people and the world would automatically go away. They would be eliminated. I was totally wrong. Other people and the world were still up in my face. They were still creating problems for me. This was a shocking discovery.

Case Study: Non-Duality According to Fred Davis (LOC 675)

Fred Davis is a popular non-dual author. He has developed a practical method for bringing people into his understanding. It seems that his technique has produced plenty of success stories. So let's ask the question "What is his understanding?"

On one of his websites, Davis defines non-duality as "oneness." This wonderful oneness is "connected." It is "flowing." It is "always moving." It reforms itself endlessly. His "oneness" is a lively dynamic fascinating happening.[56]

Davis knows that a merely intellectual grasp of this engaging concept is not enough. According to Davis, in order to live in this understanding from day to day, this oneness must be seen for yourself. It must lead to "the absence of a personal me." When you meet these two conditions, you will recognize who "you already are" and be what is called "enlightened."[57]

Other experiences may arise. For example, you may feel that you are waking up from a dream. Not everybody gets that feeling. But everybody who has awakened has seen this ever-changing oneness for themselves. They have seen that there is no "personal me" who is separate from this oneness.[58]

I'm Enlightened, But What About Our Troubled Planet?

Davis goes on to talk about the need for fixing our "planetary problems." He passionately writes that we need lots of people to wake up in order to heal and save our physical planet.

The web page I am quoting is an extract of the Introduction to his new book *Beyond Recovery*.[59] His book does a great job of expressing the LOC 600s non-dual understanding.

Davis cares about people. He wants to save the planet. He wants to quickly awaken as many people as he can to this lovely wonderful understanding that he has. He believes that we need lots of awakened people who want to save the planet.

If that's good enough for you, great. There's nothing wrong with that. But is that really all there is to enlightenment?

Is the ultimate truth really that there is just this "oneness" that is always fluctuating and changing and morphing? Is the final truth merely to merge with this foamy seascape of endlessly evolving oneness, this cavorting consommé of consciousness?

Even though Davis no longer has a personal me, he is nonetheless rather deeply troubled by the state of the planet. In fact, so concerned is he that he is strongly advocating that all of the non-doers out there do something about it!

No Personal Me? Zero. Other? Whap! World? Whap! Whap!

I am showcasing the articulate Davis as the voice for the LOC 600s spiritual teachers. His words illustrate the practical and spiritual limitations of the new sage in the LOC 600s stage.

I listened to lots of interviews. I read books by more than a dozen LOC 600s teachers. I chose Davis because his views seemed to best represent this group as a whole.

Davis is a warmhearted person who cares about other people and about the planet. That's wonderful. But his realization has not resolved the solid independent existence of "other people."

It does not seem to have done anything for him about the solid independent existence of this so-called "world," either. It's still "out there." It's still problematic for him. He writes as if other people and the world are an uncontested indisputable reality for Fred Davis, the "no self." But that is not "oneness." His "no self" lives in bounded space with multiple densities.

Other people and the world are being described as a great grand container for the Fred Davis "no self" space experience. He treats this container as "real." By this I mean he is not questioning it or challenging it. Fred is not alone in this. This is the modus operandi of LOC 600s sages. They do not see it.

The Fred Davis experience is a localized borderless space in a bigger bounded space. The boundaries of this bigger space are the invisible yet tangible densities called "people" and "world."

These densities can be felt if the sage extends his awareness outward via kinesthetic perception to "feel" or "sense" these limits to his local "no self" space. If he assumes that expanding from a local space that feels borderless is identical to being one with the universe, he will not see the value of this test.

I am not saying this is unique to Fred Davis. I am saying that he has done a great job of articulating the real life position of the enlightened LOC 600s realizer. He has spoken frankly from his heart about what is important to him, about what matters to him. I thank him for that. I applaud him for that.

My focus is on the subtext of his message, the one he carefully and thoughtfully put together in this Introduction to his new book *Beyond Recovery*. Yes, Fred Davis is enlightened. Yes, he is without a "personal self." He is LOC 675. He is awakened.

Yet this same Fred Davis is making it abundantly clear that for him "other people" remain very real and the apparent "world" out there remains very real. Not only that, although he is cool with it, they represent for him serious problems to be solved.

That is the subtext I am picking up on. Let's ask the obvious question. If Fred Davis and people like him, the non-dual teachers in the LOC 600s, are going around with an experience of oneness along with not having a personal self, then how come they are still focused on a world and on other people?

If you're in touch with perfect supreme ultimate oneness, then shouldn't that solve all of that stuff? Shouldn't living in the sublime state of direct perception of ultimate oneness bring an end to what are clearly unresolved dualistic issues?

There Are Different Types and Degrees of "Oneness"

The answer is "Yes, it should." Therefore, there are different kinds or grades of oneness. It is these different degrees of oneness that distinguish one stage of non-dual enlightenment from another.

In the LOC 600s oneness, there is "no self" but the "no" part does not extend to other people and the world. If it did, then other people and the world would have been annihilated along with the body-identified empirical separate self.

This annihilation of the other and the world takes place when the Absolute is attained. It does not take place before then. It is only after this annihilation has taken place that perfect rest is possible. Until then, there will always be some kind of "other" that is bothering you like unwelcome ants at your picnic. The "no self" is still looking back at the old self and the old world. There is a new curious duality in place. Instead of "self" versus other people, now the scenario is "no self" versus other people. Instead of "self" versus the world, now the scenario is "no self" versus the world. It seems "no self" needs a world, too.

Even if this new scenario tends to play out more smoothly in your day to day life, there is no avoiding the fact that this is a dualistic setup. The new "no self" of the LOC 600s is able to be a witness to these paradoxes, but that does not remove them.

If you do not find this limiting in any way, then the insight that Fred Davis is advocating will be adequate for you. If you are smelling something fishy with this kind of understanding, though, go to the head of the class. You see, getting rid of the empirical self or personal me does not get rid of your sense of "the other." This "other" can be a person. It can be the world.

Even Though There Is "No Me," There Is Still "the Other."

When I achieved my awakening in 1992 a few years after meeting my guru Ramesh Balsekar, I had already studied everything I could find on the state of enlightenment. I was fascinated by the subject and learned all that I could about it.

As a result, I had many expectations. After my awakening, I found out that most of them were wrong.

As for my ideas that turned out to be more or less correct, my pre-enlightenment understanding of them was so far off track that I might as well have been wrong. In short, enlightenment for me was a catastrophic and utterly shocking event.

It was catastrophic in the sense that it destroyed all that I had held dear. It was the end of the life for the person who had been born. A new person was born into this world in 1992. It was all these things, but I was quite glad it happened.

One of my chief assumptions was that if the separate self was to totally drop away, this would be the end of the matter. That would be that. With the empirical self or personal me out of the picture, then any issues having to do with other people or the world would also be resolved with deafening finality. In brief, how could "I" have problems if "I" didn't exist anymore?

What I discovered was that the disappearance of the separate self and the advent of a state of non-doership that satisfied the strict guidelines of the *Bhagavad Gita* did *not* get rid of those "other" people and it did *not* get rid of the "world" out there.

I will say that again. When my separate self ended, the feeling of there being other people and the feeling of there being a world out there did not go away. Those feelings continued!

I was now separate from activity as a soft spacious spherical awareness that expanded outward in all directions, but this had not eliminated the invisible "metaframe" of those "other" people and the "in my face" world "out there." There was "no me," there was "no self," but there was still "other" (in the form of other people and a very big planet outside of this "no me").

Your Separate Self and the Invasion by the Invisible Other

This problem is not going to arise before enlightenment. It shows up only after the separate self has been eliminated.

The natural expectation is that, since the unenlightened life has this personal me which is a pain in the butt, getting rid of it via enlightenment is pretty much going to solve everything.

An unrealistic expectation would be that life will be like magic all of the time. That's not what I mean. The rational notion is that when the personal me is gone, the other will be gone, too.

It turns out that this is not true at all. The reason is that the experience of a personal me, ego or empirical separate self was produced when you were invaded at a very early age by "the Other." This Other took the form of your parents, of your school teachers, of anybody and everybody who was bigger than you and some kind of an authority in your life.

The "you" that you thought of as you did not come first. The "Other" came first. The Other created you. This Other is your hidden context. This Other is the womb space of you as a separate self. When you get enlightened and attain to the "no self," you discover that this Other is still your womb space.

So when "you" or the little "me" goes away in LOC 600s enlightenment, the deep impact of the big Other who invaded you when you were a child still remains. Somehow this sense of Other goes on. Whether your experience as a human being is that of a self or a no self, the Other lives on as your context.

Your new opportunity in the LOC 600s is that you can finally investigate and embrace this womb space and gain liberation though it. This is expansion of pure being takes place in the LOC 700s. In the LOC 700s, you discover and embrace the outer limits of the great womb space. Later, in higher LOCs, you transcend even that realization of cosmic consciousness.

Jean-Paul Sartre Said It Best: "Hell is other people."

Now you have awakened. Now your sense of separate self has died. Now you are in touch with oneness. Now your LOC is in the 600s. And now you find out that there are still "others" and there is still a "world" out there. I don't blame you if you are confused. I know I was.

That revelation puts a rather nasty kink into your glorious experience of oneness. Although your new experience of oneness beats the pants off of anything you experienced before you got enlightened, your LOC 600s type of oneness has got two serious flaws: other people and the world.

When I found this out, it was a massive disappointment. I felt lied to and misled. It was a huge letdown for me. What was the point of this "enlightenment" crap if it couldn't do anything about all those other people, about the world?

As this new spiritual crisis escalated inside of me, this lack of self, this "no self," turned into psychological torture. I was an isolated stranded empty blank comatose "non-doing no self." I was powerless. My "no self," pure and aware though it was, felt to me like heartless void bereft of love and joy. If the price of this serenely objective clarity was that I was doomed to a soulless pointless vacant barren unfeeling state, I wanted out.

Even worse, I was enclosed and imprisoned by billions of cold loveless others in a faceless indifferent monolithic world. In contrast to Jeff Foster's hit non-dual title *An Extraordinary Absence*,[60] my "absence" was *not* "extraordinary." It was the opposite. It was worse than ordinary. It was hell. With my familiar sense of self gone, nothing anywhere brought me comfort. I was truly inconsolable. This new emptiness was my new prison cell. I was a pointless blank, a zero, a cypher.

Oneness or no oneness, life was garbage and it stunk. I was reminded of Jean-Paul Sartre and his famous statement "Hell is other people."[61] Jean-Paul, wherever you are, you're right!

I want to make it clear that I had definitely not fallen out of my state. I was not regressing. Oh, no, I was still totally the no self and the non-doer. I tested that and made sure of it.

Something else was going on. I had not been able to uncover it before my LOC 600s enlightenment. My non-doing "no self" space had not improved the quality of my life.

It had not enhanced my sense of well-being. Instead, I was trapped in a new prison, a dark empty hopeless "ghost cave" of despair.

I would have to come up with my own solution. My feelings and my kinesthetic sense were deeply refined. Like a blind person, I would feel my way into and through the darkness. One thing I could do was find out if anybody else had arrived at an authentic state of enlightenment and then suffered from a bitter corrosive emptiness and nihilistic breakdown like me.

Case Study: the Enlightened Curmudgeon U. G. (LOC 678)

U. G. Krishnamurti recently passed away. He was a walking contradiction. His dramatic awakening left no doubt that he was a genuinely enlightened person. Yet he delighted in telling people he could not help them. He traveled around the world teaching, yet he said he was not a spiritual teacher.

Here are a just a few of the many mind boggling quotes from this ruthless, godless, nihilistic, idol smashing LOC 678 rascal.

> Don't follow me, I'm lost.
>
> We are not created for any grander purpose than the ants that are there or the flies that are hovering around us or the mosquitoes that are sucking our blood.
>
> I discovered for myself and by myself that there is no self to realize — that's the realization I am talking about. It comes as a shattering blow. It hits you like a thunderbolt.
>
> You have invested everything in one basket, self-realization, and, in the end, suddenly you discover that there is no self to discover, no self to realize — and you say to yourself "What the hell have I been doing all my life?!" That blasts you.
>
> I am not out to liberate anybody. You have to liberate yourself, and you are unable to do that. What I have to say will not do it. I am only interested in describing this state, in clearing away the occultation and mystification in which those people in the "holy business" have shrouded the whole thing. Maybe I can convince you not to waste a lot of time and energy, looking for a state which does not exist except in your imagination.[62]

Born Cynic U. G. Krishnamurti Was Never a Happy Camper

U. G. Krishnamurti was not a happy camper. Ever.

If you want to be happy, then learn from happy people. U. G. Krishnamurti was not a happy person. He was not happy before his enlightenment. He was not happy after it.

I suspect that the average seeker assumes that enlightenment will automatically produce happiness for him. It will not.

There is nothing in all of the vividly documented details of U. G.'s awakening that speaks of anything other than his arrival at a profound absence of self in a context of non-doing. The reports of his experiences make for fantastic reading. Yet throughout is the same thread: absence of self, nothing more.

He never recognized that his state was not the end state. Since he was convinced that all the saints and sages were phonies, there was nowhere for him to go. There would not be a higher state or a better place for him.

Hoisted by his own petard, he lived a curiously dramatic life filled with nihilistic paradoxes. He presumed to show others the way, or to show them that there was no way, yet he lived in a dead end void that he himself could not transcend.

Even as a teenager, U. G. cast a cynical eye on gurus, religion and the whole "holy business." He was dedicated skeptic. He loved exposing human hypocrisy. His own grandmother remarked that he had "the heart of a butcher."[63]

Even though U. G. Krishnamurti asserted that there was nothing a person could do to attain his state, he evolved into the consummate anti-guru guru. "I have no message for mankind. But of one thing I am certain, I cannot help you solve your basic dilemma or save you from self-deception, and IF I CAN'T HELP YOU, NO ONE CAN."[64]

Please note that the capitalized words are in the original. He is really going all out to mess with people's minds!

For a properly prepared fortunate few, his strategy will put them into a double-bind that gets resolved in enlightenment. For the majority, though, this "no exit" strategy will produce doubt, distress, depression and discouragement.

When the skeptical cynical melodramatic melancholic U. G. Krishnamurti attained enlightenment, it did not change his personality. It did not change his tendencies. Self or no self, he just kept right on going as the nihilistic jaundiced juggernaut.

The U. G. before his enlightenment was convinced nobody could help him or help anybody else. The U. G. after his enlightenment was convinced of the same thing. This U. G. personality was so blinded by his own skepticism he could not see in his own life convincing evidence to the contrary.

In life, we get to decide if the cup is half empty or half full. U. G. decided that it was half empty. He stuck to that view until the bitter end. Indeed, what enjoyment he did have he seemed to derive from shocking people with his pessimistic insights.

U. G. Krishnamurti: Enlightened Via Grace at Satsang

The greatest paradox of all is that even though his position was that nobody can help anybody, his awakening occurred in the context of listening to Jiddu Krishnamurti speak live in Saanen, Switzerland on the morning of July 9, 1967.

In today's parlance, U. G. Krishnamurti was attending the satsang of the well-known sage Jiddu Krishnamurti. He had not intended to go, but via a curious synchronicity having to do with writing his autobiography, he attended the talk.

About halfway into Jiddu Krishnamurti's talk, when Jiddu was describing the state of a man who was free, U. G. had the sudden recognition that the famous globetrotting sage was describing U. G.'s own state. U. G. thought "What the hell am I doing listening to someone describe how I am functioning?"

Dazed and confused by this surprising turn of events, he abruptly left the meeting and headed towards his chalet. For no apparent reason, he decided instead to sit down on a bench which had a stunning view of the Saanen Valley. It was there, sitting on that bench before mountains and rivers that testified to nature's glory, his "explosion," his "calamity," happened.[65]

His entire life had been preparation for this moment. The "chance" encounter with Jiddu Krishnamurti can be seen as the cherry on top for a profound spiritually engineered event.

Even though U. G.'s interpretation of what happened to him, how it happened and why it happened is shockingly nihilistic, that is merely his interpretation based upon his unusual background and his melancholic personality. Either way, he was a born skeptic and an aggressive irreverent nihilist. Enlightened, he was still a sharp-tongued cynic with "the heart of a butcher" who did not care who he skewered or how.

An eloquent rascal such as U. G. Krishnamurti has his place in this modern materialistic world where quantum science has become the new religion. But we need to separate the man, the diehard skeptic and bitter nihilist, from his life and message.

His life can just as easily be interpreted to say that he was destined to attain enlightenment. His awakening took place through Grace.

The triggering event was listening to the deeply enlightened man who, whether he accepted it or not, was his guru. Prior to that meeting, his separate will, his drive to survive, had been slowly melting away in preparation.

Not only that, this event occurred in his 49th year. Many years previously, a respected astrologer known as the Kowmara Nadi had predicted that a great spiritual event would happen to U. G. on his 49th birthday.[66] This is a matter of record.

So when was U. G. born? July 9, 1918. In the morning.[67]

When did his spiritual event occur? On July 9, 1967. In the morning. On his 49th birthday as predicted years before.

U. G. Krishnamurti can say it is all garbage because it is the nature of his personality to do so. When he interprets his LOC 678 enlightenment as a waste of time and a farce, he is wrong. His prejudices did not allow him to investigate his state any deeper. If he had, he would have drastically changed his tune.

Enlightenment LOC 600s: Conception of the Baby Buddha

The ever cheerful and enthusiastic Jeff Foster is also at LOC 678.[68] What accounts for the difference in apparent happiness and warmth of personality between him and U. G.?

You can say it is the parents, the childhood, early influences and any other factors that create the personality and attitudes of the man he will be when he has matured. The contrast between them clarifies a point often missed: enlightenment cannot be counted on to change your personality.

If you were an unhappy, moody, bitter skeptic like U. G. before enlightenment, it is likely that you will be just as unhappy after enlightenment into the LOC 600s. For some, there is a major positive personality change. But not for all.

I am referring to the first stage of enlightenment, to the LOC 600s. The man is not yet transformed. That occurs later. I can vouch from my own experience that the desired changes, the happiness, peace and sense of well-being, are found in the LOC 700s and up. Yes, the summum bonum is LOC 1000.

That is the enlightenment project. Awakening into the "no self" is the beginning of a new kind of transformation. The ego center that would have prevented the deepest possible transformations out of its fear and its need for survival is no longer calling the shots. Deep down, we are all the Buddha.

Awakening into the LOC 600s is the conception of the baby Buddha in the "no self" womb of genuine enlightenment. If the person already has a kind, humble and charming personality, it may seem like they have completed their work. Perhaps for them it will turn out to be enough, at least in this life.

There are many excellent non-dual teachers in the LOC 600s. It is perfect that they are there living with that understanding. It is perfect that they are teaching from there. Everything is as it should be. That is the truth and the reality.

My message is an advance warning to the seeker that you may not get what you need until you go *all* the way (LOC 1000). My message is for those who sense that something is missing in the "There is nothing you can do" of the LOC 600s sages.

My message is for those who attained enlightenment and, like me, found it somehow wanting. The realization of LOC 600 about non-duality is legitimate, but it is incomplete.

I want my message out for people to hear in case it applies to them. If it applies, great. If it doesn't, then that's fine, too.

I sincerely want as many people as possible to be happy and free. To me, a state of freedom which lacks love and happiness is not a state worth keeping and cultivating. Freedom cannot be an absence of anything. It is a celebration of everything.

Those who can celebrate the missing self of the LOC 600s have it in their nature to do so. For others, it simply is not enough.

LOC 600s Gallery of Rogues, Rascals and Renegades

The LOC 600s are colorful. Fred Davis (LOC 675), Jeff Foster (LOC 678), John Wheeler (LOC 692) and Leo Hartong (LOC 692), to name a few, are kind caring heart-centered people.

They have written excellent books that share their view of enlightenment. They emphasize demystifying non-duality and making it accessible.

They and many more LOC 600 sages are doing a great job of quickly and compassionately awakening people around the planet. They are gentle loving people who clearly have the best interests of those they help at heart. The vast majority are demonstrating that the realization of non-duality goes beyond sitting on a mountain. Enlightenment changes the world.

However, more than any other non-dual stage, the LOC 600s offers a true rogues gallery of surprising "outside of the box" sages. In the LOC 600s, you are having your cake and eating it, too. You are looking back at the world and engaging the world, but from a unique and powerful non-dual perspective.

This makes for mind bending blends of spiritual attainment fused with profoundly questionable morality. These souls soar above the mundane shuffle, but their vision may be twisted.

This can be expressed as a demonstration of extreme genius. They may never say a word about "non-duality." The LOC 600s sage takes his spiritual insight and integrates it into society in his own very highly original special way.

The amorality of the LOC 600s state is a side effect of having "no self" in a worldly context. Though it is an illusion, it seems like the laws and rules that apply to the ordinary person do not apply to you. This roguish sense of freedom beyond laws and rules may be joyfully expressed as creative brilliance within a human discipline. Or it may be taken to its logical extreme of violating human rights and dashing human hopes.

In most cases, this mundane contribution to modern society is perceived as beneficial for all. But this is not always the case. Some LOC 600s sages are highly controversial. You will see what I mean. Very few therapists, psychics, occultists or cult leaders are enlightened. But a few in recent history were. One of these is in prison for masterminding multiple murders.

Jim Morrison
Rock star and lead singer of "The Doors."
LOC 693

Carlos Castaneda
Controversial bestselling author-shaman-guru.
LOC 672

Milton Erickson
Father of Neuro-Linguistic Programming (NLP).
LOC 673

Ingo Swann
Gifted Painter, Psychic and Father of Remote Viewing.
LOC 653

Terence McKenna
Botanist who taught dissolving ego knot with psychedelics.
LOC 684

Aleister Crowley
Notorious British occultist with many modern followers.
LOC 665.8 (666?)

Charles Manson
Infamous cult leader of "The Family."
LOC 653

Friedrich Nietzche
Respected "God is dead" philosopher who went insane.
LOC 662

LOC 600s Sage: Mutually Assumed Deep Hidden Structure

Whether or not you agree that these people were enlightened, their impact on our culture has been massive. They had *power*.

1000

They did what they did because of the freedom they felt. They were their own highest authority. That is what they knew.

Their unconscious assumption was that the correct play is to engage and transform society. This proves that their bias was fixed inside the context of other people and the world. They had the advantage of a higher view, of an enlightened non-dual perspective. Their emphasis on mundane achievement exposes a bias intrinsic to the realization of all LOC 600s sages.

I refer to mutually assumed deep hidden structure. You can be at a party with other people in a house as a doing self or as a non-doing no self. Either way, your focus is on the party, not the house. "House" symbolizes people and world. These contents of consciousness are not usually challenged.

Likewise, you can remain unconscious of your existential social substratum, of other people and the world, as apparent realities that you are assuming and posturing for yourself moment to moment. A deep hidden societal context or deep human cultural matrix is functioning as your environment.

You are a self or a no self, but either way your greater context, your invisible "metaframe," remains untested by you. You are aware of other people, of the world as being real, substantial and solid. You yourself may seem to exist or to not exist, but either way you have not yet understood that you are the source of the perceived substantiality of the estranged "other."

You can rebel or not rebel. In either behavior, you are validating the substance of otherness. Your options appear to be limited. The assumption of this frame is an old habit.

You will not examine this until you begin to realize that this invisible boundary condition imprisons you. This mutually assumed deep hidden structure is so embedded that the insight and ability to go beyond it and transform it does not arise until enlightenment. Even then many still project it.

You have been granting the other in the form of other people and your environment a substance that is derived from you, not from them. In the LOC 700s, you realize this substance is derived from you as the totality. But this is a dangerous insight in the hands of person who is not yet ready for it.

LOC 600s Risk: Amorality, Nihilism and Anti-Freedom

In a way, it is a good thing that the world and the other are being granted undeniable reality and substance by the LOC 600s sage. If in realizing non-doership and the no self you did not find others or a world that you needed to acknowledge, then as an LOC 600s sage you could assault people and the planet in a cold hard-hearted psychopathic or narcissistic manner and have no notion of there being any consequences.

Such self-serving solipsism offers vast potential for amoral destructive behavior. The defiant nihilism and provocative cynicism of U. G. Krishnamurti is this negative negation of the other and the world taken to the verbal interpersonal level.

In his case, his disregard for rules made him a globetrotting anti-guru. In his celebration of his freedom, he did not respect the freedom of his listeners. Because he was relating as a no self non-doer, he saw no other option available to him. Nor did he see the possibility for error on the path he chose.

Case Study: Enlightened Sociopath C. Manson (LOC 653)

This amoral indifference, love of chaos and lack of ethical brakes can be further escalated by the no self non-doer. The classic example is cult leader and convicted murderer Charles Manson (LOC 653). It is controversial for me to say Manson is enlightened. There is no question for me. He is enlightened.

The Google search "charles manson enlightened" brings up a fascinating interview of Manson by Charlie Rose. Manson offers non-dualistic answers from his state of enlightenment. Rose fails utterly when he tries to paint him as a "monster."[69]

In the Introduction to his book *Our Savage God*, R. C. Zaehner states that Charles Manson had accessed at least one time (if not several times), probably through the use of drugs, an authentic state of non-dual enlightenment. He experienced the "eternal Now" where he found all opposites transcended.[70]

Zaehner argues that Manson then interpreted the *Bhagavad Gita* in the light of this experience to say that he, Manson, could kill with impunity and without consequences. Thanks to his mystical attainment, Manson viewed himself as having transcended conventional morality, ethics and responsibility.

Manson is thought to have consulted the well-known Chapter Two, Verse 19. It says "Those who think that they can kill or get killed are wrong. You can neither kill nor get killed."[71]

A recent new biography, *Manson* by Jeff Guinn, argues that Manson was an "opportunistic sociopath" from childhood.[72]

We have a devil's brew, perhaps, of a clever psychopath with an LOC of 653 convinced by holy scripture that he is above the law. Though locked up in prison for life, Manson still attracts people and displays an extraordinary magnetism. We can learn a crucial lesson about the LOC 600s from him. His literal interpretation of the impersonal "All is One" is an eye-opener.

Enlightenment does not make you a saint. Enlightenment does not make you a better human being. You may become a better person after LOC 600s enlightenment. But you could become a much worse person. Enlightenment is not about morality.

To some extent, this streak of amorality extends to the LOC 700s sages. Power may be abused in the usual ways we are all so tired of hearing about — sexual misconduct, misuse of financial donations, abuse of drugs. It is only in the LOC 800s and above that we find the mystical love, the experience of the other as your very own beloved Self, taking over the behavior.

The LOC 600s Sage: the Master One to One Coach

It is not enough just to be enlightened. As they say in Zen, enlightened or not, you still have to chop wood and carry water. Translated to modern living, that means we still need to know the rules and abide by the rules. We still have to pay our bills and do our best to handle other people skillfully.

Maturation in the LOC 600s stage is learning how to make this work while at the same time uncovering the limitations of the LOC 600s. He is preparing for the next higher stage, the cosmic consciousness of the LOC 700s.

There, too, amorality and behavioral violations may emerge. In the LOC 700s, identification is now with the cosmic ego rather than local no self consciousness. The group is the new arena of engagement. The spiritual voltage is intensified.

The LOC 600s sages excel at one to one coaching. Fred Davis, for example, is a master at it. He is exceptionally skilled at initiating people into non-duality. That is his specialty.

John Wheeler (LOC 692) also has this skill in abundance. John works very quickly using direct pointing questions. He has had many successes. Both men show great compassion, kindness and humility in their work.

The LOC 700s Sage: Creator of New Enlightenment Tools

When a person moves up to the LOC 700s, their interest often changes from doing one to one coaching work to discovering a solution that can be applied to the individual or group with or without the LOC 700s sage present. Their interest is now in facilitating a solution that is universally applicable without their personal involvement or immediate supervision.

They train and coach others in their unique innovative awakening methods. These student coaches may or may not be enlightened themselves. The emphasis of many LOC 700s sages is on the radical methodology that they have developed.

Two examples of this approach to enlightening the world are Byron Katie and Scott Kiloby. I will explore their world, the stage of the LOC 700s sage, very soon.

I will also talk about Mandi Solk, a woman in the United Kingdom who realized that her enlightenment at LOC 657 had left her half-baked. She dedicated herself all over again to Self-inquiry. She quickly rose up to LOC 758. She now enjoys the peace and joy that her heart had yearned for at her new LOC.

But first I want to set the stage. I have kept a detailed spiritual journal since 2001. I fully intended to keep this journal private. I was writing for myself. I never expected to publish any of it.

In the next chapter, I will tell you about my transition from LOC 683 ("no self") to LOC 776 ("cosmic self"). I welcomed this movement to the next stage of awakening. The life event that triggered the spiritual shock for this shift was brutally painful.

My Spiritual Journal:

From No Self to Cosmic Self

(LOC 683 to LOC 776)

My Journey from No Self to Cosmic Self

My transition from LOC 600s ("no self") to LOC 776 ("cosmic self") took place in 2000. I did not keep a journal during that period of time. I was basically in shock for most of the year.

I have referenced LOC 776 for the title of this chapter because when I jumped from "no self" to "cosmic self," the movement was from LOC 683 to LOC 776. When this leap took place, I did not have the context for it that I do now. I was dealing with LOC 776 and its ramifications at the time.

The journal entries in this chapter show my progression from LOC 776 to LOC 793 in preparation for my next big jump to LOC 845. These excerpts show how I went back and forth as I stabilized in the LOC 700s. The later entries convey what I was experiencing once I had entered into the fullness of that level.

The story of how I shifted into the LOC 700s may not be what you expect. It was not the result of me meditating for days on a retreat. The event that produced the spiritual shock behind this big shift was as earthy as it gets. I got my heart broken.

The short version is I had fallen in love with a woman 12 years younger than me. For the first few years, this was okay. I was in my 40s. She was in her 30s. But then other differences arose.

It turned out that my idea of a good time together was to stay at home and hang out together. Her idea of a good time with each other was to go climb a mountain or do some other new adventure. Eventually, she found another lover while she was still living with me. She ended up marrying him.

1000

There is nothing new or original about this kind of story. It happens to people every day around the world. The difference was in the intensity of the impact of our breakup on me.

This impact went far beyond the fact that I was still in love with her when we separated. It was the equivalent of using a nuclear bomb to kill a fly. The emotional impact left me without the ability to feel for almost a year.

This nuclear bomb had completely fried my emotional circuits. I literally could not feel anything. I functioned in life like an efficient indifferent automaton. My body and mind were fine. Yet I no longer had emotions like before.

The funny thing was that I didn't care. This total and utter lack of emotion began to feel like a blessing to me.

At first, I was shocked by it. It seemed like a terrible thing. Then it dawned on me the extent to which I had still been pushed around and manipulated by my emotional needs. When this spiritual shock hit me in 2000, I had already been living in non-doership as the empty no self for eight years.

This devastating shock occurred in January, 2000. In October, 2000 I moved to Las Vegas, Nevada. I had seen waking visions like vivid daydreams of a city with neon lights blazing.

While watching a new TV show based in Las Vegas I realized that it was the place that was being shown to me. I had never been there before. I had no interest in it, yet the signs were beyond obvious.

The one thing that really attracted me was the non-stop sunshine. I was done with the rain that poured from the Portland, Oregon skies a full 10 months of the year.

I moved to downtown Las Vegas. That's the old part with the old casinos. One casino was from the early 1900s. I like history so I enjoyed that aspect. For six months, I talked to no one.

There was one exception. I would speak to the store clerk when I need to know the price of something. For some reason, they didn't want to put prices on things so I had to ask.

I met my wife Linda in Las Vegas in November, 2001. It was about a year after I moved there. During that whole time I had had no interest in dating or in sex or in having an intimate relationship. I didn't care if I had friends either, but there was a guy, an old TM meditator, who liked me and insisted on hanging out with me. He was a salesman. I couldn't say no.

Not dating and not caring about having a relationship may not sound like a big deal to you, but it was for me. Just think of the biggest most important most critical need that you have.

It could be money, food, reputation, love, relationships, sex, adventure, laughter, meditation, health. It doesn't matter. It just has to be the thing you want to have in your life more than anything else. Other things can go, but not this need.

Now imagine that that need has been blasted away as if by a nuclear bomb. In its place is devastation and no feeling at all. You simply cannot even muster up that feeling anymore.

Your need for that thing, that experience, has been wiped off the face of the earth. You are left with the memory of how you used to be, of what you used to feel, of what you used to do.

You are no longer that person. You will never be them again. This change is total, final and forever. That need is dead.

Anyway, I no longer needed to be in a relationship. I didn't care one way or the other at all. Sex was still of interest to me. But the whole relationship thing made no sense to me at all.

I did end up getting into a relationship. I did get married. But when I did that, I still felt the same way. You could call this experience "high indifference." I was in the relationship but I didn't feel bound by it at all. To be in the relationship felt just as free to me as not being in the relationship. Both were okay.

I could love her yet I truly did not care what happened either way. Paradoxically, this enabled me to love even more. I had no personal agendas, conscious or subconscious.

I marveled at the wisdom of the universe. Somehow I had ended up with what I wanted. I had always wanted to be able to be in a relationship without feeling needy or incomplete.

The irony was that this had come to me only because I no longer cared if I got it or not. I no longer wanted it or needed it, so I had it. I didn't care at all, it didn't make me happier, yet now I had more love in my life than I knew what to do with.

You may be wondering what this story of losing love and finding love has to do with cosmic consciousness and the transition to the LOC 700s. Sometimes life is the guru.

I tell you my personal human story because I want to make it clear that the spiritual shock that takes you to the next stage can appear in any form. God or the Self will do whatever it takes. It will use whatever It can to wake you up.

When my heart got broken in Portland, Oregon, the impact shifted me to a new level of non-attachment that I had not been able to achieve before based on my own efforts. A life shock was needed and that was exactly what I got. It came from where I least expected it, too, the relationship area.

In the next section, I have organized excerpts from my spiritual diary in chronological order. You will be able to read how I progressed from my tortured obsession with the "no self" to glorious expansion into universal consciousness. To be clear, in this book I use the expressions "cosmic consciousness" and "universal consciousness" to mean the same thing.

In my case, the process unfolded slowly and gradually. You could say it happened at a turtle's pace. But the ground that was gained was held. I mainly just moved steadily forward.

Some people move quickly and may even jump ahead. Then they have to backtrack and fill in what they didn't do.

I prefer to thoroughly test the new ground before I step on it. I know this slowed me down, but it has given me confidence in the process. I have seen the steps and stages in great detail.

Introduction to My Spiritual Diary (2001 to 2006)

When I wrote them down on printer paper, coiled student notebooks, index cards and restaurant napkins, these entries were for my own private reflection. I had no intention of showing them to friends, much less publishing them.

In the course of writing this book, I realized that these private jottings, with their naive thrill of discovery, their freshness in finding the unexpected, their rawness when shocked and disappointed, did as good a job as my words could do to convey the internal emotional life while on this journey.

The spiritual shock of losing the girlfriend I was in love with hit me in January, 2000. I was in Portland, Oregon. My LOC right before this event was 689. This shock left me without feelings. That sounds vague or impossible, but it's the best way I can describe it. My internal emotional life had been rich, lively and varied. It was now a barren wasteland. It was like the devastation after a nuclear blast. Everything is wiped out.

It took about a year, but my feelings did come back. When they did, they were different. I felt feelings, but with a detachment I had never had before. The content and sensation was there, the meaning was there, but the involvement was not there.

At first, I thought this was the entire "gift" from the traumatic spiritual shock. I believed this new dimension of "non-attachment" was the "silver lining" in the dark clouds of my suffering. I was wrong. There was more. I would soon be enjoying a new "oneness" that put the old "oneness" to shame.

Below are excerpts in chronological order from my spiritual journal. It really was a slow steady transformation over time.

I would like for you to see the progression as I move from the solo "no self" to celebrating "I am everything." In LOC terms, these private journal entries, which I wrote only for myself at the time, document my expansion from the empty "no self" space of the LOC 600s to the cosmic self of the LOC 700s. This entire stage is covered up to the next spiritual shock in April, 2006, the passage through the pitch black Void of Unknowing.

I would also like you to notice how it is not just a linear march forward. It is more like a "two steps forward, one step back." I included a few such entries so that you can appreciate how this frustrating rhythm of integration is part of the process. In spite of my subjective dramas, my LOC remained stable.

I moved from Portland to Las Vegas in October. My LOC at my arrival in the famous neon jungle was 776. I did not keep a spiritual diary during 2000. As I was so incredibly "numbed out," I had nothing worth talking about. I had nothing to say.

I returned to keeping my spiritual diary after moving to Las Vegas. My feelings had returned. For the first few years, Las Vegas was an exciting place to live. Its mirror-like qualities, its eagerness to reflect and fulfill my projections and fantasies, made it an ideal place to continue my journey of awakening.

The new diary entries in 2001 reflect a small rise in my LOC (from LOC 776 in October, 2000 to LOC 778 in March, 2001). They also show that although the shift well into the LOC 700s had taken place, I did not yet fully grasp what had occurred. I kept trying to fit my new experience of self and world into the old familiar models and concepts. It was unfamiliar ground.

My May 5, 2001 diary entry shows my skepticism about the new expansion into cosmic consciousness. For a brief time, I went back to believing that my "oneness" was an expanding outwards from an empty borderless "no self" open center.

That was my experience back during the first eight years after my awakening in 1992, but when this "big" cosmic oneness showed up, it kicked separate solo "no self" butt. Cosmic consciousness is way cooler. Even so, I was attached to my "no self" and I didn't want to let it go. Eventually, I figured out that even as the "no self" I was terrified of annihilation.

But I didn't see that until much later. Letting go of any kind of "I" whatsoever is what opens the door to the Absolute. But very few jump right to that ultimate door. Most take their time, which is probably wise. Time is what it takes for the nervous system to adjust to and integrate these spiritual shifts.

The early journal entries reveal that I'm still not sure about the size and scope of my presence. Am I just feeling a sense of being borderless and expanding without boundaries? Or could it really be true that I literally am infinite like an ocean?

Eventually, my inner knowing revealed the truth of cosmic consciousness. It was my lingering attachment to the "no self" that had been speaking.

I was not quite ready to claim being universal so I backed away from it. The infinite Self took it in stride and moved steadily forward. The moral of the story is do not settle for anything less than the Absolute. In this book I am done my very best to show you the path and describe the destination.

Please note as you read these and other excerpts from my spiritual diary that words like stillness, emptiness, no self, oneness, silence, no mind, unknowing, "I," the Self and so on keep gaining new meanings as I go deeper into the Self and rise higher in my LOC level. Absolute stillness, emptiness and oneness are not realized until the Absolute itself is realized.

My Diary: March, 2001 (LOC 778) to January, 2006 (LOC 793)

Some people may find it odd or amusing that this deep spiritual transformation took place in what is arguably the most materialistic big city in the United States. In some ways, the dreamlike neon facade that is Las Vegas made it easier.

March 23, 2001
Las Vegas, Nevada
LOC 778

So now I stand in myself, more alone and more free than ever before. In a sense, unconditionally free, without strings, without obligations but also in a positive value sense free — full and complete to overflowing with this aloneness.

Today, now that I am complete in myself, I felt myself sinking into myself deeper (at times a little "intoxicating"). I now feel how from this centerless centeredness there is the movement to expand as that.

It is like a pulsation — the supernova effect — drawing to the centerless center, then releasing in infinite expansion, only this is more gentle, natural, like a breath or a breeze. There is no effort to it, no need in it. As the leaves flutter in the wind, so do I live and move.

Ultimately, perhaps, the only difference between "alone" and "all one" is which end of the telescope you are looking into.

April 27, 2001
Las Vegas, Nevada
LOC 778

On February 28, 1992 at 9:30 a.m. in San Diego, something happened. I lost my self.

The difference now is that my "I" is now "all." There is no separate "I." There is only that which is universal, which feels like nothing and everything all at the same time. This may seem extraordinary, but it is not. It is normal and natural. It is everyday life without that irritating illusion called "the self."

All I find, everywhere, is my self. I am all. Is this a cause of bliss? No. It is... ordinary. It is, simply, the way that it is.

May 5, 2001
Las Vegas, Nevada
LOC 779

When I say "you are infinite," I am not saying you are as big as the universe. What I am saying is you are boundless, that in the experience of being nothing there is no limit, no edge to you. You cannot find out where you end.

So there is the sensation of expanding without limit, without end. You, or your sense of identity, does not stop at any point. It is no longer limited in any way to the physical body. The physical body is now furniture.

This is what I mean by "infinite," that you experience yourself as "boundless... I think, I suspect, that the sacred talk about being the cosmos, infinite, etc. comes from this. If you focuis on the "edge," the "boundary" of this boundless expanding feeling, there is just more expanding.

It is like deep currents drawing you into a vast ocean. You don't know how big it is, or if it is really infinite, but it is indescribably vast. In other words, it *feels* infinite.

May 26, 2001
Las Vegas, Nevada
LOC 779

Pure Universal "I" of the Universe. Image: stone thrown into pond. Concentric ripples. "I" is pure, complete in itself. No need to move out, extend itself. "I AM" though still, whole, contains the urge to expand (fall) into multiplicity.

There is only one I, so all it sees and experiences is itself. There is no "other." If there is no "other," then there is no "I" or "one," no one and no thing, that is separate. There is only one.

August 20, 2001
Las Vegas, Nevada
LOC 779

The pure self, pure yet isolated, pristine and unbounded (the monad), it is separate. Like a chicken egg, it has a shell around it. Invisible shell, wall, barrier. Perfect expression of the monastic ideal: aloof, detached, beyond, separate from the world. Within monastic lifestyle, no need to move out of this.

The Great Universal Cosmic Silence. The second movement. The pure, separate, indivisible silence discovers that which is greater than itself and surrounds itself — the Infinite Silence.

Eventually, the wall of separation from the world/activity melts as the self opens up to its Mother, the Immanent Silent Beauty of God. This is approached cautiously, for the separation from/disidentification with the world and activity is appropriate.

The invisible shell is melting as the self opens and expands to Infinite Cosmic Beauty Reality Ocean. Expanding out from the edge of the unbounded expandingness into that which it touches, melting, merging, unifying. There is the ever-deepening felt realization "Ah, Glory! I Am That!" The Richness of Universal Variety. Paradoxically, this is Tantra!

November 21, 2001
Las Vegas, Nevada
LOC 779

Do not assert your complexity. Be your simplicity. Be simple. Be Being itself. The One has no parts, moving or otherwise. It is not complicated. It is not a construct, It is not ever divided.

It is the one Oneness, the Beingness of Being. It knows only Itself, only Wholeness. It has never known anything else, and it never will.

April 28, 2002
Las Vegas, Nevada
LOC 780

There is only my Self. All this is me/I. Dualistic appearance is how I have my cake and eat it, too. The non-dualistic Wholeness is not compromised because world is "projected only," not solid. All I need is inside of and within me.

All suffering originates in other. Thus I am I and apparent other — simultaneously manifest and unmanifest. Hence the ability to experience the creation. There is no self-limitation involved.

The Bliss of "I Am Already Full"

All this that I see Is not a compromise of Me.
In fact, I am always Full. I do this so that things aren't Dull.
Happy am I as I Create. I do it now, no need to Wait.
I am the one and only one. I play myself as Others in Fun!

March 4, 2003
Las Vegas, Nevada
LOC 780

One of the distinct experiences has been that of the Ocean of Silence coming into the body like waves, like the tide coming in. The feeling is the body is getting filled up with substantial Silence in the same way as "external" objects...

Right now, looking at the bookshelves [in the bookstore] and so on, my feeling is not of "looking at" but of experiencing a substance (universal) of which the seer and the seen equally partake.

This all sounds like the "perception of oneness in emptiness" that I had for 11 years but it is *not*. As I recall, for years I saw the Clear Light and the world looked solid, too. Then the world looked ghost-like, lunar, dead. This corresponded to the loss of interest in life and living. Now I see the world again, but AS the Silence, AS the Emptiness.

March 23, 2003
Las Vegas, Nevada
LOC 780

The oscillation from one day (Friday in the Vastness with K. in the park... peace, bliss, fusion of fullness = substance of space all around = Wisdom vs. Saturday = dualistic = okay, but very funky and tired by 5 p.m., no special feelings, that is no "Cosmic Substance" = Vastness = that am I.

So, right now, peculiarly, one day will be in Vastness, one day will not be. To be stabilized and integrated in it to me means you are living in it — "walking through yourself" — the way Suzanne Segal talked about it. It is not an experience you *had*. It is an *experiencing* you *are*.

March 31, 2003
Las Vegas, Nevada
LOC 780

The new and unexpected "state" or condition that I was telling J. about on the phone continues: gone is the feeling of a witness, gone is the feeling of being in a "special" or "higher" state of consciousness. There is no sense of "distance" from subjective thoughts, states and moods, or very little.

<u>Specifically, the experience of a "silent background" to all experiences throughout the day is gone.</u> This is what I used to call "the witness."

I think this is the "two steps forward, one step back" syndrome, at least I hope it is. I feel as if I was dropped into a pit of dullness and dimness. Like I said to J. Sunday, it's as if I'm back to the way I was 30 years ago. In other words, back then a pen was a pen, a notebook a notebook, smog smog, blue sky blue sky, etc.

April 9, 2003
Las Vegas, Nevada
LOC 780

In the past, I had thought and believed that what I was experiencing was the pure wide open space of consciousness, of awareness. It was, but it was *with impurities*, with cloudiness, fuzziness, vagueness.

It is this pure wide open space of awareness that has been busy for the last decade plus purifying, cleansing, dissolving, eliminating that which is not itself.

So the shift that has taken place, which I am glad seems to be "permanent," is the next movement in the symphony of Self-realization. The First Movement was the Search, initiated by the lucid dream as a teenager and lasting up to 1992. The Second Movement was the Journey of the No-Self, from 1992 to February, 2003 and its fixation on Emptiness as a Spiritual Object (with accompanying moods of alienation, isolation and desire to exit the world).

The Third Movement in the Symphony has just begun! It is "Living the Vastness," not "in" the Vastness — the Whole is my Identity. The great advantage of this third movement is that, just as before I had clearly seen the contrast between old ego-self and new no-self, now I can see the contrast between the old no-self/old Emptiness and the new Vastness.

Thus, as I oscillate from fuzzily perceived subject/object experiencing and pure Vastness, the difference in quality, value and "benefits" (e.g. holistic self-union celebration) becomes self-evident. Naturally, in a relaxed and gradual effortless manner, I can relax back into and settle into the Ease of Great Being, the Vastness.

July 7, 2004
Las Vegas, Nevada
LOC 780

Why am I reading all this crap from all these "experts"? It won't help me. The whole point that I have to admit to myself is that there are NO others.

April 16, 2005
Las Vegas, Nevada
LOC 782

Today I would say that the feeling shift has stabilized as a pure "I AM" feeling. This pure "I AM" feeling has a sense of stability and solidity to it that the "I am the Universe" (or "I am All") feeling did not have.

I am no longer anything, not even the Universe. Now I just am Now, simply and purely, "I AM."

This pure "I AM" has the sense of being unmoving or non-moving. It is not just still. It is stopped. At times, as with the initial arising a few days ago, it feels utterly rock solid — like the symbolic diamond.

The "I am All" state had a sense of drama and change and involvement with it. The "I am" was identified with the cosmos, but it was still an identification. The "I am" was still intrigued by the possibilities, by the changes, by the growth and riches of knowledge.

But in this pure "I AM" there is no longer an identification with the Universe. "Let the Universe be! It knows how to manage and run itself. It does not need me for that." This is the feeling and thought.

"I am All" was busy and stressful compared to "I AM." I am happy with the change.

January 14, 2006
Las Vegas, Nevada
LOC 793

I have noticed a different experience of the body occurring. It's like I am forgetting it more. It is diaphanous. I cannot find it. Floating, light, it is pure energy. I cannot distinguish the boundaries. At those times, motor action seems out of kilter, like I couldn't reach for the coffee cup or I would drop it as the body could not be found in a substantial way. It almost seemed to "ripple" or fragment or disintegrate, so that it was not understood how the action could be performed or completed.

1000

The perception of the Self has come forward. The Self is all that matters. Nothing else is important.

The Wynn casino and other buildings, though worth billions, are like toys, like pieces on a board game, inside the greatness of the Self. The Self is glorious, it is magnificent.

The Self is the only Reality. There is only the Self.

Objects are perceived, but they have receded. They are known to be expressions of the Self, that is their only meaning (the Self). Otherwise, they have no meaning or value.

Attitude? My attitude is light, playful, easygoing, simple, gentle and carefree.

I look at a building, a truck going by, and I think "That is me. That is mine. I am that." And then let it go, no longer interested. Ownership, when it is a fact, no longer needs to be repeated in the mind.

Occasional disruption in the bodily field, like it is falling apart, then quickly reorganizes. Enhanced sense of timeless: things happen, yet nothing is happening.

People, things, buildings, events, all take place *inside* the Self. The Self is greater. They are within it. Close analogy is the snow globe paperweight where you can see a small city inside a transparent plastic dome. You shake it and there is snow falling inside.

The Self is like a big Bubble, and all of this, the entire universe, is taking place inside the Fullness-Transparency-Wholeness-Completeness that is the Self. It is all inside of it, small and toy-like. The universe is a dream floating inside this Great Serene Bubble of Wholeness. The Self exists with or without that dream universe within it, and all of the toys and toy dramas being played out on planets like Earth.

Before, I was impressed by "I am the Universe!" Now I am seeing for myself that since only the Self is Real, and there is only the Self, then this great universe is (a) itself only a dream and (2) it is a tiny dream image within the grand Vastness of the Self (Bubble). In the Self, there is no change. There is only Serenity, only Eternity, only Equality, only Infinity.

NOTE: My passage through the darkness of the Great Void of Not Knowing that took me to LOC 845 began April 13, 2006 three months after this January, 2006 spiritual diary entry.

That Void passage was shorter and easier than I thought it would be. It ended May 6, 2006 with the sudden dissolution of attention and a falling into what I call the "stateless state."

My comments about being "I Am" and "the Self" show that I am anticipating those revelations. But seeing it or tasting it or in some way getting a sample of it is not the same as living it. I could not stabilize in it until I went through the Great Void passage. Then it was like I had moved to another country!

The Cosmic Vision

LOC 700 to 799

The Cosmic Vision: LOC 700 to 799

In the LOC 700s, the subliminal limitation of your localized non-doer "no self" space in the LOC 600s is sacrificed for the more impressive and more enjoyable cosmic or universal "no self" of the grand glorious physical manifestation. Your "no self" self gets exchanged for the spiritual ego of the universe.

The localized human "no self" arose within the context of the human self and the human world. In the beginning, right after LOC 600s stage enlightenment (including non-doership), this context may not have felt limiting or confining in any way.

At some point, though, a yearning to be greater than just the "no self" emerges. There is the intuition "I am the world" or "I am the universe." There is an inner demand to claim a bigger and more unlimited identity. This is the Cosmic Ego identity.

It is radically different from the localized "no self" feeling. It was spacious and empty of self, but its expanding borderless quality was merely a sense of there being no obstacle to the outgoing feeling from a "no self" pseudo-center. This is not the same as great uninhibited identification with the world or the cosmos. The latter realization is sublime, glorious and majestic compared to the barren sterility of the "no self'" attainment.

Meet the New Boss — Same As the Old Boss (World-Other)

When "you" go, the others and the world remain. When you drop the separate personal me, that is not the end. That is the dualistic puzzle that you face living in the LOC 600s. Why this puzzle? When the other can dominate you, are you free?

There is a subtle irritation, a constant tension, induced by the undeniable continuity of the presence of the other and the world. Since there is other and world, the oneness that you are experiencing is flawed. Like I said, it may be good enough for you. You may be happy with it for the rest of your life.

Even so, this dynamic ocean of "oneness" has in it those unpredictable independent concrete "islands" called other people. More intimidating, a vast indifferent indecipherable "continent" (world) boils and roils outside of you, seething with a relentless unforgiving tension that will haunt you until you fully face its implications. As long as there is the other and the world, you are subject to them. You are their slave.

The reality is you are not comfortable with the existence of these others and this world. At a subtle emotional level, it provokes a contraction in you. Can you feel that? Even in your "no self," this knowledge of other and world causes you pain. This knowledge of the other invites instability and insecurity.

Yes, it is a puzzle. It is a problem. But is the noise, the pain, the tension, the dissonance, the harshness of this conflict, this new separation between "no self" and other/world, compelling enough for you to take action? Or is it just a mild irritant?

For those who go onto the LOC 700s, it was a problem that they had to boldly and courageously solve. They recognized that their realization of non-duality was not yet complete. The solution of the 700s is to embrace the other and embrace the world. This revolutionary solution is not anticipated by the LOC 600s sage in his non-doing "no self" happy place space.

The Amazing LOC 700s Solution to the World-Other Boss

In the LOC 700s, you expand to attain a big new cosmic self that includes both other and the world in it. Then there is no other to threaten you. There is no world to bother you. You ate it all up. You gobbled it all up. Now it's all inside of you.

This is what I call "cosmic consciousness." Your experience of pure presence blows up to include everything that you can feel, sense and know. You are now the consciousness of the world, the consciousness of the universe. This is your answer.

As a result, the problem is solved. There is no other. There is no world. You handled it. Now you are the other. Now you are the world. Now you are everything. Now You Are That.

No more puny weakling "non-doing no self." You are the 800 pound gorilla. You are the universal consciousness.

This cosmic consciousness self is pure being, too, but it is pure being set free to expand without any limits to what it is and what it can be. It has outgrown the localized context entirely. The promise of expanding outwards of the local "no self" space has been fulfilled. Now you really are the universe.

To merely be the non-doing "no self" is a severe and painful restriction on consciousness. It is filled with contradictions.

It is a level of contraction, of isolation, that sooner or later, in this life or in another life, will be seen through, dropped and abandoned. Sooner or later, the cosmic whole will consume it.

To be the "no self" in terms of having had a self is meaningful. To be the "no self" when you are intuiting that your identity is literally the whole world, the entire universe, is punishment.

If You Haven't Seen It Yet, Just Wait... You Will See It

If you haven't seen this yet, then just wait. The sages who are contentedly sequestered away in the LOC 600s haven't seen it. It seems that it hasn't come up for them. They may have noticed it, but it isn't an urgent matter. They are still involved with others and the world. That's awesome. Good for them. It's just right for them. For the people who listen to them and follow their advice, that is just right for them, too. If it's not right for you, then you will *feel* it. You will deeply *intuit* it.

It can be fun to be the "no self" in the midst of all of these endlessly fascinating others and this vast entrancing creative world. Definitely it can, but it wasn't fun for me. I loathed it.

For me the localized "no self" experience became a nihilistic "ghost cave" with me as the hopeless despairing isolated "ghost." I faced the emptiness of the no self day in and day out. In this dark night of the "no soul" I was banished to a void that was supposed to be my true self, but clearly it was not.

In the end I was thankful for my traumatic shock. I was thankful for the merciless burning pain. I was thankful for the agony, desolation and devastation. This acute pain prevented me from stopping. This pain forced me to fully transcend it.

All I can do right now is point this possibility to you. I submit these ideas for your consideration. If they are not useful to you now, they may become useful to you in the future.

The Enlightened Sucker Punch: "No Self" Is *Not* Better

The first few months of my "no self" sojourn right after my awakening were times of luminous bliss. Then the need to process negative emotions kicked in. The "no self" really was okay for awhile. The nihilistic "ghost cave" came later.

Perhaps it was just an extremely rough patch of negative conditioning. Whatever it was, it took me by surprise. In total, I was in the non-doing "no self" space for about eight years. It was about two years into being the "no self" that it hammered me. I hit depths of crushing agonizing despair, of soul dead darkness that made nihilism sound like a bubbly pop song.

When it suddenly appeared, I was not prepared for it. The spiritual literature says almost nothing about it.

In *The Experience of No-Self*, Bernadette Roberts describes her journey into a bleak emptiness that followed her unexpected fall into her "no-self." Her autobiographical account of the severe challenges she faced *after* the appearance of the "no-self" was the closest thing I could find to my own deadly implacable voidness.[73] I read her book three times. If she had survived her nightmare of nothingness, then so could I.

Although it all worked out in the end for her, at one point in her journey she concluded that to be the no-self was no better than having a self. In fact, it could be worse.[74] She observed that, contrary to popular assumptions about enlightenment, the end of separation by itself did not have value or meaning.

Finally, her journey to no-self was not the end for her at all. That no-self phase was followed by a new journey from "no-self to nowhere," and beyond.[75]

If it had been my destiny to kill myself, then I would have. I would not have felt that there was any loss. The impersonality of everything was like a heartless absolute zero freezer.

There is no love when you are dead. I was alive, and yet I was dead. Not unlike those popular film symbols of vacuity, the zombie and the vampire, I lived on death. I fed on darkness.

Somewhere somehow the unrelenting darkness, the heartless void, released me from its icy clutches. I was slowly reborn as a human being, as a feeling caring alive laughing human being. To this day, I don't know how it happened. What I know is that falling into egolessness can land you as easily into a black hole as into a white hole. Whatever you have right now in your life, be thankful for it. Be grateful you are alive.

How I Solved the Mystery of "Dead Man Walking"

My conclusions are based on my own unique path. They are colored by the dark despair that poisoned the LOC 600s stage for me. I suffered enormously from a callously invasive sense of other and the world even after I had achieved the non-doing "no self." It was not a theoretical issue for me. It turned out that a localized void can suffer, too. It was painful as hell!

Remember, I had painstakingly "validated" my enlightenment against all the classical criteria I could find. This included the *Bhagavad Gita* but it was not limited to it.

My point is simply that I was definitely an LOC 600s enlightened person. I was there, yet I was not enjoying peace, love and happiness.

So I set about solving it. The way I did that was to start questioning, challenging and investigating everything all over again from the ground up. I was determined to make no assumptions and to have no expectations. I renewed my total commitment to thoroughly knowing Reality exactly as it is no matter what it was. I didn't care about what it was. It could be the darkest most terrible most devastating truth beyond any nightmare my imagination could cook up. I didn't care. I just wanted the truth. No matter what the cost, I wanted that.

Now I was investigating any and all experiences of boundary, limitation, other, world, density, thickness, substance, shells, envelopes, layers, bubbles, bodies, walls, internal noise, "I", silence, self, identity, thought, imagery, emotion, sensation, touch, sight, hearing, smelling, tasting and much more.

I investigated more deeply this empty "no self." I found that deep within this supposed "lack of center" there was a subtle holding to an invisible pseudo-center. When I finally saw this and felt this for myself, I said "Aha!" out loud.

I knew that some kind of "somebody" had to be hiding in there somewhere. My suffering was proof of that. This "no self" I had taken at face value as "nothing" was still a "self."

The Perils of Early Crystallization: Ignorance Is Not Bliss

In that moment, I realized that the final truth for me had to be no center, no other, no limit, no boundary, no world, no "I".

If anything could be found anywhere, then that was not it. If I could touch, make contact with or sense density with *anything* in my space, then that was a limit. I needed to knock it down.

If a state or stage was going to be "it," then it could not be felt to have *any* limits of any kind associated with it. That became my criterion. That is the one I stuck with all the way through.

My advice to you is that if you are in the LOC 600s, double your efforts to investigate and transcend your state. If you are new to living in non-duality, enjoy the LOC 600s and have a short vacation. Then get back to work. It's not all that it's cracked up to be. It's just the beginning of the journey.

If you're only in the LOC 600s, it's too early to go around and talk about enlightenment. Technically, you are enlightened if you are in the LOC 600s. My real concern is that you may get stuck in the LOC 600s. It's your life and it's fine for you to teach from that level. But you are running a legitimate risk.

When you set yourself up as a teacher, you tend to crystallize in that stage. If it's in the LOC 600s, then that's where you crystallize. If it's in the LOC 700s, then that's where you will crystallize. If you're going to crystallize early, then at least crystallize in the LOC 700s. You will have missed the best part of being enlightened if you don't at least get to the LOC 700s.

LOC 700s Case Study: Non-Duality Teacher Mandi Solk

Mandi Solk is the author of *The Joy of No Self*. She is currently writing a new book on her experiences with Self-inquiry.[76]

1000

Mandi has generously allowed me to quote at length from her web site regarding her journey from LOC 657 to LOC 758. She is one of the few I have heard of who experienced a profound sense of dissatisfaction with the LOC 600s non-doer no self space in the LOC 600s and then took strong action about it. Her decisive action to raise herself into the LOC 700s took the form of an intense home-based Self-inquiry retreat.

My assessments of her LOC at each level are my own. I did not discuss the matter of LOCs with her. I think that's just as well. Her own independent assessments of these two distinct levels — the labels don't really matter — speak volumes.

Mandi specifically singles out the conveniently bland passive "neo-advaita" platitude that "there is nothing you can do." Based on her own experience, this is completely misleading.

Mandi is a good writer. Her book got glowing reviews from Jeff Foster and Scott Kiloby. Here she talks about her journey from the limitations of "no self" (my words) to the peace and joy of universal or cosmic consciousness (also my words).

I heartily recommend her 2012 YouTube video interview with Renate McNay. Mandi speaks passionately and eloquently about how she discovered the power of Self-inquiry.[77]

Editorial Note: I had a Skype chat with Mandi Solk on March 30, 2014. She told me she had gone through another shift since her 2012 video interview. I checked her LOC during our call. She showed up at a very solid and lovely LOC 879. On that same call, the enthusiastic Mandi asked to get RASA right then and there. Since that RASA, and just before this book went to press, Mandi stabilized at LOC 1000. Go, Mandi!

In Her Own Words: Mandi Solk's Self-Inquiry Journey

Mandi Solk is a happy loving person. To her, realizing Truth and freedom meant living in "abiding peace and joy."

> Since I last wrote notes for this website, a lot has been discovered and a radical deepening has occurred, and having originally believed that there was nothing that could be deliberately done to achieve Liberation, I have experienced and witnessed a total change of heart. To this end, I have made little video on You Tube, called "YES! There IS something ' you' can do."[78]

The story of her quest begins with several shocks. Life itself was her guru. Her wake up alarm was ringing. It was loud!

> Quite a few years ago I had a series of intermittent awakenings, which seemed to have arisen from various dramatic scenarios. One was a nearly fatal motor-bike accident. Another one was dying on an operating table; still more bizarre dramas occurred, and in all these incidents, I was able to see through the illusion of a life that I took to be so real. I saw that everything that had seemed so solid, was in fact unreal and transparent, including "me." I totally lost any fear of death and discovered for myself that there is no death — no end.
>
> I started speaking about all this. I wrote a book and appeared in an interview on Conscious TV, and it all appeared to be flowing. At the same time I was going to Nonduality Meetings, and I founded Nonduality-North, where I regularly invited speakers on this subject to the North of England.
>
> I made videos and started doing meetings myself. All the Nonduality speakers were saying "There's nothing you can do — the awakening will either happen or it won't. Don't worry about it. Its not important." And as this seemed to be my own experience, I concurred with this for years.

After a few years of this, I started to notice that I wasn't Liberated at all, I now see maybe I was part-way "cooked," but in no way completed! And nor was anybody else!

All the same people kept attending meeting after meeting and nobody had attained abiding peace and joy. I'd certainly had awakenings and so I knew Truth, but total freedom hadn't happened yet — there was no abiding joy.

So I decided to shut up for a while and didn't write, speak or make videos until I had inquired further. This inquiring, this looking within for who I am, was something that I'd always warned against, misguidedly thinking that this activity would strengthen the sense of identity — not diminish it. This assumption was completely incorrect, dead wrong in fact.

I became passionate and addicted to Self-Inquiry, spending hours and hours over weeks and months just looking deeply within for "Who and Where I Am," and I can only report back to you, that now the sense of identity has been "hollowed or scooped out" and what remains is an ever-deepening sense of abiding joy, peace, freedom, and bliss, and the great news is, "you" can have this too and achieve it quickly. It is not "you" who does the looking anyway even though it appears that way at first.[79]

Mandi Solk Says "Forget 'There's nothing you can do.'"

Mandi's insights on why the "There is nothing you can do" rap is useless, if not misleading, are among the best I've heard.

Even though my own guru Ramesh Balsekar told me face to face "There is nothing you can do," and this moment changed my life, it is not suitable advice for everyone. I believe that it can be damaging. I am delighted to quote from this passionate Self-inquiry advocate who speaks from her own experience.

So forget "There's nothing you can do."

It is a trick on words, because yes, ultimately it is not the human sense of "you" who can do anything, but until you see through the human sense of you, which can only happen through looking, it will initially seem like the "you" is looking, but only the "you," you THINK you are.

After all, how could Presence, Love, allow freedom for only the select few? It's ridiculous, and it would be so cruel, and that is not part of Divine Love; no part of who You really are.

You have only to look and notice the consciousness of what you are, independent of thought, and then eventually the sense of "you" the imposter, slowly but surely gives way to the sense of Being.

Having seen so many "stuck" people over the years, imprisoned into believing "there's nothing they can do," and having said that myself so many times, I now know, categorically, that the solid shift only comes from losing all sense of personal identification.[80]

Voice of Experience: Mandi Solk's Approach to Self-Inquiry

Mandi's approach to Self-inquiry is practical and profound. Anyone doing Self-inquiry will benefit from her grasp of this technique. She is clearly speaking from her own experience.

> I realized that in all my awakenings, I was also shown my True Self by Presence. It might've been in the form of a few instant looks, but looking had happened. I just hadn't realized it because the looking was so quick.
>
> Presence is the ONLY teacher and finds Itself only through your looking within. Although these "seeings" happened quickly for me, they didn't last.

The true abiding in Presence has to come from taking the time to really LOOK on a twice-daily basis until Presence becomes dominant and thoughts fade way into the background.

You are your own Guru — Guru means "remover of ignorance." Remember, it's not a personal "you" that looks — but consciousness itself. This is what you are and there is nothing and no-one else doing the looking or finding. You have the Power to do this, because you ARE Presence seeking Itself.

Thoughts will always arise and that's absolutely fine and right. When I have suggested "dropping thoughts like a hot potato," I simply mean being the witness of thought and not getting "on the ride" with each one. Not actively trying to STOP thoughts, which is an impossibility. We just cease to see any thought as important (as in one thought being more significant than another). We gradually become completely unattached to thought and thereby any personal sense of identification with them.

Try to not be so attached to everything you've ever read or heard about Nonduality, including my stuff and LOOK FOR YOURSELF. Then you will begin to see the undeniable Truth of all this. Also you cannot rush this, otherwise it will be merely an intellectual process.

Presence Itself helps us with this, then slowly but surely, a switch-around starts to occur: instead of thoughts being like a huge magnet attracting you into a vortex of deep involvement with them, Presence becomes the magnet — drawing you into to the silent spaciousness of "ITSelf into ITself."

When I say "Presence Itself helps us with this," I mean that IT can see you looking and IT is delighted, since it is Itself, looking for Itself through you. When Love sees you opening the curtains to let in some light, Presence Itself helps "you" to pull them open further so IT can see more of ITself.

> When we talk about "looking," we are simply asking ourselves the questions "Where am I? Who am I?" Find out. Sit with this for 10 minutes or so for as often as you can make the time, and watch what happens.
>
> When you really begin to look, a space in thought occurs, and with more practice, a spaciousness begins to emerge and eventually this becomes the power that transforms our "seeing" from thought dominance to Presence dominance.
>
> Although it takes a little effort initially, there will soon come a natural craving to do this, followed eventually by an abiding in THIS, and finally, no practice necessary.
>
> In fact these recommendations are set out so beautifully in "Nam Yar" (which means "Who Am I?") by Ramana Maharshi.[81] You can download the PDF for free.[82]

Many people think of Self-inquiry as dry and emotionless. Her words convey enormous energy and enthusiasm. There is nothing more exciting than the thrill of discovering your own true Self! When you investigate with passion, you get results.

Two Steps to the Supreme: Nisargadatta Maharaj Speaks

A careful reading of the teachings of Nisargadatta Maharaj will show that he acknowledged an early phase where a pure localized "I Am" presence might be experienced. He did not place value on the realization until it became universal.

According to Nisargadatta, when your realization of this pure I Am or "I Amness" or sense of Beingness is complete, then you will experience that you are "one with the whole world." You will be one with the "entire universe." It is all you.[83]

Even though Nisargadatta spoke plainly and directly, perhaps more so than any other spiritual master in modern times, his message remains poorly understood. Part of the problem is that people must evaluate his message based upon their own stage and state. If they have not yet experienced what he is talking about, they will naturally interpret his advice and views in terms of their own level of realization.

In his later talks, Nisargadatta made it clear that this achieving universal or cosmic consciousness so that you know your true identity is the entire universe is just the first big step. From his point of view, the process was simple and straightforward.

First, you realize and abide as this knowledge of yourself as the universal I Am Presence. You know you are the whole universe. You may even experience that the world or universe is inside of you. That is the first step to the Supreme.

The second step is able to take place after the first step reaches its natural maximum fullness. Then that majestic state of being the whole universe is itself dropped, discarded, donated. It is seen that the entirety of knowledge, this vast enterprise called the universe and space and time, is useless to you. When this is seen clearly, then the Supreme or Absolute is realized.[84]

Because you are able to embrace and know the entire thing, which he calls Brahman, then you can let that great universal I Am, that amazing cosmic consciousness, go. Then you realize Parabrahman, his word for the stainless Absolute.[85]

The local "I-am-ness" of Nisargadatta is "Presence." The first movement is the full complete embrace and appreciation of your true self as this Presence at the universal level.

Nisargadatta might say that a person who is established at this level is a sage, but he would not say that the sage is done until that "I-am-ness" is fully dissolved.[86]

In the second step or movement prescribed by Nisargadatta, even this identity with universal consciousness gets thrown away. Then what is left is the Absolute, the "nothingness" of "nirvana," the stateless state of "nirguna" (no "I-am-ness").[87]

In sum, Nisargadatta is saying there are two steps to the Supreme, to the Absolute. The first step is to realize the I Am as universal consciousness. The second step, taken after you have abided as that for awhile, is to drop that experience of yourself as the universe to realize true "nothingness."[88]

I am equating the LOC 700s with Nisargadatta's first step of realizing yourself as universal or cosmic consciousness. This means the attainment of a non-doing no self presence is not enough. It is not even achieving Nisargadatta's first big step.

It is preliminary to that. This was my experience. Abiding in the LOC 600s was preparation for a grand and truly majestic expansion, a movement from local pure I Am to cosmic or universal I Am. There was no mistaking it when it happened.

In this stage, the experience of "I am the universe" is not just poetry. Nor is it just the feeling of expanding out from a borderless local "no self" space with an empty non-center. It is your actual experience. "I am that" means "I am the world." Later on, "I am that" may come to mean "I am the Absolute."

LOC 700s Case Study: Non-Duality Teacher Ellie Roozdar

In April, 2003, non-duality teacher Ellie Roozdar (LOC 785) learned Reiki. This led to a Kundalini awakening. She started doing healing with this energy, but a Buddhist teacher in New York advised her to use the Kundalini for deep meditation.[89]

She meditated and observed her thoughts and emotions. After awhile, a "silent watcher" appeared that began dissolving the separate self and the stories it told about itself.

After several months, the mind was quiet. An ecstatic energy began rising up the front of her body. This went on for more than two years. She realized that she did not want to be separate from this pleasurable experience. She wanted her "I" to unite with it so that she could not lose it anymore.

When this happened, she found herself having an experience of only "the sense of I-AM-ness." She no longer felt divided on the inside. She felt that this "I AM' was reality. It was oneness and everything, yet alone. Even so, her mind still struggled. It wanted to merge with this truth of "I AM." The mind kept seeing itself as separate, so it kept trying to merge with this "I AM" or with the world.

Ellie kept meditating. She would inquire as to whether or not there really was an "I" separate from this "I-Am-ness"? Was there an "I" separate from this "I-Am-ness" that owned these stories in her head? Was there an "I" that was conditioned that needed to be unconditioned?

This went on for awhile. She liked to walk on a regular basis. One time while she was doing her usual walk, the world around her became completely silent and still.

Then she experienced that everything in her environment, including, trees, automobiles, animals and even her own body, were inside of her. She was everything, all of these things, yet they were inside of her. She was "vision" itself seeing them. She embraced all of this within herself.

The first time this happened it lasted only minutes. It was like it opened and then it shut again. The experience happened again and again. It lasted longer and longer. Eventually, to be the container for her world was her natural state. She was the Subject. All the other things were objects inside of her. These objects were not separate from her. They appeared within her as part of her. She was the reality, the true Subject.

Her mind kept trying to understand this. Finally, there came a day when it stopped. The mind gave up. Her mind accepted "the unknown." It was humbled before this great unknown. The searching stopped. The becoming stopped. She had realized the Truth.

When Ellie Roozdar first began having this experience of being the world yet having the world inside of her, she used the word "container." She was a container for all that she could see. She was the supreme Subject. Everything she could see was that Subject, yet that Subject, who is herself, was at the same time independent of the objects arising within it.

Please notice how Ellie's experience, which is now her everyday state of consciousness, is very different from just being the "no self." She is not "borderless" expanding outwards. Instead, she is the "container" for everything. Not only is she the world, the world is actually inside of her!

She is describing the experience of "I am the world" or "I am the universe." This is the experience that Nisargadatta was saying the mature sage will have. It is the realization of universal or cosmic consciousness. This is the experience of the LOC 700s sage that I am encouraging you to embrace.[90]

LOC 700s Case Study: Karl Renz and Nisargadatta's Steps

Karl Renz (LOC 1000) is that rare exception who realizes the Absolute yet never had a teacher or guru. In the 1970s, while in a lucid dream, he felt his dream body dissolving in a way that he knew meant death. He fought this impending death, but he finally surrendered to a cosmic "black hole."

When he did this, he experienced light. His sense of a separate self disappeared. After this event he felt detached and a sense of "alienation" from the world. This unsought state of "cosmic consciousness," of "impersonal consciousness," of a vast "Nothing," saw the world as an illusion. It lasted for 15 years.

This cosmic Nothing state unexpectedly shifted while he was watching the *Mahabharata*, an Indian epic, on television. He quickly stabilized in "pure Is-ness," attaining the Absolute.[91] He saw that this vast wise Nothing which saw the world as an illusion was itself an illusion. This second shift dropped him into Parabrahman, into the Supreme nothingness, the Self.

The reason I am bringing up Karl Renz is that his experience closely follows Nisargadatta's two steps to the Supreme. First, Karl entered an impersonal cosmic consciousness. This is the stage where you realize what Nisargadatta called Brahman.

Nisargadatta says that you have to fight ignorance with knowledge. This "knowledge" is universal consciousness, the great Brahman. It is the medicine for conventional ignorance.

According to Nisargadatta, after this cosmic knowledge has eliminated the ignorance, both the ignorance and this great knowledge of cosmic consciousness are discarded. They are "thrown overboard." The Absolute is what is left. He calls it the Parabrahman, which means "beyond Brahman."[92]

LOC 700s Case Study: Non-Duality Teacher Suzanne Segal

The late Suzanne Segal (LOC 782) offered a fascinating vision of a "Vastness" which ended with a brain tumor that cut her life short at the age of 42. Her autobiography *Collision with the Infinite* reveals that she spent more than a decade tortured by fear after her spontaneous awakening at the age of 27.[93]

The reign of terror by the mind persisted as long as she felt herself to be the emptiness of the "no self." In the absence of a personal self, the mind became hyperactive and filled with dread. This led to exhaustion and doubting her own sanity.

She consulted with many well-known enlightened teachers. They told her that her experience was normal. She should relax and accept it. Finally, the condition let up on its own.

The way this happened confirms the model in this book. She learned from several teachers that being stranded in spiritual isolation as the "no self" could be a very difficult phase. In this LOC 600s stage she was tortured by the absence of a self.

While driving to see some friends, her obsession with the "no self" and its absence was suddenly transformed directly and dramatically into a deep knowing that "There is no other."

The moment this insight arose, she found that she was literally "everything." This experience was so vivid that she actually felt like she was "driving through" herself with her car.

She was now "everywhere already." She was now the "infinite substance" of whatever she looked at. The emptiness that had tortured her was transformed into a joyful vastness.[94]

She had shifted into the LOC 700s. Please note that her insight was extremely specific. The insight that accompanied her self-liberation while driving her car was "There is no other."

This was my experience also. Even when the personal self was gone, the concrete sense of the existence of the other, and of being tortured by this otherness, persisted for several years.

I was able to gain freedom from this painful stress due to the persistence of the other only after I shifted into the LOC 700s. Then I experienced that I was one with the whole universe.

The other disappeared. I had absorbed it. This is why attaining cosmic consciousness is so important. Your enlightenment will not stabilize until you realize universal consciousness. The emptiness of the "no self" is not stable.

I recommend reading Suzanne's candid account for several reasons. First, it sets the record straight about the journey through the empty "no self" phase being a bed of roses.

Second, it shows that when you stay on this "no self" path and don't give up, it will expand and shift into cosmic consciousness or a vastness in which you are the universe.

Realizing cosmic or universal consciousness is not the end, either. There is still the journey through the darkness of not knowing and beyond to stabilization in the unborn Absolute. Not only is the other eliminated then, the world disappears.

Even so, it is a dramatic and welcome shift from the narrow dry focus on the unsatisfying emptiness of the little "no self." I have put a link in the Notes to an inspiring online interview with Suzanne Segal in 1996 that she gave while she was at her best and still going strong. She died on April 1, 1997.[95]

LOC 700s Case Study: Non-Duality Teacher Sailor Bob

Sailor Bob Adamson (LOC 788) is a colorful well-liked non-duality teacher who gives powerful direct pointing satsang live in Melbourne, Australia and via telephone. He was awakened in the presence of Nisargadatta Maharaj in 1976.

Sailor Bob is a brilliant non-dual teacher. He has helped to awaken at least seven people that I know of, including John Wheeler who has himself helped to awaken at least two more people. Thanks to Sailor Bob, one of the few living disciples of Nisargadatta Maharaj, the lineage of Maharaj is thriving.

What's not to like, right? He is here as a case study to illustrate some pointers that the reader can look for when learning about and learning from an LOC 700s non-duality teacher.

I think his approach is very good for getting a person into the LOC 600s. I didn't find anybody in the LOC 700s or above among his students who are currently teaching non-duality.

A teacher's stage of enlightenment and, therefore, a rough idea of their LOC, can be extrapolated from the comments they make about their own experience. I am going to use Sailor Bob's statements from a series of satsangs he gave in Florida in 2004 to illustrate how this works.

In the LOC 600s, the first stage of enlightenment, the self or identity is experienced as a "no self" or an absence of the personal empirical self. The typical LOC 600s teacher is going to emphasize the lack of a personal or empirical self.

In the LOC 700s, this experience of self expands and feels universal and unlimited. Feeling that you have a "no self" and you expand outward with no limit is not the same. That is still an LOC 600s experience. In the LOC 700s, your identity, you could even say your body, is now the world or universe.

Sailor Bob talks about how the "emptiness" or "space" or "no thing" that you are is "everywhere." There is no "center." There is no "circumference." This "no thing" is "reality." When he says this is what you are, he is saying this is his experience.[96]

He also says that nobody has ever transcended this "no thing." He includes Buddha, Christ and Ramana in this list. James Braha (LOC 675) then extrapolates from this teaching that since he attained non-duality in Sailor Bob's presence, then he is in a "space" or "consciousness" identical to those masters and to the realization of any other saint or sage. This is based on not being able to find "an independent self center."[97]

This is a classic example of confusing stage one enlightenment (LOC 600s) with stage two enlightenment (LOC 700s). It is true that neither one has a "self center." But that does not make them identical realizations of equal depth. As you may recall, I made the very same mistake when I was in the LOC 600s!

What Sailor Bob does *not* talk about is also important. He does not talk about "not knowing." He does not talk about "love." He does not talk about sahaja, the non-thought "stateless state" which is the "no mind" realization of the Absolute (LOC 1000).

Sailor Bob says that you cannot go beyond "no thing." Is that true? Even "no thing" is still a "thing." It is still a concept.

"No thing" compared to a "thing" is just a negation. This negation of something results in emptiness. This emptiness must itself be negated. Then no description is possible.

"No thing" is a concept of universal consciousness experienced as "no thing." It is the highest level you can get to as a state of knowledge. It is the peak of knowledge. It is not yet spotless "no mind." The Absolute is beyond all concepts of any kind.

He talks about pure "uncontaminated" awareness-presence or emptiness cognizing itself, but he arrives there from the state of ordinary presence-awareness. This common denominator consciousness is accessible for all human beings.[98]

This state of presence-awareness he is talking about is subtly contaminated. It is contaminated by very refined concepts. It is made impure by knowledge itself, by the micro-movements of the subtle mind, by the act of knowing itself.

The very context for this perception is the universe. Yet the universe is itself merely a form of knowledge, a projection of the pristine Absolute. The universe is a form of the mind.

Beyond the LOC 700s, it is understood that the world, the universe, is itself a concept. It is only thoughts or ideas. That is why it disappears when the Self or the Absolute is realized.

The Natural State: "Pure" Awareness as the Absolute

The natural state is not so easily glimpsed. It is not emptiness or no thought or the natural obvious feeling of presence. It is the radical death of the mind. Only "no mind" is sahaja. The way to understand "pure" Awareness is to BE the Absolute.

The universe is itself a product of the cosmic mind. The death and dissolution of the universe arises before the realization of and stabilization in "no mind." To be one with the universe is to be one with the cosmic mind, the universal mind, the great non-local supermind. It is the Creator. You must go beyond it.

This oneness with the vastness of the cosmic mind is supreme knowledge, but it is dirt and dust compared to the diamond of no mind. The Supreme is found only when the mind is lost.

"No mind" requires the transition through the darkness of the Great Void of not knowing. You may then reside in the bliss of divine or transcendental love (LOC 800s). Or you may go right into the LOC 900s and onto LOC 1000 for final stabilization in no mind (sahaja). There is no rule as to how long it will take or what the experience will be. These are the stages of spiritual growth, but they will be actualized differently by each person.

Sailor Bob is saying in a plain no nonsense way that he is this emptiness or "no thing." As that, he is literally everywhere all the time without a center or a circumference. This is the theme of the LOC 700s. I am infinite. I am the universal emptiness. I am everywhere. I am everything. It sounds cool — and it is.

It is the acme of understanding. It is tip-top knowledge. It is the supreme state of the mind. It is universal cosmic mind.

The first stage of enlightenment, the LOC 600s, is merely the absence of the personal self-doer. Different people experience it differently, but there is nothing universal or cosmic about it. It's just the sudden loss of a "personal me." That's it. That's all.

The loss of self or center can be problematic in the LOC 600s. For some (myself, Bernadette Roberts, Suzanne Segal), it can produce years of very personal impersonal hell.

This torture due to spiritual depersonalization is resolved in the LOC 700s. There is a major seeing through of the illusion of "the other." The true solution, as radical as it sounds, is "Everything is me. I am all." It was not yet the seeing at the Absolute (LOC 1000), but it is deeply liberating. Devout Catholic Bernadette held onto a divine ineffable Trinity. This is a positive affirmation of self, of a cosmic universal self.

I am all in favor of guiding people to a non-dual realization in one week. Both Nisargadatta Maharaj and Sailor Bob say that this is possible with the "serious" seeker. My concern is that the new sage will imagine that his nascent awakening is the be all and end all of enlightenment. It almost certainly is not.[99]

The Absolute is not just a static end where life gets paralyzed in some ethereal perfection. The Absolute is not merely a state of dynamic wholeness, even if that wholeness is the universe.

The Absolute is called that because it includes absolutely everything. It is beyond materialism. It is beyond spirituality. It is beyond non-duality. It is a complete return to this world exactly as it is, only at the very same time, this world is the Supreme Self, the flesh of God, pure perfection beyond mind.

As soon as there is knowing, this life is polluted. Only in not knowing, only in no mind, can the Buddha Nature come forth.

Only then can Christ be crucified, resurrected and ascend into the divine Light. Then, and only then, is this world "saved." Only then does this World literally become the Body of God.

LOC 700s Case Study: Non-Duality Teacher Mooji

Mooji (LOC 763) has a large and devoted following. He is endowed with a warm personality and natural charisma.

According to his recent interview with Conscious.tv, the life story of Mooji lends itself to two easily articulated stages. In his first spiritual stage, he met a Christian mystic named Michael. After working with Michael for awhile, he asked for his blessing. This changed his level of consciousness.[100]

From this time forward, he lived in a state of joyful flow. He was now at LOC 672. He enjoyed "bliss" and "space."[101] Next Mooji was guided by mysterious events to Papaji's satsang.

Soon after an intense conversation with the Lucknow sage, what was left of Mooji's "me" suddenly disappeared. In its place appeared a great emptiness or "infinite expanse."[102]

Instead of I am consciousness everywhere or I am the universe, Mooji describes it as I am this infinite expanse. This is a textbook description of second stage enlightenment. After this event, Mooji's LOC stabilized at 763.

It is reasonable to assume that if Mooji had gone beyond this experience, he would say so. The same can be said of Sailor Bob. Both men seem content with their realization. LOC 700s is a deep and profound level of enlightenment.

Many people stay here for the rest of their lives. One reason for this is that the higher stages of enlightenment are poorly understood and rarely discussed. Another reason is akin to the saying "It is good to be king!" It's good to be the universe. In the realm of knowledge, it is the ultimate achievement.

Zen Mountains, Zen Rivers and the Three Awakenings

The great Chinese Zen Master Ch'ing yuan Wei-hsin of the T'ang Dynasty once said "Before Zen, I saw mountains as mountains and rivers as rivers. Through Zen, I saw mountains were not mountains and rivers were not rivers. Now, resting in the Absolute, I see mountains again as mountains, and rivers again as rivers." Then he asked "Are these three the same or are they different?"[103]

"I saw mountains as mountains" corresponds to the ordinary state of the worldly person. This includes the LOC 600s sage since he sees the world as other from his "no self" perspective.

1000

In the LOC 700s, mountains are no longer mountains. Now the mountains are your self. You are the universe. This is the cosmic mind, cosmic ego, cosmic consciousness. You have gone from the world to "no self" in the world to "You are the world." This makes you the reality and the world the illusion.

This is a great negation of the ordinary world. Now this great negation must itself be negated. The little zero of the "no self" that became the Big Zero of the universe must now itself be zeroed out in order to realize itself as the Supreme Zero. In this Supreme Zero there is the absolute present, the no mind.

Just as the conventional ego died in order for the "no self" to live, and the "no self" transformed itself (died) to be reborn as infinite space, now this impressive vastness must dissolve so that a reality the mind cannot know or describe is attained.

On the wonderful web site NonDuality.com, there has been a web page for many years which includes a teaching called "Three Awakenings." The author is M. He describes himself as a lifelong devotee of Nityananda and Muktananda.[104]

To paraphrase M., in the first awakening, non-doership and an experience of oneness within the context of persistent duality is enjoyed. In the second awakening, you experience your true Self as the entire world or universe. In the third awakening, all duality is dissolved leaving only "I" or pure Awareness that transcends all constructs and concepts.[105] This model from M. closely matches my model of four stages of enlightenment. The additional stage from me is the LOC 800s phase. It can be included in the process of stabilizing in "no mind" since it introduces the step of "not knowing."

The three awakening model fitted to my map puts LOC 600s as the first awakening, LOC 700s as the second awakening and LOC 800s through to LOC 1000 as the third awakening. M.'s model appears to be taken from Kashmir Shaivism.

The key point in terms of this LOC 700s discussion is that ancient tradition sees a middle stage between "no self" and the Absolute in which there is expansion of identification to include the world or the universe. This is a precise match to my own personal experience as well as my four stage model.

LOC 700s Sages: Inquiry Systems and Coach Trainings

In this section I'm going to take a look at contemporary non-dual teachers Byron Katie (LOC 768), Scott Kiloby (LOC 754), Arjuna Nick Ardagh (LOC 773), Genpo Roshi (LOC 755) and Peter Fenner (LOC 744). I will also discuss famous gurus of the recent past, including my guru Ramesh Balsekar (LOC 764), Rajneesh aka Osho (LOC 754) and Paramahansa Yogananda (LOC 769). They all have something in common.

As I looked for patterns that would help me identify and differentiate the LOC 700s sages from those in a stage above or below them, I was struck by how many well-known sages at this level had created an original inquiry system. Not only that, they had such faith in the effectiveness of this inquiry system that they were training (unenlightened) coaches in it.

That the coaches who deliver these novel inquiry systems do not themselves have to be enlightened is a strong show of confidence in the method by the sage. In essence, the sage is "outsourcing" themselves. The method becomes the satsang.

This approach is in sharp contrast to the classical model of seekers sitting, asking questions, doing Self-inquiry and meditating in the physical presence of the enlightened sage (satsang). The sage is thought to deliver an ineffable "X Factor." In the LOC 700s model, method replaces the sage.

Let's look first at Byron Katie. She is probably the most famous and most successful of the group. Her approach is straightforward involving four questions and a reversal where you take the viewpoint of the person or situation you are having a problem with (invitation to non-dual experience). The emphasis of the questions is on challenging thoughts.

Byron trains certified facilitators in her method. It is called The Work. It is abundantly clear that The Work, while offering a vehicle that facilitates awakening, also fills the self-help void. Her spiritual technology is especially useful to someone who wants to benefit from inquiry but is not ready for Ramana.

A deeply enlightened person, Byron Katie, has provided a simple procedure where you can go through a gradual awakening as you help yourself to deeper, higher and better levels of self-liberation. It is a brilliant fusion based on LOC 700s insights. It is practical, effective and compassionate.[106]

Scott Kiloby is not as well-known but he is a rapidly rising star in the same enlightened self-help niche. His method is called Living Inquiry. He too has a growing team of certified facilitators. Scott is especially interested in the application of his method to addiction problems. By focusing on a limited set of psychological issues, Living Inquiry appears to deliver non-duality as next generation high-octane psychotherapy.[107]

Arjuna Nick Ardagh offers Awakening Coaching Training. He delivers key skills via tele-seminar, online course and optional residential course. He is taking full advantage of the Internet.

What Arjuna defines as the seven "basic skills" or "core competencies" do not sound very basic. For example, one is called "Absolute Presence." Another is called "Radical Awakening." The latter skill offers multiple "portals" that will quickly (yes, "in a few minutes") enable the client to get out of their head to discover "awakened presence."[108]

Next on the list of contemporary LOC 700s inquiry innovators is Zen Master Genpo Roshi. His approach, called Big Mind®, unites decades of hard Zen practice with Jungian psychology and the Voice Dialog methods of Hal and Sidra Stone adapted for use with a large group. Although controversial within the large American Zen community, Genpo sees Big Mind as a compassionate revolution designed to speed up realization.[109]

Genpo Roshi's motivation is to give people an experience of non-dual consciousness quickly and easily. Stabilization in non-dual consciousness is another matter, but obviously you can't stabilize in it if you don't even know what it is.

Peter Fenner offers two fascinating in-depth trainings, Radiant Mind and the more advanced Natural Awakening. The nine month course promises personal discovery of "unconditioned awareness." Beyond training coaches, he positions himself as a spiritual mentor to non-dual teachers already giving satsang who wish to intensify the potency of their "transmission."[110]

1000

Ramesh Balsekar ended up developing a system that focused on non-doership. He used it like a surgeon with a scalpel.

Although he still held to the teaching that "All there is, is Consciousness," in practice it was delivered as a catechism in which the punchline was non-doership. Either you got it or you didn't. Non-doership was a knife at the jugular of the ego.

Some interpreted this hammering away at the principle of non-doership ("Everything is God's will") as a rigid fatalism. From the point of view of the entrenched doer, it most certainly is. From the perspective of non-duality in daily life, it is a liberating "realistic" assessment of how things work.[111]

Rajneesh (Osho) was also a systems developer and promoter. His flamboyant lifestyle and global influence spoke highly of his charisma and desire for attention. Controversy still swirls around this man. The extreme life of Rajneesh illustrates the paradoxical power of some LOC 700s sages who profoundly influence and impact others both favorably and negatively.[112]

His strategy was to take the words of established spiritual authorities and deliver talks based on what this authority had said. Rajneesh is the classic example of the LOC 700s sage implementing many strategies for awakening. He was one of the first to synthesize psychotherapy and non-duality.[113]

Paramahansa Yogananda is on this list of LOC 700s system developers because he is known as the promoter of a system of meditation and enlightenment said to be both scientific and complete. It is impossible to evaluate whether or not the Kriya Yoga path delivers on all of its promises. The successful spread of this tradition in the West cannot be disputed.[114]

My LOC 764 Guru: Ramesh Balsekar and Sexual Misconduct

Along with power and position, being an authoritative guru who leads groups offers certain temptations. Who better to talk about in this section than my own guru Ramesh Balsekar?

When Ramesh himself got embroiled in a sex scandal, that seemed to confirm for his critics that he was a fallen guru.[115]

My personal experience of Ramesh Balsekar is that he was impeccable and the perfect guru for me. As for his supposed sexual shenanigans, I believe he was being his authentic self. If he was just a "horny old Indian man" to his critics, so be it.[116]

The relationship between the authentic sage and his students defies definition. Western standards that get applied to priests and psychotherapists do not apply to enlightened sages.

When the sage is married, I believe the correct ethical action is to remain monogamous and be "faithful" to your spouse. I have thoroughly researched the online reports about Ramesh's behavior. In my opinion, Ramesh was not a "fallen" guru.

If, as some say, he had a mistress while he was still married, then I would not personally "approve" of that behavior. But it does not change my feeling about his legitimacy as my guru. He has his karma just as I have mine. Likewise, God has given him a unique destiny. If I approve or not does not matter.

People who write about "fallen" gurus do not talk about non-doership. You must have at least an intellectual grasp of it if you want to understand the behavior of a realized person.

In his public talks, Ramesh repeatedly made it crystal clear that not being the doer literally meant that a person could do *anything* and, no matter what it was, it would be God's will. It seems to me that some of his followers did not believe him!

According to one report on the Internet, Ramesh replied to his accusers at a live satsang event by saying "If I have hurt you I apologize... But all this is only a happening and it does not concern me... You have created the problem. Now solve it... you have been asking me for hugs and whatever happened afterwards is your fault... I have nothing to do with it... It is you who are creating the problem."[117]

To the outsider who does not know Ramesh personally like I do, it may sound like he is just making up excuses for his apparently selfish behavior. His critics fail to grasp that his actions are in perfect alignment with his teaching. I *know* that non-doership means that *any* behavior is possible. The "perfect guru" is a fantasy. Ramesh's actions destroyed that fantasy.

For me, this is the Ramesh I know, love and fondly remember. All I can say to the people who got their feelings hurt is "If you don't want to burn and die, don't jump into the fire." Yes, I know the actions of the guru can be a rude difficult shock.

If he or she really is your guru, if that is the commitment you have made, then be in that 100 per cent. Then you are able to make use of *everything* that he or she throws at you.

My experience was that Ramesh could be difficult, yet all of his actions were perfect. They were clearly God's will for me.

The liberating spiritual shocks that he delivered to me were precisely timed, perfectly targeted and profound in impact. I got my feelings hurt numerous times in relationship to him. Yet there was never any doubt in my heart that he was my guru and that his teachings were just right for me. From the moment I saw his picture, I knew that he was the guru I had been looking for and that God had sent him to me.

This is the power of the guru. Yet you will not gain full access to his liberating power until your investment is total. The time to question is before you commit. Question all you like then. Once you commit, go all in with the totality of your being.

Apart from Ramesh having been my guru, the reality for me is also that Ramesh had an LOC of 764. This LOC tells me that he still had some work to do. This does not change the fact that he was perfect for me at the time. My alignment, trust, openness and resonance with him was ideal. As a result, I was able to receive from him everything that he could give me.

Ramesh is just the tip of the iceberg. There are many examples to choose from among popular well-known LOC 700s gurus.

Zen Master Genpo Roshi is widely known for his sexual misconduct.[118] There are reports that famous spiritual pioneer Paramahansa Yogananda had secret sex scandals.[119]

With the flamboyant Rajneesh, it barely needs mentioning.[120] The Tibetan Buddhist community reluctantly recognizes "sexual misconduct" as an issue within its ranks.[121]

My research for my four stage model shows that sexual and other misconduct is less likely in LOC 800s sages and above.

One of the questions I keep hearing from seekers is "If he really is enlightened, then how can he behave that way?" This is a variation of the bigger question: "What is enlightenment?"

The sages in the first two stages at LOC 600s and LOC 700s are still vulnerable to these tendencies. They have not gone through the purifications of the higher levels. In LOC 800s to LOC 1000, deep compassion is discovered. It is beyond the "devil may care" spontaneity of LOC 600s and the confident self-sufficiency of the LOC 700s. The total compassion that embraces the suffering of the world emerges for the first time.

The bottom line is that these sages are not acting with love, respect and compassion. They have a long way to go before they are mature sages. My Map of Awakening explains their behavior by showing that they have not gone through the LOC 800s. It is in the LOC 800s that they discover ultimate love. Until then, love and opening the heart take a back seat.

As impressive as the attainment of the LOC 700s sage is, his cosmic consciousness, his cosmic identity, is also a very subtle cosmic narcissism. He has not yet been transformed and healed by the mind melting fires of love in the LOC 800s.

LOC 800s: the Discovery of Transcendental Mystical Love

In the LOC 700s, major purification is still taking place. The sweet discovery of the transcendental or divine love (the seed "I AM") that is prior to the cosmic manifestation does not arise until the LOC 800s. No matter how wise or compassionate the teacher may be, they have not yet experienced for themselves the ultimate grace of love in its supreme mystical form.

Moving up to this higher level deepens humility. It intensifies profoundly the visceral reality of "You are my very own beloved Self," the Self in this case being the spiritual student or coaching client. Abusing the other is abusing your self.

The experience of the universe as yourself, the attainment of cosmic consciousness, is not yet the sacrifice of ego in the heart that is perhaps best described as a crucifixion. Beyond the LOC 700s the divine Beloved is encountered. In this meeting, so-called "emptiness" is filled in and transcended.

In the darkness of "not knowing," divine Love's supremacy is set free as supernatural solvent. The tenderness of humanity is enhanced. Identification with universal consciousness leads to subtle narcissism and ego inflation. The LOC 700s sage may conclude he is "the king of kings." Who shall challenge him?

To harm another when they are your very Self is unthinkable to the person who is actually having this experience of the Love supreme and transcendental. To realize that you are the world, you are infinite, is not yet that experience. Incredibly, all of that will have to be let go of, surrendered and dissolved.

Though perhaps obvious, it is worth emphasizing that when a teacher acts in a way that he or she knows has the potential to cause harm, this teacher is not acting as if the other is indeed his very own beloved Self. He is acting as if they are "other."

Based on the known behaviors of LOC 600s and LOC 700s teachers, it is clear that this kind of violation is more likely at these lower stages of enlightenment. No matter what they say about their state, the evidence says something is lacking.

This tendency as a group shows that no matter what the claim in terms of unity, some kind of duality troubles the 600s and 700s. Deep subconscious cleansing still needs to take place.

The Human Sex Drive Does Not Disappear for the Sage

When we get to the LOC 800s, LOC 900s and LOC 1000, we will see that either there are no reports of violations or that the transgressions arise in an unusual context. In the two cases I am thinking of, the "sexual misconduct" arose in scenarios that I consider poignantly vulnerable and profoundly human.

I speak of Jiddu Krishnamurti (LOC 844) and Sasaki Roshi (LOC 1000). You can decide if these men deserve sympathy.

In Jiddu's case, he had a long-term affair with the wife of his editor. In Sasaki's case, he asked female students to undress or to touch him while on intensive Zen retreats. I will go into more detail when I write about them.

In my experience, the sexual drive, the desire for physical intimacy, does not die. No matter how enlightened a sage may be, the need to reach out to "others" in this way is an essential element of what makes him human and, therefore, beautiful.

It is interesting how sexual misconduct steals most of the limelight. What about financial wrongdoing? What about psychological misconduct? What about verbal abuse?

The fact that sexual behavior gets called out but other forms of harmful behavior get ignored tells me that a cultural wound is involved. Most people, seekers or not, need sexual healing.

What about the fact that sociopaths and con artists love the guru-devotee cult paradigm? Find damaged people you can manipulate and exploit the hell out of them. Frankly, there is not much evidence of that going on in non-duality circles.

No doubt there is some, but I have not heard of it. Mainly what I have seen is a few people with LOCS below 600 playing at being the enlightened non-dual guru. If that is all that is going on, then we can feel good about our modern non-dual tradition. Its rigor is cutting through the usual garbage.

Beyond Universal Consciousness: the Kiss of the Absolute

If you have not yet experienced the "no self" of the LOC 600s or the "cosmic self" of the LOC 700s, it may seem theoretical to talk about the limitations of the LOC 700s. It may seem that way right now, but sooner or later, you will arrive there.

If you want to get to a certain place, it helps to know what that place looks like. Like the LOC 600s, the LOC 700s is a stop along the way. It is not the destination. The message of this book is that LOC 1000 is that destination. You can achieve LOC 1000 in this life if you really want to. But it will be less likely if you think you have "arrived" at LOC 683 or LOC 783.

I remember past lives in which I was enlightened. I was an enlightened monk in Thailand. I was also an enlightened guru in India. Both were centuries ago. In those lives I had attained non-duality, yet I had future lives after that in which I was not enlightened (above LOC 600). The moral of the story is do not stop until you get to the top. The spiritual top is LOC 1000.

I was forced to conclude that the only way to guarantee your freedom is to go all the way. That is what I dedicated myself to in this lifetime. Whatever happens to this body when death comes, I will go peacefully knowing that I did everything that I possibly could to attain the highest human consciousness.

This highest human consciousness is what I am calling the Absolute. It is also the Supreme Self. My experience is that there is only one "I" that is everyone and everything. There is one Universal Supreme "I." I am that "I." Ramana called it "I-I."

When I say there is only this "I," I am saying there is *only* this "I." The world can be perceived and experienced, but it does not exist separately in any way. The world and the people in it are also this one Universal Supreme I. There is only this "I" means exactly that. There is *only* the Supreme Universal I.

The Absolute can be identified. When it is attained there is total rest, total stillness and total silence. It is a *full* stop.

Previous to realizing the Absolute, there was rest, stillness and silence, but it was not like the rest, stillness and silence of the Absolute. There was still movement, shakiness, vibration.

One way it is described is that thought and no-thought are combined and dissolved. What is left is "non-thought."

In his talks, Nisargadatta Maharaj referred to this state as the "nirvikalpa" state. In this state there are no concepts at all. It is also described as the "stateless state." It is beyond "I Am," whether that is the I Am of the body, the I Am of the no self, or the I Am of "I Am the Universe." I Am is itself a concept.

Even the pure "I Am" of the LOC 800s must be transcended. There the I Am is experienced as pure love, union with the ideal Father-Mother-God-Goddess. It is experienced in different ways by different people. After the fulfillment of this ultimate love is attained, it is found that even this perfect love is not the answer. Then this super-love loves itself with such totality that it dissolves itself into "Love that knows no love."[122]

The I Am of the LOC 800s is the first big step that the Absolute takes out of itself. It manifests as the non-dual quintessence of duality, of yin and yang. It is the potential for proliferation, but this wild expansion that will become the universe has not yet exploded. It is the essence of the universe in seed form.

In the concept-free stateless state of the Absolute that is beyond even perfect divine love, you do not even have the concept I Am. There is no knowledge of any kind.

There is not even the knowledge that "I exist." This Absolute (LOC 1000) is the pristine unborn reality that is prior to any manifestation. It is prior even to the super-condensed divine "seed" essence, the potential for manifestation at the LOC 800s.

Universal consciousness (LOC 700s) is the manifestation. But nirvikalpa samadhi or sahaja is prior to that. The universal consciousness is Brahman. Sahaja is Parabrahman (LOC 1000).

Parabrahman is beyond cosmic consciousness. It is not just without thought. It is without attention. Nisargadatta says that attention dissolves. What is left cannot be described, but it can be experienced. It is the "no-attention" of the Absolute.[123]

From the perspective of the Absolute looking at the seeker, the LOC 900s are the first thin very slight veiling of the Absolute. Then, in this veiled state, the Absolute gives birth to the LOC 800s. The LOC 800s are the pure I Am, the essence of creation.

The next big step is that the LOC 700s condense into the LOC 600s. This contraction of the LOC 700s into a more localized expression at the LOC 600s holds the potential for a grand new expansion at lower levels (in the LOC 500s and below).

The whole thing is music. It resonates with itself. The lower reflects the higher. LOC 1000 shifting down to LOC 800s is reflected by LOC 700s shifting down to LOC 600s and so on.

Please Do Not Settle for Anything Less Than LOC 1000

I did not want to experience any limits, any boundaries, any content, any spaces, any densities, any anything. Don't fence me in. I want to be free. I want the wild freedom of infinity.

I knew I wanted purity, too. I needed that purity which was so pure that it did not have anything within itself with which to compare, contrast, differentiate, identify, exist or know itself.

I would not rest until I uncovered the stateless state of perfect rest that I had intuited in deep meditation. I had discerned details of its nature from reading Ramana Maharshi and Nisargdatta Maharaj. I benefited from direct contact with other enlightened beings and divine cosmic archetypes, too.

Living as that, it is, paradoxically, the true deeply satisfying fulfillment of my humanity. It is the pinnacle of love.

It is the empty "Ah" of no holds barred non-stop reality. It is the full circle, an entire 360 degrees, so that a rose is a rose is a rose. The heart knows the secret of life. When I arrived at this "destination" which I did not know existed, my heart said yes.

Spirituality is destroyed because there was never anywhere to go. There was never anything to do. This right here has been "it" all along. Yes, there is the fact that this clarity arose for me only in the context of the one Supreme Universal I, but that is not a spiritual state. It is a statement of self-evident fact. All that is here exists as the embodiment of primordial identity.

As for how to realize the Absolute, the best advice is perhaps to do absolutely nothing. The notion of sitting quietly is the beginning, but when you come across no self, and universal consciousness, and divine not-knowing, you can be forgiven for thinking they might be it. But this reality has absolutely nothing in it at all. There is no knowledge, even of existence.

When I took the final step into this, into the Absolute, I remember being afraid that I would die. Even at that point, there was still a little holding onto the notion of a separate "I."

But I took the leap. Then what I found was that the final rest had been achieved. That "I" in all of its guises and disguises — the body, the no self, the universe, the divine darkness — had been the noise, the activity, the buzz that prevented this rest.

When I settled into this ultimate rest, I knew I was finally home. I knew I was finally my true self. Up until this arrival, there had been eating at me, however subtly, the thought and feeling "This is not good enough. There is still a lack of ease."

When I fell into the Absolute, this voice was silenced. The sense of discontent dissolved and disappeared. It has not come back since. This perfection is beyond perfection. It is beyond any concept, for it is beyond attention itself.

Sages like Ramana, Nisargadatta and Papaji have tried to explain how to arrive at the Absolute. My best advice is "Don't settle for anything less." You will be offered plenty of sweet substitutes. I fell for them in the past. Maybe that is how I recognized them now. Certainly I can say I found the answer that I began searching for back in 1966 at the age of 16.

In your heart, you will know it. It cannot be different from love, from perfect, total and unconditional love, yet in saying that, there is the intuition that even love must be transcended. But this great amazing love, this universal love, is transcended naturally, meaning that first you live it, then you outgrow it.

Then you know a love "that knows no love." Even the great love has very refined duality subtly intertwined in it. As you go beyond love, you find that you are not love anymore. You are the source of love. You are that which is prior to love.

Love was the answer, but its source is beyond questions, other and world. It is beyond the beyond. Love was the answer for the embodied being, even for the cosmic being. The Absolute is the answer that love, the great universal love, is seeking.

First you embrace everything and everyone in this love. Then it is seen that this unlimited love, in loving itself, dies into itself. This infinite love dies and dissolves. What is left is the Absolute. Then even love does not call attention to itself. Even love has been caught in the supreme moment that is life itself.

The quintessence of love, therefore, is this Absolute. The kiss of this Absolute is the supreme power of love-death. In love, there is dying to become one with the other. In death, there is the disappearance of the one who would be separate.

In the supreme love-death of the Absolute, in its terminal kiss that transcends the mind and even the attention, there is the final act of union. All is utterly and absolutely dissolved.

Then everything reappears, only it is all only That. It is all only this Absolute. This is not just knowledge. This is *seen* with open eyes, *heard* with open ears, *sensed* intimately, physically and directly with all of the body's senses wide open. This is not just "knowledge." That is for beggars. This is Real True Life. The Buddha lives, Jesus lives, as this Absolute.

Symphony of Self-Realization: Four Movements to Freedom

Let's recapitulate the journey from the seeker's perspective. In the LOC 600s the experience is there is local "no self."

In the LOC 700s this local "no self" expands to a global or universal emptiness, openness or no self. The person now feels "I am the world" or "I am the universe." This is also called cosmic consciousness or universal consciousness (Brahman).

In the LOC 800s this great knowledge "I am the world" is dissolved and forgotten. It is understood that all knowledge, including the universe, is useless. Knowledge is itself the duality. This insight follows the passage from the LOC 700s through the darkness of the Great Void to the LOC 800s.

1000

Abiding in the blessed darkness of not knowing (LOC 800s) that is the aftermath of this passage, next is Transfiguration. It takes you to the LOC 900s. Then you stabilize in the Absolute as the "no mind" sage. You are the divine fool at LOC 1000.

It has the musical rhythm of a symphony in four movements. "No self" is a negation. "I am the world" is an affirmation. The void passage through the transcendental darkness of not knowing is an even greater negation. Transfiguration is a new affirmation. Then all is redeemed forever in the Absolute.

The Transfiguration offers a clear foretaste of the nature of the Supreme in which all notions of "other," even of a magnificent divine other, are burned in the sacrificial fire of relentlessly honest fearless tireless inquiry. The "no mind" of the Absolute is the ultimate affirmation, for now all is redeemed and made fresh and new as God, Truth or Self (True "I") forever.

In mathematical terms, the empirical self, the ego, goes to a solo zero. Next this solo zero expands to infinity. This infinity is then seen as a cosmic zero.

The cancellation of this cosmic zero results in an inscrutable transcendental darkness, the cosmic womb of the Buddha. Born of "no mind" as the divine fool of the timeless ultra-zero, the sage abides as the Absolute.

LOC 500s is the empirical self. The solo zero is the LOC 600s. The cosmic zero is the LOC 700s. The transcendental darkness of not knowing is the LOC 800s. "No mind" is born in the LOC 900s. It matures like fine wine into the ultra-zero of LOC 1000.

In the Absolute, no separation is known. It cannot be thought of or remembered. There are no thoughts or concepts. There is no liberation or enlightenment. There is no materiality and no spirituality. All of those things are just thoughts and concepts.

In the LOC 600s, the old material world is destroyed. In the LOC 700s, a new unity is achieved. In the LOC 800s, this unity is destroyed as it is seen as a super-conceit of the Cosmic Ego.

In the course of this great destruction, which is the end of the universe itself, there is entry into a darkness like no other. At last, the Phoenix is reborn from the ashes. A final and ultimate Unity is revealed. This primal supernal Unity is the Absolute.

In this pristine primordial perfection, the legendary Garden of Eden is directly perceived as this very world exactly as it is. In the Transfiguration or Resurrection of the sage at this stage of emergence from the cosmic womb cave of total darkness and not knowing, the world is itself also transfigured and totally resurrected. All is God. All is Jesus. All is Buddha. All is Self.

Is There a Final Destination on the Journey? Yes. "Home."

Some say that enlightenment goes on forever, that it is always changing and growing. I suppose it is possible. I can imagine a deepening of this in some way. But even if it deepened, I don't think that would really change it. In the Absolute, change is fully embraced. It is "the change that knows no change."[124]

Perhaps it is like being in love. You are already in love. It is a self-validating state. Yet this love can somehow deepen and mature the way a fine wine gets richer with age.

Perhaps that is how it works. But it would still be this love, this supreme kiss in which death is life and love is death and everything is everything now here all of the time — yet nothing is known. "Absolute" means all is dissolved.

Even when you improve your home, it is still your home. LOC 1000 is "home." It is home and it feels like home. I am certain that you will recognize it when you get here. Just like your ordinary home, this home is comfortable. It is the ideal rest.

Whoever you are, wherever you are, you can be sure of this.

RIGHT HERE... RIGHT NOW... THIS IS IT. YOU ARE HOME.

My Spiritual Journal:

Ascent into Darkness

(LOC 776 to LOC 845)

My Dark Void of Unknowing Passage

Just before this void passage through the darkness of not knowing, a gifted spiritual friend of mine, Jerry from Canada (LOC 675), gave me an in-depth intuitive reading. He predicted this spiritual transition and what it would like in remarkable detail. I will share two of his emails with you.

This void passage marks the move from the LOC 700s to the LOC 800s. As I described in an earlier chapter of my spiritual journal excerpts, the relationship induced spiritual shock in January, 2000 took me up to LOC 776. When the actual step up in LOC to LOC 845 occurred, my LOC was at 793. I referenced LOC 776 in order to be consistent with previous chapters.

From 2001 to 2006, my LOC rose slowly but steadily up to LOC 793. This positioned me for a jump up to the next level, the divine darkness of the LOC 800s.

In the LOC 800s, the accumulated knowledge of the LOC 700s is discarded and dissolved. This is accomplished by going into a unique state of forgetting. You enter into the unknowing darkness of the deep sleep state (the causal body).[125]

People get confused by this darkness. Many turn back. It will seem like nothing is there. But when you stay in this darkness and dwell calmly in the unknowing, in the ignorance that is its defining attribute, the witness to that ignorance emerges. This witness is the super-causal body, the pure "I Am."[126]

Successful passage through the causal darkness results in a preternatural clarity. You are at the threshold of the Absolute.

Even this profoundly pure knowledge of the super-causal body, the "I Am" feeling with the identity "I am the Truth," must be eradicated. As awareness remains steady, the ultimate reality beyond this final super-knowledge is exposed.

As the first emergence from the Absolute, this knowledge is subtly unstable. It is the knowledge beyond knowledge. The identification with it triggered the blossoming of the universe. In order to be free, we must drop and forget *all* knowledge.

As with the other transitions between the major spiritual stages, there are many variations in what people experience. My dark void passage of unknowing, though dramatic, was short-lived (about three weeks— April 13 to May 6, 2006)

Some people do not even notice the transitional events. Other people may remember a significant dream. For others, there are external events that trigger an internal shift. For example, my move into the LOC 700s from the LOC 600s took place after getting dumped by my two-timing live-in girlfriend.

Email Exchange: Dark Void Passage Through Unknowing

Because these emails contained repetitive or unrelated text, I edited them for relevance and brevity. Jerry lives in Toronto, Canada. At the time, I was still residing in Las Vegas, Nevada.

The remarkable thing for me is that Jerry was able to predict my spiritual transition before I knew it was going to happen. Not only that, he knew details about it that I did not grasp until much later in the process. To contact Jerry for a session, please use the reader suggestions email at the end of the book.

Date: Sunday, April 16, 2006

Subject: Spiritual Reading

Hi Ramaji,

When I got off the phone after our conversation, I was concerned that you seemed upset about the reading I gave you. At the very least, you felt that it didn't resonate with you the way other readings have done.

I have checked and double checked what I saw and am convinced that it was accurate. I saw it as quite a positive reading, even though I used words such as "dry period" and "walking in darkness."

I see walking in the dark as evidence of a further evolution for you. I know that you are already living in non-duality and operate from a perspective of spontaneous non-doership.

Imagine the difference between walking into a lit space and spontaneously interacting with everything in it, versus walking into the same space without any sensory input (blindfolded, ears plugged, lacking senses of touch, taste and smell) and doing the same thing.

Both situations are non-dualist and do not have a doer. Nevertheless, the second situation requires a deepening of faith, an inner wisdom. You are able to walk in the dark because you are the light. You no longer need the affirmation of blissful experiences, because you are becoming bliss itself.

You are moving into a time of "direct knowing" in all of your actions. I think that this is quite exciting and something to look forward to.

However, it will take some adjustment at first. As you make the transition into this deepening that I've described, the adjustment will initially have a feeling of dryness to it.

In the Self,
Jerry

P.S. I didn't get the impression that the dry period will be a long one.

Date: Monday, April 17, 2006

Subject: My Mind Is Hardly Working

Dear Jerry,

I was going to wait much longer to make these comments, but the movement to forward them to you has been strong, so I am complying. I think you hugely deserve the validation that I am happy to provide here.

However, my mind is hardly working, and it is difficult to put words together, so if in some way I don't make sense, or it seems off, please forgive me in advance. It feels like quite a chore to write this, as the mind and body don't want to move, but I want to get it to you now as I don't know what is ahead. Basically, starting Sunday evening (yesterday April 16, 2006), your predictions came true.

Prior to that, on Saturday, I could not make sense of what you were saying as nothing had yet reached my conscious mind. You were reading me at a level deeper than the conscious mind, obviously.

I could only relate it to my immediate and distant past, and so I was honestly able to say I did not see how what you described was coming up. I had seen no sign of it at all.

Now to my report. A shift took place on Sunday in which the light in the head (Ajna Chakra) started, as far as I can tell, taking a great amount of energy from the rest of the body and senses. As a result, I have been light-headed, dizzy, feeling weak, and have to move very slowly. I also lose my balance easily (haven't fallen, but came close).

The light, which was very bright and pleasant, is no longer bright, thought it's there. And the bliss I had felt is gone.

In its place is this energy drain experience. I now feel like somebody home from the hospital recuperating. Appreciate that this shift happened suddenly, within 20 minutes, last night.

Also, suddenly all the motivation, enthusiasm, drive etc. that I had felt up until Sunday disappeared, vanished, leaving me with virtually no affect. It now feels as if I am sleepwalking through everything. It is hard to keep my eyes open.

My attention is nearly all of the time drawn upwards to the forehead and into the head. Thoughts will still run out toward worldly idea, plans, etc., but they are roped back in quickly.

The attention returns to the white, though not very bright, light that glows fuzzily within the center of the head. Worldly thoughts often look and feel like ghosts. Notions of worldly success, including the book I was writing, at the moment seem silly, pointless, absurd.

I have been a witness to my thoughts for a very long time, but I have not experienced this before. I have had shifts to the third eye, seen light there and so on before, but this time, it seems as if the third eye is literally draining the power from the rest of the body to feed itself. On Thursday (April 13, 2006) when this shift first took place it was into a realm of beautiful white light and bliss. None of this [weakness] was forecast.

There was a strong and definite feeling that a real movement had taken place — a valuable leap of some kind — and that it would need to stabilize. I guess this is that stabilization phase, but it is not like anything I have heard about, read about, thought about, or expected.

As for my book [a commercial writing project], which was discussed in my reading, due to the sudden lack of affect and total disappearance of motivation, I can theoretically see myself continuing, in that it doesn't matter, but I don't know how I am going to do it as there is no energy or drive to do so.

It is as if I am in a daze, or stoned, thoughts fragmented like shards of light. Where do I even begin?

The same feeling permeates my attitude towards all worldly projects and involvements that I have been working on or thinking about or planning. Even watching TV — I don't care to do that.

It is not that I think these things are "less than," inferior or illusory. There simply is no energy in them or for them. The energy has been withdrawn from my conventional thoughts and emotions, feeding instead this hungry inner light. I am not even interested in reading books or being on the Internet, which typically I enjoy.

Also, the body is being called to sit in a strict yogic meditation posture, the spine very vertical. The eyes go to the third eye light, the breath stops, there is silence, more or less. The rest of the time, this movement takes the form of resting on my back, with the same focus. We're only talking a few hours here — not a meditation marathon....

It feels to me more like two months have passed since Saturday, not two days. I cannot explain why I feel this way. This is a strong feeling, like a significant passage of time with major dimly known events taking place — but in only 2 days.

Also, my dreams have been affected. I woke up from a dream this morning with the thought "I now have all the bright parts." In my dreams, which I partially recall, I had gone to a number of persons and negotiated or otherwise successfully and ethically retrieved from them glowing pieces of myself that for some reason they had instead of me.

The dream ended with a sense of success, that I had collected all the bright parts and now had them together all in one place, perhaps right in my hands, definitely safe. I suppose the symbolism is fairly obvious, it is more so as you will see below.

Although these experiences are not that enjoyable, they are not extremely difficult either. So far it does not appear like my worldly functioning will be affected, which is what would concern me the most (i.e., being able to hold my job, pay bills, etc.). I feel weak, but I should be able to do my job (albeit a little more slowly and carefully).

The other thing that is going on, which I think you will get a kick out of, is that a Voice, sounding like a Guru, has said repeatedly to me in a voice that is mine but not mine: "NO OUTER AUTHORITIES!" What was happening was that I was tending to follow my usual pattern of consulting books, the Internet, etc. to gather external information [about this experience]. This tendency is like an "information addiction."

After doing that information stuff for awhile, I was told to stop doing not only that, but to also totally stop referring to any external source or persona as an expert, authority, guru, regarding anything at all, even money concerns and business.

I am not to think of anyone or anything else in that way. I am to refer to this newly perceived Light within as my only valid source of information, as my "inner guru," as my true guide and real expert/authority. I think you can see how this relates to the dream I had last night about reclaiming the "bright pieces" of myself from a number of (powerful?) others.

Sincerely, Ramaji

Date: April 18, 2006

Subject: From Everything to Nothing

Hi Ramaji,

You obviously are experiencing quite a bit right now. Out of respect for the message you've received about "NO OUTER AUTHORITIES," I'm not going to offer advice about what to do. I do get the strong sense, however, that you are on the cusp of experiencing what I was talking about. The transition is just beginning, so you're probably going to find it disorienting until you've segued completely into the deeper level of consciousness that I spoke about. I get the feeling that you'll experience more changes as you undergo this transition.

My sense is that you are moving away from a sense of being absolutely everything (i.e., the universe) to a sense of being absolutely nothing. In fact everything will seem as nothing — i.e., it will feel like walking in the dark. From this you'll experience a level of freedom that few have ever experienced. That's all I feel is appropriate to tell you right now. I look forward to receiving your accounts of what is happening.

In the Self,
Jerry

Date: April 19, 2006

Subject: Thank You for Your Amazing Support

Dear Jerry,

Thank you for your comments. I find it remarkable that you can comment like that on the transition from everything to nothing. I had not conceptualized any of this, but what you say makes sense to me.

I appreciate your discipline in keeping your comments sparse, per the Ajna Guru's command. But that little piece is definitely useful to me. I would say it is exactly the right idea to share with me at this time.

The experience of "being everything" is still definitely a kind of separation and limited existing, though it feels non-dual and is on a grander scale. It is fascinating at first, compared to being stuck in identification with a human biological machine, but it begins to show its limitations. Your insight is stunning.

I agree with you that I am merely on the cusp... of what, I have absolutely no idea. There is no precedent, no way to conceive it... when if I wanted to figure it out, to create a concept of it, I could not. In fact, the very nature of this process makes it next to impossible to try to figure it out, analyze it, or even, really, "understand it" in a way that will make the mind feel comfortable. Further, there is in fact little desire to do so.

It could be said that it is nothing, and it applies to no one, so what is there to say?

Thank you for your kindness and wisdom. I feel deeply supported by Reality to have you as my spiritual friend and transcendental resource on this indescribable journey.

Do take care, many blessings, Ramaji

Journal Notes: An Overview of My Journey into Darkness

The notion of 33 steps is somewhat arbitrary.

I have more than 50 pages of handwritten notes for this three week period. I also drew crude ink illustrations that are not shown here.

Because so much was happening so fast, I would write in my journal two, three even four times in a day. On workdays I would scribble my thoughts down when no one was looking.

In reviewing my notes, I realized there was a "story" that I could extract from the chaos of my real time "blow by blow" jottings. Here is that narrative as brief as I can make it.

In sum, a bright light in the third eye (Ajna Chakra) appeared. Then it dimmed and began demanding enormous amounts of energy. The word *shoonya* (void) appeared and kept repeating itself. The mind would swoon as it entered this void that was inside the head. The ability of the mind to attach to thoughts became disabled, in part because the world was of no interest.

The experience of a dark vertical tunnel inside the center of the head was followed by the vision of a spiritual mountain sacred to Lord Shiva, Mt. Kailash, on the top of my head.

When the snow on this sacred mountain would melt, drops of blissful soothing nectar flowed into my brain and down onto my tongue. The dark tunnel or vortex at one point went as far down as my throat chakra. Eventually, a new brightness arose and blotted out all of this phenomena. It had the appearance of a spiritual sun. This sun was the revelation of "I Am."

The outcome that signaled the end of this journey was not this vision of the spiritual sun of "I Am." While at my job, I was spontaneously inspired to look at the origin of attention itself.

In that moment, attention dissolved. I realized that I was no longer in a state of any kind. I was now in a "stateless state."

Stabilization in the natural or stateless state took about two more years (February, 2008). This natural "stateless state" in which the attention itself is dissolved away is the Absolute.

The natural state is sometimes referred to as *sahaja*, a Sanskrit word that means "spontaneous, natural, simple or easy." This revelation of the natural state took place on Saturday, May 6, 2006. It was my first full clear conscious recognition of it.[127]

Journal Notes: My Dark Journey of Unknowing in 33 Steps

Because of the esoteric and disjointed nature of my original handwritten notes, I summarized the major developments. I described my Kundalini inspired visions in more detail. I have used actual journal quotations to illuminate breakthroughs.

My spiritual journey in this life began with a sudden shocking Kundalini awakening at the age of 16. In a vivid lucid dream, I was in India with a guru speaking Sanskrit. Although mystical visions and blisses may seem attractive, keep in mind that Kundalini has at other times been extremely difficult for me.

In Theravadan Buddhism, there is a teaching that there are "dry" paths and "wet" paths. A person on the dry path just goes straight to the goal. Due to the lack of experiences, the disadvantage is he may get discouraged and give up the path. A person on the wet path has many alluring experiences. Due to the temptations encouraged by these visions and ecstasies, the disadvantage is that he may get stuck or sidetracked.

April 3, 2006
Step One: Deep Silence Descends

I have an experience of deep Silence descending upon me.

April 13, 2006
Step Two: Brightness in the Third Eye

Blissful brightness appears in the third eye (Ajna Chakra).

April 16, 2006
Step Three: The Ajna Guru Gives a Strong Command

I receive firm command in a masculine voice from Inner Guru: "No External Authorities." I must trust my inner knowing.

April 16, 2006
Step Four: I Roll My Eyes Up and Discover the Third Eye Point

I find the "sweet spot" of the Light in the head. It is in, down, back and up inside the core (just below the top of the head).

April 17, 2006
Step Five: I Have My "Only the Bright Parts" Dream

I wake up from a dream where I said "Only the bright parts are me." I have successfully acquired all of the required parts.

April 17, 2006
Step 6: The Third Eye Starts Draining Energy from My Body

I feel energy is being drained from my body to feed my third eye. On and off I feel light-headed and weak "like an invalid."

April 17, 2006
Step 7: I Must Meditate with My Spine Straight

There is a strong feeling to sit with the spine straight (not my usual practice). The light in third eye is now a candle flame.

April 17, 2006
Step 8: The Candle Flame Calls to Me to Focus on It

I am called to keep my attention on this flame at all times. It seems that the light that illuminates the body, senses and world is returning to its higher source in Ajna chakra.

April 17, 2006
Step 9: I Am Sleepwalking in Shoonya

I feel like I am sleepwalking. My eyes are heavy lidded. I keep hearing "Shoonya, shoonya" (the void). I cannot think clearly.

April 18, 2006
Step 10: Now I Have a Big Black Hole in My Head

A black hole or black ball appears in the center of my head.

April 18, 2006
Step 11: The Black Hole Becomes a Spinning Black Vortex

The black hole becomes a spinning black vortex. I am guided to meditate at a spot one inch below the top of my head.

From that point, white nectar flows down. The vortex sucks my attention up into a white pearl floating at the top of the vortex.

April 18, 2006
Step 12: The Spinning Black Vortex Rises Up Out of My Head

Though the spinning black vortex clearly originates in Ajna Chakra, it now rises eight inches above my head. It feels cool.

April 18, 2006
Step 13: The Mystical Darkness Takes Over

I am now walking in deep darkness. I feel that I am climbing up a mountain path. This path is shoonya. It is invisible.

April 18, 2006
Step 14: The Mystical Guide Speaks Words of Assurance

I am in the dark alone *listening* to instructions. The path is invisible. The guide is invisible. I see nothing. Yet I feel safe.

April 19, 2006
Step 15: Thought Itself Is Dissolving

There is no doubt. Thought and thinker are dissolving. "I am being asked to surrender all my thought feeding habits.... The thought I is disappearing." I wake up from sleep remembering blackness. I was not just looking at it. I was the blackness.

April 20, 2006
Step 16: A Small Mountain Appears on the Top of My Head

The flame at the top of my head becomes a bump. The bump suddenly turns into a "miniature mountain." Lord Shiva sits at the peak meditating. Bliss flows down from the snow cap.

April 20, 2006
Step 17: Two Striking Spiritual Synchronicities in the World

I experience strange synchronicities today. I see a man dressed in white who seems to have prominent breasts (androgynous Shiva). I hear a conversation where a man is saying to a pretty woman "Where is the Here-I-U?" He repeats it over and over.

April 20, 2006
Step 18: I Am Told That I Am Shiva

I am told that "The top of this mountain where Shiva lives is your destination. Shiva lives in the Perfect State. You are Shiva." When I look closely at the mountain, I see it is bumpy on one side and straight on the other. Later I see a photo of Mt. Kailash. It is Mt. Kailash, the traditional abode of Shiva!

Editorial Note: When I first saw this mountain on top of my head that had this shape, I did not know it was Mt. Kailash. I did not yet know what Mt. Kailash looked like. I did not know it had a unique shape where the two sides are very different.

After I fully understood this Mt. Kailash at the Crown to be the abode of Lord Shiva in the North (Himalayas), I was then shown an internal passage in Mt. Kailash like the one inside the Great Pyramid. This led me to Mt. Arunachala. It is the Heart on the right and abode of Lord Shiva in the South.

April 21, 2006
Step 19: I Realize the Silence Will Be Permanent

I realize that the shift is to Silence as my natural state. I write "Silence will become my normal state, not the I-thought who thinks and plans that I have dutifully witnessed for years."

April 23, 2006
Step 20: I See Lord Shiva and His Family

The vision of the mountain on the top of my head expands. Now I see three mountains, a temple and Lord Shiva's family. My daily routine now is to meditate in silence at this place.

April 24, 2006
Step 21: I See a Busy Town in Shiva Loka

Cool sweet nectar flows down from the mountain snow. I see a busy town with many people and buildings. This is Shiva Loka (Lord Shiva's world). Sometimes the scene turns to brilliant white light. Then it is covered by fluffy white clouds.

April 26, 2006
Step 22: Unable to Focus on the Mountain, I Choose the Vortex

Even though I can still see them, I can no longer concentrate on the mountains in the clouds. The blissful relief in silence that vision was giving me is gone. I go back to the vertical tunnel, the spinning vortex, that was inside my head. I am surprised to see it goes down to the throat (Visuddha Chakra).

April 28, 2006
Step 23: Functioning in No Mind

I realize that I have been acting without an I-thought and without self-reflection. The familiar witness from earlier spiritual stages is absent. "Mindless" spontaneous action rules.

April 28, 2006
Step 24: I Violate "No Outer Authorities" and Get a Headache

I violate the "No outer authorities" command and go on the Internet. I experience a severe headache. My action ruptured an invisible inner current that is pulling my attention up and away from the world, away from analysis, thinking and the mind. I write "Instead of going up, attention is being dragged out into thinking of 'others' as solid and real ('authorities'.)... [This] fragments the world. I cannot live there anymore."

May 1, 2006
Step 25: I Am Told "No Telephone Calls or Emails"

My attention is directed to just below the top of the head. I hear spiritual sounds like tinkling bells. I am directly told "No telephone calls or emails." Suddenly, my phone goes dead.

May 1, 2006
Step 26: The Waterfall of Sweet White Nectar

I see a white dome at the top of the head above the meditation point. A waterfall of white nectar flows down. The blissful nectar nourishes and soothes my brain. It brings sweet silence and cool deep forgetfulness. The top of my head feels wide open. I feel I am breathing the void at the top of my head.

May 1, 2006
Step 27: The Black Vortex Returns (and It Is Bigger)

The black vortex returns on its own. This time it is bigger. It extends down just below the notch in the physical throat. It feels like this vertical vortex is cleaning and clearing stuff out.

May 3, 2006
Step 28: A Ring of Mini-Siddhas Circles My Head

The vortex lasted only a day. The phone continues to be weird and not work properly. A ring of eight mini-Siddhas (realized beings) circles around my head. Concentrating on them helps me go into samadhi. I see what looks like a circular array of radiant white flower petals at the top of my head. They may have writing on them. The pitch black darkness is gone.

May 3, 2006
Step 29: I See a New Vision of This Inner Path

I see a new vision of this inner path. I call it the "Path of the New Eye" through the "Valley of Not Knowing." I am now in morning twilight. I see a single sun hanging in the sky before me. I write "I see but dimly the unknown, known by no one."

May 4, 2006
Step 30: The Process Moves More Quickly Than Expected

The process has moved more quickly than expected. I no longer feel that I am walking in darkness. I feel the light is dawning. I know intuitively that this sun ahead of me is the "I Am," the super-causal body. I sense that this spiritual sun will eventually dissolve, leaving only the blue of the empty sky.

May 4, 2006
Step 31: The Joyful Pilgrim Reaches the End of His Journey

A striking image appears. It is a pilgrim at the end of his journey beholding with joy the great spiritual sun. This sun was always shining behind the darkness. It was the goal.

I write about a wonderful new feeling. "There are no others at all. There is only this ONE, the one, the one and only One." Internally, the brightness is increasing. The mind is dissolving.

May 5, 2006
Step 32: Words Like Empty Echoes Are Illusions on Illusions

The words of Siddharameshwar Maharaj have nourished me like living water on this strange and difficult journey. I try to read the same book by him again that spoke to me before. I find that I can read only a few paragraphs. I write "The words are like empty echoes bouncing around and around referring to nothing... empty husks, shells, they are dead... labels for things that don't exist, illusory labels on top of illusion."[128]

May 6, 2006
Step 33: Dissolution of Attention into the Stateless State

While at work the thought came "Let the attention be natural and loose." I let the attention go wherever it wants to go, to sounds of the traffic (instead of rolling my eyes up). I could tell that "the attention was not anywhere. It was as if attention itself, and notions of controlling it, had dissolved."

At that moment, "It occurred to me to simply take a very direct look right into the state I was in at that time. I had interpreted it to just be another 'quiet state.' But when I looked right into it, into its heart, so to speak, I realized that it was not a state at all! There was literally nothing there. It was literally a 'stateless state.'

"Now I fully focused on this apparently 'stateless state' and found it completely confirmed by my own investigation that there was no movement in it, no change, no characteristics and no concepts. Surprise came over me... I understood why it was so hard to recognize this 'stateless state' — there is nothing to recognize it by. It doesn't move at all, so it never catches the attention."

It is "the Heart of Nothingness."

The Voice of the Master in the Pitch Black Darkness

Before, during and after this three week journey into the sacred darkness of unknowing, my incomparable guide was the guru of Nisargadatta Maharaj, Siddharameshwar Maharaj.

This remarkable blessing was made possible because his simple, precise and profound teachings on the passage through the blind darkness of deep sleep, the recognition of the super-causal body ("I Am") and the transition to Para-Brahman (the Absolute) had been translated into English.

The specific body of teachings by Siddharameshwhar Maharaj that I am referring to is called "Master Key to Self-Realization." When the time comes, you will find no better guide. His words reveal the truth like a transcendental road map.[129]

The Unthinkable Surrender

LOC 800 to 899

Unthinkable Surrender: LOC 800 to 899

I am discussing the LOC 800s because they are an important part of the complete Map of Awakening. Contemporary non-dual realizers often speed through the LOC 800s. My research shows that this stage is processed, although the time needed for the transition may be only a few days, weeks or months.

You may not notice this spiritual stage at all. You may not notice your transitions into and out of the LOC 800s, either. But in my dialogs with contemporary realizers who are in this stage or just transcended it, they talk about experiencing a divine display, transcendental love, ultimate fusion. It may come in dreams or during meditation or in another way.[130]

The impact of quantum physics on our consciousness has opened a new door to scientific validation of non-duality that did not exist for religions of the past. Who knows what the great LOC 800s mystics like St. John of the Cross (LOC 878) would have realized if they had our modern advantage?

Unless you are following a traditional religious path or a bhakti path of love, devotion and surrender, there is a good chance you will blast right past this level and head on up to the LOC 900s. Even so, you will still recapitulate this stage in some way. Others will get stuck here and regard it as the ultimate reality. I will address both scenarios in this chapter.

I emphasize the non-dual mystical devotion to God aspect in this chapter. Most of the persons that I found in the LOC 800s are famous devotional mystics. But devotion to the guru can also be an obstacle. It keeps you stuck in the LOC 800s, too.

Non-Dual Devotion: Unthinkable Surrender and Sacrifice

This depth of surrender is unthinkable. The potential gain from such a massive sacrifice cannot be conceived, imagined or anticipated. You have realized your identity as the world or as the totality of the universe. What could be beyond that?

This acme of knowledge will have to be discarded in exchange for a blind journey into unknowable indecipherable darkness. As a sage in the LOC 700s, you were a spiritual king. This universe was your kingdom. In the words of comic genius Mel Brooks, "It's good to be the king."[131]

From that perspective, it makes no sense to take this new step into the mysterious passage through the dazzling divine darkness. Only sacred fools who are enchanted by the useless "non-sense" of the great divine romance will be interested. The others will stay where they are in the LOC 700s.

After "I Am It" and "I Am That," Then What?

The LOC 600s sage is fascinated by the local emptiness of the "no self." He talks about the joy of absence, the freedom of living without a center. When he examines his subjective experience, he finds that he is expanding outwards in all directions from an empty open center. Captivated by this "no self" state, his ongoing experience is "I Am It."

Most of the sages living today are in the LOC 600s. Most of them are comfortable there. Since the stage of enlightenment that you start teaching from tends to be the stage that you stay at, it is likely that most of them will stay there for life.

Sages that mature into the LOC 700s discover that the "no self" inflates to include all that can be known. You now feel that your identity includes the whole world, even the universe.

When your sense of identity expands to include the world, this is not just an experience of having no center or no borders. Now your truth is "I am the world" or "I am the universe."

This expansion of your consciousness does not give you special powers. It does not mean you can read minds. This knowledge is at the level of identity. It gives you an answer to the most important question of all: "Who am I?"

It is natural at this stage to believe that you have fully realized the meaning of the famous statement "I Am That." After all, you are able to honestly proclaim "I am the world" or "I am the universe." It sounds impressive, and it is.

Super-Knowledge: the Sweet Trap of Cosmic Consciousness

To realize that you are this vast cosmic consciousness is super-knowledge. But this super-knowledge is a trap. Even though it is amazing, it is still a limitation. You probably will not see it right away, but this cosmic consciousness is a burden.

The LOC 700s sage has attained the highest fruition of human knowledge. There is nothing beyond it. To be the universe is to know the universe. This truly is the ultimate knowledge.

When you look at the entire spiritual journey of awakening from high above with the eyes of a soaring eagle, you can see everything laid out in front of you. It is quite simply really.

What you see is that the path has two major movements. The first great movement eliminates the separate self. The second great movement eliminates the "other." The sense of an "other" gets dissolved until, like Ramana said, "There is no world."

The LOC 600s and LOC 700s belong to the first movement. It may look like the LOC 700s sage has eliminated the "other." He is identified with the universe. But that does not bring an end to the other. "I Am That" says there is still "I" and still "That." The "no self" of the LOC 600s was still a self. The "cosmic self" of the LOC 700s is an inflated version of it.

As enjoyable as the experience of self as boundless space or consciousness may be, there is still identification. The sage is identified with the world or the universe.

Duality at a very refined level still remains. Even in super-knowledge, there is duality. If there is still duality even at the level of super-knowledge, then what can you do?

The No Knowing Step: First No Self, Then No Other

In order to move on and rise above the LOC 700s, the sage must sacrifice this universal knowledge. This universal knowledge is the full blossoming of the no self. It has now expanded to include the whole world, the whole universe.

This is wonderful, but it is eventually seen that this greatest of all knowledge is a massive limitation. The universe is like a huge humming machine. It is constantly engaged in creation and manifestation. It is always vibrating and pulsating. It is very smart but it is very busy.

Even though you have achieved identification with the cosmic "I Am" so that you can say with pride and joy "I Am All," in the end it is just more stuff. This stuff is filled with very subtle tension. It is not a state of perfect rest, of absolute stillness. It is not the highest state. It is not the stateless state.

The solution is a drastic one, but it turns out to be the only one that works. If you are going to get rid of the "other" for good, you will have to get rid of knowledge, too. The experience or sense of the other is embedded in all knowledge. Therefore, you must let go of your knowledge. You must sacrifice it.

Chances are you will only take this step when you have realized that all of this super-knowledge, including this world and this universe, is useless to you. It is of no value to you.

This sacrifice of your super-knowledge and of your cosmic consciousness is a big step. It is very pleasant in the LOC 700s. This level has a lot going for it. Some of the greatest teachers alive are in the LOC 700s. It is very comforting to have all of this rich beautiful knowledge. Knowledge, after all, is power.

When the sage finally recognizes that he needs to sacrifice his super-knowledge of cosmic consciousness to go on, he leaves behind the comfort of knowing. He enters into a world of not knowing, of disconcerting darkness, of divine ignorance.

This profound sacrifice by the sage of his hard-won spiritual gains for unknown realms beyond cosmic consciousness takes the sage into the second movement where the primal seed of duality, the birthplace of the other, is exposed. In this supernal darkness, the troublesome sense of other is finally dissolved.

The other does not dissolve away easily. The other has one more surprise up its sleeve. When knowledge is sacrificed and the sense of the world as the other, as the "that" in "I Am That," vanishes, an astonishing new surprise waits for the sage in the intoxicating velvet darkness.

This big surprise is God, Goddess, Christ, Buddha, Guru. Whoever you would worship, whoever you would regard as the Father or Mother of Love, whoever is your savior, will be waiting there for you with open arms and a big friendly smile.

If You Meet the Buddha on the Road, Kill Him

The LOC 800s used to be much more popular. When I first started looking at the LOCs of contemporary non-duality teachers, I noticed that most were in the 600s, some were in the 700s and a handful were at 1000. But I was having trouble finding modern sages who were abiding in the LOC 800s.

When I looked at the great historical mystics, the spiritual giants of the past, I found many with LOCs in the 800s. Among them were famous Christian saints like St. John of the Cross (LOC 878) and St. Teresa of Avila (LOC 840).

It dawned on me that they stabilized at this stage because their spiritual path was devotion, prayer and surrender. In the East, this is the path of bhakti, the way of love, devotion, service and surrender. It is the way of the heart. This idea was confirmed when I checked contemporary mystic Bernadette Roberts (LOC 854). Her devotional non-dual awakening, described in *The Experience of No-Self*, confirms that she did not want to go beyond her divine union.[132]

I am not saying that you have to give up your faith or turn your back on God in order to realize the Absolute. Meister Eckhart (LOC 1000), the greatest of all medieval mystics, famously said "I pray God to make me free of God, for [His] unconditioned Being is above God and all distinctions."[133]

The "unconditioned Being" Eckhart refers to is the Supreme Self, the Absolute. This natural state appears after there is stabilization in the no mind. It is sometimes called "sahaja."

You can be a Christian, a Jew, a Hindu, a Muslim, and still love God and still realize the Absolute (LOC 1000). True, you will still have to kill God. But what you are killing is *not* actually God. It is your concept of God. It is just mind stuff.

You cannot kill the ultimate reality, the supreme transpersonal Godhead. Triumphantly forever transcendent yet gloriously immanent, the real God that is within is also beyond.

It cannot die. Concepts die. Thoughts die. Ideas die. Beliefs die. Reality does not die. A real God cannot die. Only phony Gods die. If you can kill your God, then It was not real God.

It is in this spirit that I subscribe to the Zen saying "If you meet the Buddha on the road, kill him." It is attributed to Zen Master Linji, founder of the Rinzai sect of Zen Buddhism.[134]

By the time you reach the LOC 800s, you have already "killed" many "Buddhas" along the path. If you do not go all the way to LOC 1000, then you have fallen for the trap of the "perfect other." This other is perfect because it is divine and it is the embodiment of love. This makes it the perfect trap.

This Beloved brings healing of your deepest wounds. But as long as you remain separate from the Beloved, you fail to receive His or Her final gift. That parting gift is that you are the Beloved. You realize "I am the Beloved." I Am That.

Allow yourself to be loved. Allow yourself to be healed. Stay awhile and enjoy the fruits of your labor. Rest in the sense of pure "I Am." This is beyond the cosmic "I Am" of the LOC 700s where you feel like you are the universe. This pure divine "I Am" is a state of wholeness that contains within it the yin and yang potentials of the universe. It is the cosmic seed state.

It is prior to the universe, yet it is poised for manifestation. It is the seed essence of manifestation. It is the divine expansion on the brink of bursting forth. Blissfully abiding within it is the perfect primal duality, ultimate primordial Mother-Father.

Seductive, beautiful and seemingly perfect, this Abode of Love is not your final place of rest. It is not your spiritual Home. There is still the veil of the LOC 900s where you know you are the Self but you have not totally resolved the "world." After that is a final step into full embrace of the Absolute.

This essential "I Am" is very subtly outward oriented. It is so close to the Absolute (LOC 1000), but this distance is further than it looks. In this place there is Perfect Love, but this Love wants to express itself, to unveil itself as the absurd generosity of the infinite universe. It cannot wait to get the party started!

Transcending God: Going Beyond Union with the Divine

It is impossible for me to give devotional mysticism, Christian and otherwise, the coverage it deserves in this book. Because the devotional way is today poorly understood and rarely practiced, I have chosen to keep my comments to a minimum.

My own spiritual path has had a strong devotional flavor to it. You will find it most clearly expressed in the excerpts from my spiritual journey having to do with Kundalini. Although Kundalini may be described as an "energy," it is equally accurate to describe it as the spiritual power of Divine Mother.

The most primal dyad, soul and God, sets the stage for an ineffable transcendence of all but that divine union itself. The mystic who attains to this spiritual height is likely to remain there, content that he has attained the supreme boon of God.

Union in God, even dissolution in God, these are possible. But surely transcending God is not. How can you transcend God?

It turns out that the Absolute, the Supreme Self, is beyond union as well. The last veil of God, the last face of God, is God itself. This is the primal projection of the divine Father-Mother Source. The universe is the living Child of this Father-Mother.

In the ancient Kabbalah, the Absolute or Supreme Self is called Kether. Just below it and branching out from it are the Mother God, Binah, and the Father God, Chokmah. In order to arrive at the nameless, we must face, attain fusion with and then forge on beyond the Divine Father-Mother, the Source of All.

Just as you empty yourself into the Divine, the Divine must empty itself into the Absolute. As you follow this river of no return, you arrive at Kether, the Crown of the Kabbalah.

1000

Here is found the Supernal Light, the Reality from which the Father-Mother God (the pure "I AM") emerged. "I Am That" means you are This. You are this Ultimate Reality.

In the LOC 700s, there was the full realization of pure Being. In the LOC 800s, there is the full mystical realization of Love. In the LOC 900s and the full blossoming in LOC 1000, Being, Love and Unknowing are fused. All sense of limitation is consumed in the fire of their meeting. Everything is reborn.

This rebirth is like no other. It is being reborn into "unborn."

Life in the LOC 800s can be profoundly blissful and amazing, for just as the LOC 700s was the acme of knowledge, the LOC 800s are the acme of love, devotion and surrender. Total and utter abandon in love leads to ecstasy, bliss, rapture and more.

Achieving oneness with the Divine Beloved is seen as the supreme attainment of the devotional mystical path. Speaking of my own path, I did not wish to move beyond the union that I felt with Kali Ma, the form of Divine Mother who had chosen me back in 1982 at a Vedanta Society Temple in California.

In Her Grace and Love, She forced me to face the hidden limitations of my humble stance. She outsmarted me.

She exposed the subtle posturing that remained even in my role as Her devoted spiritual slave and love servant. In Her Infinite Mercy, She forced me to embrace the liberating truth of Lord Shiva (a name for the Absolute or the Supreme Self).

I was content to be Her devotee. But She would have none of that. She said "I will not have you sniveling at my feet like a human worm. Be a man. The only true man is Lord Shiva. Be like Shiva. Become Shiva. Nothing less is acceptable to Me."

This was tantamount to me becoming God, and I resisted it. When union with God is transcended, then that is all that is left. I told Her that She was speaking nonsense. As always, She found ways to educate me about my error. I was forced to embrace Lord Shiva as my identity, meaning there is only "I."

The Radical Kindness of the Bloodthirsty God Killers

It was only after I sat down to write this book that the full implications of the steps in awakening that I had *already* taken registered for me. I knew that Kali Ma had demanded that I relinquish my slavish devotion to Her. I knew that She had demanded that I fully and unconditionally embrace my identity as Shiva. But I did not grasp the implications of Kali's command in terms of how people think about these things.

I followed Her orders. I took the actions. The results were as She had predicted. It all took place in such a seamless and flowing way that I accepted it as natural and normal. It was just one more step on the path. But it was more than that.

Once again, the staggering brilliance and infinite cunning of Kali Ma astonished me. I had been masterfully outplayed by Her. Knowing that I did not want to give Her up (an error that was keeping me in the LOC 800s), She made it so that the only way for me to keep my relationship with Her would be to embrace Shiva Consciousness and unconditionally be the Self.

It was not until I was discussing this with my friend Koort that I realized that Kali had turned me into a "god killer." In my email to Koort, I wrote "My Kali bhakti [devotional] streak makes me sympathetic to the LOC 800s. I was lucky with Kali Ma as she kicked my ass into kingdom come... not all forms of God are so (brutally) kind to their devotees."

Here is Koort's reply. I would say it hits the bull's eye.

> If your God/Goddess/Guru is not so kind as to remove themselves from you, then be courageous and kill them so that you do not to get stuck in this level.
>
> Don't be a coward. If you see a Buddha on the road, don't make him into a God or icon, kill him. He doesn't want or need your love or devotion. He is neither name nor form. He is never incarnated into anything. Buddha is That which is all things, but is nothing Itself. Those stuck in the LOC 800s are cowards in love with themselves, the glorious I AM, and afraid of the nothingness... that which is Self without a second.
>
> The pure I AM, God, the Light is very tricky. You have eaten the forbidden fruit from the Tree of Knowledge, and you believe that you are because of Him or Her, but no. It is just the opposite. He or She is only because you are.
>
> Those in the LOC 800s may feel good living in the state of pure I AM, but it is still only a state. If Christian mystics really have respect for their beloved God, Christ or Jesus, they would let them die once and for all.
>
> They certainly want to die, so that you will die with them into THAT which is nothingness or not knowing, into THAT in which all states exist, but is touched by no state. No God. No Jesus. No Christ. No Buddha. No Guru. No Ramana. No you.[135]

Fearlessness is not usually listed as a requirement for spiritual enlightenment. But it will be required of you sooner or later.

The LOC 800s: Dazzling Dark Womb of the Baby Buddha

Having attained to the quintessential love union, the ultimate embrace, the love higher than any other, you rest in a thrilling dazzling darkness, the mindless warmth of a womb divine.

This is the birth of unknowing, but it is not its full blossoming.

The final supreme step becomes possible: the birth of a baby Buddha, the Absolute abiding in human form. The baby Buddha grows up and leaves the Father-Mother behind.

It cannot be any other way. The end cannot be in darkness, not even divine darkness. The grand finale must be in supreme Light. The fantastic fusion with Father and/or Mother God in the dazzling darkness of unknowing recapitulates the nine months in the sentient darkness of the biological mother.

As grand as the LOC 800s are, they set the stage for true spiritual self-reliance and adulthood. The LOC 800s are the third spiritual trimester, preparation for birth of the Buddha.

When he is born, it will be into the stunning brightness of the super-real World that is both True Self and dynamic Duality.

The ultimate truth of non-duality is not non-duality. It is a Supreme Wholeness in which the ineffable value and worth of everything and everyone is understood at an existential level.

In terms of daily life, it means that the duality of the world which was previously thought to be a problem to escape from, is now seen to be the living breathing moving Body of Truth.

The World of Flesh and Blood Is "Saved" By a Mature Sage

This is why the mystical realization at the LOC 800s cannot be the final solution. The final solution must enable you to live in the world with the pristine clarity that this world is Truth itself. "I Am That" does not only mean that I am a Super-Self of Oneness, the Supreme I of the universe. Nor does it mean that now that I am one with God, I can ignore the world or pretend that it is unreal and illusory. That is not enough.

The all-consuming realization of "I Am That" must include the World too, so that the World is redeemed, is made whole, is reborn. It means that this ugly stupid crazy World is Saved.

Who "saves" it? It is saved by the mature sage who attains the Absolute. Although it appears that even love is transcended, the reality is that now the unlimited power of love has been unleashed to be itself. Love liberated becomes the World.

Even in the transcendental mystery of divine union, the world as physical world, the world as "out there," as "not I," is still not resolved fully and completely. The materialistic taint of the apparent world still fouls even this divinely blissful air.

Love wants to overcome even this primordial duality. Self and other, soul and God, divine Father and divine Mother, all roll on the road of knowledge, of knowing an other.

Only when the fire burns the brightest and the highest is all knowledge of the other consumed. Only in not knowing the other at all, in not knowing that an other exists, can Love reach its empyrean.

The secret ambition of the sacred super-love of the LOC 800s is for this supernal love to die into itself. This love wants to return to its own Source in the Absolute.

There it is utterly consumed. There it eats itself alive and puts itself out. There this eternal fire of love is renewed, regenerated and reborn.

The archetypal duality of soul and God united, of Father and Mother God transcendentally fused, is not the final home of the Supreme Love. Supreme Love finds true rest only in the Supreme Self, in the Absolute. It dies so that it may live again.

Even when Transfiguration takes you into the LOC 900s, there may still be a reluctance to merge with and embrace without any reservations at all the blood, sweat, tears and trials of the mundane world. There may still be a desire to hold onto special inner states of samadhi, purity and bliss. These pristine pleasures provide the penultimate temptation.

I call this spiritual stutter step at the final threshold to the Absolute the Hesitant Hermit phase. It corresponds to the low LOC 900s. Most of the sages who get this far keep on going to LOC 1000. I call the very few sages who fail to complete the journey at this level hesitant hermits because typically they choose to live a private isolated life where they are left alone.

I went through this phase. I think it is natural for there to be some hesitation about returning to the world. The question is whether or not the sage can see through this holy temptation.

Some LOC 1000 sages continue to live in relative isolation. It is not about the lifestyle. It is about the full naked return to the "world" so that it may be saved and reborn as World by you.

Pseudo-Dionysius, Agnosia and the Dazzling Divine Dark

The classical devotional mystics like Pseudo-Dionysius (LOC 867), St. John of the Cross (LOC 878) and the anonymous author of *The Cloud of Unknowing* (LOC 846) make the state of divine union sound like the supreme experience.[136] In a way it is, for beyond this highest union lies the total loss of union.

Indeed, what lies ahead in the LOC 900s to LOC 1000 is a non-state of non-union, for unity is possible only for that which feels it is separate and has a sense of other. If no separation is known, recognized or even remembered, then movement towards or movement away from both become impossible.

Likewise, subject and object are utterly transcended because they are not known to have ever existed. Knowledge of God becomes irrelevant. Primordial wholeness is embraced which, knowing no other, cannot know that it exists as such.

It is the other that notifies you that you exist. If the other does not emerge, if that movement, that birth of the other, never takes place, then even the bliss of divine union is consumed.

The preparation for this sublime and sacred ignorance, the no mind of the unborn Absolute, is in dazzling divine darkness.

This is the birth of the no-knowing that achieves its full flowering in the natural "only don't know" state, sahaja.

The title of one such mystical Christian meditation manual, *The Cloud of Unknowing*, is a perfect description of what lies ahead for the prayerful Christian mystic should he succeed. But the most eloquent of these writers, apart from the great and inimitable St. John of the Cross, is Pseudo-Dionysius.

Pseudo-Dionysius gets his odd hyphenated name because at one time he was thought to be Dionysius the Areopagite, the Athenian convert of St. Paul mentioned in Acts 17:34. Though it turned out he was not the author, the association with this Biblical celebrity gave the magnificent mystical writings of the anonymous author considerable clout.

Pseudo-Dionysius wrote in the late 5th century, yet his artful deception was not discovered until the fifteenth century. By then it was, as they say, too late. Pseudo-Dionysius had become iconic — a good thing for Christian mysticism.[137]

Here is a taste of the elegant mystical prose of Pseudo-Dionysius that so deliciously invites the reader into a blissful darkness beyond the mind where all knowing is forgotten. These quotations are from *The Mystical Theology*.

The term "Agnosia" refers to spiritual super-knowledge that requires the dropping of both conventional ignorance and knowledge. In short, only by "not knowing" can you ever hope to truly "know" the naked reality of the unspeakable Supreme.

The simple and absolute and changeless mysteries of theology lie hidden within the super-luminous gloom of the silence, revealing hidden things, which in its deepest darkness shines above the most super-brilliant, and in the altogether impalpable and invisible, fills to overflowing the eyeless minds with glories of surpassing beauty...

leave behind both sensible perceptions and intellectual efforts, and all objects of sense and intelligence, and all things not being and being, and be raised aloft unknowingly to the union, as far as attainable, with Him Who is above every essence and knowledge. For by the resistless and absolute ecstasy in all purity, from thyself and all, thou wilt be carried on high, to the superessential ray of the Divine darkness, when thou hast cast away all, and become free from all...

It is superessentially exalted above all, and manifested without veil and in truth, to those alone who pass through both all things consecrated and pure, and ascend above every ascent of all holy summits, and leave behind all divine lights and sounds, and heavenly words, and enter into the gloom, where really is, as the Oracles say, He Who is beyond all.

Now this I think signifies that the most Divine and Highest of the things seen and contemplated are a sort of suggestive expression, of the things subject to Him Who is above all, through which His wholly inconceivable Presence is shown, reaching to the highest spiritual summits of His most holy places; and then he (Moses) is freed from them who are both seen and seeing, and enters into the gloom of the Agnosia;

a gloom veritably mystic, within which he closes all perceptions of knowledge and enters into the altogether impalpable and unseen, being wholly of Him Who is beyond all, and of none, neither himself nor other; and by inactivity of all knowledge, united in his better part to the altogether Unknown, and by knowing nothing, knowing above mind.[138]

1000

If you detected the flavor of the *via negativa*, the "neti neti" of "not this and not that," you are right on target. As the metaphor of the statue illustrates, "by extracting all the encumbrances" and through "the mere cutting away," the true ultimate divine, "the Superessential," is inevitably revealed.

That "no mind" or transcendent wisdom beyond and prior to the mind is what this is about is made abundantly transparent in this sentence from the above pithy guidance: "By inactivity of all knowledge, united in his better part to the altogether Unknown, and by knowing nothing, knowing above mind."

As profound as "I am All" or I am the Universe" or "I am Cosmic Consciousness" may have been, this ripe crescendo of self-serving super-knowledge must give way to divinely inspired super-ignorance, to transcendental unknowing, to the nascent no mind of the baby Buddha, for progress to be made.

LOC 800s Case Study: Papaji, the Ardent Krishna Devotee

Students of Papaji may be familiar with this story. It is worth retelling. It illustrates the grandeur and subtle flaws of the LOC 800s while demonstrating ascent beyond the devotional heart to illumination of the Heart on the right and LOC 1000.

As a child, Papaji was such a strong devotee of Lord Krishna that Lord Krishna would appear to him and physical form and play with him. As an adult, the mention of the name Krishna invoked intense bliss, rapture and ecstasy in his body.[139]

During this profound devotional phase, Papaji was at LOC 878. He was experiencing the heights of devotional sadhana. Eventually, he became unsatisfied even with this attainment.

Later in life, after seeing remarkable visions of Lord Rama and other great Hindu deities where he conversed with them like they were just other human beings, his ability to repeat the name of Lord Krishna suddenly vanished. His mind would not hold onto thoughts anymore. This made repeating the divine name impossible. Nor could he read his holy books.[140]

It occurred to him to visit Ramana Maharshi. When he arrived there, he told Ramana how he could not longer chant the name of Lord Krishna. Ramana replied by asking him how he got there. Papaji replied that he took a train, a cart and so on.

Ramana then asked him where are the train and the cart now?

Papaji was confused by Ramana's line of reasoning. They "went away," he said. He was here now. They were long gone.

Ramana replied by saying that his chanting of Lord Krishna's name is a similar situation. This chanting that he had been doing faithfully for decades had been a vehicle for him to arrive here. Now that he was here with Ramana, he didn't need it anymore. It had served its purpose. Because this was so, he did not need to drop it. It went away on its own.

Papaji wanted to know if Ramana could show God to him.

Ramana answered with strong words. "No, I cannot show you God or enable you to see God because God is not an object that can be seen. God is the subject. He is the seer. Don't concern yourself with objects that can be seen. Find out who the seer is." As if to emphasize the error of seeking a God outside of himself, Ramana added "You alone are God."[141]

Ramana gazed intently at Papaji. In the sacred luminosity of the great sage's silence, Papaji felt every cell being purified. In that moment, he realized the peace of the Self (LOC 1000).[142]

In this moment, Papaji experienced a profound blossoming of the spiritual Heart, the Heart of all. He said the location matched the Heart on the right talked about by Ramana.[143]

Through the Grace of Ramana Maharshi, Papaji had realized the Absolute, the Supreme Self. Even so, he had spent many years in this life and many years in previous lives passionately engaged in deep and intense spiritual practices.

Although enlightenment is uncaused, eternal and universal, these lifetimes of spiritual practice had, as Ramana plainly said, functioned as the vehicle that brought him to Ramana's Grace and to the full realization of the Self in this life.

LOC 800s Case Study: Dazzling Dark of John Wren-Lewis

John Wren-Lewis talks about a "dazzling darkness" that sounds like the luminous darkness of Pseudo-Dionysius.

He is highly articulate and conveys his experience of the LOC 800s expert with great eloquence. As impressive as it may sound, his beloved darkness is not the final destination. The fact that he still had unresolved questions illustrates this.

While riding a bus in the jungles of Thailand with his wife in 1983, John Wren-Lewis (LOC 847) was given poisoned candy by a well-dressed young would-be thief.

His wife did not eat the poisoned candy. John Wren-Lewis did. When she saw her husband turning blue, she rushed him to the hospital.[144]

At the hospital, it was thought he might die. Instead of dying, he had an unusual near-death experience. His former identity was snuffed out like a candle flame (as in the root meaning of nirvana, to "snuff out"). When he came back, it was as an enlightened person.

His fear of death vanished, but that was not all. He found himself living in a vibrant eternal now that transcended any concerns about the future, including survival after death.

> On the contrary, it has everything to do with a dimension of aliveness here and now which makes the notion of separate survival a very secondary matter, in this world or any other. In fact it makes each present instant so utterly satisfying that even the success or failure of creative activity becomes relatively unimportant. In other words, I've been liberated from what William Blake called obsession with futurity, which, until it happened, I used to consider a psychological impossibility."[145]

His new state was not immediately obvious to him. It became apparent that he would survive the primitive concoction of morphine and cocaine that had been administered to him by the erstwhile criminal on the long distance bus.

That evening in the hospital, after his unique near-death experience, he noticed that when he had returned to waking consciousness from sleep, it was from a totally different place than before. Please note that he did not have a background in meditation. Though not an atheist, he was a skeptic.

> The fact that I'd undergone a radical consciousness shift began to become apparent only after everyone had settled down for the night and I was left awake, feeling as if I'd had enough sleep to last a lifetime. By stages I became aware that when I'd awakened a few hours earlier, it hadn't been from a state of ordinary unconsciousness at all.
>
> It was as if I'd emerged freshly made (complete with all the memories that constitute my personal identity) from a vast blackness that was somehow radiant, a kind of infinitely concentrated aliveness or pure consciousness that had no separation within it, and therefore no space or time."[146]

Wren-Lewis called this vast radiant blackness that had rebirthed him into a new life of enlightenment the "dazzling dark." He described his near-death experience as being more like an ego death experience. His separate personal self had vanished.

When memories and personality reconstructed themselves, they did so from a joyful cosmic perspective that he, as a dyed in the wool skeptic, had not thought possible. Here's how he described this spiritual rebirth.

> There was absolutely no sense of personal continuity. In fact the sense of a stop in time was so absolute that I'm now convinced I really did die, if only for a few seconds or fractions of a second... My impression is that my personal consciousness was actually snuffed out (the root meaning, according to some scholars, of the word nirvana) and then recreated by a kind of focusing-down from the infinite eternity of that radiant dark pure consciousness.[147]

In a parallel to Suzanne Segal and Bernadette Roberts, he was aware of a kind of witness faculty or presence near his head.

> That wonderful eternal life of everywhere was still there, right behind my eyes, or more accurately, at the back of my head, continually recreating my whole personal body-mind consciousness afresh, instant by instant, now! and now! and now! That's no mere metaphor for a vague sensation; it was so palpably real that I put my hand up to probe the back of my skull, half wondering if the doctors had sawn part of it away to open my head to infinity. Yet it wasn't in the least a feeling of being damaged; it was more like having had a cataract taken off my brain, letting me experience the world and myself properly for the first time, for that lovely dark radiance seemed to reveal the essence of everything as holy.[148]

Wren-Lewis found that he now took delight in everything. No matter how imperfect, ugly or stinky, it was magnificently and gloriously what it was and, for him, a source of great joy.

> I felt like exclaiming, 'Of course! That's absolutely right!' and applauding every single thing with tears of gratitude, not just the now sleeping Ann [his wife] and the small jar of flowers the nurse had placed by the bedside, but also the ominous stains on the bed sheets, the ancient paint peeling off the walls, the far from hygienic smell of the toilet, the coughs and groans of other patients, and even the traumatized condition of my body. From the recesses of my memory emerged that statement [in] the book of Genesis about God observing everything He had made and finding it very good.[149]

As the days, weeks and months passed, his "eternity consciousness" showed no sign of fading. Somehow, he had won the spiritual lottery, yet he had never bought the ticket.

He had been a scientist, humanist, spiritual cynic and a leader in the "Death of God" movement in Great Britain. Before his awakening, he saw religion and spiritual pursuits as rubbish.

When his mind, memories and personality reconstituted themselves, his deeply rational skeptical tendencies were reincarnated in him as well. This time, though, he wondered about the vast planetary enterprise called religion and spirituality from the other end of the telescope. From the perspective of the "eternity consciousness" that he had actualized, there was nothing to seek. There was only NOW.

Now he was an enlightened person. The veils had fallen from his eyes. His deeply skeptical mind wondered about all the people seeking and all the methods that they were using as they struggled to gain what he had so aimlessly and effortlessly achieved through an apparently random act of nearly lethal poisoned kindness.

Were they just wasting there time? Was it a futile fantasy? Now, in his compassion, he asked these sorts of questions.

It seems that he never arrived at an answer. He wrote a book about his experience, but it was never published. John Wren-Lewis passed away in 2006. He was 82 years old.[150]

LOC 800s Case Study: Christian Mystic Bernadette Roberts

Based upon my research, the three modern sages who most resemble the classical mystics like St. John of the Cross are Bernadette Roberts (LOC 854) Philip Mistlberger (LOC 876) and David Hawkins (LOC 874). Philip Mistlberger is a master of the Western occult mystery tradition. The late Hawkins was known as a mystical teacher of "devotional nonduality."[151]

Here I will talk about the path of Bernadette Roberts based on her spiritual autobiography. This is an extraordinary book for several reasons. It is rare for a person of this level of spiritual attainment to write with such candor about their experiences. It is also rare for them to be such a good writer.

I have already referenced her first autobiographical book in the context of the LOC 700s. Here I will look at her account of the LOC 800s. I will also look at why she stopped at the stage.

If you have not read this book, please read it. I am not aware of any other spiritual autobiography that speaks with such clarity and honesty about the trials and tribulations, about the graces and the glories, of the high levels of the spiritual path.

Beyond that profundity, which would be enough, her account is remarkable in how it balances the psychological and mystical dimensions of spiritual progress. Finally, along with walking a Western path of being a mother raising several children, she speaks from the perspective of a Christian.

Most of you reading this book were raised in a Christian, Jewish or Muslim religious heritage. These religions all have Middle Eastern roots. They are all profoundly dualistic.

As the saying goes, you can take the girl out of the city, but you can't take the city out of the girl. The parallel here is that for most students of Advaita and non-duality, it is inevitable and unavoidable that they will translate their non-dual studies in terms of the dualistic religions that they were raised in.

1000

Of all the modern sages, Bernadette Roberts stands out as the classic modern non-dual Christian realizer. She transcended all but her own devotion. As my own case shows, it is possible to "kill God" and still enjoy a relationship with Him or Her.

There is a big step beyond the LOC 800s to the LOC 900s and another big step to LOC 1000. To arrive at that quintessential simplicity, all concepts, all beliefs, all notions, all ideas, must be dropped, dissolved, burned up, destroyed. Nothing, not one thing, can be held onto. Everything must go. Your most precious religious icons and ideals must be incinerated.

The Christian sage Meister Eckhart (LOC 1000) proves that it is possible to attain the Absolute and still remain true to your faith. Muslim masters who attained the Absolute did so.

Jewish masters who attained the Absolute did so. The Absolute is not just the purview of Eastern religion, of Buddhism and Advaita. The Absolute is available to all.

The focal points for Bernadette Roberts appear to be the uniqueness of Christ, the the flow of love within the Trinity and the mystical grace of the Eucharist. In my view, she can keep all of that and still attain the Absolute (LOC 1000).[152]

Meister Eckhart was able to happily resolve this conflict and stay in harmony with Christian dogma. He boldly proclaimed "Truth is something so noble that if God could turn aside from it, I could keep the truth and let God go."[153]

As admirable as Roberts' quest is, it would appear that she preferred, at the threshold of the final step, to keep God and let the Truth go. This places her smack dab in the LOC 800s.

What she finally seems to butt up against, the mystical problem which she cannot resolve, is *not* these Christian mysteries. It is *not* her Christian beliefs that get in the way.

The evidence that she is unable to embrace, in spite of her own experience, is that she, in terms of her ultimate and final truth, is none other than God. In terms of any God that is based on concepts or dogma, she is beyond God. She is the Source of that God, for she is one with the ineffable Source itself. This Source is the Absolute, the mystic's true and eternal home.

Her argument that she is not God appears to have two parts. First, she says that it is obvious to her that she is "not the totality of God." God knows things and does things that she is not knowing and doing. Therefore, she cannot be God.[154]

The second argument is based on the uniqueness of Christ. She seems to be saying that in order for her to be God, to have her true identity in and as God in essence, she must herself be Christ. Yet clearly there was and is only one Christ.[155]

I will address her second point first. That view is like saying that because the historical Buddha was a great Avatar who came here to establish a global religion that has lasted more than 2,500 years, it is impossible for me to realize my Buddha Nature, the Absolute, the Universal I, the Supreme Self of all.

Stated in this way, the truth is plainly the opposite. Lord Buddha incarnated as an Avatar so that you and I could attain to the Truth, to realize ourselves as the Absolute Reality. In a parallel line, Roberts was called to realize her Christ Nature.

The Buddhist realizes Buddha. The Christian realizes Christ. This Supreme Reality is not separate from God. It is beyond all concepts. As the stateless state, it is beyond "God" as well.

Now I will address the first point. Roberts' says several times in her autobiography that, after the full power of the Grace of God had been dispensed into her being, all that could be said, all that was left, was the knowingness that "I am God." This was the final truth that she had become aware of.[156]

She admits to struggling with this concept. She confesses that she was unable to resolve the implications of her discovery. She is concerned that it might take her more deeply into this "I am God" state. She vigorously asserts that she does not want that to happen. This is her confession. She admits to resisting the full invasion of God's Grace in favor of religious dogma or the subtle egocentricity of dualistic devotion, or both.[157]

In the quote below from her journal, notice how she admits that it is possible for God to eliminate any view other than the knowledge that "I am God." It is possible for God to "possess" her to that point. If she allows God to go all the way with her, that could be her fate. She sees that clearly. After seeing that, she makes it plain that she definitely does not want that!

> To lose yourself is one thing, to become God is another... So what does all this mean? I don't know, but what I know for sure is that God can possess this form far more than He does at present. He can take over and obliterate any other knowing but the one that says "I am God." I don't know what to make of this... Maybe it's a foretaste of some future event. I hope not![158]

Roberts is okay with losing herself, but she is not okay with becoming God. If this is her truth and her position, that is all it will take for her progress to grind to a halt. She is blissfully comfortable in the LOC 800s, apparently. She will stay there until she sees through this subtle resistance to God's Grace.

The Christian dogma does not really support this seeing, but it is very possible for a Christian to keep going to the Absolute. The proof is found in Meister Eckhart who retained his faith and went all the way under even more difficult conditions.

"The Devotee of God Wants to Eat Sugar..." and Kill God!

In the traditional devotional path, there is a spiritual position that might be described as transcendental humility. It is the ego remnant that enables the devotee to experience the Beloved as the Supreme Source of love, bliss, rapture, peace.

It may be that Bernadette Roberts preferred to retain this highest form of humility so that she could continue to enjoy her relationship with God through her Lord Jesus Christ. If so, there is an ancient tradition that supports this.

According to this philosophy, to merge with the Divine Source will obliterate its peerless flavor. This mystical merger is incomparably sweet. It is the triumph of pure love. It is the love supreme and ineffable. In short, it is supposed to be the best spiritual enjoyment, better even than realizing the Self.

Of course, this is not true. If it was true, then this devotional position would be the Self or the Absolute. But it is not.

1000

This devotion versus non-duality confusion was wonderfully dramatized in the life of the great master Ramakrishna (LOC 1000). Ramakrishna is regarded as the Avatar for our present Kali Yuga by his devotees. He is known for rekindling the devotion to Divine Mother Kali Ma in modern times.[159]

In his role as a world teacher, he would tell people that the path of love, surrender, service and devotion is the way most suitable for spiritual aspirants today. "The devotee of God wants to eat sugar, and not become sugar," he declared.[160]

Yet Ramakrishna's own unwavering devotion to Kali Ma was seen to be a limitation. Even he, the most famous devotee of the goddess Kali in modern times, was compelled to realize the Absolute in the hands of Totapuri, a non-dual sage.

Totapuri asked Ramakrishna to forget about God and focus on the Absolute. Ramakrishna said he could not do it. Kali, the Divine Mother of the Universe, kept appearing to his inner eye. Totapuri took a piece of glass and jammed it between Ramakrishna's eyebrows. "Concentrate the mind on this point!" he shouted at the top of his lungs.

With this sharp target as his guide, Ramakrishna increased his efforts. When Kali appeared to him, Ramakrishna cut her in two by using his "discrimination as a sword." Ramakrishna stayed absorbed in non-dual samadhi for three days.[161]

This is a fantastic teaching story. Ramakrishna is highly regarded as a great bhakti (devotion to God) practitioner. He was totally surrendered to God's will. Therefore, he was able to accept the possibility that his deity, Kali Ma, could ask him to kill Her and chop Her in two right in front of his eyes.

When it was ordained that he should undergo a non-dual initiation and cut his beloved Kali in two in order to realize the Absolute, this could mean only one thing. It is what Kali, in Her infinite mercy and compassion, wanted for him!

My own story is less dramatic, but like Ramakrishna, I did not want to give up seeing Kali Ma with my inner vision. I had been devoted to Kali Ma since 1982. I liked being Her devotee and I did not want to give that up. I was content with having access to her unparalleled combination of toughness and sweetness. Being a non-dual Goddess who is ruthless in Her efforts to mercifully liberate her devotees, She used force and brilliant trickery to get me to give up my posture of surrender.

To let go of that final transcendental perch could mean only one thing. I was God. In my non-dual Tantric tradition, I am Shiva. Here Shiva means Supreme Universal I Consciousness. Lord Shiva is a name for the Absolute, for the Supreme Self.

In our Judeo-Christian cultural environment, this remains a bold statement still subject to numerous misinterpretations. Even so, there is no question that it is on the mark. Since God is the Supreme Subject, to realize the Absolute means, in the words of Ramana Maharshi, that you "Know I am God."[162]

Nonetheless, there is the cautionary tragic tale of the Persian mystic Mansur Al-Hallaj (LOC 1000). He made the "mistake" of declaring "Ana al-Haqq." In Persian, this meant "I am the Truth." Unfortunately for Mansur Al-Hallaj, the only Being who was allowed to say those words was Allah or God.

It was declared that he had committed blasphemy. He was imprisoned, tortured and cruelly executed in a public square for his bold declarations in 922 A.D. It had not helped his case that he had also gone around announcing about the cloak he was wearing that "There is nothing in my cloak but God."[163]

LOC 800s Case Study: Indiscretions of Jiddu Krishnamurti

I have asserted that teachers in the LOC 800s, 900s and 1000 are unlikely to commit the usual abuses. The trouble making teachers who abuse the power handed to them by their students are usually in the LOC 600s and LOC 700s.

Even though these teachers are sincere, they are still going through deep purifications themselves. They still need to integrate their realization. Depending on their background, their new role as spiritual teacher could be putting them in situations for which they have little or no preparation.

In order to support my assertion about the higher LOCs, I went looking for "dirt" on teachers with LOCS from the mid-800s to LOC 1000. While it is certainly possible that I missed something on someone, I could find only two documented cases of abuse of power on record for people at these levels.

Both involved sexual improprieties. The two cases are Jiddu Krishnamurti (LOC 844) and Joshu Sasaki Roshi (LOC 1000). I will discuss Sasaki Roshi's case in the chapter on LOC 1000.

It is now well documented that Jiddu Krishnamurti had a 25-year long love affair[164] with Rosalind Rajagopal, the wife of his manager and publisher.[165] There were three abortions.[166]

What are we to make of this?

What I think this means is simply that Krishnamurti was human. The sex drive does not disappear with enlightenment. The desire of the personality for human intimacy, for a tender touch, for meaningful close contact does not go away. A human being feels these things. The sage is a human being.

As enlightenment deepens, your humanity is able to expand and blossom. The rich dark soil from which that beautiful flower of human sensitivity, vulnerability and generosity grows includes all of our emotions, the negative ones as well as the positive ones. There are no "bad" desires or "bad" feelings. But there can be desires and feelings that have not been accepted, embraced, welcomed and deeply integrated.

No matter deep the enlightenment, the mature sage does not become an unfeeling spiritual robot. Though the mature sage is motivated by love and compassion, he is a human being with a human personality. He is a human being just like you.

Even if you put him up on a pedestal, he is not a god walking on the earth. He is just a human being. He has human feelings!

There is no excuse or justification for his behavior. Jiddu Krishnamurti had an extraordinary life. He was vaulted into spiritual celebrity at a very early age. It can be very lonely at the top. While I am not endorsing his long affair with the wife of one of his best friends, I am saying that I can understand it.

Many years ago, when I was in my early thirties, I worked in the music and film industries. I lived in Hollywood. I knew a number of celebrities. They are names you would recognize.

I would get invited to fabulous parties at amazing houses high up in the Hollywood Hills. These are the houses you see in the movies. There is glass all the way across. A pool shimmers in the backyard. Beyond it, the lights of Los Angeles tantalize.

What I learned about celebrities shocked me. Even though they had money and fame, they lacked something that most of us take for granted. They lacked close friends they could trust.

So although it looks like the world is your oyster when you are a rich and famous celebrity, the bitch goddess of worldly success has her own hidden way of exacting her price. Many of the celebrities I knew cultivated a very tight very tiny circle of people that they believed they could know, love and trust.

With these people, they could let their hair down and relax. They could drop the public image of the star, of being a god or goddess for the masses, and become simply and merely human. They needed this ordinary friendship time to decompress. In private, they could totally be themselves.

How does this relate to Krishnamurti?

When you are a world famous celebrity, your inner circle of intimate friends that you can trust to truly know you and love you as you are is very small. This means the circle from which you can select someone to have a sexual relationship may be extremely limited. Some celebrities go to clubs and pick up dates. For obvious reasons, Krishnamurti could not do that.

A love affair that goes on for 25 years is a situation of mutual consent. Something of value is being gained by both partners.

It is confusing and strange that this woman was the wife of his manager and publisher, yet when you live in the clouds above with the celebrated elite, your circle narrows to a handful.

Who can you trust? You can trust the people that have been with you through thick and thin. They are your real friends.

If they are a beautiful woman like Rosalind Rajagopal, then they may be the one you go to in order to experience intimacy, in order to be heard, in order to be healed. It is not justified, but it makes of the mythical god Krishnamurti a man who had feelings. Krishnamurti had been put in a position where he was supposed to be celibate. This was his secret compromise.

Was he right? No, I don't think so. Was he wrong? I believe he was trying to solve a very difficult dilemma. He had a public image of being celibate, yet he had the yearnings of a man for love and sexual intimacy. He chose someone in his inner circle that he felt he could know and trust. Rajagopal sustained their clandestine connection for 25 years. It would appear that he was correct about her. He could trust her to be his secret lover.

The topic of sexual intimacy between teachers and students goes beyond the scope of this book. That said, I would like to address a theme that keeps repeating itself. For some students, the revelation that their teacher has had sexual relations with his students will be viewed as an unforgivable breach of trust even if they are not the actual "victim." Men as well as women may feel this sexual behavior invalidates the teacher for them.

My view is that if a person has indicated that they are celibate, married or monogamous, then they should be expected to uphold their agreements just like any other person. If they are openly single and they let it be known that they are on the lookout for an intimate relationship(s), then they are being honest and out front about what they want and how they live.

In my research on sexual abuse by teachers, what I have come across again and again is that the greatest shock and outrage is not about sexual acts per se. It is about the bald hypocrisy of the teacher. He is pretending to be one way in public, but he is being another way in private. He is a stone cold hypocrite.

The real damage seems to be the lying, the deception, the duplicity, the phoniness. Even if the student was not involved in the affair, even if they do not even know the student who was abused, many students of the teacher will feel betrayed.[167]

I'm not sure what to make of this. A teacher like this is showing with his actions that he is a hypocrite and that he cannot be trusted. But it is a big step to go from knowing that he betrayed a stranger to feeling that he has betrayed you.

This kind of reaction is quite common in cases where it is proven that a teacher is guilty of sexual misconduct over a period of time. It suggests that some very deep issues are at work. We live in a culture where violence against women is accepted as the norm. It is a statistical fact that one in five American women are victims of rape or of attempted rape.[168]

We have a deep cultural wound in terms of sex. We were raised as children *inside* of this limiting cultural context. It is difficult for us to see outside of our own sexual upbringing.

Some cultures other than Judeo-Christian do have very different sexual standards and mores. This does not prove right or wrong. It shows that there are many possibilities that people, people like us, may find acceptable or unacceptable.

I think that each person must work out what they truly feel and believe for themselves about sex and relationships. In my experience, taboo issues like sex, money, religion and early childhood abuse are studiously avoided by most people.

These painful emotional injuries do not usually get resolved by people until it becomes a necessity for them. Many of us are "walking wounded" in need of deep emotional healing. When a spiritual teacher in whom we have placed our trust sexually misbehaves, it triggers these unresolved traumas.

Hypocrisy under holy robes is as old as the hills. I would fault Krishnamurti for his hypocrisy, not for his sexuality. Perhaps he was attached to his fame and lifestyle. Perhaps he wanted to have his cake and eat it, too. He did just that for 25 years.

LOC 800s Case Study: MacDonald Could Not Kill Her Guru

Spiritual teachers in the LOC 800s are universally sweet, joyful and loving. I had to look long and hard to find any "flaws."

The error in the LOC 800s is that the notion of a sacred other is allowed to remain. Somehow because it's sacred or holy or has assisted you in your awakening, you are supposed to give it a special status. If the Self is to be realized, then all notions of other and the world must be annihilated once and for all. No other, no matter how sacred it is, can remain. It all must go.

Elizabeth MacDonald (LOC 850) took over running A.H.A.M. (the Association of Happiness for All Mankind) in Asheboro, North Carolina after her guru A. Ramana (LOC 1000) dropped the body.[169] MacDonald found that after 32 years of service to A.H.A.M. she needed a break. She sustained an unexpected "burnout," took a long sabbatical and then retired.[170]

I mention her because I believe her devotion to A. Ramana and to the A.H.A.M. organization that he founded got in the way of her going all the way and attaining the realization that her guru wanted for her. She is a lovely woman who is known for saying "Once the Heart is awakened, it is simply living from this perspective. Then, *it's all about love.*"[171]

That quote is interesting because this is not what her teacher was teaching! He did not teach "it's all about love." Her love focus confirms her place in the LOC 800s camp.

When you read her book *Living From the Heart*, which talks about opening the Heart Cave and entering into deep true authentic feeling, you experience her profound emphasis on love as the expression of Self-inquiry. She really meant it, that for her, the message of the realized Heart is "all about love."

In contrast, A. Ramana was teaching Self-inquiry. You can talk all day long about Self-inquiry and not mention the word "love" even one time. They are related, but they are not the same thing. Real love is the outcome of doing Self-inquiry.

There is no doubt that A. Ramana wanted her to attain LOC 1000. After all, that is what he wanted for everybody!

I suspect that her devotion to him, her great love for him, has kept her in the subtly dualistic position of devotee subject to guru love object. Many traditions support the notion that you should always remain in a devotee position with your guru. The tough truth of the LOC numbers indicates otherwise.

The "god" that you must "kill" may not be Jesus or Buddha. It could be your own guru. It could be the very special man or woman who has helped to lift you up into enlightenment.

When your guru or teacher is the real deal, that is what they want for you. They don't want you to stay attached to them. They want you to kill them in your thoughts and destroy the house of cards called the mind. Let the hurricane force winds of the guru's Grace blow that phony facade down for good.

Ramana Maharshi said that the "Guru comes only to tell him [the seeker] 'That God is within yourself. Dive within and realize.' God, Guru and the Self are the same."[172]

This is a polite way of saying "Kill your guru." If you think you are separate from him, destroy the idea he is another. It is utterly false. Not only that, it's you blocking your own way.

My Buddha Told Me to Kill Him for Good and Walk Away!

Ramesh Balsekar made it easy for me. I adored him so much that I started thinking about living in Mumbai just so I could attend his daily satsangs and be with him. I had already received his Grace and had my awakening. But I was still attached to him. I cried tears of bliss from my love for him.

When I saw him on his final U.S. retreat, I told him what I wanted to do. I will never forget the look of horror on his face. "That is an absolutely terrible idea!" he said. "I've given you all I can give you. Now move on and live your own life!"

I gave him a hug and that was that. I never saw him again. It was tough to take. Somehow, though, I knew he was right.

Looking back, I am deeply grateful for his fierce rejection of my feverish bhakti-soaked fantasies. He knew me better than I did. I needed to move on. I needed to "kill my guru" and live free. I did as he said and discovered the wisdom of his words.

I was fortunate that neither he nor Kali Ma had a problem with cutting my sticky strings of attachment. A sudden strike with the sword of truth severs the false in one blow. The devotee learns to live on his own two spiritual feet because he has no choice but to do so! No Mama's boys or girls allowed!

From "I Am My Self" to "I Am All" to Just Plain "I Am"

Very few of you today are engaged in non-dual devotional sadhana. Nonetheless, you may spend a few months or years in the LOC 800s before moving on up. In my case, I was in the LOC 800s from May, 2006 to November, 2006 (seven months).

My love-surrender-devotion relationship to Divine Mother in the form of Kali Ma was running parallel to my non-dual meditation practice. However, it was She that terminated my devotional relationship to Her, not the other way around.

1000

When I completed the void passage through the darkness of unknowing, I found that I had arrived at a pure experience of "I Am." This was not the same "I Am" that I had felt in the LOC 700s. At that stage, I was still caught up in identification with the world and the universe. The feeling of being the world, the feeling "I am the world," involved a big expansion.

The pure "I Am" of the LOC 800s feels self-contained. It may be experienced that the universe lies within it. It may also be experienced that the divine pair, Shiva and Shakti as creators, also lives within it. It is a majestic quiescent wholeness.

It is the quintessence of duality, yet it is beyond it. But the experience is a simple one. It is just pure "I Am," pure Being.

The feeling or experience that you had in the LOC 700s of "I am all" or "I am everything" now gets condensed into an even more refined and concentrated identity. This is the pure "I Am" state. It may declare that "I am the pure I, the original essential I." Even so, this pure "I Am" is not yet the Absolute.

The pure "I Am" can be mistaken for the Absolute. Upon close inspection, it will be seen that the "I Am" state is still subtly fluctuating. In the Absolute there is no movement, no change, no fluctuation of any kind. If there is movement or change, it is not the Absolute. The Absolute is called that because it is the final distillation of all the layers and levels. That which remains after everything else is dissolved is the Absolute.

In the pure "I Am," there is still the potential for duality. It is the step that holds the invisible potential for the manifestation of the universe. It is the first big step away from the Absolute.

There is intentionally in it a slightly muted tendency towards outwardness. There is still that bias for motion, for the Shiva and Shakti principles to move and give birth to the universe. This stage is necessary for the universe to exist.

This pure "I Am" has the consciousness "I am the Truth." But just as when a man is heard to be repeating "I am Steven" over and over and over again, doubt arises as to whether or not he really is Steven and even if he actually knows who he is.

It is a cosmic paradox, but because this super-causal "I Am" body, the sublime luminous witness of the darkness and ignorance of the causal body, emerges from the Absolute boldly asserting "I am the Truth," he is immediately suspect. As it turns out, these suspicions are well founded, for this pure "I Am" is the first step of manifestation.[173]

This "I Am" is the birth of super-pure spiritual knowledge, but this very subtle "hum" of super-pure spiritual knowledge is, nonetheless, the beginning of knowledge. Because it is the birth of knowledge, it is the genesis of illusion as well.

It has another flaw. It knows that it exists. It has emerged from the Absolute. Now that door is shut behind it. Empowered by its emergence, it has a momentum to blow up like a balloon.

As beautiful as it is, this super-pure knowledge of "I am the Truth" (which is the same as the pure "I Am") must itself be eliminated. Only then is freedom possible. Even the memory of having had that knowledge must be obliterated and erased.

The liquidation of this pure "I Am" makes way for the final relaxation into the naked natural state. This unconditioned silence and stillness, ultimate freedom, birthed "I Am." When "I am the Truth" is sacrificed, you abide as the Absolute.[174]

The LOC 800s Sages: Teaching the Path of Non-Dual Love

The non-dual devotional sages of the LOC 800s enjoy the exquisite rapture of this unified fusion of ultimate sublime complementary powers. This is the highest romantic love. The union of Shiva and Shakti is the primordial archetype for the human expression of intimate love, sex and childbirth.

The mystic of love enjoys this divine ambrosial love in its sweetest and most perfect form, right at the source. Yet this divine nectar must itself have a source. That is the Absolute.

In his classic *I Am That*, Nisargadatta Maharaj summarized the non-dual path as progressing from "I Am My Self" (LOC 600s) to "I Am All" (LOC 700s) to "I Am" (LOC 800s) to "Reality Alone Is" (LOC 1000). Looked at in reverse, it is logical that the first main station that Awareness takes after leaving the sublime not knowing of the Absolute is to know itself as unlimited pristine feeling-knowing of pure Being (I Am).[175]

This pure "I Am" is prior to the more complex unfolding as the divine pair and then as their creation, the conscious cosmos. The spiritual student retraces his path by expanding his identification from the body to the no self to the universe.

On this path of return, he finally realizes that being the universe, being the "I Am All," grand as it is, lies within the state of pure Being, the pure "I Am."

1000

When he questions this "I Am," he discovers that this elegant beautiful pure Being is itself slightly restless. It is the first bold step in the majestic drama of creation. This "I Am" is seething with incomparable potentiality. It is eager to get into action.

To have "I am X," you must first have "I am." There must first be created the "I am." Then you can have I am "anything."

This "I Am" partakes of the stillness of the Absolute, yet it is bursting with loving creativity. It is the primordial impulse.

It is conscious of its existence, but it is not yet conscious of its true destiny. The "I am" is the son sent out on a mission. The "I am" is the daughter whose hand is given in marriage. They have no clue what is in store for them on the road ahead.

The foundation, the fountainhead, for this great pure "I Am" is the Absolute. Nothing else can possibly be its source.

This "I Am" is the blissfully ignorant love juice of creation. It is the cry of timeless love birthing itself as endless forms of playful energy. It is the urge to achieve union and enjoy fusion. It is the phenomenal lover with a thousand eager shining faces. It is the clock that ticks relentlessly towards death the instant that a human being is born into this world.

It is through these forms and energies that it will know itself. As this original impulse knows itself, it loves itself. For it is love and it knows itself only as that. There is great bliss, great joy, great rapture, great ecstasy. All that is known is love.

Yet this splendid experiment is bound for failure. A thousand lovers, a million lovers, it always ends the same. Try as it will, love cannot totally and truly know itself through its forms.

In the end, it returns to its own source, to the Absolute. Love dies into Truth and comes to rest. It continues, but it cannot be described. It is now love beyond love, nameless and beyond words. The search is over. Love dies and is reborn as Truth.

The gentle modern LOC 800s sages are tenderhearted. They speak of the supremacy of love. Their willingness to embrace the wounded healer in themselves and others, to put love first, may be ridiculed by the tough minded hardcore non-dualists.

Philip Mistlberger (LOC 876) is a highly regarded non-dual teacher with a Western Mysteries background.[176] In an interview he said he valued being a therapist and a healer over being an agent for enlightenment.[177] For this, for putting love first, he was criticized and his credibility challenged by members of an online forum that he had once belonged to.[178]

I sympathize with the forum members and their belief that an enlightened teacher like Mistlberger should prioritize helping people awaken who have strong potential for enlightenment. At the same time, my impression from their comments is that they themselves have not stabilized in non-duality.

Unconditional love itself cannot be fully realized, experienced and expressed until the person is enlightened. Not only that, many who take a hardheaded approach to non-duality would be well served to work on emotional healing and self-love.

In our everyday lives, what could possibly be more "non-dual" than love, especially love without any conditions attached to it? The answer, of course, is that there is nothing else that fills the bill. Like the words peace and truth, it is distilled essence.

Our word "love" is the exact right term for non-duality in action, especially when coupled with ideals like kindness, generosity and compassion. All of these can be placed under the cosmic umbrella of this crazy big thing called "love."

But love, even unconditional love, must be guided by wisdom. There is no higher source of wisdom than the Absolute.

What Lies Ahead: the Transcendental Song of the Absolute

Having attained the "I Am" on the path of return, the way is now to forget everything. The void passage in the darkness of unknowing did get you here, but it was a trembling negation of knowledge past. It was shaky sacrifices of former treasures.

What lies ahead is Transfiguration. It is an illumination, a celebration, an affirmation of the secret positive aspect of not knowing, of the wild and crazy freedom of divine ignorance. It is an encouraging foretaste of stabilization in the Absolute.

When even the forgetting is forgotten, and the notion of knowledge is itself sunk to the bottom of the sea, you stand tall and free without the limit even of knowing "I." In the Absolute, not knowing extends to not knowing that "I" exist.

To know that you exist is a symptom of the existence of an other. Even the slightest notion or concept of the existence of an other as a possibility is enough to produce this error.

In the Absolute, the other is obliterated and utterly forgotten. As a result, the Absolute does not know itself. It does not have any knowledge. The first knowledge would be to know that it exists. That knowing step is the emergence of the pure "I Am."

This knowing step, being the first of all knowledge, is pure and uncontaminated. It hides behind the causal darkness like a shining sun in the black midnight. Yet it, too, must be snuffed out if the causal darkness it supports is to be defeated.

That which is prior even to this pure knowledge step is beyond both existence and non-existence. Since it is prior to any kind of knowing or ignorance, and prior even to any concept of knowing or ignorance, it cannot be described at all.

It is Buddha Nature. It is "ISness." It is pure Awareness. It is naked Reality. That is as good as these words can do.

Now only Silence and poets can speak.

My Spiritual Journal:

Transfiguration or Radical Illumination via Amrita Nadi

(LOC 845 to LOC 932)

Transfiguration: Amrita Nadi Awakens

The step I am calling Transfiguration marks the transition from the LOC 800s to the LOC 900s. It presages the situation of living and abiding in the Absolute. It delivers a foretaste that is positive and joyful. Unlike the previous major steps, it is not a void or an ego death. It is an affirmation of the Self.

I have been asked several times by readers of this book if it is necessary for them to go through the awakening of Amrita Nadi that is described in this chapter. The short answer is no. The experience of Amrita Nadi is definitely not needed.

After all, no less than Nisargadatta Maharaj went on record as saying he has never experienced the Heart on the right. If he did not experience the Heart on the right, then he did not have the experience of Amrita Nadi either. His realization proves that this experience is not needed for you or anybody else.[179]

Even so, I am prejudiced in favor of teaching that feeling the Heart on the right and having the experience of Amrita Nada coming alive (which Ramana called aham sphurana) are both important. Ramana is recorded as saying the Heart on the right can be seen with "the inner eye" of the inquiring yogi.

> Here lies the Heart, the Dynamic, Spiritual Heart. It is called Hridaya and is located on the right side of the chest and is clearly visible to the inner eye of an adept on the Spiritual Path. Through meditation you can learn to find the Self in the cave of this Heart.[180]

This spiritual event that happened to me appears on the Map of Awakening as Radical Illumination or Transfiguration. The experience itself is not the significant part.

The primary sign for the transition is the ability to detect with unprecedented clarity the rising up of the I-thought. You do not need aham sphurana or illumination of Amrita Nadi to have that skill.

The pivotal passage from the LOC 800s to the LOC 900s is a milestone. You emerge from subtle dualistic tangles involving concepts such as "God" to the diagnostic isolation of the root troublemaker ego I-thought. This faculty can arise in the context of any tradition or style of meditation. For example, Amber Terrell (LOC 914) talks about noticing the naked rising of the I-thought yet she does not mention Amrita Nadi at all.

> When I would wake in the morning, there would be a moment when it was clear that the I-thought has not yet arisen. For some moments there would be no identification with "person" or "body" as myself, just a huge expanse of blissful Presence. Then I would watch the "I" arise. This arising would often be accompanied by a burning sensation in the body...
>
> It was not long before whole days would go by without the I-thought arising at all. I began to notice an effortlessness in action which seemed almost magical — things were getting done without the sense that "I" was doing anything.[181]

Purification of the mind to the point that the I-thought, the root of the mind, can be identified, isolated and tracked is what is needed, not this or that experience. Full mindfulness of the movement of the I-thought leads to its dissolution.

Transfiguration: Radical Illumination or Aham Sphurana

My next big spiritual event took place in November, 2006. I refer to this Transfiguration as "consummation of the Crown."

It was my fulfillment after a difficult lifelong journey of Kundalini awakening. Traditional Kundalini sees the Crown chakra as the final destination. I reached that spiritual zenith.

By any name, it was a real game changer. As a result of this liberating illumination in late 2006, my doubts regarding the path and the nature of the Self (the Absolute) dissipated almost completely. It took me from LOC 845 to LOC 932.

Now I knew beyond question that the essence of what I am is supremely positive. The true I and the world had been perceived as pure Light. I understood why Ramana Maharshi stressed that the Self, the Absolute, is happiness itself.

Ramana talked about a unique yogic channel that connected the Crown chakra and the causal Heart on the right. This secret channel is given various names including Amrita Nadi, Atma Nadi and Para Nadi. I prefer Amrita Nadi.[182]

This experience of Amrita Nadi lighting up, pulsating and radiating light was called aham sphurana by Ramana. "Aham" means "I" and "sphurana" means "radiation, emanation, or pulsation."[183] It is said to presage realization of the Self.[184]

The aham sphurana or Amrita Nadi blaze of November 5 and 6, 2006, was the most dramatic spiritual event of my life. It is possible to have several such aham sphurana events. Aham sphurana was experienced by a number of Ramana's disciples.

During aham sphurana, the Crown chakra and the Heart on the right (causal Heart chakra) fuse in a river of glowing Light.

This Light may become so strong that it blots out everything. All that is seen is pure Light. This was my experience.

> When the discerning one renounces attachment [egotism] and the identification of himself with the body [the "I am the body" idea] and pursues one-pointed inquiry [into the Self], a churning [movement of life force] starts in the *nadis* [channels of life force].
>
> With this churning of the *nadis*, the Self gets separated from the other *nadis*, and clinging to [confined to] the *amrita nadi* alone, shines forth [with clear light].
>
> When the effulgent [very bright] light of awareness shines in *atma nadi* [*amrita nadi*] alone, nothing else shines except the Self [the world is gone and only the Light of the Self is seen].[185]

Dramatic though the aham sphurana experience(s) may be, it is not Self-realization. Aham sphurana fades away. Its function is to be a bridge, a preparation for the recognition of that which is supreme, beyond all else.

In a few individuals, the blazing of Amrita Nadi leads directly to Self-realization (LOC 1000). The LOC 900s stage appears to be "skipped." In fact, it was quickly and effortlessly integrated.

This chapter also covers the consummation or opening of the Crown chakra. Many attain liberation via the stable opening of the Crown chakra without having a conscious experience of Amrita Nadi. In fact, if they are in a tradition that does not pay attention to yogic experiences, they may not even be aware of the Crown chakra opening that enables no mind.

Silence and Nothingness: A Glorious Inscrutable Dead End

I need to go back to May, 2006 to provide a realistic context.

This was shortly after I completed the void passage of unknowing through darkness. The aham sphurana experience where Amrita Nadi blazed up to provide my Transfiguration transition into the LOC 900s took place in November, 2006.

The point I want to make is that I was bewildered by the experiences of silence and nothingness I was having. Yes, they got cleared up by Amrita Nadi, but I don't want you to think that it was just cocktails and party favors. I was in a muddled state. My move to the LOC 800s left me dazed and confused.

In that passage the Crown had opened up. This passage began with an opening of Ajna chakra following by unexpectedly intense and surreal Crown chakra visionary experiences.

At that time, I had no idea that Amrita Nadi and aham sphurana lie ahead. I was just doing my best to integrate the void passage through an unknowing darkness that moved me into the LOC 800s in a short 24 days (April 13 to May 6, 2006).

After the passage through the dark void of unknowing that took me from the 700s (LOC 793) to the 800s (LOC 845), my new focus was nothingness and silence. This nothingness was equivalent to the "I Am" that had been revealed after I let go of identification with the LOC 700s state of "I Am All."

In this transition, I went from feeling I was everything to feeling that everything was nothing. This felt like a superior state, a more pure state, but my questions remained. It was not stable. I was phasing in and out of it. I was gaining and losing it. It was obvious that this was not the end of the road.

I had reached a new depth of silence. Based upon what I had heard and read, I thought maybe this was the final step. But I did not see how that was possible.

I knew that the state of not knowing I had arrived at in that journey in darkness guided by an invisible Ajna Guru was a state of "no mind." But this no mind of mine fluctuated a lot. This meant that the "no mind" state I was now in, though legitimate, still needed to be purified and cleansed.

Something else bothered me even more. I intended to keep digging until I arrived at the final answer, an answer that I could test mercilessly, an answer that would never fail me. In my heart, I just could not get excited about a big fat empty "nothingness" being the be all and end all of my life's quest.

I felt strongly that the ultimate truth could not be a negation. It had to be a supreme ultimate affirmation of all that is good, positive and beautiful. If not, then why our heart-felt pursuit of being happy? Why is it regarded as the highest good?

Being happy is more than feeling good. Being happy is being yourself and feeling you are finally free, finally home at last. Being happy is peace, love and joy, the summum bonum.

Just so you know, from May to November and during all of my spiritual transitions there was a lot of the old "two steps forward, one step back" kind of stuff. I haven't bored you with this content, but rest assured that I was going through the good days and the bad days, the days of delight and the days of doubt, the days of progress and the days of pandemonium.

At a deep level that I was barely conscious of, the steady current of spiritual life was carrying me forward. On the surface, the waves were choppy. Even though I could tell that my mind was slowly but surely dissolving, I still found myself struggling to get a firm grip on this process.

Much Ado About Nothingness — At Least in My Journal

Because this was the deepest and most stable state of silence I had ever been able to abide in while living and working in the world (in Las Vegas, Nevada, no less), I probably made a bigger deal about it than I should have. I have 100 plus pages of notes in my spiritual journal covering May 8, 2006 through October 14, 2006 (my last entry before November 5, 2006, the day of aham sphurana and the bright blazing of Amrita Nadi).

What I did not realize at the time was that this phase where I was beholding "nothingness" was itself just another transition. I was living out and integrating the impact of the internal events of the "no mind" void passage through darkness.

That passage ended when I felt my attention turn in on itself and dissolve. I called the resulting condition a "stateless state," but it turned out my assessment was premature. It was my first real taste of the natural state, but I would need to go through more steps of purification before I could stabilize in this "stateless state."

To give you the flavor of my writing at the time, here is a journal quote from May 19, 2006. I wrote this two weeks after I had completed the void passage. This is a short excerpt. My entries for May 19, 2006 alone fill up nine pages in my journal.

May 19, 2006
Las Vegas, Nevada

I noticed yesterday that the "I am everything" feeling is gone. Today I inquired into that more directly. Also, today was the first day I felt good and happy and friendly since Saturday. It has been a rough three days.

Thanks to consciousness clearing up today, I pressed the inquiry. Q: Is this "I am everything" feeling totally gone? A: Yes. Q: Then what has replaced it? Something still functions. What is it? A: Nothing. I am Nothingness. That felt right.

Q: Then I asked "If I am nothing, what is all of this, the world, everything?" It can't be "something" if I am "nothing." A: The world/everything is Nothing, too! That felt right, too.

Q: Then if "everything is nothing," then what is all this activity, doing, stuff? When a car goes by, what is that action?

A. It is nothing. Then I watched three palm trees swinging slowly in the spring breeze as I sat in the back parking area. I *knew* they were Nothing.

Then someone/something I was watching *stopped* feeling like Nothing to me. It suddenly felt real (as a gut reaction — as an impact to the gut, a crunch, a subtle punch to the stomach).

What happened? A *thought* happened!

My thought about it had objectified it and made it seem real.

My thought about it *as if* it is real (assumed it was real = I think/behave it is "real") made it go from Nothing to something (object/world) for me, in my perception (and feeling). I find this to be truly remarkable!

Then I caught myself thinking in the same way about "the world" *as if* it is real and objective — and I felt the exact same crunch/contraction/cramp in the gut.

Suddenly, I realized "I am creating the world!" In a blink, I think the world into existence. I am making the world appearance an objective reality (for me) by thinking about it as "real," meaning I assume or presume it is "real."

May 26, 2006
Las Vegas, Nevada

1000

Yesterday at work the "I Am" was busy arising with stories, memories, worries, minor anxiety. This morning more of the same, not as severe. It is so interesting how these "I Am" or "diffused I" or "mind" or "mental conditioning" experiences have been every time associated with the same phenomenon.

This phenomenon is a sense or feeling of being clouded over, of a coating or layer arising, and in a global way (as in totally covering a spherical object all at once). There is also a subtle sense of stupidity or dullness that comes with it, like awareness itself seemed to become foggy or vague.

This coating or cloud or fog seems to be at a primal level. It is a primitive feeling of existing or being in a formless way that is not yet looking at itself.

A primordial soup of "I exist" but not yet thinking "I." Perhaps like the foggy state of waking up from a deep sleep, groggy where you are aware that you exist, but you have not yet labeled it as "I" or thought about it as "I."

Then after the formless soupy existing feeling appears there seems to come the I-feeling as in "I exist!" and then the memory gets involved. Then the "personal I" stories and reactions occur, again with the same feeling of a thick layer all around and all over the Nothingness.

These steps from "formless existing" to "non-specific I" to "I associated with personal memories and stories" happens very quickly!

May 27, 2006
Las Vegas, Nevada

The short version seems to be that after my initial blessed introduction to an experience of Nothingness (the Absolute), I am kicked out and am now experiencing solidified message of "I Am." It feels like pure existing within a field of Nothingness (hence, very subtly, it stands in the center of that field).

I think this "I Am" state is a congealing of the very strange tension (felt around the solar plexus and in my whole body) that I felt yesterday. I think that was a step which led to this experience of a pure "I Am" which feels like a congealing of the Nothingness (its first expression or outpouring?).

It has a very subtle thickness or density to it. Like I said yesterday, it is a thickening of the Nothingness.

Had I not already directly experienced the Nothingness and its feeling of unqualified unconditioned freedom, I might think this "I Am" state is a desirable stabilization in contrast to the "I Am All" that I previously felt and identified with.

I found the "I Am All" to be unstable and undesirable. I am arriving at the same conclusion on this concentrated "I Am."

May 29, 2006
Las Vegas, Nevada

Every now and then, I have been shifting back into the Sunyata or Nothingness non-space ("stateless state"). These are notes from one such brief shift.

I want to say "Thank you!" for the "experience" and for the validation it brings. I have been concerned that maybe it was lost.

Characteristics of the stateless state (*unmani* or *shoonya*):

1. No sense of space
2. All reference points gone
3. No sense of time
4. During the day, actions/events appear to happen — and yet not happen.
5. No feeling of "I" or "I Am" of any kind.
6. Impression of *shoonya* moving under the I Am "cap" like an underground river and slowly dissolving it.

May 31, 2006
Las Vegas, Nevada

Walking to the grocery store, I realized that the key reason I have been getting along with my co-worker S. so well is that there is no "self-other pivot" or polarity functioning or residing underneath my moment-to-moment experience.

Previous to April 13, 2006, when I was in the "I Am All" state, there was still a subtle self-other split that was causing me extreme pain and difficulty with S. I had to face the fact that I was still stuck in a self-other trap. Somehow, being around him brought it into sharpness more than with anyone else.

Anyway, while I was walking to the store, being in a fairly clear "one sky" state, I recognized that the dualistic self-other sensations I had felt during a turbulent day had occurred while I was thinking a dualistic thought in that exact moment.

That thought then caused a coarse reflection in the front of the body (chest-belly) of tension, disruption, conflict. But this feeling disappeared when the thoughts were gone.

When there were no thoughts and I was in a "one sky" state (clear and open wide, but not the stainless pristine purity of the "stateless state"), I could not find any kind of structure or construct that corresponded to self-other. (Maybe my state in this moment is close to the "stateless state," I'm not sure).

The "stateless state" is not *my* state — it is *the* state. Other states were my state, and I was having them. There is no I, no me or mine, in the "stateless state." There is no one to claim it, to describe it, to point it out.

June 2, 2006
Las Vegas, Nevada

Well, this process is full of surprises. Today at 3:30 pm I noticed that I am having difficulty finding my body.

It was like it was dissolving from the heart out. Also the solar plexus was relaxing and releasing. It felt really good, like a deep letting-go of a very old tension.

Of course, it is not the body that is disappearing but the idea, concept, notion, image... I think this effect has been in place since this process began in April and I am now just noticing it.

June 23, 2006
Las Vegas, Nevada

It is difficult, actually, to write something. There is nothing to say. I have nothing to say.

Nothing since the recent shift and fundamental change [on Saturday, June 10]. I remain utterly at ease with the notion that this is "the final freedom" — to not exist at all, to realize supreme Nothingness (Buddhist Emptiness).

Nothing in my life has been so supremely restful, complete, content, satisfied. It is non-moving in the sense of being beyond both moving and not moving. I am utterly fulfilled for the first time in my life.

The "I" or "I Am" or "me" or sense of existing or the feeling of being that arises does so bundled with all the other content of body, emotion, mind and life. As the Nothingness, I am not that "I." I watch it appear and disappear.

You could say it appears on my surface, on my face. It is "trivial" or small — a "pinprick" as Nisargadatta Maharaj said.

This is not witnessing. It is utterly beyond the changing phenomena. Yet they are a part of it, its expression. Think of a bubble in which appears a dream. This bubble floats in a boundless vastness. Even if the bubble goes, the vastness remains. The bubble is the universe and everything in it.

The coming or going of the bubble is of no consequence to the vastness. The changing phenomena are happening due to there being a body. It is not witnessing as there is no witness (subject). Nor is there an object — for an unreal dream model of nothingness hardly constitutes a solid significant "other."

July 28, 2006
Las Vegas, Nevada

Very interesting over the last week. New step that I would call "non-differentiation." Objects and events are perceived but no distractions or differences are created (in the mind) from that pure perception. As a result, four things:

1. The mind is much more quiet because there is nothing to talk to itself about. It needs to experience objects as distinct and separate to function and start distorting and magnifying.

2. It is concluded that nothing has happened. There is no experience of anything happening, for such experiences depend upon an experience of difference. Without difference, this cannot move to that, or impact that, or change that. There is no this and that. Thus it is said that "This world is only an appearance. Nothing has ever happened."

3. Pure Awareness is a rock solid block like massive diamond. Nothing changing. Ever.

4. Mind, storytelling, noise is based on the notion of it being about somebody with separate existence. There is less and less reference to an "I." Lately, it is often forgotten.

September 25, 2006
Las Vegas, Nevada

This is a time of difficulty. Left foot hurts like hell [from onset of diabetes]. Can't do job at hospital properly (as it involves walking). Gave two weeks notice. Can't even do errands. Money remains extremely tight. Rescued by loan from C.

My wife hasn't been able to work much and now both her arms are hurting her. She is in a lot of pain. We are a MESS! If I cannot work full-time, we are screwed!

As you can see, there is nothing "spiritual" about any of this. In all honesty, there is nothing "spiritual" about my life or experience. The whole notion of "Spirit" is gone. This is why I haven't bothered to write in my "spiritual" journal. There's nothing to say!

Although at times I have judgmental or arrogant thoughts, and still can view others as spiritually "unevolved," I think it is all nonsense!

Everything is nothing. There is no God or other special something. There is only Nothing.

I don't feel nihilistic or depressed by that. I feel *ordinary*. Never have I felt so ordinary in my entire life.

Somehow I finished my commercial book proposal. As usual, I added important ideas/structure at the last minute. This was all spontaneous. It arose as/when needed, then disappeared.

I cannot talk about spirituality because (a) there is Nothing to focus on and (b) I have nothing to focus with. That loss of attention that triggered the fall into Nothingness remains.

I cannot find anyone or anything yet this personality, with its needs, wants and attitudes, persists. The world persists. The surprises persist. The drama of survival persists. Yet at another level, there only the Real, the Nothingness. There is no change, no personality (or "I Am" from the body).

There is no knowing and no not-knowing. It is beyond knowledge and ignorance, beyond existence and absence.

It cannot be described.

As I noted somewhere, I am under a Pluto transit to my natal Moon. If there is any change in the last few months, it is that I am feeling everything so intensely and feeling so many things.

Much of it is negative, as in depression and frustration. This whole week has been very difficult. Everything is a push, a struggle uphill. The negative moods sweep over my body and hold me in thrall for a few minutes or hours, rarely days.

There isn't much in terms of worry or thoughts, just the raw moods. They are like incoming ocean waves inundating me.

My anger is less pronounced. I don't enjoy anger like I used to. Sometimes I flare up, but I am not enthusiastic about it.

October 1, 2006
Las Vegas, Nevada

1000

It has been quite awhile since I wrote in my spiritual diary. This is because nothing much has been happening except "purification" — several difficult relocations, my one and a half year long Pluto-Moon transit. However, I did finally get my book proposal off. Life feels to be in a new phase.

I am writing this because I experienced a new shift.

At first, after falling into what appeared to be the final dissolution into Nothingness after the dissolution of attention itself [May 6, 2006], I made comments based on past knowledge.

At that time, I was still trying to make sense out of it based on what I had experienced in the past. Then came the disastrous move to North Las Vegas, the daytime rainbow light visions, the ride on the ugly noisy bus, the drama of the almost fight.

I would now comment that there is a stabilization taking place "over time" in that which simply cannot be described. It can be called Nothingness, or Pure Awareness or Buddha Nature or "abiding nowhere."

It is the dissolution of all frames of reference. It can be said that there is literally nothing left.

Before, I think I was still trying to "make sense" out of it, and that has pretty much stopped. I was also experiencing a kind of split, where there was this Ground of Nothingness and then there was consciousness expressing itself as a personality. I thought maybe this was how it was going to be.

However, last week a shift took place in which even this sense of personality existing vanished. The words "this is abiding nowhere" came into my brain, and I decided that "abiding nowhere" was about as good as words were going to do to describe that status. I knew it was a Buddhist phrase, and a search on the Internet did not disappoint.

This new shift took place about 2 pm on Thursday, September, 28, 2006. Mind you, in a matter of minutes, I was back out of it. But it has reappeared, briefly since, and always with the same clarity and peace.

When that shift occurred, several insights flooded my knowing. The first was that this is a state of "no-mind," quite literally. Second, it is Buddha Nature. Third, in it there is absolutely no self, no center, no "I Am," for the arising of "I Am," selfness and the mind are one and the same.

There was a sense that the shift took place in the center of the head, though I don't view that as very important, as none of this is something that can be manipulated or produced.

I was aware of how the "I Am" thought automatically coats the body with feeling, and this produces the experience of moving fluctuating emotion. Certainly I have had many waves of negative emotion rolling through my body during this long difficult Pluto/Moon period.

Also I had an intuition of how the "I Am" sense [I-thought] doesn't float around on its own, it immediately seeks out a host body, a physical human body (or other life form). It needs to be associated with something concrete.

The experience also forced me to re-evaluate my position in term of "self and other." I had to admit that I still feel this duality and the conflict it brings. I still feel a "me" of some kind in relation to "others." I feel the "me" of those "others."

In the more pure no-mind state I dropped into briefly, all of this was resolved. The subtle residual emotional remnants that would remain due to still having "I Am" in relationship to the physical body were gone. Finally, the sense of any self or center, even a speck of sand of self (as in the particle that triggers the creation of the pearl in the clam shell) was gone.

As a result, in what seemed like a very direct relationship, there was an influx of a deep peace, and a sense of joy, even playfulness. I realized that if I were to abide in this "non-abiding" that would be my natural and continuous state.

Later in the week, I had the insight "If there is no problem in thought or consciousness, then there will be no problem in reality"... There is a phrase by the Buddha, not sure of the exact quote, but what it means is "abiding nowhere, intend pure spontaneous spiritual intuition."

I feel that I am gradually living more and more in that way, from that spiritual super-intuition. I know how the mind works, by looking for facts, thinking, comparing, figuring, differentiating, like a machine, like a computer.

With spiritual super-intuition, there is none of that. I could call it "pure spontaneous knowing," but I don't like calling it a form of knowing, as there is no knower, and also no doer to apply the knowledge.

Instead, this kind of intuition, the associated action and the mandala of circumstances in which it appears all arise together, in harmonic perfection, in unspeakable elegance and in breathless beauty.

It is an easeful, wonderful, even playful way to live that I am now just beginning to appreciate, to fathom as my new path in Nothingness... There is a different feeling about living life.

When the shift into this deeper Perfect Peace (so to speak) occurred, I realized that it was accompanied by (a) no self or center at all and (b) no mind at all. When these requirements are met, then there is the life of freedom, which I am only now just beginning to taste. This Taste is not only of peace, it is of joy, of living life in mature playfulness, of lightness of being....

Lately, I have been waking up with an impression of having been in a gray space, a gray light realm which is slightly thick. It is not a negative place. There is a sense of blankness, almost numbness, associated with it. It is peaceful, but in a dull way, like it is too dumb or too numb to react to stimuli.

It is suggestive of a new dawn. But it is a murky twilight, a very early twilight, well before the breaking forth of the bright and glorious sun. There is still plenty of night left in it, almost as if it is the night just as it shifts into the dawning of the twilight.

In other words, the very beginning of the end of night. This transition has to begin at some point, and at that early twilight, it would still seem quite dark.

The Light of a Thousand Suns: the Glory of Amrita Nadi

The phrase "the light of a thousand suns" is based on Chapter 11, Verse 12 of the *Bhagavad Gita* where Lord Krishna displays his universal form to his awestruck devotee Arjuna.[186] The image of a thousand suns in the sky conveys a splendor, magnificence and radiance that far exceeds any experience of our world, including the brightness of our own sun.

I chose the phrase deliberately because the illumination of Amrita Nadi was a glorious revelation of the nature of the divine and of my true self at the same time. In the seamless and absolute unity of that state, all became pure Light.

The world disappeared. My body disappeared. I disappeared. Yet I remained as conscious awareness of this supernal Light. The word "ineffable" was invented for experiences like this. This brilliance blazed most intensely for about two hours.

Since Amrita Nadi and its blazing revelation of Light is rarely talked about today, I created a series of three videos to explain it as best I can. In these YouTube videos I also describe how the I-thought rises up from the Heart on the right.[187]

The revelation of God, the World and the Self as pure Light bright beyond description is not unique to me. Similar reports can be found in many religions and spiritual traditions including, of course, the teachings of Ramana Maharshi.[188]

Below is my written record from that mystical experience (aham sphurana). The event took place Sunday evening, November 5, 2006 in the apartment that I shared with my wife. I was home alone at the time.

Although it was at its most intense for about two hours, it did not completely fade. It continued into the next day. Aham sphurana showed up again but less intensely and always briefly about a dozen times over the next six months.

My journal entry blossomed into an essay 19 typewritten pages long. I have quoted the pithiest paragraphs I could find.

They appear here in the same order as they do in the essay in my spiritual journal. I wrote the essay during the week that followed the Sunday, November 5, 2006 sphurana event.

This Amrita Nadi experience left me speechless. I wrote nothing the day of the event. I was not able to attempt putting this event into words until the night of Monday, November 6.

Sphurana: An Event in Harmony with Ramana's Teachings

The teachings of Ramana Maharshi on the Heart on the right, the I-thought, Amrita Nadi and the spiritual phenomenon of aham sphurana are readily available in books and online.

It is remarkable to me that his descriptions, spoken in India more than 60 years ago, could apply to a Western man in his apartment in Las Vegas, Nevada. In my view, Amrita Nadi and sphurana are the ultimate esoteric mystical knowledge.

The precise details supplied by Ramana make identification of this spiritual yoga event easy. It is unlike anything else. I have experienced Kundalini phenomena since I was 16 years old. I can confidently say it is beyond Kundalini. I believe that it is the culmination, the grand finale, of the Kundalini process.

Notes I made in my spiritual journal in October reveal a tip that may help you feel and experience the Heart on the right as described by Ramana Maharshi. This practice is what I was doing when I suddenly became aware of the Heart on the right. I was not looking for the Heart or trying to access it.

The meditation practice I came up with and did for many days and hours in October, 2006 was "relaxing and sinking down into a state of deep rest while in the waking state. While doing so, I would encourage bliss."

I developed this meditation after doing Yoga Nidra a few times. I wanted to focus on and directly access the causal or deep sleep state. "It became clear to me that in order to progress spiritually I must now actually embrace bliss... I had worked from an emptiness approach... I had gone as far as I could go with emptiness per se, and now had to embrace its balancing factor, the characteristic of deep sleep... bliss."

Doing this deeply enjoyable meditation for the whole of October led to the discovery, in early November, of Ramana's causal Heart on the right. I had been sinking deep down into a state of rest in order to find the source of bliss. I found it.

Overview: From Finding the Heart to Amrita Nadi on Fire

These words are taken from my journal essay, page 19.

They were written a few days after the event. I summarized the experiences that led up to sphurana on November 5, 2006.

Tuesday, November 7, 2006
Las Vegas, Nevada

Now for a brief review. The new process began with a strong certainty that the World literally does not exist, and that somehow I must hold onto this Truth in order for me to further progress spiritually.

Doing that, especially Saturday, November 4 (aware of the tension this created since I was living in the world and having to relate to "others"), I experienced the "sizzling Sahasrara" [Crown chakra] with the "saucepan" above the head frying up apparent karmic seeds [looking like sesame seeds] and neutralizing them.

This was more radical than I realized. No longer did thought occur merely in the upper interior of the brain and inside the skull (upper Ajna chakra), now it did not even incline down into the body. It was not washing through or dripping quickly down into the body/flesh, which process would have then caused the experience of negative emotions and sensations.

The separation where the thoughts were cooking on the plate physically one-half inch above the head also prevented that downward flow of subtle, emotional body identification. Therefore, suffering was not occurring. Only detachment.

This is how it unfolded after I began sinking into the causal Heart in October. The "sizzling Sahasrara" experience started.

A crude awareness of the Heart on the right as a sensation emerged. My inner eye saw a path between Crown and Heart.

Then the illumination of the Amrita Nadi pathway arose from the shadow tracing I originally detected. Finally, the all too brief unforgettable blazing of the Amrita Nadi, transcendental self-luminosity, aham sphurana, the light of a thousand suns.

Amrita Nadi, Sphurana and Ineffable Empyreal Radiance

Now that you have the overview, I will take you through the aham sphurana experience as it unfolded for me. The Crown chakra was going through something where it seemed to be burning up "karmic seeds." I became aware of the Heart on the right. Logical in retrospect, a stunning surprise in the moment, I next saw the connection between the Crown and the Heart.

This channel, called Amrita Nadi by Ramana Maharshi, started to glow. Then it appeared to be lit on fire. This "fire" was caught by the Heart and the Crown, then total Radiance took over, blotting out everything. This was the "light of a thousand suns" for which there are no words.

This peak intensity lasted a few hours. I realized I would not be able to abide in this exalted state. The Radiance faded, but it did not totally fade away until Tuesday, November 7.

After that, I had repeat experiences of aham sphurana (blazing of Amrita Nadi) for the next six months, though none were as majestic as the Sunday, November 5 event. In my journal, I described these minor aham sphurana events as phenomena of brightness "that came and went like a light bulb flickering."

Saturday, November 4, 2006
Las Vegas, Nevada

Naturally, I became curious about the connection between the frothing of thought on the top of my head [the "sizzling Sahasrara"] and the bodily signature [sensation marker] of the Heart on the right. They definitely seemed to be connected.

Exploring this possibility in meditation, I discovered that there was a passageway between the two locations. It went from the very top of the head down over the back of the head, curled around the side of the throat and down.

It then went through the physical heart across the chest ending with a well-defined terminus in the Heart of the right center. So for a little while my meditation consisted of tracing the current or flow or nadi that went from the Crown down to the causal Heart.

Based upon my reading of Ramana Maharshi's teachings, it became clear to me that I had it backwards. The thoughts arose from the Heart, so I should instead trace Amrita Nadi (Para Nadi) from the Heart up to the top of the Crown.

Regarding the separation of thoughts, and their subtle frothing ["sizzling Sahasrara"] just above the physical top of the body and at the Crown chakra, I came to see this as very significant, and as a necessary preliminary (for me, anyway) to recognizing the Heart on the right. As long as thoughts are stuck in the head, they tend to be "my" thoughts.

The Grace here was that the thoughts themselves had self-liberated and now proclaimed themselves (based on my deep rest causal meditation, presumably) to be the terminus of a thought creation process that originated elsewhere and NOT from the head or from the lower chakras at all!

It was as if they were physically detached. I was looking at the end of some kind of long tube or hose. I could see enough of the end, where the thoughts were frothing like water foaming from a hose, and I could see enough of the long hose, to make me ask "Where is the rest of this hose?" (Or "Where is the origin of this hose? What is the source of my thoughts?").

The thoughts themselves, by the way, had a much weaker sense of I-ness to them. I would say that before these recent events they still had a directionality, a force to them, and they were still driving and pushing and pulling me. These bubbles were pale and weak, empty imitations of themselves.

Sunday, November 5, 2006
Las Vegas, Nevada

As I continued in this way, taking plenty of time to rest in and feel and be this Heart on the right, this center became more active, as if subtly pulsating. It also defined itself very clearly, a location which corresponded exactly to that described by Ramana Maharshi as being two digits to the right of center, in line exactly with the nipples.[189]

First there was a growing awareness and intensification of sensation in the right chest, two finger widths from center. In the beginning, it felt higher than the right nipple, but later clearly defined itself as being in line with the right nipple.

At this time there arose in the mind a shadow tracing of the path of Amrita Nadi from the Crown, down the back of the neck, and across the chest from left to right, ending in the terminus of the causal Heart center just left of the right nipple. This tracing was my first detection of the Amrita Nadi.

At first, the pulsation or aham sphurana was not dramatic. The Heart area took on a great aliveness. It felt much bigger than the physical point or the marker sensation itself.

It felt like it went deeper into the body — like the "heart cave" it is sometimes called. There was a feeling of vibration. There was a throbbing that was very subtle. Intuitively, I knew it meant the Heart center had come alive. It was now activated.

Right after these sphurana or throbbing, vibratory sensations occurred, the phenomena of seeing the Amrita Nadi as light, and not just as the dark tracing of a pathway along the surface of the body (as seen by the inner eye), took place.

I find it astonishing that this has all unfolded in coordination with my deep acceptance of the need for me to embrace bliss as the next step in my sadhana. I had not anticipated any kind of sudden result, and certainly not Amrita Nadi!

The entire length of the ribbon or connection between the Crown and the Heart began to take on a luminous quality. It began to look literally like a current of light, a river of light. The origin was in the Heart. The display or experiential aspect was in the head and at the very top, the Crown.

During the actual Amrita Nadi fulfillment, this self-evident filament or track that is on and in the body did more than glow. The luminescence took over the entire body and energy system. The analogy came to me several times of how when a light bulb is dim and weak, you can see the filament glowing.

But when the filament [Amrita Nadi] is at full strength, the filament itself disappears in the Radiance. There is only Light, only Brightness, and the bliss-peace that accompanies it.

It was not long after the appearance of Amrita Nadi as an illumined pathway that I found I had fallen into this state of total Radiance. What I mean by that is the Amrita Nadi was like a string saturated with gasoline that had been set on fire.

As it burned, it then set on fire that which it was linked to at both ends — the Heart and the Crown. Not set on fire in terms of burning or heat, set on fire in terms of Light and Radiance.

There now arose an experience in which it was known that there was no mind, no I-thought. Instead there was a blissful Radiance which included the Heart and the Crown, included the Amrita Nadi, and ultimately produced a state of complete Radiance from the radical and total fusion of these elements.

This Radiance completely replaced the mind, making it totally unnecessary. This Radiance could perform all of the functions of the mind, but there would be no suffering involved.

This state of Radiance was natural and effortless. I recognized it immediately as the state in which the mind is dead, gone and buried forever. However, I also recognized that I was not able to stay in this state.

Monday, November 6, 2006
Las Vegas, Nevada

Since yesterday, I have been in and out of this state. Right now I am out of it. My practice is to return to feeling and dwelling in the Heart on the right. If Amrita Nadi and the Radiance arise, wonderful! But if they do not, then I just do this simple practice of feeling the Heart and dwelling in it.

Also, I will continue my practice of resting in the Self (lucid spacious radiant awareness) at the moment of waking from sleep. This practice has helped me gain direct access to the Self and the causal dimension while in the waking state. I hesitate to describe any expectations. I am grateful for this Grace.

None of this was expected by me. However, the sublimity of the Radiance is undeniable. I see now that living as that all issues are resolved forever. In that Radiance of Amrita Nadi lies true happiness, true peace, true bliss, true and final contentment, absolute lasting fulfillment.

Emptiness is not the end. Nor is Nothingness the end. What I have learned, thanks to Grace, is that attaining true Emptiness and Nothingness sets the stage for true Radiance and genuine lasting Happiness. True Fullness is possible only after true Emptiness has been actualized, integrated and appreciated.

Now that this shift has taken place, everything else pales in comparison. I do not feel that it is within my power to stabilize in the Radiance. It must happen through Grace.

However, I feel that its sudden, spontaneous appearance in such a gentle, natural, effortless and truly blessed way signifies the likelihood of eventually being fully established in it — which will also mean the final death of the mind.

I have been afraid of the death of the mind, but more and more, specifically since the falling into Nothingness earlier this year, I have become painfully aware that it is only due to the mind, and the movement of the mind, and the notions that the mind and the world are real, that I still suffer.

Without these ingredients in my life, I would not suffer at all! I would be happy! I am now ready to claim the pure happiness, untainted by the troubled, turbulent mind. It is my birthright.

Perhaps, though, the "death" of the mind is not required. Perhaps, when it is broken, it will submit and allow seamless serenity. I will not need to destroy it. Instead, I will enjoy it.

Ramana Maharshi compared the mind of the sage to the moon when it is seen in the sky in the daytime. The sun has risen. The moon persists, but it is no longer in the way (in contrast to an eclipse, the astronomical symbol of endarkenment).[190]

Either way, the obvious point is that the sage is free from suffering. Call the mind whatever you like. Declare it alive or dead. Announce that it is annihilated or merely harmless.

The essence is that the mind's reign of terror will finally come to an end. Trouble begins and ends with the mind. It is a terrible master, that much is certain. Can it be a good servant? If it cannot, then it must hang from the gallows until dead.

The Hesitant Hermit

LOC 900

The Hesitant Hermit: LOC 900

Since most people will not tarry at the LOC 900 level, this chapter functions mainly as a placeholder so that my model of the journey of consciousness is complete. I took the "local bus" route on my spiritual journey, so I've made most of the stops that people are going to make. That includes this stage at the low LOC 900s which I am calling the "Hesitant Hermit."

At this stage, there is still a subtle veil or membrane that separates the sage from the "world." It is like living inside a room with glass walls. You can see everything fine, you know what is going on, but somehow you are not quite connected.

You remain remote. You are ever so subtly aloof and distant. You are just slightly removed. It is enough to create a gap that you can feel. This gap makes you feel safe and untouched.

It is like you are too refined, too noble, too sublime for this gross ugly coarse vulgar crass disgusting brutish planet. This spiritual windowpane is transparent. It is hard to detect.

Since you are enjoying the benefits of enlightenment without the final "tax" of giving it all up for the sake of the "world," you do not want to know about your invisible glass wall. This manifests as living a life that is simple and undisturbed.

It means minimizing your involvement with other people. You are living in a still silent glass cage of your own making.

The LOC 900s sage still wants to control his environment. This points to a duality. This is the final veil.

1000

When the LOC 900s sage tears this veil open, he is home free. Until then, he is suffocating himself. He has not yet totally embraced the full implications of his realization. The LOC 900s sage will say "It is all the Self." Good. Then live that way. Don't just talk about it.

I, Too, Was Once a Hesitant Hermit Avoiding the World

I call this stage "hesitant hermit" based on my own experience as well as my observations of people stationed here. After the life-changing revelation and Transfiguration that was Amrita Nadi ("aham sphurana" or the arising of the Amrita Nadi experience that connects the Crown and the Heart), I was not eager to return to the degenerate eclipsed world.

True, I now had an exquisitely sublime clarity that told me there was only this Light, that this radiant Unity so totally embraced the world that all that was to be seen, heard, felt and known is only the one Self. However, for reasons not clear to me, there still arose the reluctance to engage the world.

In my case, it was only after the final battle and showdown with the I-thought, described after this chapter, that I was able to unconditionally embrace the World as my Self. By then, I could not find anyone or anything else than my Self. Likewise, as the one Self, I no longer could find the world, either. All notion, taste, flavor or sensation of "other" had been erased.

What is the final obstacle for the LOC 900s sage? To put it as simply as I can, he or she is still holding onto some concept of a "world." The concept or idea of the world is being assumed and projected. To get to LOC 1000, all concepts must go.

Ramana Maharshi makes it abundantly clear that you cannot fully realize the Self and still see the world. He expresses it succinctly in his well-known 1920s essay "Who Am I."

> Question: Will there be realization of the Self even while the world is there, and taken to be real?
>
> Ramana: If the mind, which is the cause of all knowledge and all actions, subsides, the perception of the world will cease... the perception of one's real nature, the substratum, will not be obtained unless the perception of the world, which is a superimposition, ceases... There is no such thing as 'the world' independent of thoughts. There are no thoughts in deep sleep, and there is no world... When the mind emanates from the Self, the world appears. Consequently, when the world appears, the Self is not seen, and when the Self appears or shines, the world will not appear.[191]

When I am teaching this point to people, I summarize it by saying "There is no world. There only the Self." When you are stabilized in that, then you have got it and you are done.

Inscrutable Shyness of the Eloquent Infinite: Three Hermits

It strikes me as a fascinating paradox that all of the modern "hermit" sages I talk about in this chapter have written books. Two of them wrote spiritual autobiographies. They are Amber Terrell (LOC 914) and David Carse (LOC 924).

The better known *Perfect Brilliant Stillness* by David Carse is a bestseller in the non-duality niche.[192] Amber Terrell's 1997 *Surprised By Grace* is excellent and equally candid.[193] If they wanted to hide under a rock, it remains a mystery to me why they chose to write so openly about themselves.

As far as I know, neither of them is a public teacher. Although Terrell used to give public satsangs, now she apparently limits herself to writing spiritual songs that are about non-duality and devotion to the guru.[194] Carse has plainly stated that he wants to continue being just a carpenter in Vermont. He has no desire to teach or to have students.[195]

Terrell's charming obsession with writing songs of devotion about her guru Gangaji has me wondering if she is stuck in a spiritual humility trap. Her songs are wonderfully sweet and heart-centered. But they lack the all-in cutthroat take no prisoners intensity of the typical LOC 1000 achiever.[196]

David Carse: Write a Popular Book. Hide in the Woods.

Perfect Brilliant Stillness is a popular book. As a result, author David Carse (LOC 924) got invited to speak about his book. This is a rather normal chain of events. Most authors would jump at this chance. Carse said no. Here is how he explains it.

> Recently, I was once again asked to share my story... and once again declined. Good reasons: you see, it is precisely this constant creating and maintaining, telling and retelling, polishing and honing of the personal story which maintains the sense of individual self. The ego is only the story it constantly tells of itself, the experiences and difficulties it has had, the path it has followed, the wounds it carries. The invitation here is precisely to stop telling the story.[197]

Sounds pretty good, right? Except that it's wrong. Carse is confusing the story with the I-thought. The root I-thought is a contraction deep in the subconscious. It is not a "story." It is a knot. Telling or not telling the story will make no difference.

Some meditators practice quietism. They think if they can just shut off the mind so that it stops talking and telling stories, they will get enlightened. It doesn't work. The I-thought knot lives at a level that is below conscious thinking. If you stop the storytelling, you will feel better, but you won't uproot the ego.

If the story is just a "dream," then what is the problem with telling it? Dreams by definition do not impact reality.

It sounds like Carse is concerned about what will happen if he gets back into talking to people about his stories. He could get sucked back into them along with the people listening. If so, that's a good reason for him to avoid public storytelling.

Carse openly confesses to yearning for the perfect simplicity of the ideal hermit's life. As far as I can tell, all three LOC 900s sages strongly prefer the simple quiet hermit-like lifestyle.

> Ultimately, there is truly nothing to say. The dream continues; and there is re-entering the dream (not by choice but because that, apparently, is what is to occur in this dream character) with the full knowledge that it is a dream... But you just can't expect I-I to take any of it seriously.
>
> And that hermit's cave still looks awfully good. Nothing is needed. It is so completely not important that anything happen, that anything come of this. No need, no requirement, no mandate, no role. Simple. Utterly simple.[198]

Carse describes his enlightenment experience as one that involved both the heart and the head. It reminds me very much of Amrita Nadi, of the luminous fusion of Heart and Crown. He finds himself in "perfect brilliant stillness."

> There is a tearing, a searing physical pain in the chest that feels like my rib cage is being torn open; at the same time there is a tingling at the top of my head and the sensation is that the top is peeled off my skull like a tight cap being removed. There is peace, consent, no fear.
>
> The sensation is that there is an immense surge or explosion or expansion, which the body cannot contain. Something surges, spins up out of the top of the head to I know not where, to infinity; while my heart expands up and out of my chest, outward, until it fills first the forest, then the world, then the galaxy.
>
> The surge out the top of the head is noticed, but not followed. What is followed with the attention is the expansion of the heart, because with the heart's expansion the "I" sense also expands. And I find myself in what in my ignorance, without language or categories, I call Presence: expressing as Brilliance, like light but clearer and brighter, beyond light. Not white or gold, just absolute Brilliance. Brilliantly Alive, radiantly Being All That Is.[199]

In his chapter where he talks about this experience, he quotes the great Zen master Huang Po: "On no account make a distinction between the Absolute and the sentient world. Whatever Consciousness Is, so also are phenomena."[200]

That's great advice. That is what life in the Absolute is like. It turns out that Carse can't follow his own advice. In his book, he makes it clear that he thinks he is following it. But he isn't. You will see what I mean in a moment. This view where you think you are living the Absolute but you are still making a "distinction" is the close but no cigar error of LOC 900s sages.

Don't get me wrong. I think *Perfect Brilliant Stillness* is a great book. I highly recommend it.

It is the kind of book that only a person who did not have a background in these teachings could have written. It is raw, vulnerable, fresh, naive. I could not have written it. I wrote this book *1000* instead.

I like how he says that a "long gestation period" after this "nameless" awakening happens is normal and to be expected: "Ten, twelve, twenty years before any 'coming out'."[201]

When he starts talking about the contemporary Advaita non-duality scene, though, a different David Carse emerges. This David Carse holds some very strong views about money and charging for any kind of spiritual teaching. His harsh criticism of other teachers solves the mystery of why he is not teaching.

> This game of money for spirituality is a whitewash job. It's widely practiced and widely accepted, but it's the spiritual community's dirty little secret; nobody's really comfortable with it, because everybody knows in their hearts that charging money for access to spiritual teaching, even indirectly, is inauthentic and basically inconsistent with the Teaching itself.[202]

Is that true? When somebody starts speaking for "everybody" that raises a red flag, but I will let that pass. Instead, I will look at what he just said on the previous page of his book.

> Money is necessary for living in the modern world, and there's an honorable tradition of gifting money or its equivalent to support teachers, monks, ashrams, monasteries. But there's a clear line here because on a basic level money and spiritual teaching don't mix.[203]

So let me get this straight. If the money is given as part of an "honorable tradition," it's okay. But if it's given to a modern teacher who operates outside of an institution, it's not okay?

Carse is right that he must allow for "gifting money or its equivalent" (donations) to spiritual and religious institutions. But his vendetta against independent contemporary Advaita and non-dual spiritual teachers who charge money for what they do starts to sound very personal for Carse himself.

> If a teacher wants anything from you, demands anything from you, solicits anything from you, even if it is couched in the most spiritual terms of advancing your own awakening, then it is exceedingly likely that they have not awakened, that the Understanding is not there. **If they ask for money in any form...** I assure you that it is supremely unlikely that they are what they say they are, that they can have what you are seeking, or that awakening has occurred.[204]

The bolding of the words in the quote is mine. "If they ask for money in any form..." then look out! But what about teachers who offer something for free as a strategy to get you involved in some other way? Oh, right, that's covered in the quote where Carse says "If the teacher wants anything from you."

Hmm. How much did I pay for *Perfect Brilliant Stillness* new at Amazon.com? $16.47. Because I'm a publisher myself, I know that this book did not cost $16.47 to print. People are making money from this book. Carse is asking for money. Carse is making a profit. Carse is contradicting himself.

Last time I checked, most of the LOC 1000 teachers like Renz, Lucille, Spira and Gangaji charge money for events. There are multiple practical problems with what Carse is saying. If asking for money is unacceptable for these top teachers, then it should be unacceptable for all of the spiritual and religious institutions of the world bar none.

I don't think that would be a good idea. I suspect that you don't think so, either. Running religions requires money.

What it sounds like to me is that, for Carse, money is a symbol of the "world." If you are involved with money, then you are overly involved with the world. The compromise is to live a simple quiet low impact lifestyle. This is the hermit's answer.

Carse likes to talk about dream characters in a dream world. As long as you live in this dream world, you have a dream body and you have dream expenses. In order to pay those dream expenses, you are going to need dream money.

If what you do best is spiritual teaching and that is your dream calling in this dream world, then the best thing for you to do is make your dream money doing the dream job of spiritual teaching. You are a dream teacher giving dream teachings to dream students who pay you dream money.

As long as the world is "real," then choosing the hermit's life makes sense. But if there really is no "world," then there is no "dream world," either. It is a mistake to even talk about a dream world. There is the Absolute and that is all that there is.

The rent you pay is Absolute rent. You pay it with Absolute money. The body you have is an Absolute body. You feed it Absolute food. Carse is an Absolute carpenter in Absolute Vermont and that is how he makes his Absolute money.

If you want to be a hermit, fine. But don't do it because you think there is a world, or even a dream world. There is no such thing. It is gone. It never even existed. Get over it!

Dr. Jean Klein: A "Quiet Life" Too Refined for Prime Time?

The third of these low 900s "hermits" is Jean Klein (LOC 926). He is the illustrious guru of Francis Lucille (LOC 1000). Lucille is in turn the guru of Rupert Spira (LOC 1000). Assuming I am correct about Klein's LOC, this means that Lucille was able to surpass his teacher. In a parallel scenario, Cee (LOC 1000) was able to transcend the limitations of her guru Nome (LOC 711).

Clearly, Klein established a magnificent lineage. I have checked his LOC repeatedly over the years. For reasons I do not understand, his LOC has always come to me as 926.

Perhaps he had reclusive tendencies I don't know about. Between LOC 900 and LOC 1000, we are getting into murky territory. It is difficult to say much about it other than you will want to get to LOC 1000 in this life if you can.

As far as I know, the several excellent books by Klein, in my opinion some of the best in modern Advaita and non-duality, are edited transcripts of his live talks. My favorite is called simply *I Am* (compiled and edited by Emma Edwards).[205]

In the front leaf of *I Am*, published in 1989, there is one long paragraph about Klein which summarizes all we, apparently, need to know about him. The final sentence strikes me as oddly opaque: "Since 1960 he has led a quiet life, engaging in talks with groups in Europe and the United States."[206]

What does this expression "led a quiet life" mean exactly? I looked online for the answer to "What does it mean to live a quiet life?" I was surprised to find that it is a Biblical concept.

You live responsibly in the world, maintain a low profile, keep to yourself and practice some form of right livelihood.[207] If you can, you work with your hands.

Many people subscribe to this kind of low impact life one way or another. An ecological variation is the "green lifestyle." It cannot be faulted. All I am saying is that if the sage is truly the non-doer, then the externals of his lifestyle are irrelevant. Whatever he does is God's will, not separate from the will of the Universe that made his body and operates it every day.

Studying the few fragments I could find about Klein, two things do stand out. First, although he did not take a stand against being a public teacher, it was deliberate on his part that he "never solicited students." Second, he belonged to the celebrated Advaita club with reluctance. If the truth he was teaching was found to be aligned with this ancient Advaita tradition, he said that this was taking place "accidentally."[208]

Precious little has been written about Klein's life and views. In *Transmission of the Flame*, he states "People came to me. I have never taken myself for a teacher, so I never solicited students. The teacher only appears when asked to teach."[209]

If everything is the Absolute, then why would it matter if there are people asking you to teach or not? Either way you are not the doer and you are not the teacher.

Playing the role does not make it so. Taking the position that people must somehow seek you out and find you when you have not taken actions to make yourself known or available sounds quite passive. After all, Buddha and Jesus preached to the masses.

1000

Due to the lack of data, this is the only statement from Klein that supports my assertion that his relationship to teaching was ambivalent and isolationist, befitting an LOC 900s sage.

I had the good fortune to sit in his satsang twice in Santa Barbara. He was delightful and luminous. At the time, I was still seeking. My impression was that, even though he was open, benevolent and sweet, he still had a very private side.

There were eight people at a private home. Though I was new, I felt warmly welcomed. Everyone was sitting very quietly.

Klein had his eyes open. He was smiling and looking around. I figured it would be okay to ask him a few questions. His answers were brief, to the point and, for me, unforgettable.

Because of the clarity, elegance and precision of his answers, I thought of taking him as a teacher. I had not yet met Ramesh Balsekar. I decided that even though Klein was enlightened, there was no future in it for me. It would be more of the same soft delicate diaphanous radiance. There would not be the fierce forceful full-blooded face to face encounter I wanted.

In short, Dr. Klein was impressively independent. He needed no one and wanted nothing. Highly accomplished as both a musicologist and a medical doctor, he was extraordinary by any standard. He was a great man in every sense of the word.

Why did he not reach LOC 1000? It is such a fine point, but I believe his passion for independence, plainly displayed in multiple ways, belies a commitment to autonomy that did not support fully embracing the teaching life.

He did not reject the world as such, but his flair for freedom meant being aloof, alone and different. Even the most subtle veil is still a veil.

LOC 900s Sage Case Study: Totapuri Realizes the Absolute

In my chapter on the LOC 800s, I retold the famous story of how Ramakrishna chopped his beloved Kali Ma in half with the "sword of discrimination." Less well known is the story of how his non-duality guru, Totapuri, received Grace and went from LOC 917 to LOC 1000 while staying with Ramakrishna.

Totapuri was a skyclad (naked) wandering monk smeared with ashes when he showed up to be Ramakrishna's Advaita Vedanta guru and personal guide to the Absolute. His rule was to never stay in the same place longer than three days.

After he initiated Ramakrishna into the Absolute, he was so impressed by Ramakrishna that he broke that rule and stayed with Ramakrishna at his Dakshineswar Temple for 11 months. He contracted dysentery so painful he could not meditate.

Since he did not think of his body as having any value or significance, he decided to drop the body by drowning it in the Ganges river. Even though Totapuri was a big man, as he walked out into the deep river, his body would not sink.

As the story goes, no matter how far out into the river he walked, the water never rose above his knees. He ended up standing on the opposite bank of the river.

When Totapuri turned around and looked back at the Kali temple on the other side of the Ganges river that he had just walked upon, he saw that it was radiating a beautiful light. In that moment, he experienced an awakening in which form and formlessness were united. He realized that the manifested world is none other than the supreme Absolute itself.

When he had arrived at Dakshineswar Temple, he was still rejecting the world. This made the "world" real for him. It had made sense to him to reject his physical body because he was so committed to rejecting this illusory world. This view is a very subtle trap. Totapuri had not yet seen through it.

Totapuri was still stuck in the LOC 900s at LOC 917 when he met the great Ramakrishna for the first time. He was still LOC 917 until he had this breakthrough in which he realized the Absolute. In that moment, via the Grace of Ramakrishna and Kali Ma, he realized the Absolute and went to LOC 1000.[210]

The Raw Tender Skin of the Unbaked Baby Buddha

Dr. Klein has passed on. I have not talked about this subject with Terrell or Carse. There is little data on it to be found anywhere. What follows is my unsupported speculation based upon my personal experiences and how they unfolded for me.

I believe my own process contains a close parallel, meaning I went through an LOC low 900s phase. The equivalent for me was that around the time of my Amrita Nadi experiences, an intensely strong feeling to avoid the world took me over. I felt overwhelmed by it. I felt extremely vulnerable to it. I realized that the residual layers of concretized thought that I had kept about the world had functioned as my armor.

With that armor gone, I had no defenses against any notion of the "world" or "other." I felt completely naked. Because it had been hiding underneath the armor for so long, my bare skin was raw and tender. This meant I was not yet fully baked.

Jerry from Canada, my deeply intuitive spiritual friend and ally since 1994, said he saw around me a "green and black cocoon for spiritual purposes that is like a womb. You will emerge from it, with impurities released from it. Upon your emergence from this process, you will be wide open and completely available. You will no longer need to protect and isolate yourself."[211] As usual, Jerry's words were prophetic.

When I reflect on what I was going through at the time, the state which Jerry symbolically saw as a cocoon or womb, I felt fragile like a newborn child. Yes, I knew it was all One. But I did not feel strong enough to deal with that. It was tempting to isolate myself, and that is exactly what I did.

It was what I needed to do at the time. This was the theme for me for years until, for want of a better expression, I received a "direct order" from God, the Universe, the Higher Power, Kali Ma or the Self (you choose). I was liking my isolation in the desert (Palm Springs, California), but I was told that my life in retreat was now terminated. Soon after, my wife and I moved to San Diego. I began public teaching there in June, 2012.

Based on my experience of the LOC low 900s, there remained a subtle veil, a film, a birthing process not yet completed. The best image may be that of a newborn infant. The shock of the world at birth is extreme. If the sage stays in retreat based on that shock, perhaps that explains the "hesitant hermits."

The Final Step: Embracing the Painful Shadow of the World

But there is one more factor to take into account. It is a famous consideration. Every sage must deal with it. Is he or she here to "save the world" or not? Not "save the world" in a religious sense, but "save the world" by being willing to go all out for it.

Is the sage willing to embrace the global shadow of poison, pain, rage, terror, ignorance and arrogance? Is the compassion of the sage great enough that he or she is willing to do this for the sake of these ones who are transparently "my beloved true Self," the 7 billion people who are "my very own Self."

After all, that is the experience: "You Are Me." Or maybe "I Am Us." Either way, there is only *one* I, and it is Universal. To step boldly forward like this in a global embrace sets in motion the machinery of fate. Perhaps it leads to greatness. Perhaps it leads to infamy. Perhaps it leads to crucifixion.

But the reality, heart-felt to the deep deep core, that each and every person on this planet is none other that one's very own beloved Self, cannot be blithely ignored. It demands action. It requires that the sage step forward into the final birth by fire.

My theory is those who have tarried at the LOC low 900s have done so because they chose to not take this final step. Even so, they are doing enormous good. They are great sages.

I knew that I wanted to keep pressing forward until there was nothing left. It was unacceptable to me to have anything in the way. I could not tolerate any kind of barrier. The Absolute, by definition, means all is dissolved.

By the way, a sage may be reclusive and still be LOC 1000. This is not really about lifestyle. Lakshmana Swamy (LOC 1000) and his enlightened devotee Saradamma (LOC 1000) reside in seclusion on a lovely property near Arunachala.[212] It is reported that gaining access to them can be a challenge.

In such a case where it is next to impossible to study with the guru, you can meditate on the sage from a distance. If you feel strongly that their Grace will help you, there is no genuine sage who will be able to refuse Grace when you are sincere.

Obtain their picture. Pray to them from your heart. Meditate as if you are in their physical Presence. This will be enough to gain some degree of their Grace, whether they are living on the other side of the planet or dropped the body years ago.

In my case, during my Amrita Nadi phase, I was strongly drawn to pray to Lakshmana Swamy and ask for his Grace. His face appeared smiling brightly in my Heart on the right.

During another phase of my sadhana, I prayed to Papaji. I was watching a video where he was talking about the I-thought. I prayed while the video was playing. I felt the Grace of Papaji in that moment. I experienced a deep release from suffering. This took place even though Papaji had dropped the body.

In sum, I believe one of the main characteristics of the LOC 1000 sage is that he or she has decided to make themselves unconditionally available to spiritual seekers everywhere. The heart of the LOC 1000 sage has broken open. Nothing is held back. Nothing can be held back. Nothing will be held back. The LOC 1000 sage is all in all of the time in every way.

My Spiritual Journal:

Starving the I-Thought to Death

(LOC 932 to LOC 1000)

How I Starved the I-Thought to Death

In the earlier spiritual stages, you are dealing with the "mind." When you get to the 900s stage, you may find that you can observe and track the I-thought as it rises up from the Heart on the right to the top of the head. Not everybody has this experience. I am describing it here in case it happens to you.

My Amrita Nadi (aham sphurana) experiences struck me as remarkable at the time, yet the main benefit from them turned out to be my new skill at tracking the I-thought. The path that the I-thought takes from the Heart to the head is the Amrita Nadi. Since the Amrita Nadi was now awakened and visible to me, I could now detect the movement of the I-thought on it.

The I-thought moves up from the Heart to the head quickly. In my experience, it takes it about one-third of a second to cover that distance. That is fast, but it can be detected. I would see the I-thought rise up from the Heart like a spark shooting up from a fire. At other times it looked like a speeding bullet.

What I want to emphasize here is that the I-thought is an observable phenomenon. Ramana described it as the "root" of the mind. He also described it as the "I am the body" thought. By studying the I-thought in this way, I came to know it very well. I realized that the goal was to keep it down in the Heart. It did not want to stay there. If it stayed there, it would die.

It may sound melodramatic, but one of the best analogies I can think of is a life and death struggle in the deep ocean between a good guy and a bad guy. The good guy holds the bad guy under water until he drowns.

The bad guy will struggle fiercely because his life is at stake. But if the good guy persists, the bad guy dies. He sinks into the watery depths and drowns. In this analogy, watery depths are the Heart.

You do not need these same experiences to realize the Self, the Absolute. Like me, some of Ramana's devotees had Kundalini rising and a Crown chakra opening first. Then the revelation of the Heart on the right and Amrita Nadi took place. Other phenomena also associated with aham sphurana (pulsation of the Heart center) may also occur at this stage of Self-inquiry.[213]

What Is the Most Important Factor for Spiritual Success?

If you do not need to experience the Heart on the right, see Amrita Nadi or feel Kundalini, then what do you need?

Nisargadatta Maharaj was asked that kind of question. He replied that being "earnest" was the single most important factor. I agree. How much do you want spiritual freedom? In your heart of hearts, what do you care about the most?

I have seen it come true again and again. Whatever you hold closest and most dear deep in your heart is what will manifest in your life. What is your passion? Where is your fire?

My initial awakening into the LOC 683 in 1992 occurred after I began a spiritual period where I prayed to Divine Mother and flat out demanded that She set me free. I cried, I shouted, I screamed. In every way I could, I made it clear to Her that I was done playing with Her "toys" and with Her "games." At first, She tried to talk me out of it.

She said that She wanted me to continue "playing" with my "playmates" on this beautiful planet that She had made for us. It was only after I showed Her that I would *not* accept "no" for an answer that She reluctantly granted Her Grace to me.

In retrospect, Divine Mother was testing me. I proved to Her that I meant business. I believe that Her reluctance, which She made quite a show of to me, was real. She really does love Her children. She really does enjoy watching them play.

She also realizes that eventually Her children get tired of the planetary school and want to graduate. Even though it may be difficult for Her to let you go, She knows that there are many new players eagerly waiting in the wings to join in Her games.

There is no way to "cause" enlightenment the way you order a meal at a restaurant, but you can prepare. When the Lightning of God strikes, you will then be ready to make the most of it.

This journey is a fire. It will consume everything. Then it will consume itself. It will leave nothing at all behind. It will be as if nothing ever happened. Even the notion of enlightenment will be seen to be absurd. It is beyond enlightenment. You already are the Self. You cannot attain it. You are it. You can gain a recognition that you are That. That is the difference.

Ramana on the "I Am the Body" Thought and the Heart

The revolutionary distinction made by the great sage Ramana Maharshi is that the I-thought in its primordial form is the basis for the mind. This root I-thought has two critical aspects.

First, the I-thought is the false idea "I am the [physical] body." Second, this I-thought arises directly from the causal Heart or Heart on the right to the brain. This is not speculative theory.

When the spiritual yoga reaches this point, the rapid arising of the primal I-thought from its source in the causal Heart can be seen with clarity. It will be as obvious and striking to behold as a big black crow flying swiftly over sparkling white snow.

Strictly speaking, the I-thought is not the thinker thought that the average person is familiar with. The deep imperturbable Silence of the Absolute (Supreme Self) is attained as a result of the final and permanent dissolution (death) of the I-thought.

The subjective experiences of thinking and the thinker thought may go through many changes, but this does not mean that the root I-thought has been eliminated. When you are finally able to get rid of the I-thought, then the notion of the mind is annihilated. This does not mean that the functional use of the mind is lost. Nor does it mean that thoughts totally disappear.

When I first set about writing this book, my faulty memory led me to believe that the Amrita Nadi breakthrough was penultimate to stabilization in the Absolute. When I looked through my spiritual journals, I found this was not the case.

Much like the movie showdown between the hero and the villain that brings the film to a triumphant close, I had to fight one last long fierce battle with the I-thought before it was consumed by the Heart on the right and dissolved for good.

The Sacred Lotus Flower: the Crown, the Stem and the Root

The spiritual practice of tracking the I-thought via Self-inquiry is an advanced practice. The I-thought is the seed of the mind.

The "thinker thought" that is easy to identify and can be found in the mind of every person is just the tip of the iceberg. The I-thought is the hidden portion. It is very difficult to dig it out.

Most of the information that is in books about Self-inquiry is intellectual or theoretical. It is impossible to understand the mechanics of the I-thought, its behavior and how to get rid of it if you cannot personally observe the I-thought yourself.

You can attempt to explain it on the basis of Ramana's great teachings, but there will still be blind spots. One of the biggest areas of confusion is the Heart on the right itself. Even though Ramana talked plenty about it, it is still poorly understood.

I have had numerous people share that a non-duality teacher had told them that their experience of the Heart on the right was just a distraction or interruption of their sadhana. This is unfortunate. Activity in the Heart on the right, such as heat, pressure, light, bliss, opening and so on is a sign of progress.

The Amrita Nadi channel is much like the long stem of a lotus flower. The hidden root of this stem is in the Heart. The glorious flower at the top of the stem is the Crown chakra.

I believe this is one reason why the Crown chakra is called the "thousand petal lotus" flower. It is a full and complete flower with a stem, too. This stem goes down to the Heart. The lotus flower floating on a pond has its stem and roots buried deep in ineffable silence. The visible flower rests in invisible power.

The resplendent Crown chakra is well-known and it is easily observed. The Heart, hidden in the dark causal depths, is not well-known. It is the secret root. It is the ultimate spiritual secret. It is the esoteric spiritual black hole where the ego dies.

How to Track the Rapid Rising of the Sneaky I-Thought

As I explained, the awakening of Amrita Nadi in a series of classic aham sphurana events made me fully aware of Amrita Nadi, the Heart on the right and the connection between the Heart on the right and the Crown chakra. This effortless clarity enabled me to easily and meticulously track the subtle movements of the I-thought from the Heart to the head.

When the I-thought shoots up, it first makes contact with the Crown chakra at the top of the head. Next the I-thought enters the brain. It modifies the brain to produce chemicals that permeate the nerves of the body. These neurotoxins produce convincing sensations that firmly reinforce the trance state of "I am this physical body." I have covered this information in great detail in my book *The Spiritual Heart*. The first arising of the I-thought occurs when you wake up from sleep.[214]

In case you are wondering why you have not noticed these events yourself, please note that they take place very fast. The I-thought shoots up to the Crown (top of the head) from the Heart on the right in about one-third of a second.

The steps it takes in order to take over the brain and permeate the body with the "I am the physical body" feeling take about two-thirds of a second. Allowing for variations in how fast the I-thought may move, this process takes about one second.

In order to detect this movement of the I-thought, you must be stationed in the Heart. Then you can discern its initial impulse to rise up to the brain. The very best time to catch it is the first time it rises up. This is right after you wake up from sleep.

If you have made a strong commitment to stalk the I-thought and you are waiting for it, you will be able to detect its arising when you enter the waking state. You may not be able to see it rise up from the Heart on the right, but you will be able to wake up as spacious awareness and sense it rising up from somewhere in order to get to the top of the head and into the brain. To catch the I-thought as it shoots up to the head in the morning is simple, but it is not easy. My book *Waking Up As Awareness* goes into more detail, but that is the essence of it.[215]

You will find parallel observations about the Heart and the I-thought in the lucid and practical Self-inquiry manual by Sadhu Om called *The Path of Sri Ramana, Part One*. Sadhu Om is a direct disciple of Ramana Maharshi. This spiritual masterpiece is available on the Internet as a free download courtesy of its editor and translator, Michael James.[216]

If you are doing Self-inquiry meditation, please do not feel that you need to have these experiences. I am sharing them because I believe it is important for people to know that such experiences do take place and that they are legitimate.

Likewise, it is very important to me that people know that the Heart on the right is very real. It is not a spiritual trap. I am not telling you to concentrate at that point, but if the Heart on the right awakens in you in some way, I would like my words to give you assurance that you are on the right spiritual track.

If the Heart on the right awakens for you, you will find that it is calling you to be there and rest there. Allow this to happen. You will experience deep peace and rest, perhaps bliss.

The Heart on the right is the causal heart chakra. Its nature is that of deep sleep and of the causal body: bliss, peace, no thought, no knowing. The ability to experience the Heart on the right in the conscious waking state is a deep blessing. Not only that, it is a direct pathway to enlightenment.

Conscious awareness and feeling of the Heart on the right is bringing the deep sleep state into the conscious waking state. Enlightenment *is* deep sleep brought into the waking state.

This is why it can be said that you are already enlightened yet you are not enjoying or experiencing this enlightenment. Each night in deep sleep you enter into "no mind." When deep sleep is purified and clarified via sadhana, it is discovered to be the Silence, the Absolute, the Self.

Ramana Maharshi on the I-Thought and the Mind

Here is a series of direct quotes from Ramana Maharshi about the I-thought (aham vritti). There is no doubt that Ramana taught that the I-thought is the root of the mind. In order to become free of the mind, the I-thought must be destroyed.

The mind is merely thoughts. Of all thoughts, the thought "I" is the root. [Therefore] the mind is only the thought "I."

Of all the thoughts that arise in the mind, the "I" thought is the first. It is only after the rise of this, that the other thoughts arise.

Thoughts alone constitute the mind; and for all thoughts the base or source is the "I" thought. "I" is the mind. If we go inward questing for the source of the "I," the "I" topples down. This is the jnana enquiry.

The ego's phenomenal existence is transcended when you dive into the Source wherefrom arises the Aham vritti.

After the rising up of this "I"-thought all other thoughts arise. The "I"-thought is therefore the root-thought. If the root is pulled out all others are at the same time uprooted.

That which rises as "I" in this body is the mind. If one inquires as to where in the body the thought "I" rises first, one would discover that it rises in the heart. That is the place of the mind's origin.[217]

The full revelation of the bare I-thought as it really is occurs in the last stages of the enlightenment journey. The previous stages were needed in order to get to this critical point. To behold the I-thought naked, unprotected and exposed is tantamount to its imminent and final termination. It will do everything in its power to prevent this deadly revelation.

Once exposed as it really is, it has no defense. Just as with the hidden root of a tall hardy weed, when you dig and finally can see and grab hold of the root of the weed in your hand, it is a simple matter to pull it out. The real challenge was finding the root, digging it up and exposing it in the first place.

To Hunt the I-Thought: Stalk, Starve and Dissolve the Mind

You do not need to experience the Heart on the right to stalk, starve and dissolve the I-thought, the root of the mind.

Several contemporary sages have talked about the pivotal importance of identifying and dissolving the I-thought. This penultimate stage to realizing and stabilizing in the Absolute was well-defined for them.

In his book *Eternity Now*, Francis Lucille writes eloquently and precisely about how he saw the I-thought and, in that clear, direct and total seeing, the I-thought could not survive.

> In an almost simultaneous apperception, the personal entity with which I was identifying revealed itself in its totality. I saw its superstructure, the thoughts originating from the I-concept and its infrastructure, the traces of my fears and desires at the physical level. Now the entire tree was contemplated by an impersonal eye, and both the superstructure of thoughts and the infrastructure of bodily sensations rapidly vanished, leaving the I-thought alone in the field of consciousness.
>
> For a few moments, the pure I-thought seemed to vacillate, just as the flame of an oil lamp running out of fuel, then vanished. At that precise moment, the immortal background of Presence revealed itself in all its splendor.[218]

The unpredictable and mischievous Karl Renz occasionally displays his serious side. During a fascinating little-known interview, he spells out the central role of the I-thought.

> All concepts, of way, development and even cognition, appear with the first I-thought. This first idea creates time, space and thus the entire universe.
>
> And as long as this I-thought appears to be real, which means separation (twoness, suffering), there appears the desire for unity and herewith the longing for a way out, for an end of suffering.

1000

> The first false idea, the one of "I", conditions everything false which follows it. Therefore only the absolute cognition of being prior to the I-thought, and thus recognizing the false as false and removing hereby the root of all problems, is to be what one is. By being what you are, or better, as you are, absolute, prior to all and nothing, all concepts are destroyed.[219]

While giving satsang April 8, 1992, Papaji made these remarks which have been given the title "What Is The Self?" One of the most famous realized devotees of Ramana, he emphasizes that when you find out how the I-thought arises, you will discover how the mind arises also. Vigilant dedicated investigation while in the no-thought state can produce this recognition.

> Somehow this notion arises and this notion becomes mind. This notion is only mind, which is not distinct from "I." "I" arises — this is what is called mind. "I" is not separate from ego... bring everything back, bring all these tendencies back to the "I" thought. Be very vigilant and find out how this notion of "I" arises.[220]

The I-thought may sound like a theory or fanciful idea. It is not. The point is not merely that the I-thought shoots up to the brain and takes it over. The resulting body identification is what produces the experience of the world. If the I-thought has not been surgically uprooted, then the world will continue to seem real to the person even if they are in non-duality.

If it is not exposed and terminated, the I-thought will keep coming back like the bad guy in a movie. The LOC 1000 sage has confronted and destroyed with finality this sly unruly troublemaker. Then true "no mind" is enjoyed.

Until the I-thought is fully investigated and eliminated, the world and a subtle sense of "otherness" will persist. This is true even for enlightened persons not stabilized at LOC 1000.

1000

The final dissolution of the I-thought enables the enlightened person to reach LOC 1000. The I-thought no longer rises up. The sage stabilizes in the "no mind" of the Absolute. This is also called the sahaja or the totally effortless natural state.

After the "Enemy" Was Discovered, I Engaged Him in Battle

What follows is nothing less than my documentation of a war. I fought this spiritual war daily with the I-thought.

There were many battles in this war. The I-thought would keep changing it up on me. I had to keep adapting. I knew that the I-thought was fighting for its life. I suspected that, like a wild animal cornered and facing death, it would throw everything that it could at me. That's exactly what it did.

I have three thick three-ring binders filled with handwritten and typed notes from this period that goes from December, 2006 (right after my Amrita Nadi revelations) to February, 2008.

Please keep in mind that in support of my sadhana, the Self (or God) had given me a part-time security job. I worked two 12 hours days on the weekend. This job was out in the desert guarding an empty machine shop. My only work was this guard job assignment from December, 2006 to February, 2008.

Because of the isolated location, I was able to meditate at least 8 hours a day and get paid for it. The supervisor didn't mind. As long as I stayed awake and did my hourly round, I could read a book, watch TV, write in my journal or meditate.

The I-Thought: Gone With a Whimper, Not a Bang!

I will tell you right now that I was disappointed with the finale. I wanted fireworks. I wanted explosions. I wanted noise. After fighting me so hard for so many years, when it did go, it was like a tired old man taking his last thin breath.

To my vividly alert awareness, the I-thought resembled a clear oscillating bubble like you might see rising up in a soda bottle. Before my inner eye, this translucent bubble slowly collapsed like a balloon losing all of its air. Once it was flat and lifeless, it disintegrated and dissolved into its Source, the open Heart.

In those last moments, he reminded me of a man drowning in the middle of the ocean far from land or ships. He knew that he would never get out of this situation alive. He knew he had been defeated. He gave up his struggle and went limp. He slipped down into the ocean's depths, never to be seen again.

This kind of seeing is possible only when the I-thought has been isolated. Then you can know for sure that it has died.

After the I-thought bubble deflated, dissolved and dropped down in front of my inner eye, I watched and waited. Again like the bad guy in the movie, I did not trust him. I wanted to make sure that he had really drowned... that he would not be coming back up... that this was not just another sly trick.

I could be confident that he had died because I knew what he looked like. I knew his hangouts. I knew his usual behaviors. This knowledge was the direct result of tirelessly stalking him.

I use the world "stalking" deliberately. The most dangerous prey in the entire world is the I-thought. It is the trickster that is behind the mind, behind human suffering. To eliminate it once and for all is the highest and greatest of all human achievements. It heralds the end of the mind's reign of terror.

The journal excerpts that follow start in December, 2006 and go through February, 2008. As I completed this fighting phase which had demanded non-stop inquiry all day every day, I was able to shift into a different kind of relationship with the Heart and I-thought. I was finally able to abide in the Heart.

"Abiding" in the Heart means the battle is over. You are now at peace. You can now rest with ease in the Heart. The pesky I-thought causes trouble now and then, but it is dying.

As you remain stabilized in the state of abiding, it becomes permanent. The I-thought no longer arises. There is only the perfect peace of the Heart. This took place February, 2008.

You are able to know that the I-thought is no longer arising for you because you were able to be aware of it when it was arising. Typically the I-thought is very busy and active when it is coming up. If you have developed the skill required to detect it at that level, it is easy to tell it is no longer rising up.

I do not want to give the appearance that this is easy. The passive approaches to inquiry meditation like watching thoughts will never get the job done. Not only do you need to work up to noticing each and every thought, you want to confront each thought and knock it down into the Heart. In this book I refer to resources that will enable you to arrive at the thought-free state and do assertive Self-inquiry correctly.

Could These Be the Ultimate Spiritual Secrets of Humanity?

But that is telling the end of the story at the beginning. I did not arrive there easily or peacefully. It was a knock down fight from day one and every day after that. There were days when it seemed like the I-thought was winning. But I never gave up.

As you may recall, my landmark Amrita Nadi experience took place on November 5, 2006 in my apartment in Las Vegas. Prior to this revelation, I had read the teachings of Ramana Maharshi with keen interest, but I did not understand his emphasis on the I-thought and the Heart on the right.

After this Amrita Nadi event, it all became crystal clear. I was shocked by what had been revealed to me. I realized that the teachings of Ramana Maharshi are the most powerful and most revolutionary spiritual teachings on the planet today.

These are the deepest spiritual secrets. They are the *ultimate* secrets of the human race. It is only now, thanks to Ramana Maharshi, that these greatest secrets can be made public.

I believe a massive spiritual revolution is taking place on our planet right now. That is one of the reasons why these highest extraordinarily arcane top secrets have been exposed in plain sight for all to see, hear, read, feel, know and practice.

Stalking and Starving the I-Thought: Dec. 2006 to Feb. 2008

These journal entries cover the final phase from December, 2006 through February, 2008. I was living in Las Vegas.

I worked as a security guard in a remote outpost that was ideal for meditation. The conclusion of this phase coincided with a move to San Francisco to support my wife's health.

Stalking means getting to know the ways of your prey. It is a 24/7 kind of thing. All day, every day, all of the time you are stalking your prey. This kind of dedication is required because you are hunting the most stealthy prey of all, the I-thought.

You are not just watching it, either. You are stalking it intently so that you can know its habits, capture it and kill it. These may be strong words, but the I-thought must be put down. If you do not put the I-thought down, it will persist. Your mind will persist. This means your suffering will persist.

You may be an enlightened person right now, but until you kill the I-thought you are playing Russian roulette with your awakening. The I-thought can rise up again in this life or the next life and come back with a vengeance. I am speaking from experience here.

The I-thought is eliminated by studying it and stalking it. Then you starve it. Eventually it runs out of gas. Unless you are one of the rare cases of spontaneous enlightenment, the task of getting rid of the I-thought will require extraordinary and sustained daily effort, precision, dedication and diligence.

December 11, 2006
Las Vegas, Nevada

This has been like oscillating between heaven and hell on a roller coaster of day and night.

When I "lose" the Light in the Heart (it's still there, but I lost my contact with it), I return to the dim, gray limbo of the ego-ruled mental world. I feel depressed, moody, weary, unhappy, discouraged.

I am realizing that this is the defensive strategy of the ego mind I-thought. Negativity, loss, isolation, alienation and drama are all that it has to use as tools. The life of the ego I-thought is a perennial soap opera. True happiness is from the Self, from the Heart. Except for happiness secretly provided by the hidden Heart, there is no happiness for the ego I-thought!

Perhaps this emotional discomfort would stop a less determined person, but not me. I am very used to being depressed, and it doesn't bother me.

I've never based my spiritual progress on how happy I am. Instead, I've asked myself: How hard am I working? Am I staying with the discipline? Is my commitment 100% every hour of every day? Suffering is inevitable.

After the first breakthrough into the Heart on the right and Amrita Nadi in November, 2006, I was not prepared for the "shock" of being returned to the "darkness."

Before, I hadn't perceived my everyday state as darkness, but after living in the Light, even for a few hours, I saw it as dimly lit and confining old, outdated dungeon. I know I am in prison!

December 19, 2006
Las Vegas, Nevada

The Pluto conjunction to my natal Moon is exact on December 23, Saturday, so that may account for some of this weird empty blank intensity. I feel stuck between two worlds. I understand now that the Heart on the right is the source of the I-thought. I have seen that for myself. I do not doubt it.

I have experienced Amrita Nadi a number of times since early November. Now when I read Ramana or Lakshmana Swamy I understand specifically and concretely what they are talking about from my own experience of the Light of the Self. Yet... any and all of it is utterly beyond my power.

I do the inquiry, I trace the I-thought to the Heart. I am aware, on and off, of the Heart on the right. This is easily maintained every day. But nothing more comes of it, and I am realizing that I must accept this way of life. Once again I recognize that I have done all that I can do.

Ramana and Laskshmana Swamy talk about the blank that meditators find when they seek the Heart. Ramana advised "find who is experiencing the blank."

I guess that is my task. Somehow an experience of a big life blankness is occurring and for that to take place, there has to be the I-thought, the pseudo-experiencer.

Pluto conjunct Moon is a total wipe-out of whatever was there, and this super-blank that I keep coming back to fulfills that. Pluto first wipes out what was there. It is only later that spring arrives, and flowering is possible.

I can see how this living blankness could feel like massive loss or great desolation, but it strikes me as the same old negative emptiness I have struggled with since 1992 [my awakening] dressed up in new and grander clothes. This emptiness is not just a state. Now it is my entire existence. Remove the ego I-thought *totally*. This life blank is the ego's bleak nightmare of its demise.

January 24, 2007
Las Vegas, Nevada

I am already meditating about 8 hours a day on the weekend (at my security guard post job). I resolved yesterday Monday to begin meditating a minimum of 1 hour per day during the week (in the morning). This hour commitment is fruitful. Yesterday I am sure it kept me on track with self-inquiry and returning to the glowing Heart. Today it was emotional, healing, a discovery of love.

I went out to get the mail before sitting down to meditate (I watched several hours of TV before, too). I noticed something unusual. The usual very subtle stress caused by the sense of otherness was almost absent. In its place was a sense of unity, which meant that there was only my self, there were no others, there was nothing that was "other" to me.

It was not a perfect sense of unity, as there was still the experiencer, but I saw an important point: as long as there is any sense of an "other," there will be stress, suffering, lack of peace. With this brief sense of unity there was also a mild ecstasy or enhanced feeling of exhilarated well-being.

Meditating after that walk, I quickly reached a deeper level of feeling as I focused on the Heart on the right and actively did two-step self-inquiry [as taught by Sadhu Om in *The Path of Sri Ramana, Part One*] to bring attention back to the Heart.

I began to cry. I was shown that the aspiration to true and total love that I felt as a 14 year-old boy wanting to be able to love, help and heal the world, would be answered by attaining the total wholeness of the Self.

I had never before connected my yearning to love and be loved unconditionally with my aspiration to realize the Self. The two goals are one and the same. The true whole Self IS the real true Love. Ramana said this about love. Now I begin to understand!

For most of the hour (approximately 10 a. m. to 11 a. m.), I cried — literally sobbed — uncontrollably. I understood for the first time that the spiritual True Self that I have seeking since I was 16 years old [my Kundalini awakening] is none other than the pure true total unconditional love without limit my heart has yearned for.

It is not some abstraction, some non-human realm beyond feeling. It is the fulfillment of human feeling, of human love. It IS love, love incarnate.

Now I realize that my search for love and my search for truth and my search for self are all colliding in a crazy merger. Now my heart is speaking with silent feeling, telling me that as I now approach the core of my being, I equally discover the ultimate secret of true love. Love Is Unity.

I talked to God, to Lord Shiva: "Father, I am coming home. Please keep the door open for me. Please show mercy. Now that you revealed this ultimate truth, that the love I want is the Self I seek, I can't go back. I must go forward all of the way. I can't do that without you. Still, do with me what you will!"

March 14, 2007
Las Vegas, Nevada

Tempted by magic, by super-knowledge, by super-power, in the form of a Remote Viewing/Remote Influencing course on eBay. I considered bidding on it, but I felt how it kicked up an intoxicating, addictive fascination with power. I instantly felt a hard knot in my solar plexus of conflict, lack, raga-dwesha [attachment-aversion]. It acted as a reinforcer for identification with the body and of the buzzing "beehive brain."

The endless hyperactive mind chatter is tied to that knot. I let it go by meditating on it. I was surprised by the hold this temptation of "occult magic powers" had on me. I saw that for 2 weeks I have been living without this knot in my solar plexus. This coincides with my ability to stay in Silence without distraction most of the time. I believe I would have lost this Silence had I gone down that magic path.

April 3, 2007
Las Vegas, Nevada

Last night I had a Warning Dream. The context: Yesterday at the library, there was a full shelf of screenwriting books. I got excited and checked out all 15 books.

Then I went through them. I cooked up a scenario of studying the movie "Starman" and screenplay, writing a screenplay, entering script contests, getting an agent. I took the providential synchronicity of all these books together — I have never seen that in a public library, such books are popular! — as a sign of things to come, of a good and appropriate pathway for me to take.

But the Warning Dream said otherwise. Its graphic message told me that if I pursued this screenwriting path at this time, I will destroy the foundation of my spiritual work in the last six months and lose the path. I will get caught up in it, allowing the ego I-thought to take over. The symbology was I am at work at the machinery shop that I am the security guard for on weekends. "I" first observed the strange events in the shop bodiless, like an all-seeing eye (this would be pure awareness).

Then "I" as a dream character walked into the scene in my security guard uniform. A movie crew had invaded the shop. The crew was drilling into the cement floor of the building creating big holes. At center of the chaos was a flashily dressed director. I knew that he was the ego I-thought. He was arrogant with me as I tried to do my security job. I asked him why he was there, what his name was, who gave him permission. I had a sinking feeling that all was tragically lost.

He was not arrogant as in rude. He was arrogant by being aloof, snooty, dismissive. He reeked of confidence in his power and position. He was used to being in charge and in control. The location of the machine shop security job in the desert was chosen because it had been a spiritual retreat for me, where I am isolated, alone, free to meditate for hours on end. I joked with Jerry from Canada: "I am paid to meditate."

That morning the meaning was obvious. I had slept with an unusual degree of clarity and awoke with a feeling of lucidity. I woke up with the dream firmly in my mind. I instantly understood that the cement floor represented the foundation of my spiritual practice and meditation. I understood that the silver-tongued "director" was the ego I-thought (or body-I).

I understood, most important of all, that it was due to my own lack of mindfulness, my failure to guard the boundaries of my sadhana (the locked gate at the perimeter of the property that I guarded), it was I who had let him in. He did not storm the gate. He did not have to. I invited him in.

Once again, it was my writing ambition samskara, which at another time popped up as an obsession with copywriting, which was tempting me. Subtle yet requiring a busy analytical mind, doership and ego, it is the strongest form of ambition and desire that I have left. It is the result of a powerful vow I made in a past life to be a successful writer.

July 14, 2007
Las Vegas, Nevada

This is a new experience. It looks/feels to me like the Heart-Self has caught the mind like a fish and has it caught on a line. The mind-fish is struggling to get away and now and then leaps out of the water.

But the hook of the Heart is stuck deep in its flesh. Its struggles are only deepening the hook and tiring the mind out until it is exhausted.

I have never seen this or felt this relationship between Heart and mind. After pulling the mind into the Cave of the Heart, even though the mind escaped, it is like the Heart put a fishing hook in it so as to never let it get away again. At times the mind goes all the way up to the top of the head and briefly does its conventional worry, problem solving, planning.

Last Tuesday (July 10), I talked with Jerry from Canada on the phone. I gave him permission to read me for this purpose. He told me that all he could say is that "Now you are all the way inside the cave." It is four days later and I am having this experience of the mind (the I-thought) being fully inside the Cave. At the same time, there is a subtle feeling of pressure on the right, in the chest, slightly uncomfortable. It feels like this is a sign of the mind's struggle.

July 19, 2007
Las Vegas, Nevada

Sat again for meditation for one hour. It has been helpful to not have the Internet at home since the computer crashed weeks ago during Mercury retrograde. It was a distraction.

Feeling considerable clarity and encouragement. The new breakthrough over the weekend on Sunday [at the security guard shack in the desert] where I inquired with each arising thought and it opened to a mildly ecstatic experience of formless being seems to have integrated itself quite nicely.

Sri Sadhu Om's book [*The Path of Sri Ramana, Part One —free pdf online*] was very helpful. I would hazard a guess that now finally I am understanding what "abiding in the Self" is.

This a. m. meditation I was able to stay most of the time feeling the silent feeling-I at the Heart on the right. I noticed, which I think is significant, that this feeling includes the sense "This is my real I. This is where I really live. This is my home."

Also significant is how there are feelings of contentment, joy, well-being, happiness — pure trouble-free being. Not massive bliss, but definitely a direct experience of the joy of pure being untouched by thought. This being is my true identity — the silent I of pure being.

Without realizing it, not so long ago I was trying to be in the Heart, hold onto the feeling of being that is there, *from the outside*. As Sri Sadhu Om puts it, my body-I (I-thought) was still assuming first person position, therefore making the Heart an object outside of it.

This is an impossible position as the I-thought does not realize the Self! As he says, the Self is already realized. The I-thought or body-I dies. It was covering or hiding the Self. Like the sun, the Self was shining the whole time behind the clouds of ego.

July 22, 2007
Las Vegas, Nevada

Watching TV at the weekend security guard shack job. Thanks to the sharp appearance of "otherness" by the TV characters, the awareness of the Heart radiating out "I" in waves came into focus. I now have a new appreciation of why Sri Ramana Maharshi called it "I-I." It is like a pulsing radio beacon.

It is transmitting over and over again the same message — I-I-I-I-I-I-I-I-I etc. But this is not "I" with a sense of other or no-I.

But sometimes that sense of other is weakly present. Thank God there are no other human beings here to reinforce that old habit, just a neutral impersonal industrial wilderness environment psychologically removed from the city.

When the I-thought arises, it divides. It creates a schism automatically. It also precipitates Other/Not-I, leading to pain, discontent, suffering and searching. But this "I" now radiating from the Heart, sometimes strongly, sometimes more weakly, is not based on thought, is not a thought, and has with it no sense of other or not-I at all. Instead it effortlessly *radiates* "only I" — a pure I-I. Only I am. I am the only I. There is only *I* (*this* I). I am this I am (= I-I).

In this pulsing radiating of waves of I-I, there is true peace and true happiness. There is no invasion of other, no attack of sorrow. There is true contentment. It feels like a seamless joyful Wholeness.

There is some luminosity to it as well, but the feeling "I-I" or "only I" is the dominant feature, coupled with some kind of feeling in the Heart on the right of well-being, wholeness, contentment, happiness, joy, peace. It keeps changing. The feelings are there, noticeable, but they are not overwhelming. Instead, they are gently full.

I now recognize this silent radiant pulsing of I-I to be aham sphurana as described by Sri Ramana Maharshi. There could even be said to be a "sound" with it, but it is a "silent sound," the "Voice of Silence," which is this "I-I" (or "I Am").

This joyful pulsation is the true message of Being, and without the joy, however silent, it would not be the real voice of the Heart. This silent joy and silent "I-I" (only "I Am") go together, automatically rise together, again reinforcing how the blank neutral state [mental emptiness] is NOT the final state.

August 3, 2007
Las Vegas, Nevada

An interesting week! It's far from over. This is very early Friday morning. What happened is I went to work graveyard at the Convention Center [security guard job] but it turned out that they didn't have work for me. So the security company sent me home with 4 hours of pay instead of 8 hours.

I didn't have to stay — a fair compromise. The conditions at work have been optimal for meditation. You just sit there all night and get paid for it.

I told Jerry in Canada in an email I had moved from one station to another re inquiry and the Heart. The brief "schizoid" phase is over. It feels like there is only one identity again — now in the Heart, not in the head.

This is not only because of my feeling of now being there. The answer "I am" to the first step question of the two-step inquiry now always comes from the Heart on the right (instead of the I-thought). It's like the Heart just took over.

This change in the inquiry took me completely by surprise. Not only did I not expect it, I had never heard of such a thing.[221]

In retrospect, it makes sense as the movement in inquiry is from the false I to the true I. The false I is dissolved into and absorbed by the true first-person I [the Heart or the Self]. At some point there would have to be a tangible shift(s) in the experience of identity so that it comes from the true I in the Heart.

I had already felt evidence of that on Sunday. The I-thought in the head used to answer "I am" [to the question "Who is having this thought?"]. Why can't the Heart answer "I am" with its voice? The old two-step inquiry is now a one-step return to the Heart. I ask "Who is having this thought?" to inquiry into and dissolve a thought that has arises. The voice in the Heart on the right answers "I am." Wow!

I am pretty sure the first instance of the "I am" answer being in the Heart was on the bus coming home from work 7:20 p. m. last Sunday, July 29. Although thoughts still rise up to the head, for the last few days these thoughts have been trivial and not troublesome. My impression is that they have very little substance. Their coherence is gone. Its center is lost. That ancient castle now floats in fragments at and around the head.

The content seems greatly narrowed. The thoughts today were almost exclusively about my friends Jerry and Joe and my desire to resolve any difficulties there. Even these thoughts, which were imaginary problem solving conversations, were easily perceived to be superfluous.

The implication becomes self-evident that all thoughts are not only superfluous, they actually take away from the Heart and interfere with Being, essentially short-circuiting it, stealing its energy for inferior purposes.

That is what I noticed with even these neutral seemingly innocuous thoughts. Their mere arising is enough to interfere with and disturb the fullness of the Heart.

I don't know if it's because of doing all these grave shifts and sleeping during the day, which is weird for me, but the body on and off has felt light, or even like it vanished and is not there. It feels like the identification with the body has greatly weakened.

At work I was surprised how so many of these very ordinary people really wanted to talk to me and opened up to me. Frankly, I was amazed. I know I was in a very open Heart-based space, naturally outgoing and friendly, but even so, I was a big magnet without trying.

For two days now I have been in the peace of the Heart with the voice "I am" from the Heart answering the first step of the inquiry. It is not a dramatic bliss, but it is distinctively the open peaceful happiness-goodwill cum well-being of the Heart that I have learned to recognize. I feel as if this kind, beautiful openness of being is myself, my natural identity.

I feel myself to be in the Heart very firmly. Thoughts still go up to the head, but they are "lighter," less heavy, "frothy." They seem to float up there slowly, almost aimlessly, instead of shooting up to the head like a menacing determined bullet (then aggressively throwing their weight around). This floating up is like "reverse snowing." Instead of snow falling, snow rises — the weightless kiss of snowflakes, the soft silent atmosphere of a fresh snowfall.

August 22, 2007
Las Vegas, Nevada

My impression as to "where I'm at" at this time? In spite of Monday two days ago where there was notable fear and worry thoughts — all very painful, of course — what appears to be going on is that the notion of a local Heart is dissolving and with it, the notion of mind. The feeling is that I would have to stir up the mind to find it, which would be akin to hitting a big hornet's nest as hard as I can with a baseball bat. Not a good idea! In fact, to go "look for the mind" would be a form of "seeking," and it is precisely the seeking that is absent.

So thoughts arise — "working thoughts" as Ramesh would call them — but they don't present a problem. They rise up and fall away without drama like a paper towel you use to wipe up a spill on the dinner table, then throw away.

Just every now and then there is a thought that is definitely contracted, and it is inevitable painful. For functional needs, then, the Self is fully capable of providing useful working thoughts, but these thoughts are not from "egocentric demanding."

I snuck a few peeks at the Heart even though I was choosing to not focus on the Heart on the right in this meditation. In the first peek, the Heart looked like the eye of a hurricane. It had a black hole in the center with swirling spiral gray-white clouds around it. During the second meditation session, the Heart looked like a big circle covering half the upper torso — three times bigger than I have usually seen it (size of a dinner plate).

What struck me was not the appearance as much as the feeling I got when tuning into the Heart. It was as if the Heart had expanded its influence from the localized place on the right to include the entire energy field, so that the whole field around the body had become "super-heavy" (in the black hole sense, like "super-density").

The result is a more total silence, a silence in which thought based on the I-thought is having even more difficulty arising. It is not just attempting to rise up out of the Heart on the right to the head, it is now attempting to rise up in an atmosphere that is itself expressing super-gravity along with the ground (the Heart). Against this super-gravitational pull the I-thought cannot generate enough momentum or speed or thrust to actually break free into the "sky" of the head.

Not that there haven't been a few thoughts that were negative or painful (financial worries again, of course, or the occasional imaginary dialog with Joe or Jerry). But to make the point: I can't remember any negative thoughts from yesterday!

August 28, 2007
Las Vegas, Nevada

Decided to play it loose again these last two days, meaning I didn't push for the two-step inquiry or to terminate a negative experience. Instead, I allowed the experiences to "float." I suppose I'm not so afraid of the I-thought stuff arising, e.g. worries, fear, anxieties, other negative reactions. I am studying them closely.

The weekend was very intense. There is a tendency to pull back from that anyway.

But more deeply, I am recognizing that here is where the verbal, effortful phase of inquiry fades away, to be replaced by the new ease of abiding in the pure feeling "I" or the existence "I Am."

The Heart-spaciousness that came forward during the weekend that was also the "true body" in its relaxed unboundedness has been emerging, then dropping back repeatedly. When this spaciousness is here I'm allowing negative thought-emotion to run in order to study the interaction.

What I am seeing is now that I understand that the I-thought stories are based on the mental "I-am-the-body" construct, these stories, these painful mind movies, are running on the surface of Being. The Being is there, is here, and this content, which requires the I-am-the-body as its anchor, is taking place on top of it.

Sometimes when the content got too strong and I was uncomfortable with it, I intervened with the two-step and it cut through the fog of mental confusion quickly, popped the story bubble, ruptured the thought balloon, usually with one question. Otherwise, I just studied it, allowed it to run, "X-rayed" it to expose the I-am-the-body assumption underlying each and every moment of suffering.

The suffering was for the I-am-the-body concept, for the mind, and it was doing it to itself. The insight that the I-am-the-body idea is just a mental idea acting as an interloper continues to feel like a pivotal insight.

This insight means that the vivid experience I used to think i was having of being the body was not in fact being the body. It was identification with a false thought. The body I thought I was was a construct, not the real body.

The real body is the space body, the unbounded body. This is radical! It frees me not just now but in terms of my entire past, releasing the false interpretation of all of those events. I can appreciate how those feelings and experiences did not happen to the physical body as it really is. The story is not about the true body. The story is only about a false mental concept.

October 4, 2007
Las Vegas, Nevada

I no longer feel it matters what I say. I have lost the sense of a technique or method. Instead there is life... but not life as I knew it before inquiry. The life of this illusory separate one seems like it is being slowly absorbed.

I have had some success with entering the stillness when I wake up. I'm not striving to catch it at the first moment of waking up. I am staying in bed and returning to remembering the stillness-space. For example, this morning I felt myself "remembering" that I was present the whole time I slept, that I am a perfect clear light stillness present in all conditions and circumstances — so all the time, everywhere.

The Self is coming forward, and as it does that, the pseudo-self shrinks and fades away (for it is only thought, and so a dream). I will have several days go by where the Self is almost forgotten. Then that will vanish and a deep experience of the Presence emerges spontaneously.

There is apparent coming and going of the Self. Of course, it is not really that way. My experience or awareness of it is doing that.

Another thing that has been going on — quite spontaneous — is long periods of silence where I start staring off into space. I have come close to missing my stop riding the bus, but somehow I haven't.

October 16, 2007
Las Vegas, Nevada

I just went outside to get the mail. Fascinating! I thought I had looked thoroughly at my thoughts about the world and more or less completed that investigation.

Now I would say what I did before was only the first step of getting to the place of clarity where I can see that a thought about somebody else in the world being separate from me (and so opposed to me) that causes stress and tension is in fact a totally false thought.

It actually CREATES the illusion of separation that it then seeks to solve via some kind of doing, action, conquering, overcoming of human and other obstacles.

These kinds of thoughts set up the obstacle as separate and independently "real." Then they set up dualistic body-based doings that in a speculative and subtly fearful, impotent way are supposed to solve this problem.

So although my issues seem to be practical, about having enough money to take care of this body and my spouse, I am convinced that the only "practical solution" is a fundamental healing at the very root, a healing of the split between self and the world, between identity and object.

But the Big Question is exactly HOW do I do this? How do I heal the split? By seeing how I create separation with thought.

Understanding is the key. My mind is still creating concepts and images of a world that is separate, but I understand deep and deeper that I create this separation from out of my substance, my wholeness. These constructs are MY creation, MY projection, MY expression. The "world" originates from ME. It is me. There is no "lack." Lack is a concept, a construct, created from the Wholeness that is its ground.

There is also the sense at the same time that for me the spiritual next step is moving through and beyond the invisible wall/bubble that I have created around myself to protect myself against the world. In concrete terms, I now realize that action is the only solution, the only answer.

Standing by and just watching from a sterile vacuum does not work. When you understand, when you *really* know, then action, indeed, "right action," is automatic. It spontaneously emerges right from your understanding.

There is no intermediary thinking, reasoning, theorizing, speculating. To know and to do become one and the same. This is what I am beginning to see now. To know and not do has been my disease for my whole adult life.

This action I feel wanting to be expressed is not in reaction to the world. It is "moving through" the world.

The world becomes the context for the unfolding, the raw material, the floating, flowing, flowering dream, but the unfolding itself, the art, is not based on trying to get something materialistic from the world. When I am seeing clearly then the doing, the path for the doing, is revealed. It is shown. That is what I feel is happening now.

I am seeing free of the previous karmic confusion. I can see clearly now in front of me. I can see that I have powerful paths of action available to me. I can see that I don't have to do the slave or servant or serf type of jobs anymore that I have done in Las Vegas: the groundskeeper, the security guard. I don't have to because I see greater, better value is on new paths.

December 21, 2007
Las Vegas, Nevada

Loosening of the body-navel-solar plexus plug: experience "the ego is just the body identification... I am not the body, i am the Self"... the body dissolving, disappearing, falling away... definitely related to loose SP [solar plexus] plug... also plug on back directly behind causal Heart point in the front (right side of chest) is loose.. also a plug just above right shoulder blade is loose... these plugs all look like black rubber stoppers.

This afternoon walking home the body sensation is almost gone, but it felt good, hey, it felt great. I realized that here is the bliss that Ramana was talking about... all the stress is for the body.

The body is just a concept, the body contraction. It is a false definition or defining, a false boundary. Felt this bliss, knew it was the causal body. I am entering the causal body.

Intuitively knew that though this state which is blissful and feels like there is so little of the physical body is actually the direct experience of the causal body. It is still a body, of course, but it is way bigger than the mental body. It has as its characteristic this spontaneous boundless bliss.

I also noticed in a new way the usual two-way dialog between the head and the solar plexus. I saw how the plug or knot in the solar plexus (or navel or third chakra) is like a padlock on the body identification feeling. It then automatically induces fear-based emotions of survival. The head is hooked into a closed feedback loop with this SP knot where virtually all of the thoughts tend to serve this body-based survival struggle.

In contrast, yesterday I found that when I was thinking I was having the Heart on the right as the reference point instead of the navel/SP. The role of the thoughts or head was completely different. Thoughts came and went. They were not survival oriented. Even if they were problem solving in nature, there was no anxiety or struggle. There was just peace.

January 3, 2008
Las Vegas, Nevada

Over the weekend, I had experience of light and silence briefly. I did a spontaneous meditation of "This is the Self," meaning whatever I touched, looked at, heard, etc. is the Self. This produced clarity and peace Sunday night after work.

1000

This morning, after sleeping, I watched *Short Cut to Nirvana*, a documentary about the Kumbha Mela in India.[222] At some point while watching it, or right after, the Heart on the right became a bright circular Light, and this Light shot up to the head. Then there was only joy and silence.

In fact, it was impossible for the mind to form thoughts — more accurately, there was only the Light, there was no mind. This was completely obvious. My sense was this was just a tiny portion of this Light, yet it transcended totally anything I have known, anything the world can offer. The only parallel is the experience of Amrita Nadi I had last November, 2006.

This experience right now would probably be called aham sphurana. It is like a special effect, the Heart Lighting up like this, then the shooting up of the Light via Amrita Nadi to the Crown. How to describe it? It is the ultimate. I know that with utter certainty. What can I do with it, about it? It is up to God, Guru, Self. Right now, I still feel some of it. The Peace it is cannot be described. It is another world, a perfect world, where there is no mind at all. There is Eternity only, Peace only, Joy only.

Nothing the mind offers is a hundredth, a thousandth of this perfection. I don't know what else to say. It is like I am finally now absolutely my real Self. I instantly recognize this, know it. I am at final peace and rest. Not only that, I am filled with Love, I am Love itself, Love is me, I am all, I love all. It is the ultimate state, the perfect state.

One last thing: Sri Ramana Maharshi was 100% correct.

He was so precise and accurate in everything that he said. It is amazing! So much confusion in the world, even about spirituality, yet he spoke the ultimate truth clearly, simply, directly, so that I can benefit from the Truth in this life, even in the West.

January 15, 2008
Las Vegas, Nevada

To prepare for this entry, I reviewed my entries back through November 30, 2007. I discerned a definite pattern, a "building up" of aham sphurana or Amrita Nadi phenomena. In brief, the recognition that I am the "I AM" in the Heart and not the body is deepening. There is now confident knowing that I am the Heart on the right. It is my true Self. It is the source of identity. The body is only a reflection.

Thanks to the steady discernment of the mental "I am the body" program template, I am now able to feel the Heart on the right and to feel my pure beingness there simultaneous with the conventional experience of the physical body.

The equation of limited existence is the Heart + the Mental "I am the body" Template + the Physical Body = Suffering. But the equation of freedom is the same with but one element removed: the Heart + the Body = Freedom = the Heart. The physical body itself is insentient.

The experiment of feeling the Heart "I AM" and the body-based "I-feeling" at the same time has expanded. Yesterday and today I have been active and functioning in the waking state, doing errands, and have been able to retain awareness-feeling of myself as the Heart while being the body.

The body is not an obstacle, only the mind is an obstacle. Also yesterday I noticed a phenomenon which persists today of the Heart radiating a 120 degree wide beam from its position in the right chest to include the entire physical body. This radiation is the "I-feeling" or "identity feeling" going directly to the body without the intermediary of the brain or lower Ajna thought concretization projection center.

This vision of "identity radiation" direct to the body so there is experienced "Heart + Body" (without mind/I-thought/I-am-the-body interference) is a subjective percept that parallels my feeling of being at the same time my identity in and as the Heart and also simultaneously the physical body. The body is being experienced as a solid sensation, but it feels as if it is an emanation or projection of the Heart.

This radiation from the Heart is not just a pure identity feeling being painted upon the physical body but in fact somehow this radiation from the Heart is actually CREATING this physical body. So though I am experiencing this physical body still in the old terms of a separate physical unit or vehicle, my direct perception is that this sense of density attributed to the body and the body itself are both being produced by the Heart on the right. This means that the physical body IS the Heart!

I can feel the Heart right now as I type, and the radiance that produces the body "I-feeling" sensation. I observed this connection more analytically that I have before during this sitting. I noticed that even with the connection between Heart and body vague, I was able to study and tune into the I-feeling that is experienced conventionally as body identity feeling and trace it back to the pure "I AM" in the Heart.

Another way to put this is the body is the identity-feeling confined and bounded as the body, while the Heart is the identity-feeling unrestricted and unbounded, fully and purely expressed without compromise or limitation.

The recognition is that there is but one I-feeling (I AM). At the physical level or dimension this Heart of pure being-identity-existence is expressed or emanated or radiated AS the physical body.

There is in fact no limitation implied by this, as the only reason for the sense of restriction, contraction or confinement is the subtle residual holding onto the "I am the body" idea. Now that this dialog between the Heart and body via pure I-feeling is taking place, I expect that to further dissipate.

January 19, 2008
Las Vegas, Nevada

After experiencing a strong disconnect from the Heart these last two days, I was able to return to feeling purely the Heart.

When the shift occurred, I recognized it as corresponding to the thought-free blissful state of the Heart-radiance. It is not based on the I-thought or thought-movement (and so it is not based on pain-pleasure). It is utterly tranquil, peaceful, still, fulfilled, completed and happy.

Before, the I-thought was feeling profound pain and suffering because it was feeling the loss of the Heart-illuminated state (Amrita Nadi) of a few days ago. What a paradox!

So I am feeling acute suffering and depression in/as the I-thought — failure, loss, depression, discouragement. And I'm reflecting to myself "The I-thought is bemoaning the fact that it was not able to permanently destroy itself!" In this moment, I had an insight. This is the best the I-thought can do. Its very nature is seeking and suffering, so now it is going to condemn itself for still existing!

This insight broke this pattern apart. I pulled the I-thought down into the Heart on the right. Reflecting on how I had arrived at this saturation situation of suffering, I recognized it was due to my policy of laissez faire with my thoughts, of "letting the thoughts run." I saw clearly for myself that *every* I-thought when it rises up from the Heart is seeking and it will produce suffering.

I resolved today to be more in charge of my I-thoughts and to not let them run anymore. Functional thoughts and spiritual thoughts, both being spontaneous, have their natural place. I am talking about seeking-based I-thoughts rising up from the Heart creating chains or sequences of thoughts that result in subtle turmoil and agony.

How this insight and decision came about is interesting. I was feeling the acute suffering of the loss of my blessed Amrita Nadi state of a few days ago. I began to dialog with the I-thought and did a few two-step inquiries spontaneously.

Then I talked to the I-thought directly about the paradox of its position for a few minutes. I said to it "Well, do I still have to do inquiry to get rid of you?"

The I-thought responded by seemingly bending its head and then returning, without further prompting by me, to the Heart. I realized that I need to be thinking in terms of (a) intervening when thoughts run and (b) I need to PULL the I-thought down to the Heart.

I was actually a little stunned by this meekness and quick surrender by the I-thought. I was reflecting "What just happened?" As I considered the context, I realized that the I-thought had been doing the best it could with the sadhana — but it cannot kill itself. It does not know how.

It is a catch-22 cycle of energy that cannot stop itself. It is the dog chasing its tail. But it can be stopped. So this co-operation by the I-thought to then subside into the Heart made sense.

Subsequent to that surprising event where the I-thought bent its head and subsided in the Heart, I was able to notice the I-thought rising up to the head from the Heart with greater accuracy than before. I saw it shooting up like a little July 4 fireworks rocket or like a salmon trying to jump upstream.

It's hard to say what it looked like. A little fish? Black or white? Or black and white? Or a seed or an egg or a ball, something oval. Or a spark — fragments of the Light of the Heart, the fire in the Heart, diminished, darkened, estranged.

These I-thoughts were rising up every two to five seconds which is not that often compared to what I had observed in the past. Furthermore, i could see each one of them clearly.

The Heart was in sharp contrast. It was the ultimate contest.

The blessed Ground of pure feeling and genuine Identity versus the rising rogue I-thought shooting up to the head and creating contraction, stress, an impact of dense heaviness there [at the head]. But this impact did not last. Nor did the flash of negative emotions that occurred right after the impact. Both dissolved instantly.

I do NOT usually see this rising up of the I-thought, but I have seen it today many times. There is right now clear feeling of the Heart (but no Light phenomena, no Amrita Nadi).

Because I am so clearly feeling this pure feeling of the Heart on the right, then I am seeing and feeling the I-thought rise up, attempt to shoot up to the head and create thought-conditioned feeling = negative emotions = seeking and stress.

This clarity of pure feeling is a physical sensation, very subtle, as well as peace, fulfillment, stillness, happiness in conjunction with knowing this [the Heart] is the *only* place of happiness. This intuition is intrinsic to the clarity or clear feeling-seeing. I am taking a stand in and for my happiness.

January 27, 2008
Las Vegas, Nevada

Yesterday at work [the isolated guard shack in the desert] I saw that the Heart is creating the world.

It began with a familiar experience of gazing at this industrial wasteland that I am guarding in the middle of nowhere. The landscape is of grays, blacks and browns, of metal and asphalt and dirt.

I feel that I extend into it, expand out into it, and somehow "it is I." That there is a luminescence underneath it permeating it which I am and which it is. This comes in long flashes. They last about 10 seconds. It happens three times. This was the familiar experience of "oneness."

Then I saw something new. I am seeing it again today with my inner spiritual vision. The Heart on the right is radiating beams of Light outward. These beams of Light are creating the world much like a movie projector or holographic projection.

The beams seem to fluctuate but without really losing their beam-like appearance (of having a distinct width and so on). I am strongly reminded of sunbeams coming through dusty air, perhaps in a barn. The bright beams seem to dance and flash on and off. The Light itself is continuous and unbroken. Yet somehow the breams are separate and changing within it.

It has begun to rain. Right now sitting in the guard shack, the rain coming down outside, I look at the walls and window of the shack, and it is like I am seeing this physical stuff with the eyes of the Heart, not the eyes of the brain. That experience is coming and going. It seems to be a knowing from the Heart that this world is Itself and not separate. Furthermore, that It is creating this appearance of the world from Itself right now (as a projection of the Light). This "knowing" that the world arises from the Heart is turning into a "seeing" of that.

Yesterday and today I thought about two statements of Jesus: "I have overcome the world" and "I am the Light of the world." At the risk of sounding arrogant, I would say that both of these statements are equally true of anyone who has fully realized the Heart.

February 4, 2008
Las Vegas, Nevada

On a day like today where the personality has reasserted itself, it is a mildly "schizoid" or split-self experience. It is not unpleasant, as there is no conflict between the two levels of self, between the two dimensions of identity.

Also it is not the same as what I used to call "witnessing" which is just a state of watching the mind. This is really like two layers of being that function together simultaneously without obstruction.

The deeper dimension is the Heart on the right. It is like a stable ground of peace, a "peace island." I feel it in the chest, like an oval shape, on the right, about the size of a football. I don't know why I see and feel it this way. This is just how I perceive it. It is the Ground. Above functioning from the head is taking place, but it is "soft functioning" or a "soft head" flow, as the I-thought is not usually aggressive. This personality flow extends above, like the fronds on a palm tree.

At the same time, there is a distinct sense of separation, that the two identities are not the same. The ground identity is silent, peaceful, unmoved and unmoving — like a rock. The surface identity is constantly moving and changing, talking, reacting. It is clear that it is an emanation or echo or reflection of the deep ground beingness. The Beingness exists with or without the surface personality, but not vice versa. I would almost say that the surface personality is like a wind-up toy that is winding down, a toy that chatters and moves. It is winding down and it will stop.

February 9, 2008
Las Vegas, Nevada

There has been exceptional mental clarity and quiet this morning. Earlier I was watching what I knew to be the I-thought or ego element dissolving or coming to an end.

The ego sense or I-thought was perceived as a vibratory distortion of the pure awareness-space. It was sort of like a sound echo fading away or a visible heat distortion pattern on the road fluctuating then fading.

There was a long moment where this I-sense faded away totally. There was no more vibration, no more distortion.

There was only the pure space of awareness where I felt the pure "I" only. There was no entity being watched. No watcher.

There was this persistent feeling-knowing where I keep remembering that "I am this pure awareness that was awake all night." I also saw the image of a perfectly round Sun rising high in a clear and empty Sky. It symbolized ultimate peace.

I didn't want to make too much of this, but this is the first time the pure thought-free awareness state has asserted itself from *prior to* "waking up" in the physical and through forward unbroken in the "waking state" as itself *without interruption*.

It is dawning on me why this remembrance of being conscious in the night is so important.

All morning today it has been supplanting the usual tendency to cook up stories, problems, memories, dramas, internal dialogs, fear, worry, stress — that stuff has NOT been happening today. The usual arising of the ego I-thought with its stories and worries has not occurred.

Instead I am knowing-remembering that I am the pure thought-free awareness that is present now and was present continuously throughout the night. So it is NOT the ego I-thought remembering that "it' was awake. It was not.

The one that is now naturally without effort clearly remembering being "awake without a break" is the pure thought-free awareness (I Am the Heart). The implications of this are truly a source of joy!

While in the past I have had crude measures for pure and quiet states, today's quiet clarity distinguishes itself by knowing who and what it is. So there is the feeling-knowing that this calm quiet clarity is my eternal I AM Self.

I see that the fog has burned away. I feel that I was in a trance or stupor and now I have come out of it to awaken into being truly awake. I was drunk and now, at last, I am recovering from this deadly intoxication.

Though I see the ordinary world, which here is dirt, asphalt, fences, trucks, metal buildings — my industrial wasteland meditation retreat center — I feel like I see with "the eyes of eternity."

I cannot explain it. It is a feeling and a knowing. The one who writes this now is the Eternal Self, my real True I.

February 16, 2008
Las Vegas, Nevada

It is fascinating how I become aware of things here alone in the industrial emptiness that I am not conscious of at home. I had noticed during the entire week that I was fairly peaceful with very few interludes of disturbance.

This was continuous day to day so that the *continuity* that I *remember* and view for this last week as the constant since last Saturday, February 9, is peace (stillness-silence).

What is interesting this a. m. [sitting in my "Cosmic Shack" where I have been doing my weekend security guard job] is that I am specifically aware that I am having thoughts *without a thinker*. Not only that, this has been the case this whole week.

The description would be like this: "Thoughts arise purely and spontaneously without a thinker and without the need for one." The context is that we [my wife Linda and I] are getting ready to move to San Francisco so she can get health benefits.

This has been challenging. There have been lots of thoughts and they have arisen for the practical purpose of getting the moving truck and so on.

But the thought that would arise about a *thinker* (ego I-thought entity) or his *story* have NOT been arising. For me, they are of no practical value. A thinker source for them is not needed. My observation is that it is only when there is a thinker that thoughts produce suffering.

When the thoughts are about the thinker (and his story), then the thoughts are about "somebody." Then they automatically result in suffering. The I-thought itself is in a constant state of pain due to its separation from the Heart. Thoughts reinforce that pain, amplify it and multiply it.

The I-thought cleaves in two the Wholeness of the Self. This results in the agony, confusion and desperation of the split state. In order to reinforce its existence, the I-thought produces secondary thoughts about second person ("you") and third person ("us" and "them") people and the world (all "others").

In order for it to maintain and justify its existence it needs the "other" and "others." Without movement, there is no mind and creating the other invokes a track the mind can move back and forth on. Without the other, the mind or ego I-thought or thinker is just an abstraction whose only support is space.

The other delusion or false identification is with the physical body. Once it appears, the I-thought needs a basis or a ground so it can have the illusions of solidity, density and locality.

So it takes ownership of a body and claims it as its property and its identity. But the I-thought cannot really own or control this body. It is owned by God, so this is a form of stealing. Giving this physical body back to God, then there is freedom.

The experience I am realizing and recognizing that I am having and have had all week is thoughts arising without a thinker. These thoughts do not create suffering. There is not a sense of thoughts originating at or near the head. Instead, they arise from Spacious Presence.

While I am delighted to be recording my thoughts here, at the same time I am finding there is little to say. That which IS has no need to comment on itself. That which is not (the thinker) is not worthy of comment (for it does not exist). There is the sense of space and presence as described, but most significant is the sense of Peace.

(1) There is not the "me feeling" of being "the me" [separate I] with the name and the personality. "I" am here. That is all.

(2) The body is here, but it feels like an energy pattern of very light density, like heavy smoke or fog. It can be felt, but it has little substance.

(3) I am Presence-Stillness-Peace. Even if a thought or other experience arises, I am still that Peace.

I had the thought "I am moving to San Francisco" which is the conventional description. Then I had this startling insight.

"No! 'I' am not 'moving' to 'SF' — there is no 'San Francisco' — not like that. San Francisco is just a thought inside of me. So is Las Vegas. It is inside of me. So 'I' am not moving at all. I am here and I am not going anywhere. SF and LV are both inside of me, as thoughts. Since I encompass the Whole, the Whole remains Whole and there is neither movement nor change. In fact, nothing happens at all. I do not move. I do not change. Thoughts arise and fall within me."

February 17, 2008
Las Vegas, Nevada

My guard shack retreat is coming to an end.

My last weekend retreat at the post is February 23 and 24. I feel sad. I am a bit worried how I am going to do without it. So much clarity, so many insights and experiences and breakthroughs have taken place here after hours of silent alone time in this industrial wilderness. But it is destiny. Just as the timing of my working here has been perfect (since November, 2006 which equals about 16 months), I have to assume that the move to San Francisco will be "mysteriously beneficial" (in unknown and unexpected ways) as a Grace, a Blessing, the Way.

If is funny, but I have to say it — I am running out of things to say! The Silence-Stillness speaks for itself. There is nothing you can add to it. There is nothing you can say about it. It just IS — but it is NOT a blank or a void — it is Fullness, true final rest and fulfillment.

February 24, 2008
Las Vegas, Nevada

Today is the last day of my "paid spiritual retreat" security guard shack job. It's a mixed and strange experience.

The weather is crummy, cold, windy with spots of rain. But there is something else than suggests a strong synchronicity in the timing of my departure. I find it rather remarkable. I gave notice in order to move to San Francisco with my wife, but here is what is happening. On the exact radio channel that I was being required to keep open at all times in order to stay in touch with my supervisor or respond to an emergency, the maintenance crew of a nearby casino has started chattering.

This chattering is non-stop. It was going on all day yesterday, too. The female operator's voice is irritating and distracting as she calls the maintenance guys about six times a minute. "PBX to Bill. 1137 has a toilet overflowing. 1137 has a toilet overflowing." Bill replies "Copy." This goes on the whole day!

I believe that if I had this distraction going on every weekend like this [my final] weekend, I could not have done the paid spiritual retreat that I did for a year and change. I could not have reached the same depth of Self-inquiry meditation.

The message is clear. It is time to move on. What was to be done is done. It sounds a loud and clear note to end this chapter of my life.

It is an appropriate farewell. I would not want this job if I had to listen to this crap every day. I do not want it now as I listen to "PBX Mary" at the casino. Nothing vague about any of this. It is time to move (even though, in reality, nothing has happened and nothing will ever happen).

The Rising I-Thought Creates the World Experience

When the I-thought rises up in the morning to take over the body, the result is not just an identification with the body. The real damage to happiness is that this I-thought then produces a hypnosis in which the external world seems to be reality.

This is why the I-thought must be eliminated before a person can stabilize in the Absolute. As long as the I-thought is lurking below, the conditioning that projects a "world" and "others" will continue to wield its hypnotic control.

The mind can be greatly purified on the spiritual journey without the I-thought itself being identified and eliminated. The I-thought is the last form of conditioning or limitation to go. It is the origin of the mind. When it goes, the mind goes.

This does not mean functionality is lost. Your ability to be functional and take effective action was never based on the power of the mind. Any ability the mind seemed to have was being siphoned off from the Self, from the Absolute. It is this true Self which has no thoughts in it that all along was the real Source of your power and ability to produce results.

No Mind Does Not Mean No Thoughts

It is natural to think when you hear about something called "no mind" that you will not have thoughts. That is not correct.

You can relax. No mind means just what it says. No mind.

You see, there was never really a mind. All along, there were only thoughts. These thoughts were coming and going in space. The only thing that gave you the idea that you had a mind was that clever trickster troublemaker, the I-thought.

When the I-thought gets eliminated, the experience people have of something called the "mind" dissolves. In its place is a spacious Silence in which thoughts may or may not show up.

I personally have gone for days without thoughts. There are great masters who are said to go for a much longer time than that without a single thought. My experience was that I could do everything I usually did in my daily routine without having any thoughts at all. Thoughts just weren't needed!

The best metaphor remains the timeless classical example of the wide open sky. It is fine without clouds and it is fine with clouds. It is fine if thunderclouds gather to make lightning and noise. It is fine when a rainbow appears after the storm.

It is fine with all of that. It remains pristine and pure. Effortlessly, it remains as it is, untouched, unpolluted, unsullied. It is the stainless primordial Absolute.

Yet at the same time, all of these events are somehow mysteriously a part of its functioning. So there is no separation in all of this apparent activity.

It is one glorious supreme seamless Wholeness. It is beautiful. It is love, peace and happiness. It is perfect. It is divine. It is life. It is the natural state. It is your very own beloved Self.

Lost in the Absolute

LOC 1000

Lost in the Absolute: Living at LOC 1000

LOC 1000 means the person has realized and stabilized in the Absolute, the Universal I, the one supreme Self. But what does that mean exactly?

Earlier in this book in the chapter on the LOC 700s, I said "The Absolute is not just a static end where life gets paralyzed in some ethereal perfection. The Absolute is not merely a state of dynamic wholeness, even if that wholeness is the universe.

The Absolute is called that because it includes absolutely everything. It is beyond materialism. It is beyond spirituality. It is beyond non-duality. It is a complete return to this world exactly as it is, only at the very same time, this world is the Supreme Self, the flesh of God, pure perfection beyond mind."

That's the best I can do. Alas, words fail utterly. This dilemma is intensified because non-dual teachers at different levels of understanding tend to describe enlightenment in the same way. Once you get to know a teacher well, you can decipher subtle differences that reveal their depth of realization (LOC).

Here are eight factors that I believe differentiate LOC 1000.

- No mind.
- No knowledge.
- No other.
- No world.

- No enlightened person.

- Nothing has ever happened.

- Everything is perfect just as it is right now.

- There is only the Absolute (the Self).

No mind means the notion of mind has been utterly dropped. There will still be thoughts that come and go. The deciding factor is that the I-thought has been put down. Whether or not the sage is conscious of the Heart and Amrita Nadi, there is no I-thought rising for that person. For example, Nisargadatta Maharaj said he knew nothing of the Heart on the right.

No knowledge is divine ignorance. You are the divine fool. You do not know what anything is. You are in the "only don't know" state all of the time. Because you do not know what anything is, you have no knowledge. Because you have no knowledge, you do not get stuck in what is arising. Because you have no knowledge, there is total rest and no seeking.

No other is true for you. If you knew about an other, that would mean you had knowledge for knowledge is of the other. If there is no other, then you are free to be the pure true universal "I" which has no definitions, boundaries or limits.

No world means there is only the one supreme Self. There is not anything which can be called a world. That which people call the world is just an expression of the Self or Absolute. It is an adornment of it, like a jeweled necklace. But it is not in any way separate from the Self. It is the Self. There is only the Self.

1000

No enlightened person refers to both subjective and objective dimensions of your experience. In Zen, there is an expression "the stink of enlightenment."

In the Absolute, enlightenment and no enlightenment are both transcended and forgotten. If you are hanging onto the notion that you are enlightened, you may well be enlightened, but you are not at LOC 1000.

Beyond this understanding that enlightenment or the lack of it are both just concepts in a strange dream that never really existed, there is the human or objective side. Here this stink of enlightenment takes the form of "holier than thou."

It has many variations. In essence, it boils down to the fact that you as an "enlightened person" think "I am better than you." Laughable as this sounds when plainly stated, this is the secret position of non-dual teachers who exploit their students or feel that they are entitled to special treatment from them.

Nothing has ever happened is not easily understood. But if there is no knowledge, no other and no world, then it is possible to appreciate that nothing has happened, either.

Since the Self is beyond knowledge of time and space, the intuitive feeling that arises in relationship to the apparent world phenomena is that it is an appearance only. Nothing has happened to, in, for or with the Self. It remains as it always was and always will be. It is stainless, perfect, pure, pristine, full, whole, supreme.

Everything is perfect just as it is right now is not as obvious as it sounds. The import is that *everything* you are experiencing in your life, no matter what it is, is perfect *exactly* as it is. This includes the most ugly, painful, negative experiences. A tendency to compare and contrast this experience with some other experience that would be better has been aborted.

There is only the Absolute (the Self) is self-evident. There is nothing for you to figure out. There is nothing to understand. When you sit down to eat a meal, you just eat it and enjoy it.

There is nothing to "figure out" and "understand" other than you are hungry and this is some good food. If "reality" is not not crystal clear for you beyond any doubt, then it isn't. Be honest with yourself and get back to work. When you finally "arrive" at the Absolute, it will be impossible to change or improve anything. It will be what it is, and that will be that.

"This very world is the Absolute" is related. It is like saying everything is perfect as it is with the emphasis on this physical world. This physical world appears to have many limitations and flaws. Yet the understanding from the standpoint of the Absolute, of LOC 1000, is that this world does not need to be redeemed as some kind of non-dual dream or symphony of oneness. The duality of this world is itself God, divine, the Absolute in the flesh. There is no other world. This is it.

Realization of the Absolute: Going Beyond Non-Duality

The word "non-duality" is used a lot these days. It is a good thing that we have such a handy expression. As you know, it means "not two." So it describes what something is not, but it does not say what something is

1000

A problem arises because a non-something is not something. If I offer you a "non-apple," can you eat it? No, you cannot. If I then offer you an orange, then "non-apple" is understood.

Realization of the Absolute leads to an understanding that embraces and destroys both duality and non-duality. In this unique understanding, duality becomes rejuvenated on its own terms as the original home that was never left. No matter where the quest has taken you, you return here to duality.

The stages of enlightenment below LOC 1000 are still embracing non-duality and, therefore, tacitly acknowledging that duality still plays a role in their world. The usual struggle is understood in terms of rising above and transcending duality. For the sage who has realized the Absolute, worldly *duality* embodies the ultimate truth down to the last drop.

LOC 1000 embraces this world just as it is with easy totalness. The dualistic appearance is embraced as the very divine or Buddha Nature itself. In a way that is next to impossible to explain, duality emerges once again to be fully appreciated in all of its magnificently dirty glory. Like an artistic masterpiece that depicts an ugly scene or person, this dualistic appearance is embraced as the flesh, bone and blood of the ultimate real.

Sometimes I call this "transcendental duality," but that can be misleading. It is the same duality that the ordinary person sees. The difference is that this Duality as it is is supremely transcendental without any change or adjustment of any kind.

As I said, this extremely difficult to explain, at least for me.

As long as there is a concept of duality and non-duality in your experience, then you have not yet fully and totally embraced *this* experience right now exactly as it is.

This promotes a very subtle (or not so subtle) seeking for something bigger, better, more perfect, more ultimate. This spiritual seeking takes place even for enlightened persons until they "land" in the Absolute.

This Perfect World Does Not Need to Be Saved or Redeemed

I am *not* saying that this world is redeemed because there is something wonderful hidden behind it that is giving it beauty and meaning. No, this world, with its foul stench, brutal ways and ugly displays is quite literally God, divine, the Absolute.

The primal pure Duality as it is is perfect. The ego, the mind, cannot accept this. It will mean a total end to the search. It will mean a total end to the ego I-thought, to the mind, for they *are* the search. If this gross imperfect world IS perfect, then what?

It will mean that the great noble quest for meaning and significance to this life is permanently terminated. Please note that people who are enlightened in the middle stages are still seeking. But there is nowhere to go. This is it. This broken battered dualistic world is it. The great quest ends here.

This understanding is the natural consequence of no mind, no knowledge and no other. If I drink a cup of coffee, that cup of coffee is everything. There is nothing else. Its perfection does not derive from the fact that it is an "expression of the Self." Its perfection is not derived from anything. It is IT just as it is.

Its perfection results from the fact that it is a cup of coffee. As ordinary coffee that it is hot in a cup, it is not the world's best and most expensive coffee. If I don't drink it soon, it will cool down. It is not perfect in any conventional sense of the word.

The point I am attempting to make is that the cup of coffee is perfect precisely because it is NOT perfect!

Prior to realizing the Absolute, you will still be looking for perfection. You will still believe there is some perfect place, some perfect state beyond this dark dismal bizarre place called earth. But there is no other place. You have arrived.

Going Beyond All Spirituality, Materiality and Seeking

The realization is that this is it. Its very flaws are what make it perfect. This is how the absolute rest of the Absolute is enjoyed. This Duality just as it is is ultimate truth. You cannot dream or imagine anything else. You cannot even come up with the notion of "non-duality." To focus on non-duality is a subtle rejection of this splendid majestic extraordinary duality.

Hope is for fools. Dreams are for idiots. Drop your hopes. Kill your dreams. Live in the abyss of no knowing. That will bring a swift end to all that you know, to everything you hold dear.

As the Absolute rides through your town, it announces "I bring a sword. I am not here to help you sleep. I am here to help you die. Behold, you are already dead. This is Nirvana."

If it is not here, in this world, then it is not anywhere. The Self, the Absolute, the divine, is difficult to find because it is naked right in front of you.

You look right at it yet you see through it and beyond it in your search for something perfect *other than* this funky place. It is all and everything that you enjoy with your five senses. Be just this and nothing else. This is it. Welcome home!

Spiritual and material are nonsense. They are a game that somebody invented because life had become a problem for them. They made it up in their head, then found other fools to play this silly game with them. There is no spirituality. There is no materiality. There is only *this*. It cannot be described.

But until you arrive at this understanding, you will be on a spiritual quest. After you stabilize in the Absolute, then you will drop spirituality, materiality and non-duality the way you drop the match you used to light a candle. Your focus will now be on the candle, on its beautiful dancing flame and the light that it brings. Your discarded match is utterly forgotten.

You will want nothing and seek nothing. That which arises as the here and now will be so astonishing in the opulence of its presentation that you will almost be embarrassed to accept it.

But accept it you must and accept it you will, for it is all your very own beloved "self." It is your true identity as essence and expression in one. It is all HERE. It is all NOW. It is all YOU.

LOC Stages and the Great Quest for Ultimate Happiness

Let's try looking at this another way. In a moment, I am going to introduce what some spiritual teachers I have identified as being at LOC 1000 have to say about realizing the Absolute.

But first I want to put this "place" that is at "the end of the road," that is the full flowering of the spiritual journey, in the context of the LOC model that I have proposed in this book.

- 500s: Seeking an answer to end suffering.
- 600s: Empty open spontaneous living.
- 700s: Enjoyment of cosmic wholeness.
- 800s: Divine love union and unknowing.
- 900s: Constant peace safe from the world.
- 1000: Transcendental perfection of ordinary life.

LOC 1000 is the end of the road. In one of life's stunning paradoxes, this means it is exactly equivalent to true zero.

You go through all of this so that you can end up zero. You go from hungry zero (seeker) to conquering hero (enlightened) to big fat zero (life just as it is). Your great triumph is to become nobody and nothing. In this mindless frenzy of non-rational fulfillment, you are free. In the lower enlightened LOCs, you were still something. You had attainments, knowledge, vision.

These were still all just the consolation prizes. They were the acceptable substitutes. It takes awhile to realize that the Grand Prize, the realization of the Absolute, is going to take it all. It is going to take everything. You must give ALL of it up.

It is a little like being in love. If you are thinking about it, chances are you are not deeply in love. If you are simply smitten, if you have been decimated and destroyed, if you have fallen in love beyond all reason and logic, if your passion is unreasonable and impractical, then you are in love.

As you progress through the stages of enlightenment, there are many rewards along the way. Even so, in the LOC 600s, there is felt a subtle shakiness. A still small voice whispers "This is not quite yet complete. I am not there."

The LOC 700s in particular are alluring. This stage has the stability of the middle position. It acts as a kind of resting place before the great quest fires up again.

In the LOC 800s, the movement towards the Supreme has been initiated again. Yet it does not feel truly whole. This total divine love is based on a twoness. It is ever so subtly dualistic.

You drink in primordial love-essence. It heals you and makes you whole. But it is not the destination. It is a way station. You must let go of the god, goddess or guru. You must give up the breast. Drink deep this perfect love. Enjoy its sweetness. But you must move on. This Love is wanting to manifest as the cosmos, and it will sweep you along with it sooner or later.

In the LOC 900s, you are on the brink. You are at the very edge. But you still do not accept that you must give all of it up. You are like the man who, upon hearing that he must throw everything into a blazing inferno, takes off all of his clothes and throws them in the raging bonfire. He even throws his wallet, his cell phone, his jewelry into the hungry flames. He believes he has thrown all he owns and has into it.

Then a voice speaks from out of the darkness. "I said throw everything into the fire. Now you jump in." When you jump into the fire ready to drop it all and lose it all, that is LOC 1000. That is the final death. That is the final resurrection.

When you are reborn, this world is reborn with you. Just as you cannot know the fire if you don't jump into it, you cannot know what it is like to live in a Dualistic world that is utterly and perfectly divine, whole and complete in its very flaws.

It transcends all rationality and logic. There is a reason for this, of course. The mind which would find the flaws, find a problem, find a way to justify its own existence, is no longer running the show. This is "no mind." This deep unshakeable comfort with everything exactly as it is then made possible.

The Quest for Perfection and the Invisible "Flaw Finder"

It could be said that there is a quest for perfection because this innate ultimate perfection is intuited. Even though that is true, the reality of it is known only when you have gone full circle.

You end up where you started, but there is now a difference. The mechanism that was seeing flaws, that created long lists of imperfect things, that yearned to change the way things are, that launched itself upon a quest for the deepest depth and the highest high, has been disabled. It is dead. It does not work.

As a result, you are looking now at exactly the same world. The world has not changed from what it was. It is the same world. It is exactly the same world. Nothing has changed.

What is different now is that your "flaw finder" machine has stopped. This flaw finding machine is called the mind. You can and will still have thoughts. You do not need a mind to have thoughts. All you need to have thoughts is thoughts.

The mind is that which sees something wrong, something missing, something lacking, something incomplete. It is the mind that see problems and then sets out on a seemingly endless quest to solve them. After one problem is solved, somehow there is always a new problem to solve. After that new problem is solved, somehow there is another problem.

In worldly terms, this is called "job insurance." The mind wants to survive at all costs, so it makes sure it always has a job. The job of the mind is solving problems. To make sure it always has something to do, it is also an expert at creating problems or, more accurately, the unsettling sense of problem.

The Death of the Machine and the Birth of Buddha Planet

When this machinery called the mind stops, then the sense of problem comes to a halt. No matter what shows up, it is not stimulated into action. This is one of the signs that you have realized the Absolute. No matter what kind of crap you may go through, your talent for seeing this as a problem to be solved, as a search for something else, has come to a full stop.

It is a bit shocking to finally realize that there are no flaws in this world and there never were. The flaws were all in your perception. Like looking through filthy glasses caked in mud and dust, all you saw was the filth, the mud and the dust.

Now you thoroughly clean your glasses. They are transparent. Your medium of perception has been cleansed. Now that you can see clearly, you stand before a glory so unprecedented and novel that it would stop your mind if you still had one.

It does stun you. It stops your breath. You are in love all over again. You are now, finally, totally and forever, in mad love with life, with things, with the world, with it exactly as it is.

Since this is the way it is, the way it was, and the way it will be, this mad love will go on forever. God is gone. Truth is gone. Spirituality is gone. Materiality is gone. Non-duality is gone. Everything is gone. Everything is burnt up. Everything is dead. Everything is reborn. Everything is alive. None of it can be explained. Before the spring, there was a winter.

All have been consumed by a fire so majestic, so final, so eternal, that the poet ceases to speak. The supreme secret is found only in infinitely intimate ineffable ultimate Silence.

The poet plows on, the winds of fate forcing forward his bodily sail. The uncharted future awaits. Yet this much is known. It will take place here, in this Buddha palace, on this Buddha planet. There is no other place. This world is it.

All concepts, all ideas, all notions, all thoughts bow their heads. Their usefulness has come to an end. When the sun rises, the night disappears on its own. It does not have to be chased away.

When the Absolute is realized, the darkness vanishes. What remains cannot be described, but it is the end of seeking.

It is the full stop not dependent on stopping. It is the final rest not dependent on resting. It is perfection not dependent on perfection.

Like a Rock: Reality Transcends Everything and Nothing

The great spiritual master Nisargadatta Maharaj is eminently quotable. In *I Am That* he makes an emphatic declaration.

> To me nothing ever happens. There is something changeless, motionless, immovable, rock-like, unassailable; a solid mass of pure being-consciousness-bliss. I am never out of it. Nothing can take me out of it, no torture, no calamity.[223]

My awakening occurred in 1992 after receiving Grace from Ramesh Balsekar. It was not until 2008, as documented in this book, that I found myself finally at rest and at a full stop.

Prior to arriving at this "place," I was still experiencing the subtle (or not so subtle) pangs of dissatisfaction. Somehow, in spite of all my realizations and breakthroughs, I was restless and still looking for something else. As a dedicated student of both Nisargadatta Maharaj and Ramana Maharshi, I knew this meant there was more work to be done.

In late 2006, Amrita Nadi awakened to reveal the path from the Crown to the Heart on the right. I then embarked on the most demanding period of meditation discipline in my life. I was finally able to identify, study, track and eliminate the stubborn I-thought that Ramana had so often talked about.

Ever since this spiritual milestone, I have lived in the rock-solid stability that I had intuitively sensed was my birthright.

Yet this status has still had its surprises for me. For example, to abide in this "perfect peace" does not mean that painful sensations and experiences are barely felt and easily ignored.

On the same page of *I Am That*, Nisargadatta continues the theme on a related question by saying "There is peace — deep, immense, unshakeable. Events are registered in memory, but are of no importance. I am hardly aware of them."[224]

No sage has been as bold in his declaration of the nature of the Self. I personally could not use the same words. If anything, the experiences of life are for me more rich, more refined, more intense. More is noticed than ever before, not less.

There may be pain, but it is exquisite poetic elegant living singing pain. As I write this, I have a toothache. The right side of my face aches. My whole body vibrates to the pain like a tight guitar string. Yet the Silence, the Peace, the Rock remains as it was. For That, which I Am, it makes no difference.

The eye-opener for me has been that the senses, the experience of so-called pain and pleasure, this artistic symphonic three-dimensional "world," are all more astonishing and more amazing. This is true even though I experience it to be literally the Self. It is true even though "nothing ever happens" for me.

Perhaps it is because my path has been a Tantric non-dual dance from even before my first enlightenment experience at 16 years of age courtesy of Mother Kundalini. I am a poet, a musician, a bhakti yogi, a lover... as well as a philosopher.

For me, the World is my Self, God, the Absolute, the Divine, the Supreme. It is Love. This World is the very divine.

Much of my path, not emphasized in this book, was lived in the fires of surrender, sacrifice and devotion to Divine Mother Kali Ma. If it had been required of me to give up love in order to realize the Absolute, I could not have done it. I would have refused. Instead, I was happily shown it is love's fulfillment.

I make no claim to be a great master like Nisargadatta Maharaj or Ramana Maharshi. We have been extremely blessed to have two such extraordinary masters with us in modern times. No doubt we needed them!

All I can offer you is my experience, the honest truth about how I live. I found my "rock" in 2008. It was a long 16 years!

Perhaps the "rock-like" Truth of which Nisargadatta speaks is something deeper or greater. I do not know. What I do know is without the guidance of Ramana and Nisargadatta, I would have been lost in a dim lackluster middling realization of non-duality and never found my true Self.

What I do know is that even the mere idea of seeking strikes me as utterly and totally absurd. Yet I embrace the possibility of a deepening in the human dimension like the evolution of an artist or writer. In Nisargadatta's case, it was his humanity — his shouting, his swearing, his smoking and selling of bidis [cigarettes], his complete naturalness — that drives home for us the poignant paradoxical beauty of our fleshy vulnerability.

This true Rock would not evolve, it would be as it always Was and Is. It takes courage to be vulnerable, to be human, to shine as this Rock with the flimsy human body.

Along with "Be the Absolute," Nisargadatta is shouting "Be yourself. Be a natural human being." Can you look at Nisargadatta and see the man?

After all, Nisargadatta means "natural state." He was married and had a family. His life is a message also. Do not run from anything. Face everything. Be a complete human being. Give all, live all, be all. "I Am That" means be a human being, too.

When I say this world is it, this world is the Absolute, I mean being a human being is it, too. Yes, this world really is it. The way Nisargadatta lived his life proves it.

When the Absolute is allowed to blossom, It celebrates your humanity. It make full use of it. There is no "where" to go. This Is That. Yes, Nisargadatta sold "cancer sticks." Get over it!

Whoever you are, please do not stop until it is just no longer possible for you to work through, eliminate or move on from what is in front of you. Then the way it will be for you is that you literally cannot find anything.

You will not have a choice about "stopping." You won't be able to find anything to work on, bust through or transcend. In fact, you cannot find anything at all. Yet it is firm and rock-solid like a hard strong flawless clear diamond.

Contemporary Spiritual Teachers at LOC 1000

For your convenience, here is an alphabetical list of LOC 1000 teachers that are alive today and officially teaching. Two of them — Lakshmana Swamy and Mathru Saradhamma — are at the time of this writing available only on a limited basis.

The other teachers, as far as I know, are public and accessible. Most have written books. Quite apart from my intuitive ability to assess the LOC of a spiritual teacher, I can tell when I read their work that they are at LOC 1000.

I have struggled to identify a key marker in their teachings that differentiates the LOC 1000 teachers. About the only one I can proclaim for sure at this point is that each, in his or her own words, affirms *ajata*, the Vedantic word for "no creation."

Nothing is happening. There is no coming and going. It is a "full stop," but nothing was moving or evolving in the first place. *Ajata* makes no sense ahead of time as a theory, but when the mind goes it is seen that it cannot be any other way.

The pure and total ISness of the Absolute simply... IS. This is true now, forever and always. Therefore, there is "no creation."

In truth, nothing started. Nothing stopped. Nothing has ever happened. Not even the appearance of something moving or evolving has happened. I know it sounds strange.

When I first heard about *ajata*, I could not make any sense out of it. The only kind of "nothing" that I could think of was a "nothing" compared to a "something." When you arrive at the understanding that is *ajata*, though, you realize it makes total sense. You realize that it is the *only* view that makes sense!

Many non-dual teachers imply an evolution is taking place. Right before your eyes, they may change their position. They will talk about the changes they are going through — the new opening, the deeper awakening, the higher breakthrough.

At the risk of sounding dogmatic or absolutist, at LOC 1000 there is no position. There is no interest in one and there is no need for one. You cannot find a position in order to grab hold of it. This is stability in "only don't know" mind (no mind).

I know of other people at LOC 1000 who are not teaching. These teachers are not the only people at LOC 1000 on the planet today. There could be another dozen or so. It seems that when a person reaches LOC 1000, they usually feel the call to teach publicly due to their compassion and destiny.

This list has one glaring flaw. For a teacher to appear here, they will have to be somebody who is being talked about in the modern Advaita and non-duality scene. As a result, there may be many great LOC 1000 sages in Tibetan Buddhism, Zen Buddhism, Chan Buddhism, Jainism, Advaita Vedanta, Shinto, Sikhism, Sufism, Judaism, Christianity, Muslim, Bahai Faith, Native American traditions, shamanic traditions and so on that I did not mention. For this profound limitation in my attempt at a comprehensive list, I apologize in advance.

Alphabetical List of Living LOC 1000 Spiritual Teachers

A. H. Almaas
Amma (Mata Amritanandamayi)
Anadi (Aziz Kristof)
Cee
Chetananda (Kashmir Shaivism)
Colin Drake
Dr. Pillai (Dattatriya Siva Baba)
Floyd Henderson
Francis Lucille

Gangaji
Gian Paolo Girardi
Karl Renz
Lakshmana Swamy
Lama Tsultrim Allione
Llewellyn-Vaughan Lee
Mandi Solk
Mathru Saradhamma
Namkhai Norbu
Peter Brown
Rajiv Kapur
Ramaji
Rupert Spira
Sri Sri Ravi Shankar
Stephen Jourdain
Sundance Burke

Voice of the Absolute: What LOC 1000 Teachers Report

Although you cannot accurately describe the Supreme Self or Absolute with words, you can still talk about it. I've included some stories and quotes in an attempt to illuminate what makes the experience of the LOC 1000 sage unique from his brethren in the "lower" stages (LOC 600s, 700s, 800s and 900s).

When you get to LOC 1000 you will understand exactly what I've been trying to convey. But until then, it may escape you.

Peter Brown emphasizes some of the same points that I touched on in this chapter in his friendly readable *Dirty Enlightenment: the Inherent Perfection of Imperfection.* His subtitle is spot on. Sublime radical "perfection" here now as *this*. Yes!

> The reality of our experience can look like being a yogi in the Himalayas, or can look like sitting in front of the TV drinking a beer and watching Seinfeld reruns. But in reality there's ABSOLUTELY no difference between the two... And when you SEE that, you can't lose it or find it or anything, because you and everything ARE it; there's nothing to find and nothing to lose....
>
> Yes. It's unending opening by its very nature. But you DO arrive at certainty, that you hadn't had previously: then finally you see the truth directly... and that certainty stays with you. You know you ARE it, and have always been it. And with that certainty you lose all need for anything more. There IS an end of the searching, but no end to the opening.[225]

There is a fascinating little story about Francis Lucille that is a window into the way the LOC 1000 sage experiences life. I'm guessing that the average reader did not pick up on it. I am happy to shed light on what is behind a curious dialog.

Early in the Conscious.tv interview, Lucille gives an exceptionally lucid definition of awakening. Late in the conversation, the interviewer, Iain McNay, says that unlike most of his interviews, this has been difficult for him.[226]

Then McNay asks Lucille, in the final seven minutes of their meeting, do "You have something you would like to say?"[227]

I find Lucille's reply most illuminating in terms of LOC 1000. Lucille has been wonderfully eloquent all along, yet McNay is having trouble with him.

Lucille replies with disarming simplicity that, in essence, he has nothing to say. All that he does is spontaneously reply to sincere earnest questions.

> I just answer questions... because it is the questions that trigger the answers. You see, if there is not the urgency, intensity in the question, the answer doesn't come. In a way, it is the desire from which the question originates that pulls the answer out of presence. I'm not answering questions — I'm listening to questions, and then I'm listening to the answer.[228]

The LOC 1000 sage does not build up an organization, train enlightenment coaches or promulgate a system. He functions in the way that Francis Lucille describes. He doesn't know the question. Therefore, there is no answer (other than Silence). When a question arises, an answer appears in response to it.

LOC 1000 has to do with stabilizing in the Absolute. On his website, Lucille offers the following reply to a thoughtful and detailed question from a student that begins with "How can one even know that one is in the absolute state?"

> One is always in the absolute state, knowingly or unknowingly, for there is nothing else. To be knowingly in the absolute state means to be happy, content and at peace without the slightest restriction. What is said here has to be understood experientially, not theoretically. Theoretically, you are right. The use in pursuing a state? No use at all. The use in pursuing the truth about our real nature? Happiness, plain and simple. The firm conviction that 'there was nothing ever to pursue and to gain' is not liberation, as long as there is the slightest sense of lack. However, it is an important milestone on the path to it.[229]

Stephen Jourdain, like Karl Renz, was brought to the Absolute and sudden decisive termination of the egocentric "I" via an unexpected spontaneous awakening. Reminiscent of Renz, his perspective is both irreverent and original. He butchers sacred cows right and left, yet his uncompromising clarity triumphs.

If the Absolute is difficult to grasp until you have known it directly for yourself, then how much more difficult will it be for you, my beloved reader, to grasp the fact that after the conventional "other" is totally destroyed, it gets resurrected as... "the Other." I referred to this earlier as transcendental or primal pure Duality. Let's see what Jourdain says about it.

> There's the falsified otherness which is destroyed. As far as being a consciousness separate from my own, you're [the interviewer] destroyed. In the depths of the Other, we plant an objective substratum — something truly astonishing because we plant it in the heart of a subjectivity — but there is no objective substratum!
>
> One could define the hallucination [the view of the conventional person] as the all but ineradicable belief in an objective substrata. 'But,' one cries, 'there must be a form....' No, there is not! 'Yes, but the Other? Your wife?' Nothing, nothing, I tell you!
>
> From the instant the void returned to its abode of nothingness, the good duality makes its appearance and the Other resurges — with the difference that now it's an Other who objective substratum has been definitively eliminated.[230]

Are you confused yet? There is a reason I quoted Jourdain. There is a good reason for talking about his "good duality."

You see, there is a "Garden of Eden." It is right here. It is this. This it it. When you have "eyes to see," then you will SEE!

When you are not yet able to see it that way, then you don't see it that way. But when you are finally able to see it as it is, then the "duality" that was so irksome to you, that was the thorn in your spiritual shoe which propelled you on your quest, does a complete 180. It becomes the very Body of God.

This is not different from saying that it is Your Very Own Flesh. This is how duality and non-duality get resolved. They gets resolved with a bang, with an explosion, in a resurgence which could not have been anticipated or experienced before.

The fatal flaw, the subject/object split, the self/other dilemma, the me versus the world cold war, all of it gets annihilated in a startling vision of reality so radical it stuns you into Silence.

This majestic Silence reigns supreme in all its glory. This dark dirty imperfect world becomes, right in front of your eyes, Heaven. The world is redeemed into World by its beloved Redeemer, the one supreme Self, the Absolute, the Heart.

Jourdain has another turn of phrase that I appreciate very much. When asked what changed for him after realizing the Absolute — was he in bliss, for example? — he replied that the difference was that now everything has "infinite value" for him. He could be feeling blissful or not in a given moment, but what remained stable, what was always inexplicably and mysteriously present, was this sense of "infinite value."[231]

This completely resonates with my own experience. No matter what my mood or state, in every moment there is a sense that every sensation, every perception, every object has an infinite value that is utterly beyond bliss. My life does not have this value because I'm happy.

My life and everything in it is irrepressibly and explosively asserting this infinite supreme value. I am happy, even beyond happy, because of this value.

I looked out the window from my kitchen today. Across from me are some apartments. I looked at a door. Infinite value. I looked at a window. Infinite value. I shifted my attention to the oranges in a basket on the table in my kitchen nook. More infinite value. I studied the dirty dishes sitting in the sink. Still more infinite value. Not only that, each thing that I behold is splendidly one of a kind. There is no other like it anywhere.

Call it infinite, over the top, off the scale. Call it whatever you like. This gift of "infinite value" sets everything right again. In the Absolute, true, lasting and stable happiness is possible because absolutely nothing is rejected. It embraces everything. Far from being a negation, it is the super-positive affirmation.

Zen master Ikkyu Sojun (LOC 1000) expressed the paradox of the primal pure Duality experienced as the Absolute in his poetry. Sweetness is sweeter and roughness is rougher, yet sublime beyond conception, fully resolved with no conflict.

> if there's nowhere to rest at the end
> how can I get lost on the way?
>
> this ink painting of wind blowing through pines
> who hears it?
>
> clouds very high look
> not one word helped them get up there
>
> a well nobody dug filled with no water
> ripples and a shapeless weightless man drinks
>
> here I am simply trying to get into your head
> you think you were born you die what a pity
>
> oh green green willow wonderfully red flower
> but I know the colors are not there[232]

Living in Truth is a paradox. Zen master Ikkyu expresses it best. In the end, the poet has the last word... then Silence.

1000 Case Study: Meister Eckhart, Radical Christian Mystic

Meister Eckhart (1260-1329) was a Christian mystic who realized the Absolute under life-threatening conditions. Typically, Christian mystical attainment is allowed to be devotional and dualistic only. It is heresy for the soul to claim identity with God. Eckhart taught that an "uncreated aspect of the soul" abides in perfect oneness with God at all times.[233]

Eckhart's God is transcendental and immanent at the same time. This theology of "all in God, God in all" is known as panentheism.[234] It turns out to be quite radical as it means that God is not only beyond this world, God is in this world as this world. This accords with the Absolute view as I understand it.

This means the drug dealer lurking near the school is... God. This means the pimp slapping his ho is... God. This means the dictator who kills millions of people is... God. Maybe you don't agree. But this is what I think it means. It is radical. If you assert that everything is God, you better mean *everything*.

Meister Eckhart did a good job of hiding his realization while still talking about it. Nonetheless, when you read between the lines of Meister Eckhart's cleverly worded sayings, realization of the Absolute is precisely what he is talking about. He plumbed the depths of Being to arrive at a final Reality that transcended all concepts. This included the concept of God.

This realization is not merely no self, no center and oneness. This realization is not merely cosmic openness, emptiness and void. This realization is not merely perfect divine love union with God. This realization is not merely the enjoyment of no mind with just a hint of that irksome ugly world "out there."

It is True I. It is Supreme I. It is Universal I. It is the one I that is all that is and Source of all that is. This ultimate foundation I is what Meister Eckhart discovered for himself. It is the real primordial human identity. It is the authentic human nature. Yes, there is something beyond God. That something is I.[235]

Some Non-Dual Sayings of Meister Eckhart

> When I am come into the core, the soil, the stream, and the source of the Godhead, no one ask me where I am coming from or where I have been. No one has missed me in the place where "God" ceases to become.
>
> The treasure of the Kingdom of God has been hidden by time and multiplicity and the soul's own works, or briefly by its creaturely nature. But in the measure that the soul can separate itself from this multiplicity, to that extent it reveals within itself the Kingdom of God. Here the soul and the Godhead are one. The whole scattered world of lower things is gathered up to oneness when the soul climbs up to that life in which there are no opposites.
>
> All that a man has here externally in multiplicity is intrinsically One. Here all blades of grass, wood and stone, all things are One. This is the deepest depth.
>
> God's ultimate purpose is birth. He is not content until he brings his Son to birth in us. The seed of God is in us. Given an intelligent and hard-working farmer, it will thrive and grow up to God, whose seed it is; and accordingly its fruits will be God-nature. Pear seeds grow into pear trees, nut into nut trees, and God seed into God.

If the soul knows God in creatures, night falls. If it sees how they have their being in God, morning breaks. But if it sees the Being that is in God himself alone, it is high noon! See! This is what one ought to desire with mad fervor — that all his life should become Being. The Ground of God and the ground of the soul are one and same.

Oh wonder of wonders! When I think of the union of the soul with God! The divine love-spring surges over the soul, sweeping her out of herself into the unnamed being of her original source. In this exalted state she has lost her proper self and is flowing full-flood into the unity of the divine nature. Henceforth I shall not speak about the soul, for she has lost her name in the oneness of the divine essence. There she is no more called soul. She is called infinite being.[236]

My essential being is above God insofar as we comprehend God as the principle of creatures. Indeed, in God's own being, where God is raised above all being and distinctions, I was myself, I willed myself, and I knew myself to create this man that I am. Therefore I am cause of myself according to my being which is eternal, but not according to my becoming which is temporal.

Therefore also I am unborn, and according to my unborn being I can never die. According to my unborn being I have always been, I am now, and shall eternally remain... In my eternal birth all things were born, and I was cause of myself as well as of all things....

And if I myself were not, God would not be either: that God is God, of this I am a cause. If I were not, God would not be God... For in this breakthrough, it is bestowed upon me that I and God are one. There I am what I was, and I neither diminish nor grow, for there I am an immovable cause that moves all things.[237]

Okay. It's time to put on your seat belt. We are going to get into some heavy stuff now.

Some of you may even find that the discussion that is coming up about abuse, abusers and the abused triggers something for you. Please appreciate that I have been through some very painful scenarios myself.

If you were victimized or mistreated in any way, especially by a spiritual teacher, then my heart goes out to you. I feel for you. I really mean that. I've been there.

No Victim? No Crime? It's Non-Doership Plus *Ajata* Time!

My conclusion after studying the lives and teachings of more than 200 non-duality teachers is that teachers in the LOC 600s and 700s were responsible for most of the misconduct cases. Here misconduct is defined as an abuse of sex, money, power or authority that the consensus would agree is a violation.

As you go up in LOC, there is significantly less misbehavior. You do find it with some teachers in the LOC 700s. But in the 800s and 900s it is rare. In the 1000s, it is almost nonexistent.

These observations have led me to the conclusion that the more mature the sage, the more likely it is that they will "behave" themselves. This still leaves the difficult task of defining "mature." Even the sages in the 600s or 700s do not all act the same. Some are paragons of virtue. Maturity goes beyond awakening to include integration and ripening. The human dimension must be embraced. It cannot be denied.

The flip side of this discussion is that nobody is the doer. The realized sage, whatever his or her LOC, is not the doer.

The person who has had the experience of being a "victim" is not the doer, either. This is the practical reality of non-doership. Both sage and seeker are non-doers. There is a difference, though. The sage *knows* that he is not the doer.

If nobody is the doer, then there is nobody to blame. Nobody is guilty. In legal terms, everything is an "act of God."

When in 2004 an earthquake in the ocean produced a tsunami that killed more than 250,000 people, nobody said we should arrest the ocean for murder. Nobody said we should sue the ocean and take it to court. Nature gives life and takes it away. She is both mother and killer. We are born branded by this enigmatic paradox. Someday our own mother will kill us.

Of course, the legal system sees things differently. Sage or not, each sentient adult human body is expected to act as if it is totally responsible for its decisions and actions.

For an immature unbaked sage in the LOC 600s, non-doership may look like an opportunity to exploit others without any consequences for himself. I mentioned this in relationship to the infamous enlightened cult leader Charles Manson.

This interpretation of the reality of non-doership is selfish. It is a "wrong view." The actions of the immature sage are self-serving and self-destructive as well as profoundly ignorant. The sage is being naive. There will definitely be karma to pay.

The record shows that our legal system does not like to prosecute cases that mix sex and love with religion. Even so, it is likely that the sage will suffer damage to his reputation.

He has violated the gift of trust from his students. His career as a spiritual teacher may even come to an end.

Obviously, the suffering of victims needs to be recognized if things are to improve. The silence of the victims helps to perpetuate the problem and amplify the lie. Nobody is telling the truth. The aggressor is not telling the truth. The victim is not telling the truth. Even though everybody knows that the truth will set you free, the price can be high indeed.

The best advice I can give you if you have gotten hurt is for you to totally face that hurt. Own it. Heal it. Transform it. If it happened to you, then it was your destiny. It is *your* hurt.

You cannot argue with that. I would even say it was definitely God's Will for you. If you allow for the possibility, if you work hard for your freedom, it will also be God's Will that your trauma, no matter how terrible, will bring you closer to God.

Sages Byron Katie and Scott Kiloby have developed potent inquiry tools that are highly effective with traumatic pain. I know from personal experience that the poison of a traumatic event like infidelity and intimate betrayal can be transformed into sacred "nectar" that propels you even higher spiritually.

I'm not saying it is easy. It isn't easy. What I am saying is that you can do it. I am deeply sympathetic. I have been through it myself. What I can tell you is that I discovered for myself that the only way I could be free was to transcend both victim and abuser. That said, I still had to work through the feelings and thoughts associated with being a "victim." I had to dig up and own every last detail about how I contributed to these events.

In yet another paradox, even though the mature sage is fully aware that he is not the doer, he must act as if he really is the doer. By that I mean behave according to the highest ethical and moral standards. Of course, not all sages agree on this!

I've been speaking about non-doership, yet even that level of discussion does not convey the ultimate viewpoint of the Absolute on these controversial matters. The abuse can be sexual, financial, emotional or something else, it will not change how it is perceived by the Absolute, by the one Self.

What is that view? What is the perspective of the Absolute on these touchy disturbing subjects? As best as words can say, at least from me, it would be that the abuse, the abuser, and the abused are all simply just the Absolute. They Are That.

There is an apparent flow of events. There is an apparent story that can be told. There is apparent evidence and proof, or the lack thereof. In the view of the Absolute, of the Self, since there is not even a world, then nothing has ever happened.

It may sound like I am just saying something like "It is what it is. Stuff happens. Deal with it." I am going beyond that. I am saying that nothing has ever happened to anyone. No you, no me, no abused, no abuser, no victim, no crime. NO WORLD!

These are the straight up conclusions that any rational person must make once they understand, at least intellectually, the Advaita doctrine of *ajata*, meaning "no creation." I discussed it earlier in this chapter. Now the rubber meets the road. Now we deal with the full human emotional implications of it.

Ajata is not an abstract concept. *Ajata* is how to be free in any and all conditions. Those conditions include being the victim and being the abuser and all the rest of it. The viewpoint of the Absolute, of the Self, on all this drama is that it is *ajata*.

1000 Case Study: Sasaki Roshi, Zen Bad Boy of the Absolute

If you have followed American Zen, then you know that sexual misconduct is nothing new for a Zen master teaching in the United States. The difference with Sasaki Roshi is that he represents the pinnacle of modern Zen. When the allegations of sexual misconduct came out, there were many who saw him as the greatest living Zen master in the world.

Before I say anything else, I should admit to being biased for two reasons. First, one of my most influential teachers was Venerable Shinzen Young (LOC 797). I studied with him in Los Angeles before he became well-known. Joshu Sasaki Roshi is his guru. Because I think so highly of Shinzen, and he thinks so highly of his guru, I'm not really sure that any kind of objectivity about this great Zen master is available to me.

There is a second reason. Even though I personally feel that sexual misconduct is a significant and harmful error on the part of the teacher, I believe that it is not so easy to define "sexual misconduct." When somebody says that Sasaki Roshi abused his authority to exploit naive female students, what are we to make of it? He had power. They didn't. Is that it?

Sasaki Roshi's response to one Zen student was "Zen is not the way of the saint." He was, apparently, an intensely sexual man who did not care what other people thought.

Nor, apparently, did he care about the moral standards of others. He was going to live his life the way he wanted.[238]

There are dissenting voices. One female Zen student is quoted as saying "I 'suffered Roshi's abuse' – and it was the closest I ever got to god." This statement implies that Sasaki Roshi may have engaged in potent Tantric "crazy wisdom" practices.[239]

Another thing to keep in mind is that the discipline at the Mt. Baldy Zen Center is severe and extreme almost beyond imagination. If you are interested in knowing more, you can read the first-hand account by Ed Muzika (LOC 723).[240]

Even if you currently meditate eight hours a day, your discipline is on the mild side compared to what people willingly endure on "Thunder Mountain." It all adds up to a complex and paradoxical situation. Given the extraordinary discipline that Sasaki Roshi inspired and himself maintained, there is no question that in other ways he was the real deal.

If he was the genuine article in terms of his enlightenment, then what are we to make of his sexual abuse of his female students? In many ways, his behavior reflects the Japanese Zen tradition itself. He trained in Japan. He found himself a mountain and continued to act like he was still in Japan.

I see it as mainly a cultural issue. Rinzai Zen is a warrior tradition. His behavior reflects his cultural upbringing.

Does it excuse his behavior? No. Does it help explain his behavior? Yes, I think it does. His behavior reflects his very old tradition. Many behaviors based on practices widely accepted hundreds of years ago would shock us today.

Certainly at this point in the history of American Zen, a new female student should be prepared for the possibility of sexual misconduct on the part of her venerable Zen master. It would be a good idea to do some research ahead of time.

Obviously, not all Zen masters and not all spiritual teachers are abusing their power and authority! But some definitely are. Resources on the Internet and elsewhere will reveal who they are and what they are accused of. If this kind of thing is of concern to you in the slightest, then do your due diligence.

The sexual mores of other cultures can be radically different from those of people raised in Judeo-Christian America. For example, Mahatma Gandhi is known to have "slept with" 14 year-old virgins for esoteric reasons. By "sleep with" is meant sleep naked in the same bed with but not have sexual relations. These virgins also massaged and bathed him.[241]

But there is another factor that Western students approaching Japanese Zen masters need to take into account. Japanese Zen is a *Japanese* cultural phenomenon. Japanese culture has an authoritarian dimension. It emphasizes social hierarchy.[242] That is why they bow to each other! To illustrate, I will relate a well-documented event that took place in Tokyo.

As you probably know, Zen masters may hit their students with special sticks. A particularly arrogant and difficult monk was hit with such force that he died on the spot.

The top monk under the Zen master told the police about what happened. The Zen master was never charged.

In the spiritual culture of Japan, what goes on between master and disciple is considered sacred and untouchable. It is, to an extent unfathomable to us, above and beyond the law.[243]

Years ago, I went on on a short traditional Zen meditation retreat (sesshin). I did not care for it. I think Zen is perfect for some people. For me it was macho, militaristic and bizarrely group oriented. Later it was explained to me that this group bias reflected the pervasive Japanese cultural influence in Zen.

Keeping this confrontational semi-sadomasochistic dominant-submissive dynamic in mind (I said I didn't like it!), consider this report by a female Zen student. According to her well seasoned view, everything from Sasaki Roshi was a "test."

He asked her for a sexual favor. She said "No." He asked her "Why not?" She said "Because I have a boyfriend. Roshi is not my boyfriend." Roshi smiled. "Good answer," he said.

He did not bring the subject up again. Her friend responded in the same way to Roshi. Her experience was also that it was a simple matter of saying "No." She, too, was left alone.[244]

None of this excuses or condones Sasaki Roshi's behavior. I do hope I have made my point that this situation is complex. It does not justify the simplistic self-righteous assessment that (1) "Sasaki Roshi is a sexual predator." (2) "He must be a fake."

My goal is not to excuse Sasaki Roshi. I believe there are in this mix multiple messages, nuances, layers and textures, not the least of which is our own myopic Western cultural bias.

I also believe that it is entirely possible for a man or woman to be at LOC 1000 and be as sexually aggressive and demanding as Sasaki Roshi is reported to have been. I place Genghis Khan at LOC 1000. He went around killing people right and left!

I would like to close this discussion of Sasaki Roshi's sexual misconduct by referring to comments by one of my teachers, meditation master Venerable Shinzen Young. Shinzen studied with Sasaki Roshi for many years. He says that Sasaki Roshi's direct transmission of spiritual energy was incredibly clear, forceful and strong. According to Shinzen, "ishindenshin" is the term used for this faculty of the guru (transmission of consciousness by consciousness) in Japan.[245]

Shinzen has a knack with words. He also describes it as getting a "direct vibe" or a sudden "zap of the flow of nothingness," especially during the one on one student interview with the teacher. From Shinzen's point of view, Sasaki Roshi was a legitimate deeply realized teacher. His transmission was highly effective in Shinzen's case.[246]

What do you do when you are with a teacher whose talks "blow the top off your head" yet you find out that he is a "sexual predator"[247] with 42 first person reports of sexual abuse on file (out of perhaps hundreds unreported)?[248]

If it turns out that he has a history of sexual misconduct with women that you did not know about, does that invalidate his life-transforming spiritual transmission for you?

The decision is unique for each of us. About Sasaki Roshi and his misconduct, I have no answers. All I can hope to do is raise good questions.

Some say he was a sex monster. Some say he was a God-Man. The truth, almost certainly, lies somewhere in between.

I believe he is a LOC 1000 sage. I get this from watching videos of him and reading his teachings. It is not a casual assessment. He has the look and feel of a LOC 1000 sage.

My truth is I cannot reconcile his reported behavior with what I know to be the gentle caring compassionate behavior of the typical LOC 1000 sage. I stand before you empty handed.

There is a Buddhist tradition where deeply realized teachers may make use of "crazy wisdom." This may include drunken or irrational behavior. It may involve transgressing traditional sexual boundaries for the sake of direct spiritual transmission.

Was Sasaki Roshi's flagrant sexual aggression, at least on some occasions, a true spiritual blessing disguised as transcendental crazy wisdom Tantric sex? Only Sasaki Roshi knows for sure.

1000 Case Study: Rajiv Kapur, Sage with a Four Stage Model

Rajiv Kapur is a young spiritual teacher of Self-inquiry who developed his own model of spiritual progress. He calls it the "Structure of the Self." An impressive graphic of his model is available. This link includes an excellent interview.[249]

My interest here is to share the four stage spiritual model that he teaches and show how it parallels my own (more elaborate) model. There is something to be said for the simplicity of his outline. It is the bare bones, the simple essence.

Rajiv Kapur's Four Stages of Self-Inquiry Meditation

(1) Recognize Now Presence or Now Space [LOC 600s].

(2) Recognize Void and become one with it [LOC 700s].

(3) Open Heart, drop Void and and be pure I AM [LOC 800s].

(4) Integrating love and transcending fear, let go of spiritual methods and embrace Being itself by "bringing the Unknown, Timeless stateless state into all states" [LOC 900 to 1000].[250]

In support of describing a spiritual journey with four levels or stages, Kapur quotes Ramana Maharshi: "Effort is necessary up to the state of Realization. There is a state beyond effort or effortlessness. Until it is realized effort is necessary."[251]

Kapur is articulate and brings a high level of passion to his teaching. Here is his definition of the Absolute (true "I") from an interview with Pierre Bonnasse for a French spiritual magazine: "The real 'I' is the UNKNOWN itself where all knowingness, experiences and concepts are dropped."[252]

Rajiv Kapur founds his four stage model on the traditional esoteric bodies: gross, subtle, causal and supra-causal. He says that each body must be fully experienced, studied and stabilized in before moving onto the next higher body. If you are working in traditional Advaita Vedanta, such as with the *Mandukya Upanishad*, his approach may prove quite useful.[253]

1000 Case Study: Sundance Burke and Gradual Awakening

Sudden versus gradual awakening has been a discussion topic for as long as I have been on the path. The consensus is that awakening is sudden, but integration and deconditioning are gradual. There is life-changing impact. Then you deal with it.

The advent of Advaita and non-duality teachers who imply that the full enchilada can be realized in a convenient blink has made waves. The emphasis on a mindset of "get it" right now has its place. The traditional paths can support endless seeking, surreptitiously pushing away the desired results.

What my research revealed is that the enlightened teachers who emphasize rapid awakening are, with a few exceptions, in the lower end of the LOC spectrum. Their students who awaken under them seem to get stuck in the LOC 600s.

In 1992, I myself first awakened into LOC 683. Awestruck by the experience, I deemed myself ready to teach. In 1994, I gave a 9-day Advaita retreat deep in the woods of Canada. While the event was well-received, lessons from the experience convinced me that I was not yet ready for prime time.

Put into words, my feeling at the time was "This realization can't be it. There has to be more!" Although I worked with the occasional individual or small group, I went back to focusing on my own sadhana. My intuition told me that if I positioned myself publicly as a non-duality teacher at that level, I would tend to stay there. I would become crystallized there.

I went back to Nisargadatta and Ramana, studying them from the ground up. This was tremendously useful. All of this hard work paid off finally in 2008. It took 16 years (from 1992).

1000

In his interview with Iain McNay of Conscious.tv, Sundance Burke comes across as a humble and truly honest man. While I would expect nothing less from someone I assessed at LOC 1000, personalities even at 1000 can be less than transparent. I very much enjoyed the sincere lucidity of his message.[254]

He talks frankly about how long it took him. He believes, as I do, that many of the teachers giving satsang today have not completed their spiritual training. What he calls "realization of source," I would call realization of the Absolute. I emphasize that it means stabilization in no mind. He says the same thing.

McNay had asked a question about presence and intelligence. Burke replied "[In] realization of that source... the doubt drops and the clarity is. [This happens] only when you are directly encountering the source nature of who you are... there is no substitute for discovering that directly. You must finish the job. That's why it took seventeen years."[255]

Naturally, McNay wanted to know more about the end of the road to the spiritual quest. Burke obliged him.

> It took me seventeen years of trial and error, before my mind gave up latching on to who I am... I was trapped until one particular moment that I didn't realize had happened until maybe six, seven months later, where the thinking mind no longer could trap me. All doubt went away, all confusion went away, because I was no longer going into the mind at all to find out who I am... it's beyond the mind.[256]

This is a huge point. The mind is not just your daily thoughts. Experiences of "oneness" are also experiences of the mind. If you do "finish the job" like Sundance Burke did, you know it. This is what he says and I agree wholeheartedly with him.

Burke did not hold back regarding the half-baked realizers who teach. He, too, yearned to teach early on but stayed silent.

> In fact, I always wanted to share, but I never dared, because I was honest with myself. I knew I couldn't share because I wasn't complete in the understanding. I see so many people now sharing enlightenment, just because they've had a glimpse, and they haven't really been truthful with themselves to look within and be honest to know when they're finished. You will know.[257]

If you are on the spiritual quest and wondering if there is more, keep on going. If you are an enlightened person and still wondering if there is more, then keep on going. If there is something left to investigate, then investigate it. When you arrive at the end of your journey, everything will go.

It will not be like the void. It will not be a blank or neutral emptiness. It may seem like it is Nothing, but it is a Fullness. You will have confidence in this destination because at long last all of the yearnings of your heart will be answered. You are finally home. You know you are home. You know it.

1000 Case Study: Lama Tsultrim Allione and Dakini Power

A glance at my list of LOC 1000 teachers shows it is mostly men. In these case studies I wanted to represent at least one woman. Amma and Gangaji are widely known. Cee in Hawaii prefers to keep a low profile. I've already featured Mandi Solk. Public access to Mathru Saradhamma in India is limited.

Lama Tsultrim Allione is an extraordinary woman for whom I have enormous respect and admiration. Born in America, she has had a full life, but it has not been an easy one.

In addition to being recognized as an emanation of Tibet's greatest female spiritual master, yogini Machig Labdron (11th century), she was married, had children and is now a grandmother. She was Allen Ginsberg's meditation teacher in the 1980s.[258]

One of her children, Chiara, died of Sudden Infant Death Syndrome at the age of two and a half. Coming to terms with this tragedy motivated her to write her groundbreaking book *Women of Wisdom* about six great Tibetan female mystics.[259]

At 19, she felt strongly guided to go to India and Nepal. She found the Kagyu Monastery in Katmandu and sat there each morning. She enjoyed the rituals and observed them closely.

She was living with the well-known American yogi Bhagavan Dass when the then Dr. Richard Alpert (who was to become "Baba Ram Dass") showed up. Alpert and Bhagavan Dass went off to see Neem Keroli Baba. Allione instead yearned to meet His Holiness the Dali Lama in Dharamsala. Hitchhiking under extreme and dangerous conditions, she made it there and began a lifetime of Tibetan Buddhist study.

She studied with many of the greatest Tibetan masters of our time. These included Chogyam Trungpa, the 16th Karmapa Rigpai Dorje, Lama Thupten Yeshe and Lama Zopa Rinpoche, to name only a few. In Italy, she settled down with the famed Dzogchen master Namkhai Norbu Rinpoche (LOC 1000). In 1994, in conjunction with her late husband David Petit, she began building Tara Mandala, her Tibetan Buddhist retreat and teaching center located in Southwest Colorado.[260]

Allione's life illustrates several principles that I believe we can all learn from. First, she has followed her heart. Second, she has always been very determined. She does not give up once she has started something. Third, she has worked tirelessly for the benefit of others as well as for her own spiritual success.

I bring these principles up because there is a tendency in Western non-dual circles to want things to be fast and easy. The Advaita perspective that the Self is here right now is a two-edged sword. The correct utilization of this insight presumes maturity on the part of the spiritual student.

Even if your initial insight shoots you up to the LOC 600s, that does not mean that school is out. It is typical for someone in the lower spectrum of enlightenment to talk about how their sense of limited self comes and goes, the process is unfolding, their ability to stay present is increasing and so on.[261]

There is nothing wrong with that. It is what they are experiencing. But if they choose to teach from this place, it does raise the question "Is this the best choice for their students and for themselves?"

My empirical observation is that when a teacher goes public, they tend to stay at the level they emerge at. Likewise, their students tend to realize only up to or below the LOC of the teacher. I don't know why this is, but it is what I've observed.

I believe there is tremendous psychological pressure involved in being out in the public and having one on one exchanges with students. This pressure forces the teacher to take some kind of "position" if they have not completed their spiritual education. They embrace a subtle yet fixed ego stance.

This teacher can then get into trouble because it may end up that they will need to defend their position. The "power trips" that students have experienced with some non-dual teachers illustrate this counterproductive position fixation.

Allione's work has two other important elements I want talk about here. They are emotional healing in the context of non-duality and our need as a culture for more "dakini power."

Machig Labdrom originated a powerful practice called Chod. In its original form, it is esoteric and ritually complex.

In her book *Feeding Your Demons*, Allione modernizes this powerful thousand year-old process for "resolving inner conflict" and makes it available for anyone to practice with ease.[262]

If someone else had written this book, they might be accused of reducing a profound practice into self-help pablum for profit. In Allione's case, since she is the recognized emanation of Machig Labdrom, the founder of this meditation technique, she is precisely the right person to make it available to us.

I have utilized this very simple five-step process. It seems counterintuitive to turn your sense of conflict into a demon and then feed it, but that is the process and it is shockingly effective. If you have issues you have not been able to resolve in any other way, I suggest you try Allione's approach.

Her ancient self-healing process is extremely useful. It is a non-dual way to include emotional healing and resolution of persistent inner conflicts in your non-dual journey.

Any self-help technique can be given a non-dual foundation. There is no limitation imposed by the use of such a method. For example, at the conclusion of her elegant process, Allione invites the reader to embrace non-dual awareness.[263]

Non-dual methods for resolving long-standing mental and emotional conflicts can be of enormous help to a person with a non-dual awakening who is having trouble stabilizing in their realization. Due to the intensity of the negative content, the new sage may become convinced that they have lost their understanding. In fact, it is an autonomous psychological complex that can be transformed via a method like Allione's.

While I have been critical of the decision to teach from the lower LOCs, especially the 600s, I am nonetheless delighted to see so many women teaching publicly. Allione is a leader in this growing trend of women asserting their spiritual power.

Dakini power is also the name of a book by Michaela Haas that Allione endorses.[264] It is playful enlightened feminine activity. "Dakinis tend to appear during moments of transitions when we might not know what to do next," says Allione. "The dakinis will remove the blockage."[265]

As I understand it, an enlightened female teacher is a dakini and embodies dakini energy. However, dakini energy is not exclusive to female practitioners. It is beyond gender.

Men can access it also. It is probably safe to say that when you see the the more mysterious, nurturing and playful aspects of Being expressing themselves, you are witnessing dakini power.[266]

The world desperately needs dakini energy. Patriarchal constructs permeate established spiritual traditions. Allione gave up her monastic vows in order to become a mother. In spite of her success with Tibetan Buddhist disciplines, she speaks strongly for the need of woman-specific practices.

> Women need to become aware of what practices actually work for us, what practices are adapted to our energies and our life situations. We cannot be satisfied with just doing something because it is supposed to lead to enlightenment or blindly obeying the edicts of teachers and administrators. We need to observe what actually works.[267]

Allione is speaking directly to female spiritual practitioners. I believe she is saying that the standard practices a woman on the non-dual path will be exposed to have been adapted for men. They may or may not be suitable for a woman.

The fact that women tend to have a richer experience of their embodiment can work against them in classic Advaita, but it can be a great advantage when the body is itself used as the medium for accessing subtle and transcendental dimensions.

On the cutting edge of the awakening feminine spirituality is Judith Blackstone (LOC 776), a non-dual psychotherapist and spiritual teacher who used to be a dancer. She offers an original program for embodied spiritual practice.

I highly recommend her books and in-depth training called the Realization Process. Because it is body-centered, her approach avoids classic non-dual "head trips" and traps like abstraction and overthinking.[268]

It may seem odd to bring up feminine spirituality at this point, but it is the force that will save us. We need this courageous feminine power to save our culture, to save our planet, to save our future. The phrase "dakini power" emphasizes that the feminine has a power of its own. We need that power now.

I think it is instructive that of all the enlightened teachers I have mentioned in this book, there is not one case of serious misconduct by a female teacher. All of the well documented cases of misconduct with power, sex and money have been men. To me, this says that the nurturing healing dakini power of the women expresses itself naturally whatever their LOC may be. This has not proven to be the case with the men.

Remember, I am talking about 200 people I sincerely believe are enlightened. I am not saying that women at all levels of consciousness are archetypes of purity. But I am making a strong statement in support of our need for more female non-dual spiritual teachers and their sacred (dakini) power.

This Map Is Not the Territory: You Are Totally Unique!

Alfred Korzybski, the founder of General Semantics, famously said "The map is not the territory." This book describes a map. It is a model of reality that has its merits, but it is not reality.[269]

This may sound obvious, but the tendency for some people when faced with a comprehensive detailed map is to think that the map is telling them what they should be experiencing. This means they are treating the map as if it describes reality.

The spiritual journey is different for each and every person. There is no map that fits everybody and there never will be.

1000

The best application of the spiritual map in this book may be to tell you where you have been and where you are now. It cannot predict what is going to happen next.

I am not saying to you "You should have these experiences in this order." Not at all. What I am saying is "I believe there is an inherent logic and order to this process that is universal. It is being displayed and demonstrated by my experiences. You may be able to learn something useful about your own unique path by studying the long and detailed journey I went on."

It took me 16 years to complete the process described in the map. It took my good friend Koort less than one-fifth of that time. Plus he breezed through challenges that I got stuck in.

My method of using my own life experience for these levels or stages enabled me to document my model, but the drawback is that your actual experience of the map may be completely different from mine. Koort completed the journey from the LOC 600s to LOC 1000 in one and a half years. Nisargadatta took a grand total of three years from start to finish!

In my case I laboriously slaved away at a level clearing away what seemed to be the detritus of my subconscious. Koort's stages were taken care of spontaneously in ways that had very little structure. Some major transformations occurred quickly via dreams. He was not burdened by knowledge like I was.

If Only I Had a Good Guidebook Like This Back Then!

Please learn from me, especially my mistakes. I spent much of the 16 years *after* my awakening in a stew of boiling confusion.

My problem was that many of my experiences did not match any information I had been exposed to — and I had read just about every book on the subject that was in English!

I did not have the benefit of a teacher. Ramesh Balsekar was kind enough to acknowledge my awakening, but then he told me to move on. "I've given you all I have to give. Move on. Study with other teachers if you want. Or just live your life."

It turned out he was right. I did need to move on. I adored him. My bhakti with him could have kept me stuck for a long time. Not only that, I did not find out about the higher LOCs until much later. I prayed for a book that would explain the differences between the stages or levels as well as the nature of the Absolute. There wasn't one, so I wrote it myself.

If I Had to Leave You With One Thing... Well, Here It Is.

Hopefully it's obvious that success on the spiritual path will require enormous passion, sincerity and dedication. Even if you luck into some kind of "quickie awakening," I would not trust it very much. The door may have opened... but you don't have the keys. You want to *own* this, not just go to visit it.

So what's the one thing? It's pay attention to your sense of other. As long as you have *any* sensation of otherness, then you are *not* done. The classic definition of the Absolute by Ramana Maharshi that says "Only the Self, no world," is talking about this very thing. Only the Self means no other. No world means no other. There is only supreme universal "I" or whatever you feel like calling it. There is *only* the Absolute.

1000

"Otherness" is a product of the mind. If you are experiencing it, then you are still stuck in the mind. When you realize the Absolute, you can do everything just like normal because it is all the Absolute. The car you drive is an Absolute car. The food you eat is Absolute food. There is NO other at all.

This is why just getting rid of the separate self is not enough. Your separate self is a by-product of an invasion by "the other" at a very young age. You could say it begins in the womb, but it really gets going as your parents raise you, you go to school, you learn how to be this body with this name and personality.

So "no self" in the LOC 600s isn't it. Even cosmic or universal identification in the LOC 700s has not resolved otherness. If I am one with something, there is still me and a something.

In LOC 800s, you are getting warm. You drink deep from the original love essence that created the universe. This heals you. People in the LOC 800s don't act out like those funky 600s and 700s gurus. You know who I'm talking about. In the LOC 800s, they are filled with love. Their lives are saturated with love.

In LOC 900s, so close yet no cigar. Why? There is still in place that thin veil, that envelope, that skin, that membrane to hide them and protect them from this gross physical manifestation.

At LOC 1000, you finally get it right. "No mind" really does mean NO MIND! If you want to call it an "enlightened mind" or a "Buddha Mind," fine. Just understand you still need to pull the plug on the mind. The "enlightened mind" is a mind in name only. It is the Absolute performing the functions of the so-called "mind" without any of its draconian limitations.

Advanced spiritual seekers in the LOC 560s, 570s or 580s need to understand about the "other," too. Self-inquiry mediation will not get off the ground if your thoughts always run off to the other. You will not be able to understand the I-thought.

After all, what would the I-thought be all by itself? Imagine your I-thought just floating in the space by your head. It does not move outward anymore. It has lost its interest in the other, including the world. It's sort of like a body floating head down in a swimming pool. What kind of I-thought is that?

That is pretty close to a *dead* I-thought! The I-thought stays alive via the other. As long as there is still a sense of other, it will have a chance to rejuvenate itself. The "other feeling" is a sign of the mind being present. Knowledge has accumulated.

What were the eight pointers of the Absolute?

No mind. No knowledge. No other. No world. No enlightened person. Nothing has ever happened. Everything is perfect just as it is right now. There is only the Absolute (the Self).

If this is too much for you to digest, just keep in mind "No other. No exceptions."

Let me close with some humor. At my San Diego meetings, sooner or later somebody will ask me about relationships. The way they ask seems to imply that even if this non-duality stuff works on everything else, relationships will be too much for it!

Since they know I've been married for over a decade, they ask me something like "How does this stuff apply to marriage? How does it work when you have a wife like you do?"

I answer "I don't have a wife." They shoot back "But you're married!" I say "Yes, it's true, I am married. But that doesn't mean I have a wife! There is no other for me. There is only my Self, the Absolute, the pure Universal I Consciousness."

Let me quickly clarify that by saying my wife tells me that I'm a wonderful husband. As far as I can tell, the people in my San Diego group see her as a happy wife.

The secret is that, just like you, I truly do love my Self above all else. Since my wife is literally my own Self, then I love her as my Self. Everything works out.

You see, the problems arise when when you place your self above or below the self of another. Such a gesture means you see them as a separate self.

When you cannot see an "other" of any kind anywhere, and all you can see is just your very own beloved Self, then the problem is solved. Love flows naturally, effortlessly and endlessly towards "them" for they are the Self.

I am being quite literal about this "no other" thing. No other means no sense of other, no feeling of other, no experience of other, no impression of other. NO other! ONLY (universal) "I."

The RASA Transmission and the Power of Divine Mother

The purpose of this book is to provide an overview and paint the "big picture" for the journey of enlightenment. I hope you will send me feedback about it so I can make it even better.

As I conclude this book, I want to make it clear that I have another ability beyond being able to easily and accurately assess the LOC of a teacher or student. It is called RASA.

Many seekers report that the RASA transmission of Grace from Divine Mother in support of non-dual awakening has accelerated their spiritual progress. I deliver RASA via video Skype or in person to groups.

In the next chapter, I will talk about the origins of RASA and share what some people have to say about it. It is impossible to make a guarantee for a process like this, but it is true that some people have awakened as a direct result of receiving the RASA Grace transmission.

1000

The RASA Opportunity

The RASA Opportunity

Spiritual transmission is a familiar idea to some, but not all, in the Advaita and non-dual community. Its most familiar form is probably the notion that being in the presence of or "sitting with" an awakened teacher will facilitate and somehow help to precipitate your own stabilized awakening.

The popular term "satsang" is used to encapsulate these and other benefits that may arise in the context of an enlightened person. The Sanskrit word means "in the company of truth."

My contribution to this time-honored method of spiritual empowerment is RASA. The term RASA is an acronym for "Ramaji Advaita Shaktipat Attunement." Rasa, as you may know, is also a Sanskrit word. It means "essence."[270] If you would like to see me delivering RASA in San Diego in 2012, there is a link to a YouTube video in the Notes.[271]

I have received feedback from a few people that they are concerned that the RASA Blessing is associated with the Hindu religion and Hindu gods and goddesses. It is true that my devotional relationship is with Kali Ma, a Hindu goddess.

That is personal for me. I believe that if your religion includes a feminine form of God, it is that universal divine power that is being accessed via RASA. Our planet needs Her Grace!

The Spiritual Power of Silence: Ten Minutes to Freedom?

Ramana Maharshi is known for demonstrating the power of Silence. It is the most elegant effective spiritual transmission.

However, in our busy modern world where the average spiritual student suffers from a limited attention span, the fulfillment of this ideal is not easy. Furthermore, great masters like Ramana who can transmit the Self in Silence are rare.

RASA is able to meet Ramana's high standard of excellence for several reasons. The RASA transmission is given in Silence over the Internet via video Skype. It takes only ten minutes.

RASA can be given to groups as well as individuals. It does not require any talking other than a brief introduction. The recipient does not have to believe in RASA or, for that matter, in anything at all. No background in spirituality is required.

All that is asked is a willingness to receive. In the beginning, RASA was given for free. A small donation is now requested so that more people can receive RASA in support of their non-dual awakening. In the current format, I include a one hour Skype chat and consultation. I give RASA at the end.

The Story of the RASA Grace Transmission

The RASA story begins Spring, 2011 in Palm Springs, California. It began with a heart-felt gesture for my wife.

She had come down with an immune system disease for which no cure could be found. It hurt my heart to see her suffering. I figured it was time for me to try healing again.

Even though I had learned complicated energetic techniques, the form of spiritual healing that I had always come back to was also the most simple. I could easily do it from my heart.

You may be familiar with this healing format. I place my hands above the person's head and pray for the Divine Light to come down. According to the Will of God, bring healing or another form of Grace that will help this person's situation.

My wife sat in a chair. I stood behind her. I held my hands above her head. I prayed from deep in my heart for a healing.

I held my hands straight out with the palms vertical. They were above her head about a foot on either side. Based on what I knew about keeping the Crown chakra open, I did not want to cover it up by holding my palms over her head.

I was surprised to feel an energy above her head. My hands moved spontaneously back and forth. When I felt the process had completed itself, I sat down. I had felt something new and different. I was eager to know what she had experienced.

"I could really feel that!" she said. "There was strong heat. It went all through my body. I am feeling really good now."

I was very encouraged by her report. A few days later, she told me "I'm sorry, but even though I was feeling better, I think I'm back to where I was at before."

Still believing that I was performing some kind of physical healing, I began giving the "healing" sessions to my wife three times a week. She would feel much better for about the next 24 hours. Then the positive changes would decline. While she did seem to gain an overall cumulative benefit, it was not life-changing for her at a physical health level as I had hoped.

Then it struck me that what might be happening is that somehow the treatments were raising her LOC for a brief period of time. At this point, I had already started assessing the LOCs of various teachers and other public personalities, but I had not yet conceived the idea of writing a book.

I began tracking and recording my wife's LOC before the treatment and in the hours and days after the treatment. My suspicions were confirmed. Her LOC was going up. When it went up, she felt better, but she was not able to hold onto it.

In early 2011, after a hiatus of more than a decade, I had gone back to being a public non-duality teacher. I was now talking to people from around the world via the Internet on Skype. It struck me that the next logical step was to give RASA to these spiritual students, track the results and get their feedback.

The results were consistent. The LOC of every person that I gave RASA went up into non-duality levels for a short period of time. Some were able to hold onto this boost into levels above LOC 600. For these people, RASA changed their lives.

RASA By the Numbers: Brief Summary of Top Results

I have been keeping meticulous notes since I began giving RASA in earnest in early 2012. These are my top RASA "performers." I give their starting LOC (before their RASA session) and their LOC after several months time.

Subjects were contacted to discuss and confirm the results. I also received unsolicited emails confirming a major shift.

My research included getting concrete feedback from RASA recipients. If I was going to say this worked for people, I did not want to rely solely on my subjective assessments.

All of the subjects received RASA at least two times. Subject names are fictitious to preserve privacy. Location is accurate. These students experienced unusual level of success. The RASA transmission cannot promise the same results for you.

Subjects are considered stabilized. Daily fluctuation is unlikely. Month to month or year to year, there may be variations up or down (still within non-dual limits). After the subject stabilizes at LOC 1000, no fluctuation has been seen.

Subject - Location - M/F - Starting LOC - Stabilized LOC

1. Bill - Australia - M - LOC 581 - LOC 674
2. Darla - California - F - LOC 558 - LOC 674
3. Erik - Canada - M - LOC 578 - LOC 685
4. Eve - United Kingdom - F - LOC 584 - LOC 746
5. Frank - Canada - M - LOC 582 - LOC 788
6. Laura - California - F - LOC 576 - LOC 847
7. Mary - United Kingdom - F - LOC 589 - LOC 884
8. Nathan - Norway - M - LOC 583 - LOC 888
9. Steve - California - M - LOC 583 - LOC 897
10. Robert - Hong Kong - M - LOC 582 - LOC 1000
11. Stewart - California - M - LOC 578 - LOC 1000
12. Theresa - California - F - LOC 583 - LOC 1000

RASA By the Numbers: Tracking the LOC Response

In January, 2014, a Skype RASA student from Oslo, Norway asked me for more specifics about RASA and how it worked.

He had received excellent results from his RASA Grace transmissions. I reproduced our email exchange here. I added a few sentences to my email for the sake of this book.

Question: What kind of LOC jumps are "normal" after receiving RASA based on your experience? Are we talking about +10, +20, +50 or +100 LOC jumps? I would guess it is highly individual. Does it make a difference where they start on the LOC scale?

Answer: I believe the biggest thing with RASA is the preparation and readiness of the person, their receptivity.

How much of the RASA can they absorb? For me on my end doing a group RASA is not any more difficult than for one person. I do not believe there is a limit to RASA per se.

A man in Hong Kong went from LOC 582 to LOC 1000 in less than a week! It is six months later and he is still at LOC 1000.

I talked to him on Skype and asked him questions to verify his state. There is no doubt for me that he really is at LOC 1000. His own subjective assessment confirms it as well. His is an exceptional case, but it shows the potential.

Regarding RASA and LOC, usually the person goes up into high non-duality LOC immediately. The RASA raises their LOC to 1000 (at least 900s) at the beginning. It's just that most people cannot stay there. Then they come down, only not as far. So there may be permanent gain of 1, 2 or 5 points. This is still a big gain. Five points equal a lifetime.

Some people do stabilize in the higher non-dual LOC. What I mean is they go up and stay up and do not come down. The usual pattern is to go from the LOC 580s to LOC 600s or 700s. Once they get to LOC 700s, they can find their way from there.

There is no extra effort for them to stabilize at the non-dual LOC. It is just time for it to happen to them.

A few people who stay up at a non-dual LOC still have deep unresolved traumas and fixations. They have a more mixed experience. They may have to work hard to achieve full stabilization in non-duality, but they do feel the higher LOC.

If the person is not in the LOC 580s yet, they can still benefit from RASA. Repeated RASAs will help move them up from LOC 550s, 560s or 570s. After they get to LOC 580s, they are in launch position to attain and stabilize in non-dual levels.[272]

A Global Phenomenon: RASA Reports and Testimonies

Since you do not know me personally, I can appreciate that you may be skeptical about the benefits of RASA for you. To be sure, no "guarantees" can be provided for RASA or any other spiritual transmission. Even so, I can say that, in spite of its spiritual power, RASA is surprisingly soft and gentle.

Some of the people who received the RASA transmission in support of non-duality kindly provided me with feedback that I could publish here. In most cases, the names of the RASA recipients have been kept private at their request.

The original emails are on file at my office in San Diego, CA. They have been edited for spelling, sense and continuity.

MR. K. FROM AUSTRALIA

The session itself was simple and short. Resting into the breath I soon noticed that my state had shifted, subtly more even and brighter. I felt/saw as if three fire pokers were removed from the top of my heart and then a greater spaciousness was obvious around the top of my head.

I then noticed there was an energy descending, or perhaps emerging in and as me, because there was no front edge to it, no wave as it entered and transformed, it just smoothly became me. It had the quality of deep relaxation and a subtle yet thick bliss. It was profoundly subtle and extremely full field of Goddess Love, as if an ocean was above me pouring into/through/as me with the barest golden hue, if it ever glinted in the immense darkness, and despite the sense of scale it felt utterly intimate.

The sense of the descending field of love continued through a brief meditation, and then uninterrupted through an argument with my partner where I got quite emotionally triggered. Experiencing that was remarkable.

It reached a point hours later, around sundown, where the vibrational impact felt so deep and full that I needed to lay down. Some organic processing or subtle-digesting occurred over a few hours.... phone call from my partner, a completely unexpected breakthrough between us into deeper harmony, and then I noticed I felt clear, brighter and smoother throughout my inner awareness.

MR. H. FROM NORWAY

The RASA session was excellent. I could feel the energy lift. The tension in the Heart [on the right] area was reduced. I was surprised that I hardly had any thoughts during our session. My experience afterward is that I encountered a new deeper layer of tension in the Heart area. Things are going well!

Now I feel the Self is more and more taking over - no need for "effort meditation" - feels more spontaneous - and feeling in Heart of melting and opening up. In meditation it feels like open space/sky, peaceful/silent but still full, with body tensions melting and a flowing/pulsating energy inside - feels like Self is slowly melting "Me" away - and I cannot do anything about it - I feel completely helpless - LOL :)

MR. K FROM THE UNITED STATES

RASA took me out of my head and threw me into a blissful state. I felt more alive than ever. I saw auras and experienced a deep, peaceful energy that I had no idea could be accessed so quickly and easily.

My consciousness reoriented from ego-based perception to pure being. As my false sense of self began to fall away, my overall experience of reality felt brighter, livelier, more peaceful, and ever-expanding.

MR. B. FROM CANADA

I did notice a shift after our RASA session. That evening I had trouble sleeping because I had a major wave and anxiety and fear.

By the next day it lifted. What happens now takes priority, with greater clarity about what is important.

In fact, nothing really feels to be of great concern — everything seems to have the same degree of presence. Anxiety about what has happened or what might happen down the road has fallen away to a great degree.

It is like going through the motions of being in a movie and watching a movie at the same time — nothing is really personal, it is all a script. At the same time, everything feels more personal, insofar as everything feels more present. To use an analogy, in this frame of mind, I would perceive an elephant and a mouse as equally present with equal priority.

CLAIRE CERRIDWEN DAVIES FROM UNITED KINGDOM

I have had a big shift in consciousness. I was wondering if the Shaktipat was taking place already!

I keep feeling my crown chakra tingle. Thank you so much for the blessing the other day ;). I really felt the energy and had such beautiful dreams… sort of interspersed with energy surges and slipping in and out of different realities.

I do feel different ;) it could of course be that I have someone to connect with on the earth plane that has answers to my questions! Usually people expect me to have the answers lol. Did you suggest three shaktipats [RASAs]? If so I'd like to book another one and two of my friends would like one too… Let me know how best you think it is for me to continue to raise my LOC with you ;).

Effects are subtle but profound! I've actually felt a little bit on shifting sands and experienced a change/shift. With clients amazing insights pop into my head I've really noticed that! With clients so emotional as I've untangled there blah!

I've been more aware of my thoughts... Sometimes I can spin into a spiral when the old tape starts playing but I've been able to halt that process and examine what the belief system is that creates the thought and so on... I've managed to close a door on a very old wound rather peacefully. I'm not yet enlightened I think I slip in and out and experience moments of non duality! I'd like to progress further certainly.

My intuition is razor sharp! Like a laser beam! I feel really connected and most fears have dissipated. I'm willing to follow my bliss and silence my ego.

Also and this is a big shift! I always wanted to escape my ego and 'get out of it' but recently I've been do grateful to it for how it has served me so far and I feel more like integrating and living it rather than stepping out of it! It's served me well rather than being my enemy.

What else? I've met or connected to a man who's evolved and a vibrational match... I never thought that would occur and just a whole series of people have been drawn to me.

I love it but I have felt the initial euphoria and wowness subside which made me think, yeah, it's integrated! Time for my next leap lol.

Feel free to add my testimonial to the website. I'm happy to promote and support you in getting this energy out there! Thank you for your generosity of spirit and your energy!

MRS. A FROM UNITED KINGDOM

I just wanted to thank you again for your RASA via Skype. I feel it deeply. Even as I am writing this email, I feel extreme happiness that starts within the Heart but spreads like wildfire within me. There is also a feeling of pressure on top of the head. My husband reported that I was glowing. I cannot even express the gratitude I feel at the moment for what you have given me.

Talking with you has appeased my confusion and frustration. Before getting in contact with you I had promised my self that you would be the last teacher and teaching I would seek as the road has been so long and difficult. Thankfully I am happy to report that I feel a deep connection to you which I will trust.

You asked me to be specific and detailed about my experience. RASA felt soft yet very strong. It was powerful and forceful yet feminine. Even though I say forceful, it was not aggressive. It was a descending force down from above.

I felt it was the energy of Kali Ma. This energy is merciless. It is merciless mercy, mercy without mercy. It is all done with infinite love. It is merciless Love Absolute.

It is a fierce fearless force unforgiving to anything that is not aligned with Truth. It will destroy everything that keeps you in the illusion of separation.

MR. M FROM THE UNITED STATES

Very gentle and relaxing. The RASA sessions opened my body and awareness to more of the downward flow of Shakti — tingling, soft, and expansive. Later in the following days, unpleasant emotional activity showed release and settling.

While my energy system was already in various states of openness, the RASA helped further stimulate the Crown and Heart on the right. This was new to me and is just in the beginning stages. It helped calm recently elevated automatic movement activity [involuntary purifying motions of the body, or kriyas]. A side effect was the increased awareness that what occurs in the flow of life happens on it's own.

MR. Z FROM HONG KONG

I had been experiencing non-doership before the RASA session. Yet after the session, the detachment was more pronounced, and life flows effortlessly and miraculously.

Last night, intuitively I turned all my senses inward, and I arrived at this place just like the gap between thoughts or the place of pure awareness. The bliss was immense. It was like the RASA session had cleared a path for me to get there.

My meditation happens mostly at night and in bed these days. The gap between sleeping and waking becomes longer everyday and the bliss is massive. Still working on bringing that bliss and peace to daily life.

I hope I can have a chance to talk to you for clarification on the practice of self-inquiry. The sessions with you have really speed up the journey leaps and bounds. I am so grateful for your guidance and blessings.

The RASA sessions have helped me tremendously. My life right now is full of moments of non-doership with the realization that "I" is just a concept. Thank you once again.

RASA Is a Mystery: A Direct Non-Dual Download of Grace?

It is possible that a good description of RASA is that it is a "direct non-dual download of Grace from Divine Mother." But if you don't believe in Divine Mother, meaning the feminine side of God, or you have a problem with the idea of a spiritual blessing, I don't want you to miss out. Labels don't matter.

What really matters is the experience itself and you can get that no matter what form of God you believe in and even if you don't believe in any kind of God at all. As long as you believe in yourself, in the sense that you exist, then you are qualified to receive the revolutionary spiritual blessing that is the RASA Grace transmission. There is no other qualification.

A loving Higher Power is involved with RASA that wants to help people become spiritually free. If you are interested in spiritual freedom, especially if you've been working at it for awhile, then RASA is worthy of your serious consideration. There are no qualifications. Just relax and receive. That is it.

All 12 people who have stabilized in non-dual LOCs so far, including the three who went all the way to LOC 1000, were advanced seekers who had been working hard for a long time.

In my conversations with them before delivering the RASA transmission, all of them impressed me with their humility. They were not full of spiritual ego. They were deeply sincere.

RASA is very gentle. Sometimes people see a white, gold, or white-gold light. It is felt to be a descending spiritual Force that is powerful yet distinctly feminine. It is assertive. It is not aggressive. This is how it can be so gentle, yet still accomplish major transformation and upliftment.

I recommend three RASAs. Once a month or one a week seem to work best. Then after you get three RASAs, you can decide if you need anymore. They are still helpful even if you are already established in non-duality.

Since it is typical for the RASA to take the recipient up to LOC 1000 at least briefly at the very beginning, RASA is a special opportunity for you to rise to higher enlightened LOCs swiftly and easily whatever your current LOC may be.

My Goal Is to Make Myself Obsolete. Your RASA Is It.

Since my Kundalini awakening as a teenager in Los Angeles, I have been involved in the spiritual world. I am very familiar with the marketplace and with the problems that go with it.

Since I do what I do out of love with the intention of helping people to be happy and be their true Self, I have zero interest in building an organization, cultivating lots of followers or organizing a system of teachings with multiple levels.

As I have told numerous people during their RASA session, my goal is to make myself obsolete. It is clear to me that you are the Self.

If somehow you are confused and do not see that you are the Self today, tomorrow is a new day. It is very likely that you will wake up and come to your senses tomorrow.

Then I would just look foolish calling you a "student." So I do not have any students. What I have are friends and people who, for the moment, have forgotten that they are the Supreme Self. Maybe they got knocked on the head. Maybe they got drunk. But they are definitely the Supreme Self!

The other thing is that I am working to do all of this right now today. I am not aware of any tomorrow that is going to show up. What we have is today and, really, we don't even have that. The reality is that we have *this* moment. That's about it.

The spirit of RASA is to act fast and totally deliver. So that means you could be the next RASA recipient who goes to LOC 1000 after receiving RASA. Of the three people who went to LOC 1000 after receiving the RASA transmission, one took one and a half years, one took six months and one took six days to get to LOC 1000! To be honest, these amazing people blew my mind! I did not even know that this was possible.

Act fast and totally deliver means that when I deliver RASA, it is in the spirit that the RASA will do its thing, raise you into a non-dual LOC and you will stay there. Once you stabilize in non-duality, my work is done. In other words, this is it right now. There is no training, no next level. RASA is it.

Some people come to me for coaching. Some people continue to get RASA and work with me until they get to LOC 1000.

I am here for you. I can help and I'm good at it. There is no obligation. I am not looking for "students." I have no students. You are already the Self. If you get RASA, it may help you remember or recognize that fact. That is its purpose.

If you would like to schedule a RASA transmission in support of your non-dual awakening, you can go to my web site. Click the PayPal button to pay the reasonable requested donation.

Ramaji.org

Next Step: Deliver RASA Grace Transmission to Groups

This book has described a spiritual map to help seekers and teachers know where they stand on the path. It is not a book about methods and techniques for spiritual advancement.

When I give a satsang group, I usually talk about something having to do with Self-inquiry and non-doership. I also give the RASA Grace transmission at each meeting to the group.

What I do now is give the RASA Grace transmission to the whole group at the same time. My first test of group RASA was with my local San Diego satsang group.

After delivering the group RASA, I went around the group and asked each person if they had experienced RASA. All of them did. I also checked to see if their LOC numbers went up quickly like they would with an individual RASA. They did.

When I give the RASA transmission, I do not feel that my energy is involved at all. I am functioning as a "channel" for a spiritually uplifting Force that is divine or universal.

It is the same for me to give RASA to one person, to 10 people or to 100 people. It does not make any difference to me how many people are receiving. Each person is receiving from their own place. I am not sending it to them. It is direct from the Higher Power, from Divine Mother, to them.

Thanks for reading my book.

If you want to send feedback on this book or request the LOC of a living teacher, please go to the section of the book called "If You Have Suggestions or Feedback." Use that email. It has been set up for that purpose.

If you want to contact me personally, then use the email found in the section at the back of the book called "Meet the Author."

Take Care, Many Blessings in the Self, Ramaji

If You Have Suggestions or Feedback

If You Have Suggestions or Feedback

Hi. I welcome any and all comments, thoughts, feedback, criticisms, opinions and suggestions regarding this book *1000*.

It's okay to request the LOC of a living spiritual teacher. I don't have the time to assess people from the past, but if it is somebody you know and work with or somebody you would like to see included in a later edition of this book, that's fine.

Please use this email to contact the *1000* book editorial staff:

advaitaforidiots@gmail.com

Please appreciate that we receive a large volume of emails and cannot be expected to provide a personal reply. *Also note that submitting your email to us gives us full rights to quote you in a new edition of the book or in some other related medium.*

Don't worry, we will quote you anonymously. Just please be aware that the submission of your content to us, since it is for the purpose of improving and enhancing this book *1000*, may end up being used by us without further notice to you.

Appendix One:

Music of Ramaji Unity

Appendix One: Music of Ramaji Unity

I'm delighted to tell you about my music. The best thing I can do is let my songs speak for themselves. The web site where you can listen to all of the songs for free is RamajiUnity.com. The album is called *Supreme Self*.

The songs are *Supreme Self (1000), Everything Is God, I Am That I Am, Ishvara Pranidhana, Feel the Love, Non-Dual Truck, Who Am I* and *One*. These spiritual songs are high energy with a contemporary sound. They are meant to be fun, playful and entertaining. More songs on the way for a total of eight.

I conceived the project, wrote the lyrics and shepherded the production to completion. Many years ago, I was in the music business. I worked at Capitol Records in Hollywood.

On the web site, I provide full lyrics for the songs. I talk about the production team, including my vocalist Kellian Cross. You will find all of this and more at RamjiUnity.com.

I programmed my songs to transmit enlightened frequencies of consciousness. It seems some people can feel the difference and some people can't. Either way, I think you will find them enjoyable and inspiring. Plus they are totally FREE for you to listen to online at RamajiUnity.com as my love gift to you.

I thought it would be a cool challenge to write a song about this book *1000*. I'm not aware of very many books that have had songs written about them. I figured it would be a good way to let people know about the book and its message, too. Remember, you can listen to the complete song online for free.

THE LYRICS FOR "SUPREME SELF (1000)"

CHORUS

I Don't Want the Five Hundreds,
Grimly Seeking Truth.

I Don't Want the Six Hundreds,
Stuck in Their "No Self."

I Don't Want the Seven Hundreds,
Playing Cosmic Games.

Eight Hundreds... Nine Hundreds...
More of the Same.

Joy of Universal Supreme Self One Thousand
I Am Free... Free to Be.

VERSE ONE

In the Five Hundreds Stage, You Are the Seeker,
Yoga, Inquiry, Meditation, Still You Are the Doer.

In the Six Hundreds Stage, the Doership Is Gone,
With Your Special Missing Self, You Are Enthralled.

In the Seven Hundreds Stage, Your Open Self Expands,
You Are the Universe, the Great Cosmic I Am.

BRIDGE

Everything Is Perfect, Just As It Is,

I Love Me... Infinitely...
All of This — Is My Bliss!

CHORUS

VERSE TWO

In the Eight Hundreds Stage, You and God Are One,
Kill the Buddha on Your Road, If You Would Go On.

In the Nine Hundreds Stage, Remains the Thinnest Veil,
Trapped by Your Sacred Peace, You Hide from the World.

BRIDGE

CHORUS

CODA

Free to Be As You Are...

FADE

Appendix Two:

Planetary Awakening

Appendix Two: Planetary Awakening

The level of consciousness on our planet is based on the level of consciousness of our world soul or earth spirit. She is often called Gaia. This is the Greek name for the goddess of the earth. She is also called anima mundi or the planetary Logos.

The entire population of the earth is being powerfully pulled up to the 500s and beyond. As the energies of consciousness accelerate on this planet, it will be "World Peace — Or Bust!" Our planet rushes towards its non-dual enlightenment at 600.

This acceleration of LOC by our planetary logos is intensely demanding on its human inhabitants. It is unprecedented in recorded human history. If we allow it, our LOC will rise with it. It is the greatest free ride of all time. The gate is open. The window of spiritual opportunity has arrived. This is it.

The LOC of Gaia, the World Soul, Is Moving Up Quickly

In 1900, the world soul was at LOC 209. In 1930, it was at LOC 212. In 1939, at the brink of World War 2, it was at LOC 239.

In 1950, it was at LOC 400. In 1960, it was at LOC 440. In 1970, it was at LOC 470. In 1980, it was at LOC 480.

In 1990, it was at LOC 490. In 2000, it was at 500. In 2013, it was at 545. As I write these words in March, 2014, Gaia is at LOC 559. She will awaken with or without us. She will go to LOC 600 and beyond with or without us. The New Earth is coming. The non-dual planetary rebirth is on its way.

Forthcoming Planetary LOCS and Dates: 580, 590 and 600

I expect planetary LOC 580 in 2016. Next I anticipate LOC 590 in the year 2020. Finally, I foresee that the planetary LOC will explode into non-duality at LOC 600 in 2024.

This shift will be shocking to most human nervous systems. However, even LOC 580 in 2016 is an enormous adjustment.

Many gifted human spiritual teachers are in the 580s or below. Even at LOC 580s there is a tremendous demand to enter into the Silence and to practice love without conditions or limits.

If the human transition during the LOC 590s is any indication, it will be a rough ride starting with 2020. That frequency is the consciousness of the "black hole." Whatever enters it and goes through it, does not return. Our planet will continue on. It has been preparing for this for a long time. It will go to LOC 600.

What Corrective Action Will Our Planetary Soul Take?

With the average human LOC currently at 210, there is a vast discrepancy. This gap will not be tolerated by our great world soul. I do not know how Gaia intends to handle this problem.

I am convinced that She will take matters into Her own hands at some point if the gap remains this big. What this will look like I don't know. Rather than talk about "safe lands" and "survival prepping," I suggest that you get right with God.

The basic idea is you do the same spiritual preparation that you would do if you knew you were going to die tomorrow.

What would you do if you knew for certain that you were going to drop your physical body the very next day?

Even if you found the perfect safe place at a physical level, that does nothing for your spiritual life. Surrender your life to God. Surrender your ego to God.

Take the attitude of "Not my will but Thy Will." I believe there will be an intense spiritual cleansing upon the planet. What this will entail in the physical dimension I have not seen.

What I have seen played out as a possibility for our future is an intensification of the Spiritual Light on this planet such that only persons who are enlightened or nearly so will be able to tolerate it. It can be compared to the intensity of the Sun.

If you cannot handle this intensification of the sacred Spiritual Sun everywhere on planet earth that I believe will happen in the next decade or so, then you could get burned up. Your nervous system will not be ready for it. This would result in your transition to a denser realm more compatible with you.

This is one possibility I have seen. The window remains open to turn your heart to God. That is the real purpose of all of this. Surrender to God. Turn to God. Be at one with God.

At the time of this writing, it is 2014. There is still time. But that will change. In the not too distant future, the spiritual clock will run out of time. The alarm will sound. The old will end. The new will begin. The New Spiritual Earth will appear.

You are very fortunate to be on our planet at this time. Please make the most of it.

You will be amazed by the years that are soon to come. You will see things you could not have even imagined. Even Hollywood has not imagined these things.

Get ready. This is all coming very soon. Surrender your heart to God now. Surrender your will to God now. Do not wait. If you wait too long, it will be too late. This is it. This the time.

Do it now. Take spiritual action now. You have your body today. Make the best use of it. Stay awake. Act now today.

Do not be passive. Walk the razor's edge. Take action. Go all out. Make maximum effort. Take risks. Go for it. Wake up!

Appendix Three:

Journey to the Heart of Truth

Ramaji's Journey to the Heart of Truth

Note: This short autobiographical piece appears in my other books. In 1000 I have focused on my journey through the non-dual stages. "Journey to the Heart of Truth" will give you the "big picture" of the seeker stage of my life (LOC 580s). You will see that I went through the same struggles and confusion many seekers endure.

When I was 16 years old and living in a suburb of Los Angeles, California, I had a lucid dream that changed my life. In this dream, I was in India. I was with a yoga guru who spoke to me in Sanskrit. He took me through many hatha yoga postures, then I ended up sitting in padmasana, in lotus posture.

Then next thing that happened was literally mind-blowing. Everything exploded and my sense of separate self that I had been feeling in the dream dissolved totally and completely into a blissful peaceful Ocean of White Light.

When I woke up the next morning, my Kundalini was awakened. I also had amazing psychic powers. I'm not going to go into details, but I will say having this sudden unexpected Kundalini awakening was very difficult. It was hard enough just being a teenager. The extremes of emotion from the Kundalini were astonishing.

I managed to muddle my way through this crisis. I was in high school. I was still living with my parents. Though I knew next to nothing about yoga, meditation or Eastern religion, I knew enlightenment was real and that it was better than anything else.

I had a reading by a gifted spiritual psychic. She told me that I would have to wait a long time. She predicted that I would not see fruition of my spiritual yearnings until my 40s or 50s. She said I would have to be very patient.

It turned out she was right. To a teenager, waiting for the fulfillment of your heart's desire until you're 40 or so sounds like an eternity. Yet I sensed this delay was in my destiny.

What this experience did is force me to recalibrate everything in my inquisitive young life. Now life was transparent. It was just going through the motions. All the usual things that a young man could get excited about didn't amount to a hill of beans.

I had experienced a blissful transcendental Light that made everything else meaningless. All that life offered was now nonsense. Life was a cosmic joke, but I didn't know the punchline.

It was a paradoxical situation. It made me laugh. It made me cry. It made me doubt God. It made me love God. But one thing was for sure. I could never go back.

In the 1970s, I got involved with some marginal gurus. I made mistakes and I learned from them. I became a vegetarian. I started doing hatha yoga every morning.

In the early 1980s, I ended up living in a Sivananda ashram in Hollywood, California. It was there that my spiritual practice began to stabilize. The assistant head of the yoga center was studying Vipassana meditation. I learned about it from her.

I took up Vipassana ("Insight") meditation in earnest. I would meditate one or two hours a day. I developed my own style of Vipassana that expanded on mindfulness while walking to include the tactile contact with sensory objects during the day.

The kind of Vipassana that I studied focused on fleeting body sensations. The goal was to detect the impermanence in these ever changing body sensations. This realization of spiritual science becomes possible when concentration is built up.

I had the good fortune to study with the Venerable Shinzen Young. He is a wonderful human being and a brilliant enlightened spiritual teacher. He has achieved much success as a meditation master. His success is well-deserved.

Even though he taught a contemporary approach based on science, I was drawn to an old Buddhist text *Vishuddimagga* (Path of Purification). I studied it and learned about the classical stages of the unfolding of impermanence. This traditional sequence of spiritual events or milestones on the road to Nibbana (Nirvana) is described by a few modern Vipassana teachers, too.

I was living in a huge bustling Western city. I still went through the stages *exactly* as described in this book. These stages culminated precisely as the old book had predicted in the flash of Nirvana. I was doing walking meditation on a driveway in the back of the meditation retreat house in downtown Los Angeles when it happened. Since Vipassana had been good to me, I stuck with it for seven years. But there came a time when it began to feel restrictive and limiting.

There was not anything "wrong" with it. It is a brilliant practice. My clock of destiny was ticking. It was time to move on. Advaita and Vipassana totally agree on the universal factor of impermanence as being key ("Anicca" in Pali). Vipassana is the Buddha's version of Self-inquiry meditation.

I was deep into my Vipassana meditation lifestyle when I met Kali at the Sri Ramakrishna Advaita Vedanta Temple in Hollywood, California. I was meditating there and the statue of Kali they keep up at the front moved. I saw Her walk by. Then I smelled the most lovely fragrance of sandalwood. Then She started talking to me.

Mother Kali has a very distinct way of talking. She talks like she is in total command, like she is the general and you are the private. She said to me, "You are mine. I own you. Your body is mine. I am in control of your destiny."

I was surprisingly at ease with the sudden turn of events. In my mind, I calmly replied "Okay, I believe you. If that is true, then what is next?"

Whispering in my ear again, Kali added "If you agree to this spiritual contract with me, then I will totally fulfill my side of the bargain. I can guarantee that you will attain spiritual liberation in this lifetime. You must be willing to surrender unconditionally to me from this point forward. Anything less than total surrender is unacceptable."

I was hearing Her voice from outside of my head. It was not my voice. It was a female voice that I had not heard before.

Though she sounded stern and demanding, I could feel her boundless love and compassion for me. "If you comply, then I will control your life circumstances in order to guarantee your realization. But I cannot force this on you. You must choose it. What is your decision?"

I seriously doubt She said all of this. She is a Divine Mother of few words! But that is the essence of what She said to me. Without hesitation, I said "Yes. I surrender completely to you. I give my life over to you. My life is yours now."

She smiled. Then just as quickly as She had appeared, Her Presence was gone.

When I asked somebody on the grounds about the Temple being open with the statue of Kali there, he acted surprised. The next time I visited the temple Her statue had been moved behind an iron fence. Kali in jail! I laughed out loud.

In early 1988, out of the blue the thought came to me that "My last name has the name of God, Ram, in it, so my guru is going to have Ram in his name." The thought just kept repeating over and over.

At this same time, I experienced a strange but not unpleasant metallic taste in the middle of my tongue. I have not felt that taste since. My impression is it was from Akasha (the etheric element).

A few months later I saw Ramesh's picture in a Hollywood paper. I instantly knew it was him. I intuitively knew with total certainty that meeting him was my destiny. He was going to change my life.

So what did I do? I decided to wait a year because I wanted to have one last year before I ran into the spiritual freight train called Ramesh! Looking back at it, it was a bizarre reaction. My thought at the time was "I'm not quite ready."

Fast forward to my encounter with Ramesh Balsekar in Solana Beach, October, 1989. I saw him later at other group meetings. This first time was at "Joe's Crab Shack" with about 50 people.

I have never loved a man like I loved him. I felt that he was my spiritual father. I love my biological father totally, yet the spiritual connection with Ramesh transcended everything. The feeling was like an ocean of love. I would cry and cry tears of joy.

The last event I went to took place in Pennsylvania, USA. I finally had a chance to talk to him one on one in a way. He was hanging out after giving a talk to the large group.

I walked rather timidly up to the small group that had gathered around him in the back of the room. He abruptly stopped talking to them and turned to me.

I remember his penetrating gaze locking my eyes in place. There was no escaping those magnificent eyes! I told him how much I loved him and how I wanted to come to India to be his servant. He looked genuinely shocked. "Oh, no," he said, "that is nonsense! You should not be lingering around. I have given you everything I can give you. Go study with other teachers if you like. Or just do whatever you want. It won't matter. I have given you everything. Now you must move on with your life. I cannot help you anymore."

I said "Thank you" and reached out to give him a hug, which he accepted. The joy and gratitude you feel with the person who has revealed the Self to you simply cannot be described. So even though this was the last thing I wanted to hear, I intuitively knew he was right. I never saw him again. He lives on in my heart and in my life.

My journey then took me back to Sri Nisargadatta Maharaj and Sri Ramana Maharshi. I studied their teachings all over again and practiced the unique meditations they taught. In 2006, Kundalini completed Her journey to the Crown chakra. A passageway from the Crown down to the Heart on the right called Amrita Nadi was revealed to me.

There was a life-transforming flash of Amrita Nadi. It was the ultimate spiritual experience of my life. Amrita Nadi ("channel of immortality") and Hridayam (the causal Heart on the right side of the chest) are talked about by Sri Ramana Maharshi. The awakening of Amrita Nadi has been described as "the light of a thousand suns." The world turns translucent and disappears in a blaze of Divine Light.

When the world returns, it is not the same world. That world is gone forever. There is only the one supreme Self. You can still perceive the world and function in the world, but for you the world is literally the universal Self. I have come full circle.

The Light that was revealed in 1966 was the Light that was realized in 2006. In February, 2008, I completed the quest. In 2012, I moved to San Diego and began giving public satsang.

Many Blessings in the One Supreme Self, Ramaji

Notes

1. Hawkins, David. *Transcending the Levels of Consciousness*, Veritas Publishing, Sedona, AZ, 2006, 295.

According to this online list, Dr. Hawkins put Gangaji (LOC 1000) at LOC 475. This absurdly low assessment of Gangaji by Hawkins further motivated me to start working on this project.

Bragin, Nancy, Dr. David Hawkins Calibrated List, http://nancybragin.com/2012/12/29/dr-david-hawkins-calibrated-reading-list/, accessed March, 2014.

2. Thie, John. *Touch for Health*, Devorss & Co., 1987.

I have been a student of holistic health and the human energy field since I was a teenager. This is in part because I have been able to see the human aura and chakras since my Kundalini awakening at the age of 16. Not only that, I have been doing professional reading of the human energy field since that time. This book by Thie is the tip of the iceberg for me.

My experience is that there is a global function of pure intuition. In the enlightened person, it awakens and gains the capacity to operate at full strength. This occurs when the person is at LOC 1000.

Below LOC 1000, there is still some degree of mind involved in their interpretation and calibrations. I am not saying that this means my results will be perfect or always be accurate. My point is that the process is pure whole-body intuition with no thought involved. The use of the finger ring biokinesiology is secondary to the intuitive direct knowing via totality.

I began using biokinesiology in the 1980s. I began evaluating well-known spiritual figures of the past and present in the last six years. Initially I was using biokinesiology as a supplement to my aura readings. When the idea of doing LOC evaluations showed up, since that output was a simple number, I switched over to using the finger ring technique.

When I make contact with the subject, there is first the feeling that they are right here with me. They are right next to me in the room with me. I get a whole-body sense of them, which includes the density of their mind. It is density of mind that determines LOC. When density of mind is at zero, that is LOC 1000. The functions of the mind are then taken over by the Self or pure Being.

3. Kinesiology Self-Testing Techniques - Part 1, http://youtu.be/fYGzLapQw7E, accessed March, 2014.

When I do it there is a very subtle "weakness" feeling first. I am not relying on the gross muscular response. The mistake I see people making is that they think this is a physical technique. It is not. It is based on being attuned to the energy of the person you are assessing.

If you do not have the required awareness and sensitivity, along with being able to do it free of interfering thoughts, then your results will be unreliable. In the right hands, it is an objective technique that will produce reliable and repeatable results.

4. http://nonduality.org/2012/01/06/deepak-chopra-introduces-nonduality-or-non-dual-consciousness/, accessed March, 2014.

See also by Jerry Katz:
http://nondualityamerica.wordpress.com/2011/07/23/jerry-katz-on-the-ever-expanding-world-of-nonduality/, accessed March 2014.

Chopra distinguishes himself from other self-improvement gurus because he had a close relationship for many years with Maharishi Mahesh Yogi (1000 LOC). Even though he moved on, this exposure would enable him to transcend his LOC in a way and have access to a deeper than intellectual grasp. I believe he intuitively accessed an inner knowing about the Absolute by being with the Maharishi. This has proved enormously useful for him when talking about non-duality and Advaita and how they are related to modern quantum physics.

5. Real and False Spiritual Teachers, http://www.lightwinnipeg.org/Spiritual%20Writings/REAL%20AND%20FALSE%20SPIRITUAL%20TEACHERS.pdf.

This is an excellent summary. It features lists of the characteristics of false and genuine teachers from a wide variety of trusted sources. It is short (16 pages) and supplies a Bibliography of little-known books and articles on the subject. Certainly I was not familiar with many of these references.

For an excellent discussion on sexual misconduct that promotes an intelligent book on this controversial and confusing subject, please see:

Sex and the Spiritual Teacher, A Tricycle Book Club Discussion with Scott Edelstein, http://www.tricycle.com/community/sex-and-spiritual-teacher, accessed March, 2014.

Edelstein, Scott. *Sex and the Spiritual Teacher*, Wisdom Publications, Somerville, MA, 2011.

The fact that sexual misconduct gets emphasized suggests that the emotional triggers are specific to our cultural taboos. It is reported on the news that corrupt politicians and "banksters" have stolen billions yet hardly anybody seems to care. Instead, they talk about a celebrity's latest sexual shenanigans. A fallen guru provides dirty laundry and a kind of celebrity gossip. This subject is so emotionally charged it is almost beyond discussion. The roots of this quagmire are in early childhood. Only those who really want to know themselves will dig down that deep. The rest cross their fingers and hope for the best as water and electricity mix.

6. Hippocratic Oath, http://ancienthistory.about.com/od/greekmedicine/f/HippocraticOath.htm, accessed March, 2014.

If "First do no harm" was followed literally, it would be the end of life and modern civilization as we know it. The notion that the ends justify the means is so embedded in our culture that most people cannot think any other way. True non-violence of necessity requires giving up the fruits of your actions as counseled by the *Bhagavad Gita*. Only then can you hope to see the other as they are rather than as either friend or foe, as a co-conspirator with or obstacle to the fulfillment of your self-centered short-sighted desires.

Ultimately, if you cherish the other as your self (Self), then you will not want to cause them harm and you will embrace things the way they are. Promoting harm is based on the notion that the current situation is so terrible that some kind of drastic measure is required in order to set things right or arrive at something even remotely acceptable. This is nonsense, of course, as it is the very formula for unhappiness, an unhappiness that is self-perpetuating.

The three-prong analysis of the Buddha — in any given moment, a human being is being driven by ignorance, greed or aversion — applies admirably here. Greed is also rendered as craving. Neither should be understood to be an organic "desire" like hunger which arises in the natural functioning of the human organism.

This is in contrast to the authentic sage who is living spontaneously and functioning moment by moment in non-doership. Non-doership is *the* marker of enlightenment and permanent entry into non-duality. If you are not clearly established in non-doership, then you are not enlightened.

Enlightenment is not conceptual. It is not intellectual. When the separate self goes, the doer goes. There are no ifs, ands or buts about this. I have cited the *Gita* because Krishna goes out of his way to emphasize this point. He is not talking philosophy. He is describing an empirical marker that the student can use as a yardstick to evaluate and validate his enlightenment.

In the enlightened person, all desires are "natural" although this does not fully apply in the practical sense until they have completed the integration and deconditioning process which could take 10 or 20 years. Until that maturation phase is completed, some kind of "acting out" of unresolved residual subconscious blocks, drivers and traumas is entirely possible. Put some people into the pressure cooker of being the "enlightened guru" with fawning disciples and you can count on it.

7. Caplan, Mariana. *The Guru Question: the Perils and Rewards of Choosing a Spiritual Teacher*, Sounds True, Boulder, CO, 2011.

See also Caplan, Mariana. *Eyes Wide Open: Cultivating Discernment on the Spiritual Path*, Sounds True, Boulder, CO, 2009.

My own experience with a guru who had a popular spiritual cult revealed to me that I had projected onto this person that he was a magic man, a God-man, with special powers to set me free. He was encouraging this projection, but it was my own fantasy wish for a father figure to rescue the child-like me that made me vulnerable to him.

Even after he slept with my wife, which resulted in the breakup of my marriage, it still took me a year and a half to get free of him and leave the cult community. Knowing intuitively that the future of my spiritual life depended on me fully resolving this tragic turn of events, I worked very hard to take full responsibility for stepping into this pile of poop. I kept on forgiving the offending parties and myself until I felt fully released.

In the reports of abuse that I have read, what I see lacking again and again is the taking of full responsibility for one's involvement in the first place. To own your role in it, to acknowledge your fantasies, projections, unfulfilled wishes and blinded drives due to your upbringing and family system, does not detract from the abusive teacher's responsibilities. His life is his and he must come to terms with what he has done.

What you must do is come to a full resolution of your story with that person which will include but not be limited to unconditional forgiveness. What then can take place is that the bitter deadly poison of that very real abuse can become a transformational agent, lifting you higher than ever before. Spiritual work is for adults. It requires maturity, self-discipline and honesty as well as lots of hard work. This includes doing your emotional work based on your family system. If you do not know about your family system, I recommend the works of John Bradshaw.

8. Kazlev, M. Alan, Inflation and the Delusional Guru, http://www.kheper.net/topics/gurus/inflation.html, accessed March, 2014.

This is an enormously important topic. If more people took the time to educate themselves about the psychology of power, it would make a huge difference. What makes a group a cult is a question of degree. The same techniques of manipulation are involved. We are awash in the psychology of power and manipulation. The media use it on us each and every day.

The fact that five per cent of the population is born sociopathic is vastly underappreciated by the average spiritual seeker. I bring it up because if you do not know how a sociopath (old name: psychopath) operates (meaning no shame, no guilt, no regrets, no remorse, no empathy and no morals — you might as well be a block of wood as far as he or she is concerned), then you could be surrendering your life and your well-being to a callous charismatic sociopathic leader and not even know it.

This well-written popular psychology style article by holistic health advocate Mike Adams will give you a good start if you don't know what I am talking about. People don't want to believe that one in 20 people are like this, but it is a fact of biology. Look it up.

Adams, Mike, How to spot a sociopath, http://www.naturalnews.com/036112_sociopaths_cults_influence.html#, accessed March, 2014.

Here are are two classic books you may not know about that I have found quite illuminating on the subject of how one individual can have power over a group of people.

Inflation per se is an idea from Carl Jung based on his theory of archetypes which can occur privately and not get expressed in terms of influencing and controlling others. It can remain quite internal.

Canetti, Elias. *Crowds and Power*, Farrar, Straus and Giroux, New York, 1962, 1973.

Kramer, Joel and Diana Alstad. *The Guru Papers: Masks of Authoritarian Power*, Frog Ltd., Berkeley, CA, 1993.

9. Muzika, Ed. An interview with Jean Dunn (1981), http://itisnotreal.blogspot.com/2011/09/interview-with-jean-dunn-jean-dunn.html, accessed March, 2014.

Jean Dunn was very humble. Since she was an enlightened person (LOC 748), she was in a very good position to talk about Nisargadatta Maharaj and the guru-disciple relationship.

10. Rumi Quotes, http://quotestreasure.blogspot.com/2009/11/rumi-quotes.html, accessed March, 2014. The brilliant poetry of Jalal al-Din Muhammad Rumi (LOC 1000) is highly recommended as a description of the natural state and living in the Heart.

11. Hawkins, David. *Power Vs. Force*, Hay House, Carlsbad, CA, 2002, pages 76 - 77.

Hawkins starts his scale at 20. I checked the LOCs of several serial killers to arrive at the lowest point on my Map of Awakening LOC scale. My emphasis is on non-duality levels. I do not know who or what Hawkins was measuring that had an LOC of 20.

For a video describing the contribution of Lester Levenson to the emotion scale, please see:

samuk1000, PACMAN Sedona Method Chart Of Emotions & Lester Levenson, http://youtu.be/HOJJqVcj6Mg, accessed March, 2014.

Working with a clearly articulated scale of emotions that ascend from very negative to very positive and then to the transcendence of emotion into high neutrality is a major feature of Lester Levenson's work. The books of Larry Crane emphasize this aspect of Lester's teachings.

12. Hawkins, David. *I: Reality and Subjectivity*, Veritas Publishing, Sedona, AZ, 2003.

Human spiritual evolution has been a popular topic for many centuries. For another interpretation of the lower levels of human spiritual evolution with similarities to Theosophy, please see:

Posner, Roy, The Vertical Scale of Human Consciousness, http://www.gurusoftware.com/GuruNet/KnowledgeBase/Personal/MakeupHuman.htm#VERTICAL, accessed March, 2014.

Here's a succinct summary of seven bodies or stages of consciousness that may be loosely based on Osho's model with the same terminology. This article gets points for its simplicity.

Calder, Christopher, The Realms of Consciousness, http://meditation-handbook.50webs.com/realms2.html, accessed March, 2014.

13. Aileen Wuornos, http://en.wikipedia.org/wiki/Aileen_Wuornos, accessed March, 2014.

14. Victor Lustig, http://en.wikipedia.org/wiki/Victor_Lustig, accessed March, 2014.

15. Alfred Nobel, http://en.wikipedia.org/wiki/Alfred_Nobel, accessed March, 2014.

16. Leonard, Tom, Secret life of a bitter billionaire, http://www.dailymail.co.uk/news/article-1380252/Secret-life-bitter-billionaire-Eclipsed-fellow-Microsoft-founder-decades-Paul-Allen-finally-steps-Bill-Gates-shadow.html, accessed March, 2014.

17. Cialdini, Robert. *Influence: Science and Practice*, Pearson, 5th Edition, 2008.

18. About the Author, http://www.drwaynedyer.com/about/, accessed March, 2014.

The guidelines for fulfilling desires with divine help taught by Dyer can be found in his new book *Wishes Fulfilled*. These teachings are also the subject of a public television special.

Dyer, Wayne. *Wishes Fulfilled: Mastering the Art of Manifesting*, Hay House, Carlsbad, CA, 2012.

19. Jim Rohn, http://getmotivation.com/rohn.htm, accessed March, 2014.

20. The Living Legacy of Don Riso, http://www.enneagraminstitute.com/DonRiso.asp#.UjuR58bAvAs, accessed March, 2014.

I have found the Enneagram to be accurate as a description of the ways in which people avoid their essence or true spiritual self. I am a Five. At the same time, it does tend to devolve into pop psychology almost like sun sign astrology. It is a serious tool if you approach it seriously.

While there are many good books on the Enneagram, I believe the best one is by A. H. Almaas. It is perhaps also the most challenging and the most advanced, but it is well worth the effort. For emotional healing, depth psychology and early childhood/family system work, I have found Margaret Keyes book to be original, practical, fun to use and spot on.

Almaas, A. H. *Facets of Unity: The Enneagram of Holy Ideas*, Diamond Books, Berkeley, CA, 1998.

Keyes, Margaret Frings. *Emotions and the Enneagram: Working Through Your Shadow Life Script*, Molysdatur Publications, Muir Beach, CA, Revised Ed., 1992.

21. Jack Canfield, Inspirational Writer and Speaker, http://simplereminders.com/blog/post/jack-canfield, accessed March, 2014.

22. Noble Eightfold Path, http://en.wikipedia.org/wiki/Noble_Eightfold_Path, accessed March, 2014.

Many people do not realize that there is an enormous amount of free information about Buddhism and Buddhist teachings on the Internet. Based on my training in the Theravadan tradition of Thailand, that is where I would recommend going first. The practical tools of ancient applied Buddhist meditation are unequalled by any other tradition.

The free teachings on the websites I recommend below are sufficient for generating liberating insight and entry into non-duality if you do them with perseverance. In particular, the Buddha's teachings on mindfulness (satipatthana) and breath meditation (anapanasati) are precisely designed to generate awakening, especially in conjunction with the cultivation of impeccably ethical behavior.

They are easily applied by Westerners as no rituals or other exotica are required. Since these profound teachings are totally FREE, you can start meditating today, get enlightened and never spend another nickel on anybody or anything of a spiritual nature again.

I did Vipassana very seriously (one to two hours a day plus 10 day retreats) for seven years. I can vouch for these 2,500 year-old techniques from my own personal experience. They work!

Along those lines, although it is not an insight method per se, the Buddha's Loving Kindness meditation greatly facilitates the emotional healing and integration that will provide a solid foundation for the path. Keep in mind that Buddhism is also a path of action, not just of reflection.

Access to Insights, Readings in Theravada Buddhism, http://www.accesstoinsight.org/, accessed March, 2014.

Also recommended (free audios): Dhamma Talks, http://www.dhammatalks.net/, accessed March, 2014.

23. Ken Wapnick: On Dissuading People from Doing the Course, http://www.avaiya.com/2013/03/ken-wapnick-on-dissuading-people-from-doing-the-course/, accessed March, 2014.

24. What It Says, http://acim.org/AboutACIM/what_it_says.html, accessed March, 2014.

25. Jon Kabat-Zinn, http://en.wikipedia.org/wiki/Jon_Kabat-Zinn, accessed March, 2014.

26. Jon Kabat-Zinn, http://en.wikipedia.org/wiki/Jon_Kabat-Zinn, accessed March, 2014.

In keeping with my enthusiastic endorsement of practical Buddhist meditation in these Notes, Kabat-Zinn excels at explaining these methods to Westerners. After you learn from him, go to the Theravadan sources. Then what they are saying will not seem so strange.

Kabat-Zinn's point that the Buddhist dogma is not required for success with these ancient methods is correct. You can keep your old religion or have no religion. You do not need to become a Buddhist. Of course, somebody needs to be supporting Buddhism somehow for these teachings to continue to thrive and spread. Traditionally, that is the local community.

The Vipassana I studied is known as "body sweeping" meditation. Taught by S. N. Goenka at dhamma.org, they offer free 10 day meditation retreats.

I originally learned it from Venerable Shinzen Young. I do not know if he is still teaching it or not. I give Shinzen the highest recommendation. I worked closely with him for several years. Meeting him was a major turning point in my spiritual life. He can be found at Shinzen.org.

Here's a great example of Shinzen's style and offerings. This post is from February, 2014. Hint: He's offering you a free one day breath meditation workshop. This stuff is pure gold!

Young, Shinzen, Breath Focus: Advanced Perspectives on a Basic Practice, http://shinzenyoung.blogspot.com/2014/02/breath-focus-advanced-perspectives-on.html, accessed March, 2014.

27. Orsatti, Mario, Oprah Winfrey talks TM with Dr. Mehmet Oz, http://www.tm.org/blog/people/oprah-winfrey/, accessed March, 2014.

28. Hay House Daily Meditations, https://www.facebook.com/HayHouseDailyMeditations/posts/121817701236949, accessed March, 2014.

29. Near Death Experiences, http://www.dannion.com/dannion-brinkley-near-death-experience/, accessed March, 2014.

30. Page, Ken, An Interview With Marianne Williamson: The Essential Steps To Finding Love, http://www.psychologytoday.com/blog/finding-love/201201/interview-marianne-williamson-the-essential-steps-finding-love, accessed March, 2014.

31. Enlightenment: An Unlearning Process—Marianne Williamson, 2013 Winter — Inside Enlightenment, *Integral Yoga Magazine*, Buckingham, Virginia.

32. Ramdas, Swami, Sayings of Papa Ramdas, http://saranaagathi.files.wordpress.com/2008/02/sayings-of-papa-ramdas.pdf, Anandashram, Ramnagar, Kanhangad, Kerala, India, 2008, Saying 47, page 8.

33. Godman, David, Editor. *Be As You Are: The Teachings of Sri Ramana Maharshi*, Arkana, London, England, 1985. This book is widely regarded as the essential guide to Ramana's teachings.

34. Muruganar, Guru Vachaka Kovai (The Garland of the Guru's Sayings), http://davidgodman.org/rteach/gvk_intro.shtml, accessed March, 2014.

I have a minor criticism of David Godman in regard to the Heart on the right and Amrita Nadi since he is talking like an expert about something that he has not, to the best of my knowledge, experienced. Nonetheless, his contribution to the tradition and teachings of Sri Ramana Maharshi is monumental and overshadows everything else.

In Godman's defense, Ramana himself would go silent or give apparently contradictory answers when the subject of the Heart on the right or Amrita Nadi (aham sphurana) came up. This is probably because he did not want people to get distracted from the Self and make the common mistake of focusing on dramatic and fascinating spiritual experiences as their goal.

Even so, at other times Ramana spoke at length and in great detail about these topics. Therefore, he was not merely discounting them as useless fantasies or as meaningless deadends.

For example, in V. Ganeshan's *Ramana Periya Puranam*, Amrita Nadi is described as "the immortal nerve - the nerve believed to be associated with Self-realization that has been extolled by yogic texts and the Hindu scriptures as being similar to the kundalini." In that same highly esteemed document, it is reported that Ramana talked to a Tamil scholar about the Amrita Nadi for four days in a row in 1942!

Ganeshan, V., *Ramana Periya Puranam, Inner Journey of 75 Old Devotees*, Sri Ramanasramam, Tiruvannamalai, Tamilnadu, India, 402 - 403.

Note: This big and very unique pdf ebook is available for free download here: http://aham.com/RamanaPeriyaPuranam/, accessed March, 2014.

Godman is a true workhorse. His writing and publishing accomplishments are astounding. He has received full support for his writing by numerous enlightened beings including Sri Ramana Maharshi, Sri Papaji and Sri Lakshmana Swamy.

35. Muruganar, Guru Vachaka Kovai (The Garland of the Guru's Sayings), Verse 154, The Nature of the Ego and the Self, http://www.davidgodman.org/rteach/GVK154-265.pdf, accessed March, 2014.

Read this free pdf and you will see that when I describe the ego I-thought as a thief or con artist, I am not exaggerating in the slightest. Nor am I off the mark. You will find that Sri Muruganar speaks of the deceptiveness of the ego I-thought in extremely strong language.

36. Attar - Conference of the Birds, yilmazalimoglu.com/2011/01/19/attar-conference-of-the-birds/, accessed March, 2014.

See also this clever creative insightful summary:

Quinn Arts Presents, The Seven Valleys, http://www.quinnarts.com/valleys/press/presskit6.pdf, accessed March, 2014.

This appears to be the performance notes for a play called "The Seven Valleys" by Mírzá Husayn 'Alí (Bahá'u'lláh) Produced and Performed by Wendy, Marty and Caitlyn Quinn.

37. Five Ranks, http://en.wikipedia.org/wiki/Five_Ranks, accessed March, 2014.

38. The meaning and origin of the expression: Power corrupts; absolute power corrupts absolutely, http://www.phrases.org.uk/meanings/absolute-power-corrupts-absolutely.html, accessed March, 2014.

39. Koller, John, Ox-Herding: Stages of Zen Practice, http://www.columbia.edu/cu/weai/exeas/resources/oxherding.html, accessed March, 2014.

This excellent summary is available at this website as a free pdf download. Start with this resource. There are other versions of the pictures. This resource is simple and straightforward.

40. Seven Stages of True Insight, http://jessicasunshineyoga.blogspot.com/2011/11/meditation-with-saraswati-and-chitra.html, accessed March, 2014.

The best modern translation and commentary on the Yoga Sutras is the one by Swami Satchidananda (LOC 1000). He is extremely clear and precise regarding samadhi, the nature of enlightenment, non-doership and the seven stages of yoga.

Swami Satchidananda, *The Yoga Sutras of Patanjali*, Integral Yoga Publications, Buckingham, Virginia, 1978, 1984, 1990.

41. Aiyar, K. Narayanasvami. "Thirty Minor Upanishads," Varaha Upanishad of Krishna Yajurveda, http://www.sacred-texts.com/hin/tmu/index.htm, accessed March, 2014.

The best and most readable translation in English of the *Yoga Vasistha* is by Swami Venkatesananda. It is available in the massive 767 page full edition or a condensed but still complete edition. There is no other book like this. It is a book of towering spirituality that leads to realization of the Absolute. It describes the ultimate state as being totally without concepts. It is considered an advanced text, but if you are ready to hear about going beyond all concepts, notions and mental constructs, then it is for you.

Venkatesananda, Swami. *Vasistha's Yoga*, State University of New York Press, Albany, NY, 1993.

42. Farrell, Nick, Seven Stages of Spiritual Unfoldment, http://www.omegaproject.info/nickfarrell/nick-farrell-seven-stages-of-spiritual-unfoldment.html, accessed March, 2014.

Note: This Tarot card sequence was first discovered by Paul Foster Case, founder of Builders of the Adytum. Magician Nick Farrell has greatly expanded on the original and found new applications for it.

43. Monomyth, http://en.wikipedia.org/wiki/Monomyth, accessed March, 2014.

Campbell, Joseph. *The Hero with a Thousand Faces,* New World Library, Novato, California, 2008. For the in-depth treatment by the myth master himself, read this book. It should prove eye-opening.

Mythology the way Joseph Campbell (LOC 684) teaches it is more like we are living a waking dream and the myths and mythic symbols are magical expressions of this cosmic dream. It integrates nicely with Jungian notions such as synchronicity (versus cause and effect). So it's immediate, personal, very much about our day to day lives. It smoothly interfaces with non-dual ideas (such as "life is a dream."). Campbell's scholarship is impressive.

44. Vogler, Christopher. *The Writer's Journey: Mythic Structure for Writers,* Michael Wiese Productions, Studio City, CA, 3rd Ed., 2007.

Vogler has adapted the Hero's Journey for the popular movie audience. Since film requires everything to be visually demonstrated, and not all of the parts of Campbell's original 17 step sequence allow for that in a dramatically satisfying way, Vogler chopped off the parts that slow things down or lack visual impact, especially elements of the Return that describe how the process of the Hero involves embracing the world all over again.

For example, in his 12 stage model for writers, Vogler has Resurrection and Return with Elixir as the last two stages. Most of the subtle transitions in the Road of Return have been dropped.

To be fair to Vogler, what he did works great for screenwriters. But it will be misleading to mystics. Hopefully I've helped to set the record straight and given Campbell's version some much needed new life.

Campbell's original deserves to be remembered, even by novel writers and screenwriters. Vogler's version is too simplistic for my taste, even from a writing point of view. I ended up going back to Campbell for the richer psychological textures, mythic resonances and dreamlike synchronicities.

For a handy in-depth summary of Vogler's writerly surgical modifications and the famous story of how he came up with his modern streamlined version (and why), please see:

Vogler, Christopher, The Hero's Journey Outline, http://www.thewritersjourney.com/hero's_journey.htm#Hero, accessed March, 2014.

45. The Shadow Side of Krishamurti, http://www.tricycle.com/the-shadow-side-krishnamurti, accessed March, 2014. A lively and revealing interview with author Radha Rajagopal Sloss, the daughter of Krishnamurti's long-time mistress.

Sloss, Radha Rajagopal, *Lives in the Shadow with J. Krishnamurti*, Bloomsbury Press, London, 1991.

46. Henry Kissinger, http://en.wikipedia.org/wiki/Henry_Kissinger, accessed March, 2014.

47. Sri Sadguru Siddharameshwar Maharaj. *Master Key to Self-Realization*, Sadguru Publishing, 2008. When you read this book, it becomes clear that the great Sri Nisargadatta Maharaj had a great guru. If you want to understand Nisargadatta, get this amazing book.

48. H.W.L. Poonja Satsang, Sri Harilal Poonja ♥ Papaji ◦ The Beauty Of No Mind (1993-01-31) ◦ Gangaji at 1-40, http://youtu.be/KSAcY1oRve0, accessed March, 2014. I was watching the VHS videotape that I had purchased from eBay for five dollars plus shipping.

49. Nisargadatta Maharaj, Frydman, Maurice and Sudhakar S. Dikshit, Editors. *I Am That: Talks with Sri Nisargadatta Maharaj*, The Acorn Press, Durham, N. C., Third Ed., 1981, pages 90, 230.

50. Martinez, Joshua, The Fibonacci Sequence For Forex Traders, http://www.forexcharts.net/fibonacci-sequence-markettraders/, accessed March, 2014.

51. Be Here Now, http://en.wikipedia.org/wiki/Be_Here_Now_(book), accessed March, 2014.

Ram Dass. *Be Here Now*, Lama Foundation, San Cristobal, New Mexico, 1971.

Ram Dass came out as a teacher in very public way while still in the LOC 600s. This may have crystallized him too early for his own good.

Lots of interaction with people along with having a major media focus on you will not "un-enlighten" you, but it does tend to keep you in a house of mirrors as everybody reflects back at everybody else. In other words, it will reinforce the subtle holding onto the feeling that "the other" is "real" and keep you where you are in spite of your strong sadhana efforts.

For some people, the only solution is long periods of isolation so that the "people" and "world" can be totally forgotten. Otherwise, the constant reminder due to daily activities keeps reinforcing the trance. These echoes can go on for a long time even after you've gone on retreat. There are many layers to it. The root? The I-thought, of course.

That is probably why the old masters emphasized simple living and keeping a low profile. Until you're done, you're not done, and it's easy to fool yourself into thinking you're already done when you are not.

Take another five years or so before you make any announcements just to be on the safe side! What's the rush? If you truly are there, it will make no difference to you.

And if you're not there, it's a good thing you waited. Not just for them, your prospective students, but most importantly for you. Any lifetime you manage to make it into non-duality needs to become an all out effort to go all the way. It's not time to do the happy dance yet.

52. Veeraswamy Krishnaraj, Chapter Five: Yoga of Renunciation of Action, http://www.bhagavadgitausa.com/bg05.htm, accessed March, 2014.

The online original reads "5.8: He is steady in yoga, knows the truth, and thinks without doubt that he does not do anything, while seeing, hearing, touching, smelling, eating, moving, sleeping, breathing... 5.9: speaking, discharging (evacuation), grasping, opening, or closing his eyes. He realizes the senses act in the realm of sense objects."

This is a good free translation of the *Gita* with lots of useful related information and insights provided along with the text. I have modernized the language a bit. Also, some translations avoid the fact that Krishna specifically includes the bodily functions of elimination, e.g. going to the bathroom, in his list of human voluntary and involuntary behaviors.

53. Goode, Greg. *The Direct Path: A User's Guide,* Non-Duality Press, Salisbury, United Kingdom, 2012, 25, 113.

Goode's approach is streamlined and precise. The error is not in his procedure but reading too much into the results. Fred Davis does the same thing. Space has many different expressions. The conclusion that both men arrive at makes perfect sense since all they can go on is what they have experienced so far, but they are imposing their ideas on their data.

If the biggest hole you know about is in your neighborhood, and you have never heard of the Grand Canyon, then it's the biggest hole. But once you've been to the Grand Canyon, all of that is changed forever. Nisargadatta kept saying "There's a Grand Canyon! There's a Grand Canyon!" but obviously not everybody heard him or understood what he was talking about.

I was not able to break out of the LOC 600s until I reviewed the raw data of my experience and went over it meticulously and with brutal honesty. It was only then that I realized my "borderless" experience was taking place inside of a consciousness "container," the local space "unit." This is the hole left by the sudden departure of the empirical thinker-decider-doer self.

54. Meizer, Bobby, John Wheeler, May, 2004, Santa Cruz, http://www3.telus.net/public/sarlo/ReportsJW.htm, accessed March, 2014.

This review of a live encounter with John Wheeler pretty much says it all — the good, the bad, the beautiful, the ugly. Instant enlightenment? Yes, more or less. What is it worth? Good question. I wonder what Nisargdatta would have to say about it. I mention Nisargadatta in all seriousness as I'm pretty sure these people have all read *I Am That.*

55. Adam Brunt, John Wheeler Full Interview on Let's Get Real, http://youtu.be/fL9MRoySZ2g, accessed March, 2014.

Allin Taylor extracts a crystal clear presentation from Wheeler. She is said to have had an awakening during this program or around the same time while hanging out with Wheeler. My favorite part is around the 15 minute mark, give or take a few minutes.

This is the video equivalent of the face to face satsang with John Wheeler referred to in Note 54. Pure gold if you like John Wheeler's approach. To tell you the truth, I am a fan. John is articulate and compassionate — he even writes beautiful songs. What's not to like?

John can't dictate the experience or realization of somebody he talks to. All he can do is deliver the goods, which he does. Excellent direct pointing conversation in the spirit of Sailor Bob, John's Aussie guru.

But then there is his "you are an open space of clarity and awareness" bit as if that is the whole enchilada. This goes back to the limitations of the LOC 600s "local space" view. I've said enough on that. You either get it or you don't. Either way, it's still a step in right direction, right? No worries, mate.

56. Davis, Fred, Beyond Recovery, Non-Duality and the Twelve Steps, Introduction, http://www.beyond-recovery.org/extracts/, accessed March, 2014

57. Davis, Fred, Frequently Asked Questions, 2 – What is awakening?, http://www.beyond-recovery.org/FAQ/, accessed March, 2014.

58. Davis, Fred, Frequently Asked Questions, 2 – What is awakening?, http://www.beyond-recovery.org/FAQ/, accessed March, 2014.

59. Davis, Fred. *Beyond Recovery: Non-Duality and the Twelve Steps*, Non-Duality Press, Salisbury, United Kingdom, 2012. This is a very good book. Fred has a knack for making non-duality relevant to everyday life. It is certainly for anybody who is working a 12 step program.

If you're not sure about getting this book, take a look at the Table of Contents on Amazon.com. Notice how he has provided Chapter Synopses plus there is a Foreword by Rupert Spira. Fred is a *good* writer.

60. Foster, Jeff. *An Extraordinary Absence: Liberation in the Midst of a Very Ordinary Life*, Non-Duality Press, Salisbury, United Kindgdom, 2009.

61. No Exit, http://en.wikipedia.org/wiki/No_Exit, accessed March, 2014.

Sartre, Jean-Paul and Stuart Gilbert, Translator. *No Exit and Three Other Plays*, Vintage, New York, International Edition, 1976, 1989.

To quote from paragraph two of the Wikipedia entry, "The play is a depiction of the afterlife in which three deceased characters are punished by being locked into a room together for eternity. It is the source of Sartre's especially famous and often misinterpreted quotation "L'enfer, c'est les autres" or "Hell is other people," a reference to Sartre's ideas about the Look and the perpetual ontological struggle of being caused to see oneself as an object in the world of another consciousness."

In sum, we suffer because we are thought to be the helpless submissive object for "the other" rather than enjoying the self-liberation of being the Supreme Subject for all of the subject-object incidences. When you are the ocean, you are okay with, and perhaps even delighted by, the waves.

This is a brilliant play. I recommend it for anyone who is a student or teacher of non-duality. Sartre's discovery of "the Look" articulates how we are tortured and oppressed by the other in our being seen by the other. In our constant thinking of the other and jockeying for position with or against the other, we are shamed, blinded and disempowered by the other.

He had no solution for this since he still believed in the separate existence of the other, but he described the angst that must be addressed extremely well. It is a brilliant and highly useful exposition of that agonizing non-stop dilemma. Very useful for those who are still not clear why all this hoopla about "the other" and why I keep harping on it in this book.

Sartre explains better than I can *why* you must come to terms with it. You were invaded in early childhoood. You have been at a disadvantage ever since due to this stealthy invasion of "otherness." Even a genius like Sartre could not extricate himself from its deep subconscious clutches on his own.

62. U. G. Krishnamurti Quotes, http://www.goodreads.com/author/quotes/30268.U_G_Krishnamurti, accessed March, 2014.

U. G. Krishnamurti put his books in public domain, so if you like him, there's plenty more where the quotes in the body of the text came from. Just do the Google search "u g krishnamurti pdf."

"Your constant utilization of thought to give continuity to your separate self is 'you'. There is nothing there inside you other than that." - U.G. Krishnamurti.

There is a moral ambiguity to the LOC 600s that gets resolved in LOC 700s and higher. In full bloom, it can become quite a power trip, including the ability to access the void for massive influence. The tone may not just be nihilistic. There can be a love of chaos, even anarchy. It is a unique zone.

63. Newland, Terry, Mind Is a Myth, Disquieting Conversations with the Man Called U. G., A Note at the Beginning, Part 2., http://www.ugkrishnamurti.net/ugkrishnamurti-net/intro.html, accessed March, 2014.

On this web page, U. G. Krishnamurti is quoted as saying "My teaching, if that is the word you want to use, has no copyright. You are free to reproduce, distribute, interpret, misinterpret, distort, garble, do what you like, even claim authorship, without my consent or the permission of anybody. U.G."

64. Newland, Terry, Mind Is a Myth, Disquieting Conversations with the Man Called U. G., A Note at the Beginning, Part 6., http://www.ugkrishnamurti.net/ugkrishnamurti-net/intro.html, accessed March, 2014.

65. Newland, Terry, Mind Is a Myth, Disquieting Conversations with the Man Called U. G., A Note at the Beginning, Part 4., http://www.ugkrishnamurti.net/ugkrishnamurti-net/intro.html, accessed March, 2014.

66. Newland, Terry, Mind Is a Myth, Disquieting Conversations with the Man Called U. G., A Note at the Beginning, Part 3., http://www.ugkrishnamurti.net/ugkrishnamurti-net/intro.html, accessed March, 2014.

67. Acharya Vasudev, UG Krishnamurti's Horoscope, http://www.indiadivine.org/audarya/vedic-astrology-jyotisha/308740-ug-krishnamurti-s-horoscope.html, accessed March, 2014.

68. Jeff Foster – Falling into the Mystery, http://urbangurucafe.com/2008/09/18/15-jeff-foster-falling-into-the-mystery/, accessed March, 2014.

In this half hour podcast, the ever effervescent Foster talks about such tasty tidbits as why he is not a teacher. He also "looks at people falling into nihilism when they hear that there is nothing to get and nobody to do anything." This is, of course, the trap that U. G. Krishnamurti fell into or, perhaps more accurately, was born into as his prophesied destiny.

69. Heistman, Ted. The Enlightenment of Charles Manson, http://disinfo.com/2013/05/the-enlightenment-of-charles-manson/, accessed March, 2014.

70. Doc Chubbs, Our Savage God by R.C. Zaehner, truthontatelabianca.com/threads/r-c-zaehner.4063/, accessed March, 2014.

71. Zaehner, R. C. *Our Savage God*, Sheed and Ward, New York, 1974, 89.

72. Maslin, Janet, Long Before Little Charlie Became the Face of Evil: A New Look at Charles Manson, by Jeff Guinn, www.nytimes.com/2013/08/07/books/a-new-look-at-charles-manson-by-jeff-guinn.html?_r=0, accessed March, 2014..

Guinn, Jeff. *Manson: the Life and Times of Charles Manson*, Simon & Schuster, New York, 2013.

73. Roberts, Bernadette. *The Experience of No-Self*, SUNY Press, Albany, Revised Edition, 1993.

74. Ibid., 32.

75. Ibid., 49, 62.

76. Solk, Mandi. *The Joy of No Self*, Empty Books, London, 2008.

77. conscioustv, Mandi Solk "Self Enquiry Know Yourself," Interview by Renate McNay, http://www.youtube.com/watch?v=zYTx8SOChZc, accessed March, 2014.

78. conscioustv, Mandi Solk "Self Enquiry Know Yourself," Interview by Renate McNay, http://www.youtube.com/watch?v=zYTx8SOChZc, accessed March, 2014.

79. Solk, Mandi, Who Am I?, http://mandisolk.com/about/, accessed March, 2014.

The extensive quotations are used with the kind permission of Mandi Solk in the United Kingdom provided via email in 2013. I am looking forward to her book on Self-inquiry. I'm sure it will be a good one. It will deliver her trademark honesty, enthusiasm and playful fun loving attitude to what is so often treated as a dry, difficult, subdued and esoteric practice.

80. Ibid.

81. Ibid.

82. T. M. P. Mahadevan, Who Am I? - (Nan Yar?), The Teachings of Bhagavan Sri Ramana Maharshi, http://allspirit.co.uk/whoami.html, accessed March, 2014.

83. Nisargadatta Maharaj. Maria Jory, Editor. *Beyond Freedom*, Yogi Impressions Books, Mumbai, India, 2007, pages 36, 37, 48, 55, 88.

84. Nisargadatta Maharaj. Robert Powell, Editor. *The Experience of Nothingness*, Motilal Banarsidass Publishers, Delhi, India, 1996, 36, 68 - 69.

85. Ibid., 49 - 50.

86. Ibid., 47 - 48.

87. Ibid., xii, 2 - 3, 17 - 20, 31.

88. Davidya, 3 Levels of Non-Dual Reality, http://davidya.ca/2013/05/21/3-levels-of-non-dual-reality/, accessed March, 2014. Davidya has a similar model to mine. It may be based on the Maharishi Mahesh Yogi model.

See also: Davidya, Stages of Development in Consciousness, http://davidya.ca/2014/01/25/stages-of-development-in-consciousness/, accessed March, 2014.

89. Roozdar, Ellie, Kundalini Experience, http://www.meditationerfan.com/kundalini-experience.html, accessed March, 2014.

90. Roozdar, Ellie, My Path, http://www.meditationerfan.com/my-path.html, accessed March, 2014.

91. Renz, Karl. *The Myth of Enlightenment*, Inner Directions Foundation, Carlsbad, CA, 2005, xviii - xxi.

92. Nisargadatta Maharaj, Robert Powell, Editor. *The Experience of Nothingness*, Motilal Banarsidass Publishers, Delhi, India, 1996, 36.

93. Segal, Suzanne. *Collision with the Infinite*, Blue Dove Press, San Diego, CA, 1996.

94. Suzanne Segal, Information and Excerpts taken from Collision with the Infinite, Part 4., www.nonduality.com/suzanne.htm, accessed March, 2014.

95. "The Awakening West" Interview with Suzanne Segal, http://www.spiritualteachers.org/segal_interview.htm, accessed March, 2014.

96. Braha, James. *Living Reality*, Hermetician Press, Longboat Key, Florida, 2006, 106 - 108.

97. Ibid., 163.

98. Ibid., 271.

99. Ibid., 305.

100. Gilbert, Eleonora, Editor. *Conversations on Non-Duality*, Cherry Red Books, London, U.K., 2011, 222.

101. Ibid., 228.

102. Ibid., 228.

103. Jijimuge, An open window into the understanding of Zen, http://sped2work.tripod.com/AllThingsZen.html, March, 2014.

104. M., Celebration of the Self, Three Awakenings, http://www.nonduality.com/m.htm, accessed March, 2014.

105. Ibid.

106. Certified Facilitators, http://www.thework.com/facilitators.php, accessed March, 2014.

107. Facilitators, http://livinginquiries.com/facilitators/, accessed March, 2014.

When you compare Byron's web page and Scott's web page side by side, you can see that they are putting into action the same model. The home page on Scott's site has a headline at the time of this writing which drives home my point about how the LOC 700s love to develop universal inquiry tools, techniques, systems and methods that people can learn and apply themselves or be coached to do. It reads "Discover the Tools that Change Everything." The focus is on the *tools*, not the teacher or the teaching.

Discover the Tools that Change Everything, http://livinginquiries.com/, accessed March, 2014.

108. Basic Skills, http://awakeningcoachingtraining.com/basic-skills, accessed March, 2014.

109. Facilitation, http://bigmind.org/bmfacilitators-old, accessed March, 2014.

110. Timeless Wisdom Brochure, http://www.radiantmind.net/wp-content/uploads/2014/01/AwakeningNondualTraining_RadiantMind_Presentation_2014.pdf, accessed March, 2014.

Peter's work is impressively logical, systematic and deeply compassionate.

Radiant Mind Course, http://wisdom.org/radiant-mind-course/, accessed March, 2014.

What is Natural Awakening?, http://www.nondualtraining.com/, accessed March, 2014.

Welcome, http://peterfenner.com/, accessed March, 2014.

111. Tom, The miracle of nondoership, http://awareconsciousness.blogspot.com/2010/06/miracle-of-nondoership.html, accessed March, 2014.

I've referenced Tom's post because it is a good example of a smart person investigating the truth about doership for themselves. The comments by others are also of interest.

Ramesh has been criticized because he narrowed the universal scope of Nisargadatta's message down to the "one trick pony" of non-doership. If you are a seeker and you have not yet realized non-duality, then you have no clue how significant non-doership is.

For me, Ramesh's emphasis on non-doership at the empirical daily life level (as opposed to the abstraction called "non-duality") was just what I needed to hear as a spiritual seeker. It matched *exactly* what I was going through at the time. When I say Ramesh put an emphasis on non-doership, what I mean is he *hammered* it into you if you gave him half a chance.

He struck some people as an effete intellectual, others as a materialistic knockoff of Maharaj. After all, he had been President of the Bank of India and he sported a gold Rolex watch. Maharaj had bidis but not much else.

In my experience he was the kung fu killer of consciousness, a divinely ordained and precisely guided sacred guru assassin who knew exactly how to kill the ego if you gave him the opportunity. He has a book called *Your Head in the Tiger's Mouth*. Who is the tiger? Ramesh, of course!

Balsekar, Ramesh and Blayne Bardo, Ed. *Your Head in the Tiger's Mouth: Talks in Bombay with Ramesh S. Balsekar*, Advaita Press, Redondo Beach, CA, 1998.

During the period I studied with Ramesh, he was advising students to reflect on the events of their life to see just how much they really were the captain of their ship of destiny. Consider the major events of your life, the big turning points. Did you cause them? The answer, of course, is no, you did not. They fell upon you as fate or destiny. Call it what you like, for in terms of whatever really mattered to you, you were not the doer like you thought you were.

Who cares if you feel like it is you that are brushing your teeth in the morning? When you met your wife or husband at that social event and fell in love, you were magnetically sucked into it. What's that you say? It was what you wanted to do, it was what made you feel good, it was your desire? That's a good one. Where did the feeling good about it come from? God.

This is a powerful modern form of Self-inquiry. Of what use is the ego if you are no longer the doer? It sucks the gas out of the ego's gas tank.

Once it sees that it is not the doer, not the "author" (as Wayne Liquorman puts it), then what is the point? This inquiry "Who is the doer?" and "Am I the doer?" strikes at the heart of all that the ego wants, desires, yearns for, stands for, values. It targets the ego's false belief in its separate power.

My contention is that Ramesh, like so many other LOC 700s sages, did develop an inquiry system. His emphasis on digging deep to discover the truth about the lie of doership was the laser targeted tool that he taught. Destroy that delusion and non-dual realization is just around the corner.

Some people call Ramesh's view "hard determinism" as if it matches up point by point with that Western philosophical position. I can see the similarities, but this interpretation is reductive and it is based on faulty reasoning.

Because the reader cannot understand what Ramesh is talking about (since they have not yet realized non-doership for themselves), they reduce it to something they are familiar with (comfortably Western and conveniently intellectual). Then they criticize this handy diminution.

Ramesh was from India. The Indian culture has a special non-Western flavor in terms of past lives, karma, God's will and doership that the individual raised in the "Do it now!" and "One life to live!" Judeo-Christian West has difficulty comprehending. I would recommend that people who want to make the best use of Ramesh's teachings keep in mind the hidden cultural differences.

Non-doership is not a teaching that is compatible with Judeo-Christian dogma. It violates that dogma in numerous delightful, incisive and thought provoking ways. That is a good thing, but you will need to examine the roots of your belief in your doership in terms of your childhood family system, your parental models and the psychology of your (I assume) particular Western culture.

The Western person is deeply invested in the idea that he or she can "make things happen." He is, basically, a cowboy who thinks he is riding a wild range of endless opportunity. Therefore, non-doership is threatening.

Non-doership is 100 per cent supported by quantum physics. Correctly understood, non-doership is comforting and leads to emotional healing. It increases your sense of freedom, not the other way around. The universe is behind every action that you think you are doing. How's that for backup?

In quantum physics, non-local synchronicity, not cause and effect, applies. The Buddha called it "simultaneous dependent arising." Here's an article that explains it in practical Western terms.

Linda Blanchard, A Secular Understanding of Dependent Arising: Table of Contents, http://secularbuddhism.org/2012/06/07/a-secular-understanding-of-dependent-arising-table-of-contents/, accessed March, 2014.

Why am I bringing up early Buddhism when I was just talking about Ramesh? Because it is all connected. It is all complementary. As the saying goes, "All roads lead to Rome."

The brilliance of early Buddhism is that it uses the analytical investigative strengths of the mind to break down the mind. By the time the mind realizes that it's been tricked, it's too late (hopefully).

When the sense of separate entity goes, the feeling of being the doer must of necessity go also. If the old familiar feeling of "I am doing this and that" has not vanished, then you are still holding onto the separate entity in some fashion. If you don't believe me, then believe Krishna and the *Gita*.

Non-doership is the reliable time tested proven marker of stable real enlightenment. It you don't know what I'm talking about, then chances are you have an intellectual grasp of non-duality, but you are not living it at the moment to moment, day to day level. You are *not* awakened.

Some people describe the state of non-doership as living spontaneously, being in the flow, living in a total let-go state and so on. That's all right, but you have to make sure you're not getting too sloppy with your self-observation and, as a result, just fooling yourself. That's why I reference over and over Krishna's strong precise words in the *Bhagavad Gita*.

"Some people believe we are something beyond neurons, but of course we are not. We are just the sum total of the activity of neurons. We assume that we have free will and that we make decisions, but we don't. Neurons do." - Rodolfo Llinás, neuroscientist

112. Rajneesh, http://en.wikipedia.org/wiki/Bhagwan_Shree_Rajneesh, accessed March, 2014.

113. Calder, Christopher, Osho, Bhagwan Rajneesh, and the Lost Truth, http://meditation-handbook.50webs.com/osho2.html, accessed March, 2014.

Although written in the style of an exposé of Rajneesh, Calder has some deep things to say. It is a very thoughtful essay. Consider the following direct quote: "Many enlightened humans have become fooled by the reduction of the space localization function of the brain and believed they no longer had personal selfishness that could cause trouble."

114. The Kriya Yoga Path of Meditation, http://www.yogananda-srf.org/Kriya_Yoga_path_of_meditation.aspx#.Um3HjvnRtpI, accessed March, 2014.

This web page does a great job of conveying the unique style of Yogananda's approach. He seems to have done a better job of blending Yoga and Christianity than anybody else. The offering is seamless and harmonizes both traditions, yet takes nothing away from the greatness of the path of Yoga. A brilliant and highly marketable synthesis that fires on all cylinders. Contemporary teachers can learn a lot from Yogananda's marketing genius.

115. Conway, Timothy, On neo-advaitin Ramesh Balsekar, http://www.enlightened-spirituality.org/ramesh_balsekar.html, accessed March, 2014.

The full title for this in-depth online essay by Conway is "On neo-advaitin Ramesh Balsekar: Advaita, ethics, authentic & inauthentic sages." I gather from the fact that he labeled Ramesh as a "neo-advaitin" that he is unceremoniously dumping Ramesh into the "inauthentic sage" dust bin.

This is even though he has the pedigree of the illustrious great sage Nisargadatta Maharaj. This pedigree, I might add, includes having been told in no uncertain terms *more than once* by Maharaj that he wanted him to start teaching. As I heard the story, Nisargadatta raised up on his deathbed and shouted at Ramesh something like "I told you to teach! Do it!"

This puts the latter questionable and controversial goings on with Ramesh in an interesting light. If he was indeed endorsed by Nisargadatta in such an unassailable way, could the Ramesh at that time have been an enlightened person who has since "fallen" and lost his way?

People would challenge Nisargadatta about his smoking and he would tell them it was none of their business. As I recall, he told one such erstwhile critic something like "After you get enlightened, see if you feel the same way about my smoking. If you do, let me know."

Nisargadatta knew that the stabilized sage is living in non-doership. In human terms, that means he simply cannot do a thing about what he is doing other than watch it play out in front of his eyes just like it does for anybody else. He has zero power to change his actions.

Whatever happens is literally 100 per cent God's will. That means everything all of the time. *Every* happening is God's will! This is the flavor of the total surrender of the sage. That's a big pill to swallow for non-sages who prefer their holy sages to be sweet, saintly and sexless.

In my experience, once a person is stabilized in non-duality, they stay there. Ramesh (LOC 764) was definitely stabilized, but it's safe to say he was pretty lively for an old dude. He was not ready to be put out to pasture yet! He still had some surprises up his senior sleeves.

The problem that Conway addresses is not a new one. It goes back as far as the history of spiritual teachers and spiritual students. There is no simple easy "one size fits all" answer.

The challenge for the student is that he is trying to evaluate the teacher yet all he has to go on are the teacher's actions and words plus his own fuzzy intuitive feelings about the apparently enlightened one. The difficult and confusing truth is that behavior is not that good of an indicator.

In the top masters like Ramana and Nisargadatta, we see the perfect fusion of Truth and humanity, but that is at the top level. At lower levels, the enlightenment can be legitimate and liberating yet the teacher flawed and contradictory.

This massive dilemma for the student was one of the motivators for me to write this book that offers a more practical approach based on LOC numbers and ranges. If lots of other people could easily assess LOCs like I do, then it would be an ideal solution. Unfortunately, that does not appear to be the case. Even gifted intuitive types struggle with getting LOCs.

116. Ibid.

117. Revelatory Letter on Ramesh from Patrick / Nirodhananda, March 25, 2005 [with some editing by DM], http://www.enlightened-spirituality.org/ramesh_balsekar.html, accessed March, 2014.

118. Nathan, Genpo Roshi Falls Again, http://dangerousharvests.blogspot.com/2011/02/genpo-roshi-falls-again.html, accessed March, 2014.

119. Yogananda's Sexual Indiscretions, http://srfblacklist.yuku.com/topic/269/Yoganandas-Sexual-Indiscretions#.Um3JIPnRtpI, accessed March, 2014.

I was not aware that Yogananda (LOC 769) had any dirty laundry until I was discussing sexual misconduct and famous gurus with a student of mine. He asserted that, contrary to his official image, Yogananda was sexually active, at the very least.

I went on the Internet and dug up this forum discussion. What it all means in terms of Yogananda I cannot really say other than it suggests that he was human after all.

At a certain phase of my sadhana, I went on a two week retreat at the SRF center in Encinitas, California. It was a wonderful healing experience. I felt that the spiritual energy was strong and positive. As far as I am concerned, whatever Yogananda did privately was his business. It does not seem to have affected his transmission of Grace or the presence of Shakti.

120. Rawat, Prem, Rajneesh (Osho, Bhagwan), http://www.prem-rawat-bio.org/gurus/rajneesh.htm, accessed March, 2014.

I don't know if it is even possible to have an objective critique of Osho-Rajneesh at this point. He loved controversy and it will stay around him for a long time to come. This article provides plenty of rare details and some good references.

Rawat offers useful comments regarding the rise and fall of Osho-Rajneesh and how the rapidity of the events exposed more clearly some of the dynamics of spiritual cults. As I have made clear in the body of this book, there is no doubt in my mind that Rajneesh was enlightened (LOC 754). His shenanigans require neither justification nor explanation. At the same time, his bizarre life and extreme teaching style issue a clear warning to the spiritually naive.

121. Harderwijk, Rudy, Controversial 'Buddhist' Teachers & Groups, http://viewonbuddhism.org/controversy-controversial-teacher-group-center-questionable.html, accessed March, 2014.

If only the Buddhists could keep it in their pants. Then I could say it is the perfect religion as well as the pinnacle of non-duality on the planet. But the truth is they cannot. Sordid stories, even about some very famous and acclaimed Buddhist teachers, abound and resound.

Remember, I was a very serious Buddhist for seven years. Personally, I love Theravadan (early) Buddhism very much. Buddhist mind training is without equal in our world.

It just proves that Buddhists like everybody else are human. I have a pet theory that Eastern monks do not know how to handle the sexuality of Western women. This leads to some rather painful misunderstandings. Once again, cultural differences raises its pretty little head.

The best advice I can give to a female seeker who is wondering about all of this is do not have sex with your spiritual teacher or perform sexual favors for him. A friendly loving hug is fine, but draw the line. Some women seem to think that having sexual relations with their enlightened teacher will be like "having sex with god." This is pure sexual fantasy.

Forget it! There is a 99.99 per cent chance that you will be disappointed. If you do decide to become sexual with a teacher, treat it just like any other date or fling. His enlightenment does not make him a great mystical lover.

If he has come onto you or he has responded to you coming onto him, then it's the very human part of him that is showing up. You are not going to get an increase of Grace or a life-changing Tantric transmission. What you are going to get is a big fat wad of disappointment.

Then when you have sex with your teacher, if that is what happens, you can go in with all of your eyes open and take full responsibility for it. He was good in bed or he was not good in bed — that sort of thing. When all the fantasy projections by the women upon the guru and the guru upon the women have been removed, then what is left?

Precious little. Just human beings trying to stay warm in a cold world. Sex is fantastic food for fueling fantasies, but what it delivers is short-lived and not what was expected or hoped for.

There is no spiritual sexual "sugar daddy" or "sugar momma." That is just another romantic fantasy suitable for the cover of a paperback Tantric romance novel. You will not be "saved" by having sex with your guru. Sex is just sex. Love is an entirely different matter. Pure love is God.

If you want to get enlightened, do the work and don't expect anybody else to do it for you. Only you can save you. Grace may come, but if it does, in one way or another you will have "earned" it.

Act as if it is all up to you. Surrender like it is all up to God. Enlightenment will happen somewhere in the middle.

The most important thing about sex is that we are all here because of it. Mother nature put it on the front burner for us day after day to make sure we will keep reproducing. Beyond that, I would say it's pretty much a personal matter, like food or clothing preferences.

By the way, just in case you're gay — yes, you can get enlightened if you're gay. It makes no difference at all. Like I said... it's a personal matter. It's just sexual preferences.

Sex is not going away, that much is for sure. Come to full terms with it on your own. Own your sexuality before you start projecting it onto others.

This applies to teachers and students both. Bringing consciousness to sex and shining the light on sex will bring the answer. Until then, as long as people do it in the dark they are bound to fumble and hurt each other.

122. This expression "Love that knows no love" is from Koort, a former student of mine who is now my good friend and the editor for this book. In another one of his notes to me when this book was still in manuscript form, he commented "There is no I in Truth." Perfect!

123. Nisargadatta Maharaj, http://nisargadatta.org/photos2/nisargadatta_maharaj_photo_67.html, accessed March, 2014.

There's a fantastic photo of Maharaj on the page. Here's the full quote. It is brilliant and pretty much says it all. It summarizes the message of this *1000* book. The sources are not given.

"This primary concept, 'I amness' is dishonest, because it is still a concept only. Finally one has to transcend that also and be in the 'nirvikalpa' state, which means the concept-free state. Then you have no concept at all, not even of 'I am'. In that state one does not know that one is. This state is known as 'Parabrahman': 'Brahman' transcended. 'Brahman' is manifest; 'Parabrahman' is beyond that, prior to that; the Absolute. Do you understand what I am driving at? Whatever you caught in your attention, that attention should eventually turn into no-attention. The state that is finally left over is Awareness, 'Parabrahman.'"

124. This is another expression from Koort that he casually put in his notes to me when he was editing *1000*. He is wonderfully pithy with his words. I wanted to give him credit.

125. Siddharameshwar Maharaj. *Amrut Laya (The "Stateless State"), Discourses on "Dasbodh" (Includes Master Key to Self-Realization)*, Shri Sadguru Siddharameshwar Adhyatma Kendra, Mumbai, India, 2000, 33.

126. Ibid., 33 - 35, 51 - 52.

127. Sahaja, http://en.wikipedia.org/wiki/Sahaja, accessed March, 2014.

I refer to Ramana's use of this word. It has been given other meanings by other teachers.

128. Siddharameshwar Maharaj. *Amrut Laya (The "Stateless State"), Discourses on "Dasbodh" (Includes Master Key to Self-Realization)*, Shri Sadguru Siddharameshwar Adhyatma Kendra, Mumbai, India, 2000.

129. Now available on Amazon.com in a new edition. It is the only spiritual guide through the upper (causal or deep sleep) darkness that I know of. It appeared in my life in conjunction with the awakening of an inner guru that gave identical advice but in a different way.

In my opinion, the wisdom in this spiritual manual is unparalleled. It may, however, be rough going if you're not ready for it.

The part that spoke to me the most and which I made maximum use of during this transition is called "Master Key to Self-Realization." It gave me amazingly precise guidance.

130. Koort (LOC 1000), the editor for this book, kindly shared the details of his transition through the LOC 800s with me in an email. His initiatory LOC 800s experience took place in April 21, 2013. The concluding LOC 800s experience was in August 6, 2013.

I received this report from Koort on November 1, 2013 as a document attachment called "Koorts Spiritual Progressions." Koort moved through the four stages very rapidly. I have made a few minor edits for grammar, sense and continuity.

Dear Ramaji,

You asked if I had any LOC 800s experiences. At first I wasn't sure, then I realized that these two events definitely applied.

Spiritual Experience with Kali
April 21, 2013
Approx. 10 pm

I have never classified myself as a bhakti, but if pressed, I would admit to having a long-time attraction to the Goddess Kali. Ramaji wrote a short Kindle book, "Warning From Kali." I read it and posted the following review of the book the night before.

"I have been devoted to Kali for a long time, but have never before seen any words attributed to her, let alone a message from her channeled directly through one of her chosen. Although she wears bones, she makes no bones about TRUTH and says, 'I take devotees but my standards are very high. There is a very good chance that you will not meet them. I demand nothing less than your whole life and by that I mean everything.' What are you willing to give? She is an all or nothing Goddess... and I loved reading her words. I highly recommend reading "Warning From Kali: Fierce Global Grace 2013" if you dare. OM KALI MA!"

As I laid on the couch with the television on, I closed my eyes and dared to give everything to Kali. My head started spinning like I was doing somersaults through space and time. Every little thing that came up... I gave to Kali. This went on for hours. I eventually got up from the couch, walked to the bedroom, got into bed where the experience continued uninterrupted by the move. She took every little nook and cranny of myself, concepts, experiences, and the last thing she took was herself.

Spiritual Experience with Divine Mother
August 6, 2013
Approx. 10:50 pm

I went to bed early. As I lay asleep in bed, whoosh, through the void, and the first thing I remember was hearing "Mama loves you, Mama loves you," as Mother murdered her children on a very large scale without care, understanding or sentimentality. If one was born... one was murdered... plain and simple. Newborns, cut in half by her sword one after another. No mercy.

Then the murder happened on a massive scale, as if the entire planet was endlessly birthed and consumed in a large rolling motion over and over and over. It was clearly seen that both the idea of an individual self and a world is only a joke of an experience, because in the midst of all the creation and destruction, no one is born... nothing is created... no one dies... nothing is destroyed. Nothing is happening in all the happening. That is undisturbed by all of it.

Nothing is added to That... nothing is taken from That. That which IS realizes itself in creation and destruction, life and death... but It is never created nor destroyed, never born and never dies.

It is all never ending because it never started. No final resting place because there was never any movement. No idea of enlightenment or finality belong to IT.

No history, no future, no Mother, no Father, no Koort, no Ramaji, no Ramana, no Buddha, no Jesus. All a funny, funny joke. Beyond simple.

Love, Koort

131. http://en.wikipedia.org/wiki/History_of_the_World,_Part_I, accessed March, 2014.

Incredible movie. The scene with the Old Testament tablets still makes me laugh out loud.

132. Roberts, Bernadette. *The Experience of No-Self*, SUNY Press, Albany, Revised Edition, 1993, 156 - 158.

133. Conway, Timothy, Meister Eckhart (1260-c1328) — Nondual Christian Mystic Sage, http://www.enlightened-spirituality.org/Meister_Eckhart.html, accessed March, 2014.

134. Schell, Brian, If You Meet The Buddha On The Road, Kill Him, http://www.dailybuddhism.com/archives/670, accessed March, 2014.

135. "Notes on LOC 800-899" by Koort, this book's editor, received via email December 9, 2013.

136. Gallacher, Patrick J. (Editor), The Cloud of Unknowing, Introduction, http://d.lib.rochester.edu/teams/text/gallacher-cloud-of-unknowing-introduction, accessed March, 2014.

Gallacher, Patrick J., Editor. *The Cloud of Unknowing*, Medieval Institute Publications, Kalamazoo, Michigan, 1997.

137. Pseudo-Dionysius the Areopagite, http://en.wikipedia.org/wiki/Pseudo-Dionysius_the_Areopagite, accessed March, 2014.

138. Dionysius the Areopagite with John Parker, Translator. *Dionysius the Areopagite, Works (1897)*, Christian Classics Ethereal Library, Publisher: Grand Rapids, MI, pages 84 - 86.

139. Godman, David. *Nothing Ever Happened, Volume One*, Avadhuta Foundation, Boulder, CO, 1998, 94.

140. Ibid., 119.

141. Ibid., 106.

142. Ibid., 121-122.

143. Ibid., 106-107.

144. John Wren-Lewis, http://en.wikipedia.org/wiki/John_Wren-Lewis, accessed March, 2014.

This is a very good biographical article if you want to learn more about John Wren-Lewis. There are references and links to his writings from both before and after his awakening.

145. John Wren-Lewis, The Dazzling Dark, A Near Death Experience Opens the Door to a Permanent Transformation, http://www.angelfire.com/electronic/awakening101/dazzledark.html, accessed March, 2014.

146. Ibid.

147. Ibid.

148. Ibid.

149. Ibid.

150. John Wren-Lewis Biography, http://www.angelfire.com/electronic/awakening101/dazzledark.html, accessed March, 2014.

151. Hawkins, David. *Discovery of the Presence of God: Devotional Nonduality*, Hay House Inc., Carlsbad, CA, 2007.

152. Roberts, Bernadette. *The Experience of No-Self*, SUNY Press, Albany, 1993, Revised Edition, 150 - 163.

153. Meister Eckhart, Quotes, http://en.wikiquote.org/wiki/Meister_Eckhart, accessed March, 2014.

154. Roberts, Bernadette. *The Experience of No-Self*, SUNY Press, Albany, 1993, Revised Edition, 157 - 158.

155. Ibid., 159 - 163.

156. Ibid., 157 - 158.

157. Ibid., 157 - 158.

158. Ibid., 158.

159. Sri Ramakrishna, http://www.srv.org/index.php?option=com_content&view=article&id=4&Itemid=237, accessed March, 2014.

160. Ramakrishna, The Gospel of Sri Ramakrishna (1942), p. 132, http://en.wikiquote.org/wiki/Ramakrishna, accessed March, 2014.

161. Totapuri, http://www.ramakrishnavivekananda.info/gospel/introduction/totapuri.htm, accessed March, 2014.

162. Godman, David, Editor. *Be As You Are: The Teachings of Sri Ramana Maharshi*, Arkana, London, England, 1985, 84.

163. Mansur Al-Hallaj, Teachings, arrest and imprisonment, http://en.wikipedia.org/wiki/Mansur_Al-Hallaj, accessed March, 2014.

164. The Shadow Side of Krishnamurti, http://www.tricycle.com/the-shadow-side-krishnamurti, accessed March, 2014.

165. Anand, J. Krishnamurti and Beautiful Rosalind Rajagopal, http://www.theosophy.com/theos-talk/200806/tt00112.html, accessed March, 2014.

166. The Shadow Side of Krishnamurti, http://www.tricycle.com/the-shadow-side-krishnamurti, accessed March, 2014.

167. Ibid.

168. U.S. Statistics, Fact #5, http://www.feminist.com/antiviolence/facts.html, accessed March, 2014.

169. Elizabeth MacDonald, http://www.aham.com/usa/sharing/elizabeth.html, accessed March, 2014.

170. Love Note From Elizabeth... continued, http://www.aham.com/usa/sharing/ppt/love_note.pdf, accessed March, 2014.

171. MacDonald, Elizabeth. *Living From the Heart*, AHAM Publications, Asheboro, N.C., 2005, page 167.

172. Is a "living" Guru necessary?, http://bhagavan-ramana.org/guru.html, accessed March, 2014.

173. Siddharameshwar Maharaj. *Amrut Laya (The "Stateless State"), Discourses on "Dasbodh" (Includes Master Key to Self-Realization)*, Shri Sadguru Siddharameshwar Adhyatma Kendra, Mumbai, India, 2000, 51 - 52.

174. Ibid., 33 - 35.

175. Nisargadatta Maharaj, Frydman, Maurice and Sudhakar S. Dikshit, Editors. *I Am That: Talks with Sri Nisargadatta Maharaj*, The Acorn Press, Durham, N. C., 3d Ed., 1981, 90, 230.

176. P.T. Mistlberger, Bio, http://www.ptmistlberger.com/, accessed March, 2014.

177. David Quinn and Dan Rowden, The Purpose of Gurus with Guest Philip Mistlberger, http://geniusrealms.com/reasoningshow/show6.htm, accessed March, 2014.

Podcast is available for listening online or download. Lively discussion well worth the listen.

178. The Purpose of Gurus - Philip Mistlberger, http://www.theabsolute.net/phpBB/viewtopic.php?f=23&t=3196, accessed March, 2014.

179. David Godman Interviewed By Helaine Melnitzer, Remembering Nisargadatta Maharaj, http://www.davidgodman.org/interviews/Nisargadatta_interview.pdf, page 8, accessed March, 2014.

Here is the exact quote. This interview is filled with great Nisargadatta stories. It is free to download at Godman's website.

David: With regard to the teachings [of Ramana] he [Nisargadatta] once told me, "I agree with everything that Ramana Maharshi said, with the exception of this business of the heart-centre being on the right side of the chest. I have never had that experience myself."

180. Sanskrit for Heart, HRIDAYA: hrid=center ayam=this, http://www.angelfire.com/indie/anna_jones1/hridaya.html, accessed March, 2014.

This quotation, taken from the autobiography of Mercedes De Acosta, was reprinted in *The Maharshi*, Vol. 4 Nos. 5 and 6 (Sept./Oct. and Nov./Dec. 1994), adding to its credibility. The full story of De Acosta's meeting with Ramana Maharshi can be found on this web page.

Here Lies The Heart by Mercedes D'Acosta, http://www.beezone.com/Mercedes/here_lies_the_heart.html, accessed March, 2014.

181. Terrell, Amber. *Surprised By Grace*, True Light Publishing, Boulder, Colorado, 1997, 234 - 235.

182. Heart and Mind, http://www.beezone.com/Ramana/heart_and_mind.html, accessed March, 2014.

183. Godman, David, 'I' and 'I-I' - A Reader's Query, http://davidgodman.org/rteach/iandii1.shtml, accessed March, 2014.

184. Ganesan, V. *Moments Remembered: Reminiscences of Bhagavan Ramana*, Sri Ramanasramam, 1994, 52 - 53.

In reply to a question about "Hridaya," T. K. Sundaresa Iyer wrote a letter to a devotee in England. It was approved by Ramana. Here is a paragraph from that letter that summarizes the "aham sphurana" spiritual phenomenon in relation to realizing the Self. The entire letter is reproduced in V. Ganesan *Moments Remembered* cited above.

"In the course of tracing ourselves back to our source, when all thoughts have vanished, there arises a throb from the Hridaya on the right, manifesting as 'Aham' 'Aham'. This is the sign that Pure Consciousness is beginning to reveal itself. But that is not the end in itself. Watch wherefrom this sphurana (throbbing) arises and wait attentively and continually for the revelation of the Self. Then comes the awareness, oneness of existence."

This unique in-depth online article by Peter Holleran offers a survey of esoteric topics related to Ramana's life and teachings. These include aham sphurana, the Heart on the right and controversial issues rarely discussed.

Holleran, Peter, The "Lost Years" of Ramana Maharshi, http://www.mountainrunnerdoc.com/page/page/5213285.htm, accessed March, 2014.

185. Muni, Sri Vasishtha Ganapati and K. Swaminathan, Translator. *Sri Ramana Gita*, Sri Ramanasramam, Tiruvannamalai, India, 2011, 73 - 75.

See also: Severing the Heart Knot, http://bhagavan-ramana.org/heartknot.html, accessed March, 2014.

I also utilized this chapter "Severing the Heart Knot," Verses 12 - 14 from another translation of *Sri Ramana Gita* that is available online. The chapter cited in the body of the text is entitled "On Cutting the Knot." The verses are 12 - 14 and only slightly different.

See also: Godman, David, 'I' and 'I-I' - A Reader's Query, http://davidgodman.org/rteach/iandii1.shtml, accessed March, 2014.

186. The Vision of the Universal Form, http://www.bhagavad-gita.org/Gita/verse-11-11.html, accessed March, 2014.

To paraphrase: If a thousand suns were to blaze in their glory and splendor all at the same time in the sky, that might be like this astonishing blissful vision of the radiant Truth.

187. Ramaji Satsang, Ramaji's Original Drawings Part One Amrita Nadi I-Thought Ramana Enlightenment Advaita Satsang, http://www.youtube.com/watch?v=3v8oyKJppRE, accessed March, 2014.

Ramaji Satsang, Ramaji's Original Drawings Part Two "I-Thought Rising" Ramana Enlightenment Advaita Non-Duality, http://www.youtube.com/watch?v=NoPqmEOYkSs, accessed March, 2014.

Ramaji Satsang, Ramaji's Original Drawings Part Three "Amrita Nadi Light" Ramana Enlightenment Advaita Non-Duality, http://www.youtube.com/watch?v=tqQtYX0kyhY, accessed March, 2014.

188. Holmes, Christopher, 2. Consciousness: Light of the Self, http://www.zeropoint.ca/heartIV2light.html, accessed March, 2014.

See also Almaas, A .H. *The Inner Journey Home: Soul's Realization of the Unity of Reality*, Shambhala, Boston, MA, 2004, 328 - 333.

189. Sri Ramana Maharshi on Self-Enquiry, Self-Enquiry – The nature of the Heart (Hridayam, Sphurana), http://www.angelfire.com/space2/light11/diction/ramana.html#11, accessed March, 2014.

190. Osborne, Arthur, Editor. *The Teachings of Ramana Maharshi*, Red Wheel/Weiser, York Beach, Maine, 1962, 1996, 190.

191. Who am I?, http://davidgodman.org/rteach/whoami1.shtml, accessed March, 2014.

192. Carse, David. *Perfect Brilliant Stillness: Beyond the Individual Self*, Paragate Publishing, Shelburne, VT, 2006.

193. Terrell, Amber. *Surprised By Grace*, True Light Publishing, Boulder, Colorado, 1997.

194. Michael Read from The Way Station, Highlights #916, http://www.nonduality.com/hl916.htm, accessed March, 2014.

195. About David Carse, Author, Read by Terence Stamp, Perfect Brilliant Stillness Audiobook, http://www.silksoundbooks.com/authors/david-carse/, accessed March, 2014.

196. Terrell, Amber, Eyes Like the Sun, http://www.broadjam.com/artists/songs.php?artistID=4334&mediaID=15059, accessed March, 2014.

You will find about 22 songs online for free listening. Terrell's deep understanding is clearly expressed in the lyrics. They accurately express her realization via the vehicle of sweetly luminous heartfelt poetry.

197. Carse, David. *Perfect Brilliant Stillness: Beyond the Individual Self*, Paragate Publishing, Shelburne, VT, 2006, page 11.

198. Ibid., 24-25.

199. Ibid., 51-52.

200. Ibid., 63.

201. Ibid., 100.

202. Ibid., 118.

203. Ibid., 117.

204. Ibid., 121.

205. Klein, Jean. Compiled and edited by Emma Edwards. *I Am*, Third Millenium Pub., St. Peter Port, Guernsey, C. I., 1989.

206. Klein, Jean. Compiled and edited by Emma Edwards. *I Am*, Third Millenium Pub., St. Peter Port, Guernsey, C. I., 1989, 1.

207. Pollock, Dennis, Called to a Quiet Life, http://www.spiritofgrace.org/articles/nl_2012/quiet_life.html, accessed March, 2014.

208. Dr. Jean Klein, from Rawlinson, Andrews, *The Book of Enlightened Masters: Western Teachers in Eastern Traditions*, Open Court, Chicago and LaSalle, Illinois, 1998, quoted on http://www.nonduality.com/klein.htm, accessed March, 2014.

209. Klein, Jean. *Transmission of the Flame*, 3rd Millenium Books, 1994, xx, quoted on http://www.nonduality.com/klein.htm, accessed March, 2014.

210. Totapuri, http://www.angelfire.com/electronic/awakening101/totapuri.html, accessed March, 2014.

211. Private email communication from Jerry in Canada, December 11, 2006.

212. Lakshmana Swamy, http://arunachalagrace.blogspot.com/2006/08/laksmana-swamy.html, accessed March, 2014.

Godman, David. *No Mind, I Am The Self*, Sri Lakshmana Ashram, India, 2005.

213. Subramanian.R, Aham Sphurana - John Grimes - Mountain Path, July-Sept, 2013, http://www.arunachala-ramana.org/forum_2/index.php?topic=8131.0, accessed March, 2014.

See also Notes 183, 184, 185 and Holleran, Peter, Kundalini: Up, Down, or ?, http://www.mountainrunnerdoc.com/kundalini.html, accessed March, 2014.

V. Ganesan's *Ramana Periya Puranam (Inner Journey of 75 Old Devotees)* available exclusively from AHAM via pdf download offers a few mentions of Kundalini and Amrita Nadi, but there are precious little details.

Kundalini is mentioned in relation to Kavyakantha Ganapathi Muni, Jataki Mata and Suria Nagama. Nagama is reported to have had experiences of Amrita Nadi. Kavyakantha Ganapathi Muni is also known as Sri Vaisshtha Ganapati Muni, the author of *Sri Ramana Gita* cited earlier.

Ramana Periya Puranam (Inner Journey of 75 Old Devotees), http://aham.com/RamanaPeriyaPuranam/, accessed March, 2014.

214. Ramaji. *The Spiritual Heart*, Ramaji Books, San Diego, 2013.

215. Ramaji. *Waking Up As Awareness*, Ramaji Books, San Diego, 2013.

216. Sri Sadhu Om, The Path of Sri Ramana, Part One, http://www.happinessofbeing.com/The_Path_of_Sri_Ramana_Part_One.pdf, accessed March, 2014. Chapter 8 recapitulates the art of Self-inquiry.

This wonderful book is also available as a physical book: Sadhu Om and Michael James, Editor. *The Path of Sri Ramana, Part One*, Sri Ramana Kshetra, Tiruvannamalai, 1971, 1981.

To learn more about Sri Sadhu Om, you can visit this website:

About Sri Sadhu Om, http://www.sadhuom.net/latest/sri-sadhu-om, accessed March, 2014.

217. unity22, Sri Ramana Maharshi on Self-Enquiry, http://www.angelfire.com/space2/light11/diction/ramana.html#14, March, 2014.

218. Excerpt from *Eternity Now*, by Francis Lucille, http://www.francislucille.com/, accessed March, 2014.

Lucille, Francis. *Eternity Now*, Non-Duality Press, 2008.

219. Karl Renz No Spiritual Knowledge, http://daoyoga8.blogspot.com/2012/11/what-is-enlightenment-and-your.html, accessed March, 2014.

220. What Is the Self?, http://www.satsangbhavan.net/main.htm, accessed March, 2014.

This short talk is highly recommended as a explanation of Self-inquiry step by step. There are plenty more brief yet powerful talks by Papaji here.

221. The two-step inquiry is taught by Sri Sadhu Om in *The Path of Sri Ramana Part One*. It consists of asking (1) "Who are you?" or "Who is having this thought?" followed by (2) "Where do you come from?" Some people prefer to do only the first step. If you are able to challenge a rising thought, it means you are not that thought. You are the Self (awareness).

222. Day, Nick and Maurizio Benazzo, Directors. *Short Cut To Nirvana*, Zeitgeist Films, 2004. DVD. 85 minutes.

223. Nisargadatta Maharaj, Frydman, Maurice and Sudhakar S. Dikshit, Editors. *I Am That: Talks with Sri Nisargadatta Maharaj*, The Acorn Press, Durham, N. C., Third Ed., 1981, 191.

224. Ibid.

225. Brown, Peter. *Dirty Enlightenment: The Inherent Perfection of Imperfection*, CreateSpace, 2007, 2013, 196 - 197.

226. Gilbert, Eleonora, Editor. *Conversations on Non-Duality: Twenty-Six Awakenings*, Cherry Red Books and Conscious TV, London, U.K., 2011, 259.

227. Gilbert, Eleonora, Editor. *Conversations on Non-Duality: Twenty-Six Awakenings*, Cherry Red Books and Conscious TV, London, U.K., 2011, 260.

228. Ibid.

229. Francis Answers - 222 - How can one even know that one is in the absolute state?, http://www.francislucille.com/advaita_channel_item.php?id=644, accessed March, 2014.

230. Jourdain, Stephen and Gilles Farcet, Editor. Translated by Candace Lyons. *Radical Awakening: Cutting Through the Conditioned Mind*, Inner Directions Publishing, Carlsbad, CA, 2001, 64.

231. Jourdain, Stephen and Gilles Farcet, Editor. Translated by Candace Lyons. *Radical Awakening: Cutting Through the Conditioned Mind*, Inner Directions Publishing, Carlsbad, CA, 2001, 56 - 57.

232. Berg, Stephen. *Ikkyu: Crow With No Mouth: 15th Century Zen Master*, Copper Canyon Press, Port Townsend, WA, 1989, 2000, 19, 23 - 24.

233. Conway, Timothy, Meister Eckhart (1260-c1328) — Nondual Christian Mystic Sage, http://www.enlightened-spirituality.org/Meister_Eckhart.html, accessed March, 2014.

234. Ibid.

235. Carse, David. *Perfect Brilliant Stillness*, page 385. This is a very close paraphrase of Carse's language, so I wanted to give him credit. This is powerful wording that makes for a strong statement.

236. From the Western Mystical tradition, Meister Eckhart, http://www.gnosis.org/library/coll.htm, accessed March, 2014.

237. Carse, David. *Perfect Brilliant Stillness: Beyond the Individual Self*, Paragate Publishing, Shelburne, VT, 2006, 384 - 385.

238. O'Hearn, Bob, Post 10, November 23, 2012, The Conscious Process, Zen and the Emotional/Sexual Contraction, http://sasakiarchive.com/, accessed March, 2014.

239. A female student (head quote under Sasaki Roshi's picture), http://sasakiarchive.com/, accessed March, 2014.

240. Muzika, Ed, Thunder Mountain, http://www.wearesentience.com/sasaki-roshis-mt-baldy-zen.html, accessed March, 2014.

241. Chaudhry, Lakshmi, The other side of the 'naked fakir': Remembering Gandhiji's grand-niece, http://www.firstpost.com/living/the-other-side-of-the-naked-fakir-remembering-gandhijis-grand-niece-1149535.html, accessed March, 2014.

242. Sulonen, Petteri, On Authoritarianism, Democracy, and Zen, http://primejunta.blogspot.com/2010/08/on-authoritarianism-democracy-and-zen.html, accessed March, 2014.

243. Janwillem van de Wetering, *The Empty Mirror: Experiences in a Japanese Zen Monastery*, St. Martin's Press, 1973, 1999, 135.

244. Formerinji, Post 13, November 26, 2012, An Anonymous Post on Sweeping Zen, http://sasakiarchive.com, accessed March, 2014.

245. Young, Shinzen, Direct Transmission, http://shinzenyoung.blogspot.com/2012/11/direct-transmission.html, accessed March, 2014.

246. Billings, Al Jigong, Another Side of Sasaki, http://www.openbuddha.com/2012/11/27/another-side-of-sasaki/, accessed March, 2014.

247. Shane, Charlotte, http://sasakiarchive.com/PDFs/20130106_Sex_with_Sasaki.pdf, page 8.

Another Former Inji, Post 29, January 7, 2013, An Essay By "Another Former Inji", Submitted To The Sasaki Archive, http://sasakiarchive.com, accessed March, 2014.

248. Giko, David Rubin, Post 21, December 11, 2012, Some Reflections on Rinzai-ji, http://sasakiarchive.com, accessed March, 2014.

249. Kapur, Rajiv with Pierre Bonnasse, Structure of the Self, http://www.rajivkapur.com/downloads/Structure-of-the-Self-Interview-Rajiv-Kapur-by-Pierre-Bonnasse-2012.pdf, 2012, accessed March, 2014.

250. Kapur, Rajiv, From the Known to the Unknown, http://www.rajivkapur.com/downloads/Practical-Course-Intro.pdf, 2011, 3 - 4, accessed March, 2014.

251. Ibid., 1.

252. Kapur, Rajiv with Pierre Bonnasse, Structure of the Self, http://www.rajivkapur.com/downloads/Structure-of-the-Self-Interview-Rajiv-Kapur-by-Pierre-Bonnasse-2012.pdf, 2012, 5, accessed March, 2014.

253. Ibid., 6.

254. Sundance Burke ~ Buddha at the Gas Pump (1:54) minutes, http://www.sundanceburke.org/FreeAwakeningVideos.html, March, 2014.

Free Advaita Video: Sundance Burke is interviewed by Rick Archer at Buddha at the Gas Pump on the life situation, spiritual awakening, enlightenment, Non-duality, Self-realization.

BuddhaAtTheGasPump, Sundance Burke - Buddha at the Gas Pump Interview, http://youtu.be/bkB9DvObpcY, accessed March, 2014.

This is the same video but on YouTube. This video interview conveys how genuine Sundance is. Rick Archer insists that Sundance tell his "story" for the listeners. The humble Sundance does so with reluctance.

255. Gilbert, Eleonora, Editor. *Conversations on Non-Duality: Twenty-Six Awakenings*, Cherry Red Books and Conscious TV, London, U.K., 2011, 351.

256. Ibid., 347.

257. Ibid., 351.

258. Lama Tsultrim Allione, http://taramandala.org/about/lama-tsultrim/, accessed March, 2014.

259. Allione, Tsultrim. *Women of Wisdom*, Snow Lion Publications, Ithaca, NY, Revised Edition, 2000.

260. Lama Tsultrim Allione, http://taramandala.org/about/lama-tsultrim/, accessed March, 2014.

261. Trip Overholt - Buddha at the Gas Pump Interview, http://batgap.com/trip-overholt/, accessed March, 2014.

The articulate Overholt (LOC 678) gives an illustration of this type of unfolding in his comments between 5:05 to 5:35. Overholt demonstrates exceptional clarity in his self-observation. He is just describing what is happening to him and sticking to the "facts." He is not falling into the trap of assuming or projecting that this space he is in is more than it is.

262. Allione, Tsultrim. *Feeding Your Demons: Ancient Wisdom for Resolving Inner Conflict*, Little, Brown Co., 2008.

263. Ibid., 260.

264. Haas, Michaela. *Dakini Power: Twelve Extraordinary Women Shaping the Transmission of Tibetan Buddhism in the West*, Snow Lion Publications, Ithaca, NY, 2013.

265. Lama Tsultrim Allione, http://www.dakinipower.com/tsultrim-allione/, accessed March, 2014.

266. Dakini (Sanskrit): A Female Messenger of Wisdom, http://www.dakinipower.com/what-is-a-dakini/, accessed March, 2014.

267. Lama Tsultrim Allione, The Enlightened Feminist, http://www.dakinipower.com/tsultrim-allione/, accessed March, 2014.

268. Blackstone, Judith, An Integrated Approach to Psychological Healing, Embodiment and Spiritual Awakening, http://www.realizationcenter.com/index.htm, accessed March, 2014.

269. Map–territory relation, http://en.wikipedia.org/wiki/Map%E2%80%93territory_relation, accessed March, 2014.

270. Rasa (aesthetics), http://en.wikipedia.org/wiki/Rasa_(aesthetics), accessed March, 2014.

271. Rasa Story, Ramaji Giving RASA Transmission in 2012, http://www.ramaji.org/rasa-via-skype-from-ramaji/ramaji-rasa-transmission-story/, accessed March, 2014.

The direct link on YouTube: Ramaji Satsang, Ramaji Satsang RASA With Arms Wide Open Creed San Diego Enlightenment Non-Duality Advaita, http://youtu.be/b4hfpLGTp_o, accessed March, 2014.

272. Since going public as a non-duality spiritual teacher in San Diego in June, 2012, the lowest LOC of one of my students who has stabilized in non-duality was LOC 558. It took them a year and a half to go from LOC 558 to LOC 674. As of this writing (March, 2014), they are at LOC 756.

The more common scenario is that the student starts out somewhere between the mid-570s and the mid-580s. Whether the student starts off in the LOC 580s or they move up to the LOC 580s from a lower LOC, once they get to the LOC 580s, I sense transparency, openness and availability in them. This is apart from the numerical assessment for their LOC.

One way to describe this is that now the wall or veil between them and non-duality is paper thin, I can feel the fragility and vulnerability of this weak barrier. I intuitively sense that it is ready to be broken through or to come down. RASA will help, but it is still up the student.

If the student is able to overcome their fears, doubts and temptations (such as wanting to hold onto the enjoyable openness of the LOC 580s), then jumping up to the LOC 600s or higher is likely. I cannot guarantee it, of course, but this is the pattern I have seen again and again.

1000

730

Bibliography

Allione, Tsultrim. *Feeding Your Demons: Ancient Wisdom for Resolving Inner Conflict*, Little, Brown Co., 2008.

Allione, Tsultrim. *Women of Wisdom*, Snow Lion Publications, Ithaca, NY, Revised Edition, 2000.

Almaas, A. H. *Facets of Unity: The Enneagram of Holy Ideas*, Diamond Books, Berkeley, CA, 1998.

Almaas, A .H. *The Inner Journey Home: Soul's Realization of the Unity of Reality*, Shambhala, Boston, MA, 2004.

Annamalai Swami and David Godman, Editor. *Final Talks*, AHAM Publications, Asheboro, NC, 2000.

Arjuna Ardagh. *The Translucent Revolution*, New World Library, Novato, CA, 2005.

Arjuna Nick Ardagh. *How About Now? Satsang with Arjuna*, SelfXPress, Nevada City, CA, 1999.

Balsekar, Ramesh. *Confusion No More for the Spiritual Seeker*, Watkins Publishing, London, 2007.

Balsekar, Ramesh. *The Bhagavad Gita: A Selection*, Zen Publications, Mumbai, India, 1997.

Balsekar, Ramesh and Blayne Bardo, Ed. *Your Head in the Tiger's Mouth: Talks in Bombay with Ramesh S. Balsekar*, Advaita Press, Redondo Beach, CA, 1998.

Bartlett, Richard. *Matrix Energetics*, Atria/Beyond Words, New York and Hillsboro, OR, 2007.

Berg, Stephen. *Ikkyu: Crow With No Mouth: 15th Century Zen Master*, Copper Canyon Press, Port Townsend, WA, 1989, 2000.

Bly, Robert. *Iron John: A Book About Men*, Addison-Wesley Publishing Co. Inc., New York, 1990.

Bradshaw, John. *Creating Love*, Bantam Books, New York, 1992.

Braha, James. *Living Reality*, Hermetician Press, Longboat Key, Florida, 2006.

Briggs, Rex. *Transforming Anxiety, Transcending Shame*, Health Communications, Inc., Deerfield Beach, FL, 1999.

Brown, Peter. *Dirty Enlightenment: The Inherent Perfection of Imperfection*, CreateSpace, 2007, 2013.

Buddhadasa Bhikku with Stephen Schmidt, Translator. *The Meditative Development of Mindfulness of Breathing*, 1972.

Buddhagosa with Nyanamoli, Translator. *Visuddhimagga (The Path of Purification)*, Buddhist Publication Society, Kandy, 2010.

Byrne, Rhonda. *The Secret*, Atria Books/Beyond Words Publishing, New York and Hillsboro, Oregon, 2006.

Campbell, Joseph. *The Hero with a Thousand Faces*, New World Library, Novato, California, 2008.

Canetti, Elias. *Crowds and Power*, Farrar, Straus and Giroux, New York, 1962, 1973.

Caplan, Mariana. *Eyes Wide Open: Cultivating Discernment on the Spiritual Path*, Sounds True, Boulder, CO, 2009.

Caplan, Mariana. *The Guru Question: the Perils and Rewards of Choosing a Spiritual Teacher*, Sounds True, Boulder, CO, 2011.

Carse, David. *Perfect Brilliant Stillness: Beyond the Individual Self*, Paragate Publishing, Shelburne, VT, 2006.

Cashdan, Sheldon. *Object-Relations Therapy*, W. W. Norton & Co., NY, 1988.

Cee. *The Way of Knowledge*, Booklocker.com Inc., 2007.

Cialdini, Robert. *Influence: Science and Practice*, Pearson, 5th Edition, 2008.

Cunningham, Keith. *The Soul of Screenwriting*, Continuum, New York, 2008.

Davis, Fred. *Beyond Recovery: Non-Duality and the Twelve Steps*, Non-Duality Press, Salisbury, United Kingdom, 2012.

Davis, Fred. *The Book of Undoing: Direct Pointing to Nondual Awareness*, 2013.

Day, Nick and Maurizio Benazzo, Directors. *Short Cut To Nirvana*, DVD. Zeitgeist Films, 2004.

Diamond, John. *BK: Behavioral Kinesiology*, Harper & Row, Publishers, New York, 1979.

Dionysius the Areopagite with John Parker, Translator. *Dionysius the Areopagite, Works (1897)*, Christian Classics Ethereal Library, Publisher: Grand Rapids, MI.

Drake, Colin. *Awareness of Awareness - The Open Way*, lulu.com, 2013.

Dyer, Wayne. *Wishes Fulfilled: Mastering the Art of Manifesting*, Hay House, Carlsbad, CA, 2012.

Easwaran, Eknath. *The Bhagavad Gita*, Nilgiri Press, Tomales, CA, 1995.

Edelstein, Scott. *Sex and the Spiritual Teacher*, Wisdom Publications, Somerville, MA, 2011.

Epstein, Mark. *Thoughts Without a Thinker*, BasicBooks, New York, 1995.

Fenner, Peter. *Radiant Mind: Awakening Unconditioned Awareness*, Sounds True, Boulder, CO, 2007.

Foster, Jeff. *An Extraordinary Absence: Liberation in the Midst of a Very Ordinary Life*, Non-Duality Press, Salisbury, United Kingdom, 2009.

Frawley, David. *Vedantic Meditation: Lighting the Flame of Awareness*, North Atlantic Books, Berkeley, CA, 2000.

Gallacher, Patrick J., Editor. *The Cloud of Unknowing*, Medieval Institute Publications, Kalamazoo, Michigan, 1997.

Ganesan, V. *Moments Remembered: Reminiscences of Bhagavan Ramana*, Sri Ramanasramam, 1994.

Gangaji. *You Are That! Satsang with Gangaji*, Volume I, The Gangaji Foundation, 1995.

Gangaji. *You Are That! Satsang with Gangaji*, Volume II, The Gangaji Foundation, 1996.

Gangaji with Roslyn Moore. *Just Like You: An Autobiography*, DO Publishing, Mendocino, CA, 2003.

Gilbert, Eleonora, Editor. *Conversations on Non-Duality: Twenty-Six Awakenings*, Cherry Red Books and Conscious TV, London, U.K., 2011.

Godman, David, Editor. *Be As You Are: The Teachings of Sri Ramana Maharshi*, Arkana, London, Englad, 1985.

Godman, David. *No Mind, I Am The Self*, Sri Lakshmana Ashram, India, 2005.

Godman, David. *Nothing Ever Happened, Volume One*. Avadhuta Foundation, Boulder, CO, 1998.

Godman, David. *Papaji Interviews*, Avadhuta Foundation, Boulder, CO, 1993.

Goleman, Daniel. *The Meditative Mind: the Varieites of Meditative Experience*, Jeremy P. Tarcher, Inc., Los Angeles, CA, 1988.

Goode, Greg. *The Direct Path: A User's Guide*, Non-Duality Press, Salisbury, United Kingdom, 2012

Guinn, Jeff. *Manson: the Life and Times of Charles Manson*, Simon & Schuster, New York, 2013.

Haas, Michaela. *Dakini Power: Twelve Extraordinary Women Shaping the Transmission of Tibetan Buddhism in the West*, Snow Lion Publications, Ithaca, NY, 2013.

Harrigan, Joan Shivarpita. *Kundalini Vidya: The Science of Spiritual Transformation*, Patanjali Kundalini Yoga Care, Knoxville, TN, 6th Ed., 2005.

Harper, James and Margaret Hoopes. *Uncovering Shame: An Approach Integrating Individuals and Their Family Systems*, W. W. Norton & Co., NY, 1990.

Hawkins, David. *Discovery of the Presence of God: Devotional Nonduality*, Hay House Inc., Carlsbad, CA, 2007.

Hawkins, David. *I: Reality and Subjectivity*, Veritas Publishing, Sedona, AZ, 2003.

Hawkins, David. *Power Vs. Force*, Hay House, Carlsbad, CA, 2002.

Hawkins, David. *Transcending the Levels of Consciousness*, Veritas Publishing, Sedona, AZ, 2006.

Hay, Louise and Mona Lisa Schulz. *All Is Well*, Hay House, Inc., Carlsbad, CA, 2013.

Henderson, Floyd. *From the I to the Absolute*, Henderson Books Publishing Co., Lake Conroe, TX, Third Edition, 2005.

Hopkins, Jerry and Daniel Sugerman. *No One Gets Out Alive*, Warner Books, New York, 1980.

Horner, Althea. *The Wish for Power and the Fear of Having It*, Jason Aronson Inc., NY, 1986.

Jaxon-Bear, Eli. *The Enneagram of Liberation*, Leela Foundation, Bolinas, CA, 2001.

Janwillem van de Wetering. *The Empty Mirror: Experiences in a Japanese Zen Monastery*, St. Martin's Press, 1973, 1999.

Jenkins, John Major. *Galactic Alignment*, Bear & Co., Rochester, VT, 2002.

Johnson, Stephen. *Character Styles*, W. W. Norton & Co., NY, 1994.

Johnson, Stephen. *Characterological Transformation: the Hard Work Miracle*, W. W. Norton & Co., NY, 1985.

Jones, Dantalion. *Building Your Cult: Power, Politics and People*, BuildingYourCult.com, 2010.

Josephs, Lawrence. *Character and Self-Experience*, Jason Aronson, Inc., Northvale, NJ, 1995.

Jourdain, Stephen and Gilles Farcet, Editor. Translated by Candace Lyons. *Radical Awakening: Cutting Through the Conditioned Mind*, Inner Directions Publishing, Carlsbad, CA, 2001.

Kabat-Zinn, Jon. *Wherever You Go There You Are*, Hyperion, NY, 1994.

Katie, Byron with Stephen Mitchell. *A Thousand Names for Joy*, Harmony Books, New York, 2007.

Katie, Byron with Stephen Mitchell. *Loving What Is*, Harmony Books, New York, 2002.

Keyes, Margaret Frings. *Emotions and the Enneagram: Working Through Your Shadow Life Script*, Molysdatur Publications, Muir Beach, CA, Revised Ed., 1992.

Kiloby, Scott. *Love's Quiet Revolution: The End of the Spiritual Search*, 2008.

Kinslow, Frank. *Beyond Happiness*, LucidSea, 2008.

Klein, Jean. Compiled and edited by Emma Edwards. *I Am*, Third Millenium Pub., St. Peter Port, Guernsey, C. I., 1989.

Klein, Jean. *Transmission of the Flame*, 3rd Millenium Books, 1994.

Knight, Curtis. *Jimi*, Praeger Publishers, New York, 1974.

Kornfield, Jack. *A Path with Heart: A Guide Through the Perils and Promises of Spiritual Life*, Bantam Books, New York, 1993.

Kramer, Joel and Diana Alstad. *The Guru Papers: Masks of Authoritarian Power*, Frog Ltd., Berkeley, CA, 1993.

Krishnamurti, Jiddu. *Freedom From the Known*, HarperSanFrancisco, NY, 1969.

Krishnamurti, Jiddu. *Talks and Dialogues*, Avon Books, New York, 1968.

Kwong, Jakusho. *No Beginning, No End: the Intimate Heart of Zen*, Harmony Books, New York, 2003.

Lal, P. *The Bhagavadgita*, Orient Paperbacks, Delhi, India, 1965.

Lao Tzu and Victor Mair, Translator. *Tao Te Ching*, Bantam Doubleday Dell Publishing Group, Inc., 1990, 1998.

Liquorman, Wayne. *Acceptance of What IS: A Book About Nothing*, Advaita Press, Redondo Beach, CA, 2000.

Linssen, Robert. *Living Zen*, Grove Press, New York, 1958.

Lozowick, Lee. *Spiritual Slavery*, HOHM, Tabor, NJ, 1975.

Lloyd, Virginia. *Choose Freedom*, Freedom Publications, Phoenix, AZ, 1983.

Lucille, Francis. *Eternity Now*, Non-Duality Press, 2008.

Maharishi Mahesh Yogi. *Love and God*, Spiritual Regeneration Movement, Oslo, Norway, 1965.

Marks, Dara. *Inside Story: the Power of the Transformational Arc*, A & C Black, London, 2007, 2009.

Master Charles. *The Bliss of Freedom*, Acacia Publishing Corporation, Malibu, CA, 1997.

Merton, Thomas. *The Seven Storey Mountain*, Harcourt Brace Jovanovich, Inc., New York, 1948, 1976.

Merzel, Dennis Genpo. *Big Mind, Big Heart*, Big Mind Publishing, Salt Lake City, UT, 2007.

Mindell, Arnold. *Working On Yourself Alone*, Arkana, London, 1990.

Moore, Roslyn. *Meeting Papaji*, DO Publishing, Mendocino, CA, 1999.

Morrison, Scott. *Open and Innocent: the Gentle, Passionate Art of Not-Knowing*, Second Edition Revised, 21st Century Renaissance, 2000.

Muni, Sri Vasishtha Ganapati and K. Swaminathan, Translator. *Sri Ramana Gita*, Sri Ramanasramam, Tiruvannamalai, India, 2011.

Namgyal Rinpoche. *Body, Speech & Mind*, Bodhi Publishing, Kinmount, Ontario, Canada, 2004.

Naranjo, Claudio. *Character and Neurosis: An Integrative View*, Gateways/IDHHB, Inc., Nevada City, CA, 1994.

Naranjo, Claudio. *Enneatypes in Psychotherapy*, Hohm Press, Prescott, AZ, 1995.

Nelson, John. *Healing the Split*, Jeremy P. Tarcher, Inc., Los Angeles, CA, 1990.

Nisargadatta Maharaj, Frydman, Maurice and Sudhakar S. Dikshit, Editors. *I Am That: Talks with Sri Nisargadatta Maharaj*, The Acorn Press, Durham, N. C., Third Ed., 1981.

Nisargadatta Maharaj, Robert Powell, Editor. *The Experience of Nothingness*, Motilal Banarsidass Publishers, Delhi, India, 1996.

Nisargadatta Maharaj, Maria Jory, Editor. *Beyond Freedom*, Yogi Impressions Books, Mumbai, India, 2007.

Ophiel. *The Art & Practice of Caballa Magic*, Samuel Weiser, Inc., York Beach, Maine, 1976.

Osborne, Arthur, Editor. *The Teachings of Ramana Maharshi*, Red Wheel/Weiser, York Beach, Maine, 1962, 1996.

Parker, John. *Dialogues with Emerging Spiritual Teachers*, Sagewood Press, Fort Collins, CO, 2000.

Parsons, Tony. *Invitation to Awaken: Embracing Our Natural State of Presence*, Inner Directions Foundation, Carlsbad, CA, 2005, 2005.

Pierrakos, John. *Core Energetics*, LifeRhythm Publications, Mendocino, CA, 1990.

Prasad, Ramananda. *The Bhagavad-Gita (The Sacred Song), A Modern English Translation*, International Gita Society, Fremont, CA, 2001.

Ram Dass, *Be Here Now*, Lama Foundation, San Cristobal, New Mexico, 1971.

Ramaji. *The Spiritual Heart*, Ramaji Books, San Diego, 2013.

Ramaji. *Waking Up As Awareness*, Ramaji Books, San Diego, 2013.

Ramana, Arunachala. *Consciousness Being Itself*, AHAM Publications, Asheboro, NC, 1995.

Ramana Maharshi. *Talks with Sri Ramana Maharshi*, Sri Ramanasramam, Tiruvannamalai, India, 1978.

Rawlinson, Andrews, *The Book of Enlightened Masters: Western Teachers in Eastern Traditions*, Open Court, Chicago and LaSalle, Illinois, 1998

Renz, Karl. *The Myth of Enlightenment*, Inner Directions Foundation, Carlsbad, CA, 2005.

Roberts, Bernadette. *The Experience of No-Self*, SUNY Press, Albany, Revised Edition, 1993.

Rosenberg, Larry with David Guy. *Breath By Breath: The Liberating Practice of Insight Meditation*, Shambhala, Boston, MA, 1999.

Sachdeva, Santosh. *Conscious Flight Into the Empyrean: A Visual Journey in Meditation*, Volume 1, Yogi Impressions, Mumbai, India, 1999.

Sadhu Om and Michael James, Editor. *The Path of Sri Ramana, Part One*, Sri Ramana Kshetra, Tiruvannamalai, 1971, 1981.

Sakyong Mipham. *Turning the Mind Into an Ally*, Riverhead Books, New York, 2003.

Salzberg, Sharon. *Lovingkindness: The Revolutionary Art of Happiness*, Shambhalla, Boston, MA, 2004.

Samenow, Stanton. *Inside the Criminal Mind*, Times Books, NY, 1984.

Sarkar, P. R. *The Way of Tantra*, Ananda Marga Publications, Manila, Philippines, 1988.

Sartre, Jean-Paul and Stuart Gilbert, Translator. *No Exit and Three Other Plays*, Vintage, New York, International Edition, 1976, 1989.

Segal, Suzanne. *Collision with the Infinite*, Blue Dove Press, San Diego, CA, 1996.

Siddharameshwar Maharaj. *Amrut Laya (The "Stateless State"), Discourses on "Dasbodh" (Includes Master Key to Self-Realization)*, Shri Sadguru Siddharameshwar Adhyatma Kendra, Mumbai, India, 2000.

Sloss, Radha Rajagopal, *Lives in the Shadow with J. Krishnamurti*, Bloomsbury Press, London, 1991.

Snyder, Stephen and Tina Rasmussen. *Practicing the Jhanas*, Shambhala, Boston, MA, 2009.

Solk, Mandi. *The Joy of No Self*, Empty Books, London, 2008.

Spira, Rupert. *The Transparency of Things: Contemplating the Nature of Experience*, Non-Duality Press, Salisbury, United Kingdom, 2008.

Sri Sadguru Siddharameshwar Maharaj. *Master Key to Self-Realization*, Sadguru Publishing, 2008.

Sui, Choa Kok. *Advanced Pranic Healing*, Samuel Weiser, Inc., York Beach, Maine, 1995.

Suzuki, Shunryu. *Zen Mind, Beginner's Mind*, Weatherhill, New York, 1970, 1999.

Swami Chinmayananda. *The Holy Geeta*, Central Chinmaya Mission Trust, Mumbai, India, 1970.

Swami Satchidananda, *The Yoga Sutras of Patanjali*, Integral Yoga Publications, Buckingham, Virginia, 1978, 1984, 1990.

Swami Satyananda Saraswati. *Yoga Nidra*, Yoga Publication Trust, Munger, India, 2001, 2009.

Swami Shyam. *Vivek Chudamani: Light of Knowledge*, Shyam Space, Ottawa, Canada, 1976.

Swartz, James. *How to Attain Enlightenment: the Vision of Non-Duality*, Sentient Publications, Boulder, CO, 2009.

Tarthang Tulku. *Hidden Mind of Freedom*, Dharma Publishing, Berkeley, CA, 1981.

Tendzin, Ösel. *Buddha in the Palm of Your Hand*, Shambhala, Boston, MA, 1987.

Tenzin Wangyal Rinpoche. *The Tibetan Yogas of Dream and Sleep*, Snow Lion Publications, Ithaca, NY, 1998.

Terrell, Amber. *Surprised By Grace*, True Light Publishing, Boulder, Colorado, 1997.

Thich Nhat Hanh. *Transformation & Healing: Sutra on the Four Establishments of Mindfulness*, Parallax Press, Berkeley, CA, 1990

Thie, John. *Touch for Health*, Devorss & Co., 1987.

Thompson, Berthold Madhukar. *The Odyssey of Enlightenment: Rare Interviews of Enlightened Teachers of Our Time*, Wisdom Editions, San Rafael, CA, 2003.

Tolle, Eckhart. *A New Earth: Awakening to Your Life's Purpose*, Plume, New York, 2005.

Trungpa, Chogyam. *Cutting Through Spiritual Materialism*, Shambhala, Boston, MA, 1987.

Venkatesananda, Swami. *Vasistha's Yoga*, State University of New York Press, Albany, NY, 1993.

Vitvan. *Self-Mastery Through Meditation*, School of the Natural Order, Baker, NV, 1982.

Yongey Mingyur Rinpoche with Eric Swanson. *The Joy of Living*, Harmony Books, New York, 2007.

Vogler, Christopher. *The Writer's Journey: Mythic Structure for Writers*, Michael Wiese Productions, Studio City, CA, 3rd Ed., 2007.

Wilber, Ken. *Integral Spirituality*, Integral Books, Boston, MA, 2006.

Wolinsky, Stephen. *Quantum Consciousness*, Bramble Books, Norfolk, CT, 1993.

Yapko, Michael. *Trancework: An Introduction to the Practice of Clinical Hypnosis*, Brunner/Mazel Publishers, NY, Second Edition, 1990.

Zaehner, R. C. *Our Savage God*, Sheed and War, New York, 1974.

Meet the Author

RAMAJI

Ramaji teaches Advaita and non-duality in San Diego, California. There is a monthly satsang meeting in the area organized via Meetup.com.

Ramaji's first awakening was at the age of 16 via Kundalini in a lucid dream. Since that time, he has kept a detailed journal of his spiritual journey. Ramaji took the "local bus" to LOC 1000. He personally went through many steps slowly and with precision. This put him in a perfect position to provide an accurate map of the stages that the spiritual student encounters on his journey from seeker to realizing the Absolute.

Ramaji is the author of *1000*, a groundbreaking guide to the path of enlightenment and the levels of consciousness from the lowest to the highest. This unique guide to the evolution of human consciousness is based on a lifetime of intuitively evaluating people. Ramaji has a natural gift for accurately assessing a person's LOC or Level of Consciousness.

Ramaji also offers a powerful unique spiritual transmission called RASA in support of rapid non-dual awakening. RASA is easy and effortless. All that is asked is that you be relaxed and receptive. Nothing else is required. The best way to reach Ramaji is via his web site Ramaji.org.

Ramaji works with students all over the world via email and Skype. He has students in Australia, United Kingdom, Scotland, Hong Kong, India, Japan, Russia, Canada and the United States.

The RASA transmission in support of non-dual awakening includes a one hour consultation where you can ask any questions that you want. After your Skype RASA session with Ramaji, you have access to him via email.

The new direction in 2014 and beyond for Ramaji is delivering RASA to groups. This is the result of the discovery that the benefit is the same. It makes no difference if you get RASA one to one or in a group. Since giving RASA to a group enables many more people to benefit at the same time, it is the next step for Ramaji in his mission to deliver the powerful yet gentle spiritual benefits of the RASA transmission to as many people as possible.

RASA (Ramaji Advaita Shaktipat Attunement) delivers the Grace of Divine Mother for accelerated spiritual awakening. Even though this Grace or Blessing has the power to quickly raise your level of consciousness, it is very gentle. Some people have shifted into enlightenment (stabilization in a non-dual LOC above well above 600) immediately after receiving RASA.

Ramaji is also the author of *The Spiritual Heart*. It explains the path of Self-inquiry meditation for the Western seeker and goes into depth about the I-thought, the Heart on the right, Kundalini and other important factors that Ramana Maharshi talked about but rarely get discussed in the modern non-duality scene.

His one of a kind meditation guide called *No Mind No Problem* reveals an effortless new way of dealing with the mind that embraces the moment while allowing your natural happiness to emerge in an enjoyable fun way. People tired of repetitive methods will enjoy his approach. It encourages the rejuvenating joys of curiosity, creativity and inspired "doing nothing."

Waking Up As Awareness by Ramaji emphasizes the "gap" at the moment of waking from sleep where the Self or lucid aware presence is naked. This opportunity was emphasized by Ramana. It is a key part of his teachings.

During the seven years that Ramaji studied Vipassana meditation, one of his Buddhist meditation teachers taught him a radical self-healing system developed long ago by a great Buddhist master. This little-known method applies the power of the mind directly to a physical, emotional or mental problem for surprisingly fast easy powerful results. Ramaji delivers a full training course in the technique in his book *Heal Your Body, Free Your Mind*.

Ramaji also offers free high energy spiritual music at RamajiUnity.com. Attuned to non-dual frequencies, this unique uplifting music is designed to facilitate your enlightenment. The eight songs are free to listen to online.

Many Blessings in the One Supreme Self,
RAMAJI

Ramaji.org

Meetup.com/Ramaji-Satsang-Group/ (San Diego meetings)

YouTube Channel: Ramaji Satsang

Email: satsangwithramaji@gmail.com

Download the Spiritual Maps of Awakening

You can download the spiritual Maps of Awakening found in this book for free online in pdf or jpeg format. Just go to Ramaji.org/ramaji-books/.

Subscribe to the Free *LOC Insider* Newsletter

Would you like to get the latest updates in Ramaji's LOC research without waiting for the next edition of *1000*? The *LOC Insider: Enlightenment By the Numbers* newsletter offers new LOC studies of established and upcoming teachers plus insights into non-dual news, media and personalities. Ramaji replies to reader's questions and offers fresh insights into spiritual stages. Get early notice about events with Ramaji and the latest developments with the RASA Grace transmission in support of non-dual awakening.

To start receiving your free email newsletter, just send an email with the subject line "LOC INSIDER" (in CAPS) to advaitaforidiots@gmail.com.

Susanne Pepal: "Kollision mit der Unendlichkeit"

The mature sage regards all as his self! (5.39)

Printed in Poland
by Amazon Fulfillment
Poland Sp. z o.o., Wrocław